UNITED NATIONS

ECONOMIC AND SOCIAL SURVEY

OF

ASIA AND THE PACIFIC

1987

Bangkok

1988

Since the 1957 issue, the *Economic and Social Survey of Asia and the Pacific* has, in addition to a review of the current situation of the region, contained a study or studies of some major aspect(s) or problem(s) of economies of Asia and the Pacific, as specified below:

1957: Postwar problems of economic development
1958: Review of postwar industrialization
1959: Foreign trade of ECAFE primary exporting countries
1960: Public finance in the postwar period
1961: Economic growth of ECAFE countries
1962: Asia's trade with western Europe
1963: Imports substitution and export diversification
1964: Economic development and the role of the agricultural sector
1965: Economic development and human resources
1966: Aspects of the finance of development
1967: Policies and planning for export
1968: Economic problems of export-dependent countries. Implications of economic controls and liberalization
1969: Strategies for agricultural development. Intra-regional trade as a growth strategy
1970: The role of foreign private investment in economic development and co-operation in the ECAFE region. Problems and prospects of the ECAFE region in the Second Development Decade
1971: Economic growth and social justice. Economic growth and employment. Economic growth and income distribution
1972: First biennial review of social and economic developments in ECAFE developing countries during the Second United Nations Development Decade
1973: Education and employment
1974: Mid-term review and appraisal of the International Development Strategy for the Second United Nations Development Decade in the ESCAP region, 1974
1975: Rural development, the small farmer and institutional reform
1976: Biennial review and appraisal of the International Development Strategy at the regional level for the Second United Nations Development Decade in the ESCAP region, 1976
1977: The international economic crises and developing Asia and the Pacific
1978: Biennial review and appraisal at the regional level of the International Development Strategy for the Second United Nations Development Decade
1979: Regional development strategy for the 1980s
1980: Short-term economic policy aspects of the energy situation in the ESCAP region
1981: Recent economic developments in major subregions of the ESCAP region
1982: Fiscal policy for development in the ESCAP region
1983: Implementing the International Development Strategy: major issues facing the developing ESCAP region
1984: Financing development
1985: Trade, trade policies and development
1986: Human resources development in Asia and the Pacific: problems, policies and perspectives

UNITED NATIONS
ECONOMIC AND SOCIAL SURVEY OF ASIA AND THE PACIFIC
1987

ST/ESCAP/585

UNITED NATIONS PUBLICATION

Sales No. E.88.II.F.2

ISBN: 92-1-119456-3   ISSN: 0252-5704

Price: $US 21.00

FOREWORD

This is the forty-first annual *Economic and Social Survey of Asia and the Pacific* (until 1974 titled the *Economic Survey of Asia and the Far East*). The *Survey* is divided into two parts, as in previous years. Part one presents a survey of current economic and social developments in the region in a global economic context. Part two contains a study on problems of international trade in primary commodities.

Amid increasing uncertainties in the world economy and despite the damaging effects of unfavourable weather, the developing economies of Asia and the Pacific substantially improved their economic performances in 1987. Economic growth reached an enviable average of 6 per cent, or about 2 per cent higher than in 1986. However, this should be viewed in the perspective of the great diversity in performance of the region's developing economies, with double-digit growth being achieved by China and the newly industrializing economies of East Asia, on the one hand, and stagnation or decline in many least developed and Pacific island countries, on the other.

Two factors had a particularly significant bearing on the region's 1987 growth performance. One was the sizeable increase in exports of manufactures, especially from countries in East and South-East Asia. The other factor was harsh climatic conditions, mainly the unprecedented drought, the effects of which were widely felt across the region but most severely in South Asia. However, the region today can derive some satisfaction that the vulnerability to capricious weather has been significantly reduced. In India, for example, the unprecedented drought slowed the GDP growth rate, but did not cause famine or a sharp drop in per capita incomes. Nevertheless, the costly drought, plus floods in Bangladesh and eastern India, are likely to cause a considerable set-back to the development efforts of many countries in the region. The region's growth prospects for 1988 will, however, be considerably weaker, due largely to slower growth in the world economy.

Part two of the *Survey* deals with the problems of international trade in primary commodities. Despite the increasing role of exports of manufactures, non-fuel primary commodities still provide a major source of employment, exports and incomes in many developing countries of the region. Notwithstanding a limited revival in 1987 in the export earnings of primary commodities, especially metals and minerals, most commodity prices in real terms remained at a low ebb. The main focus of part two of the *Survey* is on the structural problems facing the economies in the region that are dependent on primary commodities. It analyses the long-term trends affecting demand and supply in commodity markets, trade patterns and technological changes and their effects on the economies of the region and suggests some policy options emerging from the analysis.

Like previous issues, this *Survey* is published on the sole responsibility of the secretariat, and the views expressed herein do not necessarily reflect those of the Governments of the members and associate members of the Commission.

S.A.M.S. Kibria
Executive Secretary

February 1988

EXPLANATORY NOTES

The term "ESCAP region" is used in the present issue of the *Survey* to include Afghanistan, Australia, Bangladesh, Bhutan, Brunei Darussalam, Burma, China, Commonwealth of the Northern Marianas, Cook Islands, Democratic Kampuchea, the Federated States of Micronesia, Fiji, Guam, Hong Kong, India, Indonesia, the Islamic Republic of Iran, Japan, Kiribati, the Lao People's Democratic Republic, Malaysia, Maldives, Mongolia, Nauru, Nepal, New Zealand, Niue, Pakistan, Papua New Guinea, the Philippines, the Republic of Korea, the Republic of the Marshall Islands, the Republic of Palau, Samoa, Singapore, Solomon Islands, Sri Lanka, Thailand, Tonga, Tuvalu, Vanuatu and Viet Nam. The term "developing ESCAP region" excludes Australia, Japan and New Zealand.

The designations employed in this publication do not imply the expression of any opinion whatsoever on the part of the Secretariat of the United Nations concerning the legal status of any country or territory or of its authorities, or concerning the delimitation of its frontiers.

The abbreviated title *Survey* in footnotes refers to *Economic and Social Survey of Asia and the Pacific* for the year indicated.

Figures relating to national accounts and public finance are on a fiscal year basis and are assigned to the calendar year which covers the major part or second half of the fiscal year.

Reference to "tons" indicates metric tons.

Values are in United States dollars unless specified otherwise.

The term "billion" signifies a thousand million.

In the tables, three dots(. . .) indicate that data are not available or are not separately reported, a dash (–) indicates that the amount is nil or negligible, and a blank indicates that the item is not applicable.

In dates, a hyphen (-) is used to signify the full period involved, including the beginning and end years, and a stroke (/) indicates a crop year, a fiscal year or plan year. The fiscal years, currencies and 1987 exchange rates of the ESCAP countries are listed in the following table:

Country or area	Fiscal year	Currency and abbreviation	Mid-point rate of exchange for $US 1 as of June 1987
Afghanistan	21 March to 20 March	Afghani (Af)	50.600
Australia	1 July to 30 June	Australian dollar ($A)	1.388
Bangladesh	1 July to 30 June	Taka (Tk)	31.000
Bhutan	1 April to 31 March	Ngultrum (Nu)	12.934
Brunei Darussalam	1 January to 31 December	Brunei dollar ($Br)	2.240
Burma	1 April to 31 March	Kyat (K)	6.722
China	1 January to 31 December	Yuan renminbi (YRMB)	3.722
Cook Islands	1 April to 31 March	New Zealand dollar ($NZ)	1.692
Democratic Kampuchea	1 January to 31 December	Riel (KR)	. . .
Fiji	1 January to 31 December	Fijian dollar ($F)	1.305
Guam	1 October to 30 September	United States dollar ($US)	1.000
Hong Kong	1 April to 31 March	Hong Kong dollar ($HK)	7.809
India	1 April to 31 March	Rupee (Rs)	12.934
Indonesia	1 April to 31 March	Rupiah (Rp)	1.648
Iran, Islamic Republic of	21 March to 20 March	Rial (Rls)	72.195
Japan	1 April to 31 March	Yen (Y)	147.000
Kiribati	1 July to 30 June	Australian dollar ($A)	1.388
Lao People's Democratic Republic	1 July to 30 June	New Kip (NK)	35.000
Malaysia	1 January to 31 December	Ringgit ($M)	2.524
Maldives	1 October to 30 September	Rufiyaa (Mal Rf)	9.340
Mongolia	1 January to 31 December	Tughrik (Tug)	2.830
Nauru	1 July to 30 June	Australian dollar ($A)	1.388
Nepal	16 July to 15 July	Rupee (NRs)	21.600
New Zealand	1 April to 31 March	New Zealand dollar ($NZ)	1.692
Niue	1 April to 31 March	New Zealand dollar ($NZ)	1.692
Pakistan	1 July to 30 June	Rupee (PRs)	17.350
Papua New Guinea	1 January to 31 December	Kina (K)	0.901
Philippines	1 January to 31 December	Peso (P)	20.456
Republic of Korea	1 January to 31 December	Won (W)	808.9
Samoa	1 January to 31 December	Tala ($WS)	2.123
Singapore	1 April to 31 March	Singapore dollar ($S)	2.122
Solomon Islands	1 January to 31 December	Solomon Islands dollar ($SI)	2.026
Sri Lanka	1 January to 31 December	Rupee (SLRs)	29.265
Thailand	1 October to 30 September	Baht (฿)	25.840
Tonga	1 July to 30 June	Pa'anga (P)	1.388
Tuvalu	1 January to 31 December	Australian dollar ($A)	1.388
Vanuatu	1 January to 31 December	Vatu (VT)	111.160
Viet Nam	1 January to 31 December	New Dong	15.000

Sources: United Nations, *Monthly Bulletin of Statistics, January 1988;* and national sources.

CONTENTS

Part One

RECENT ECONOMIC AND SOCIAL DEVELOPMENTS

Part Two

INTERNATIONAL TRADE IN PRIMARY COMMODITIES

BOXES

Part One

BOXES

Part Two

TABLES

Part one

TABLES

Part Two

FIGURES

Part one

FIGURES

Part Two

ABBREVIATIONS

ACP	African, Caribbean and Pacific
APCC	Asian and Pacific Coconut Community
ASEAN	Association of South-East Asian Nations
ATPC	Association of Tin Producing Countries
CCCN	Customs Co-operation Council Nomenclature
CDI	Centre for Development of Industry
CMEA	Council for Mutual Economic Assistance
DAC	Development Assistance Committee
ECDC-TCDC	Economic and technical co-operation among developing countries
EEC	European Economic Community
FAO	Food and Agriculture Organization of the United Nations
GATT	General Agreement on Tariffs and Trade
GDP	Gross domestic product
GNP	Gross national product
GSP	Generalized system of preferences
IFPRI	International Food Policy Research Institute
IJO	International Jute Organization
ILO	International Labour Organisation
IMF	International Monetary Fund
IPC	Integrated Programme for Commodities
ITC	International Tin Council
LIBOR	London Interbank Offered Rate
NMP	Net material product
ODA	Official development assistance
OECD	Organisation for Economic Co-operation and Development
OPEC	Organization of the Petroleum Exporting Countries
SDRs	Special drawing rights
SITC	Standard International Trade Classification
STABEX	System of stabilization of export earnings
UNCTAD	United Nations Conference on Trade and Development
USDA	United States Department of Agriculture

Part One

RECENT ECONOMIC AND
SOCIAL DEVELOPMENTS

I. WORLD ECONOMIC DEVELOPMENTS AND THEIR IMPACT ON THE DEVELOPING ESCAP REGION

A. DEVELOPMENTS IN THE WORLD ECONOMY

1. Increasing risks of a recession

Hopes for continuing growth in the world economy were dampened considerably in the last quarter of 1987. Although it is too early to predict how lasting will be the impact on the world economy of the turbulent events of October 1987 in the stock exchanges and key currency markets, they did signify a watershed in the emerging perceptions about the future. In their own way, the financial markets clearly indicated their lack of confidence in the adequacy of efforts to co-ordinate the macro-economic policies of the major industrial countries.

The imbalances in the world economy proved too persistent to be reduced through the narrow scope of co-ordination on the exchange rates among key currencies. The expectation that the depreciation of the dollar since 1985 would soon have significant favourable effects on the balance of payments turned out to be as misplaced as the earlier hope that the imbalances would be self-correcting and no interventions in the currency markets would be needed. Policy interventions, however, often prove to be self-defeating if they appear to the markets to be too little and too late. This is the inherent danger in the present situation in the world

economy which, more than at any time since 1982, is facing increasing risks of sliding into a major recession.

Underlying the efforts to co-ordinate international economic policy has been the assumption that the current account deficit of the United States of America and the surpluses of the Federal Republic of Germany and Japan are merely two sides of the same coin. As a corollary to this, the basis for policy co-ordination has been the view that the surplus countries should reduce their savings ratio by expanding domestic consumption while at the same time taking up the slack caused by fiscal restriction in the United States.

However, there is no reason to consider the outflow of Japan's — and other countries' — savings, which are by no means excessive by historical standards, as a threat to the world economy. What the world economy is suffering from is not a glut of savings but a lack of appropriate allocation of those savings consistent with the aims of world development and sustainable growth. What is required, therefore, as a necessary complement to the reduction of the external deficit of the United States is not so much a reduction of the surpluses of Japan and other countries but increases in balance-of-payments support to developing countries. thus enabling them to resume their development process. This would restore the pattern of

capital flows disrupted in 1982, and at the same time counterbalance the slackening world demand that would be caused by the much-needed reduction in the fiscal and trade deficits of the United States (see box I.1).

The worst scenario — and the one that needs to be avoided the most — is that in which the surplus savings would be reduced through income reductions caused by a world-wide recession. In late 1987, the immediate challenge facing the developed market economies was to arrive at a consensus on policies to forestall this threat. A major recession would lead to a further increase in the fiscal deficit of the United States making any stimulation of the economy to counteract a deepening depression virtually impossible. Such a recession would be equally detrimental to the growth of the developing countries as it would stretch to the breaking point their ability to service their debts and pay for their imports. Through a further fall in the prices of primary commodities and the strengthening of the protectionist backlash in developed market economies, which this scenario would necessarily entail, the capacity of the developing countries to service their debts could be totally crippled, leading to much more serious and widespread consequences than those portended by the events of October 1987.

The outlook for the world economy for 1988 is clouded by

Box I.1. Recycling the trade surpluses of Japan

Although the financial world holds its breath before each month's announcement of trade figures of Japan and the United States of America, it is increasingly clear that the imbalances in the world balance of payments are likely to continue to be with us for some years. Efforts to reduce them within the narrow framework of macro-economic policy co-ordination among the major developed market economies have so far failed to produce the desired results.

Taking a long-term view, Professor Saburo Okita of Japan and his colleagues at the United Nations World Institute of Development Economics Research have proposed the recycling of the surpluses of the Federal Republic of Germany and Japan to finance the development of Third World countries. This would also enable the developing countries to increase their imports from the United States, thus reducing the trade gap of that country.[a]

Professor Okita's proposals are based not only on the intrinsic reasons for helping the developing countries, but also on the grounds that the recycling would help to reduce the imbalances in the global economy. His proposals involve recycling $125 billion over the next five years.

The need for capital transfers to developing countries on this scale is

---

[a] Saburo Okita, and others, World Institute for Development Economics Research, *Mobilizing International Surpluses for World Development — A WIDER Plan for a Japanese Initiative* (The Okita Report) (Study Group Series No. 2, Helsinki, 1987). See also his Third Paul Prebisch lecture, "The emerging prospects for development and the world economy" delivered to the United Nations Conference on Trade and Development at its seventh session held at Geneva on 9 July 1987.

evident from the sharp turnaround in capital inflows to developing countries to the extent that there now are substantial net capital outflows from them. The developing countries are paying more in principal repayments and interest payments on their long-term debt than they receive in new loans. According to the calculations made in the Okita Report, in the 1990s these net financial transfers will rise to around $40 billion. To reverse this trend, large net transfers of resources to developing countries are needed — to improve their capacity to increase imports from developed countries, reduce the hardship caused by net transfer from developing countries, and to ease the adjustment process. The Report argues that a well co-ordinated international economic policy for the orderly development of the world economy should provide for the generation of substantial current account surpluses in industrial countries to facilitate needed resource transfers to developing countries.[b]

The surplus countries, such as the Federal Republic of Germany and Japan, have genuine problems in domestic expansion in a non-inflationary manner. Despite the efforts of Japan to restructure the economy towards domestic demand, the necessary adjustment cannot be achieved in the short run. For quite some time, Japanese savings will exceed domestic investment and seek investment in foreign countries. Moreover, the increasing foreign investment income will add to the surplus. A precipitous decline in the Japanese savings and external surplus could hardly be in the interest of world economic growth. Therefore, it is argued, the total elimination of these surpluses is

---

[b] Saburo Okita, and others, *op. cit.*, p. 15.

neither necessary nor desirable for the world economy.

Neither can the United States deficit be eliminated in the short run. United States imports are more than 50 per cent higher than exports and therefore the turnaround will be massive and, the United States net foreign debt, now estimated at $300 billion, is projected to be around $500-$600 billion by 1990. Interest payments on this debt ($16 billion in 1986) will, by 1990, be in the region of $45-$70 billion.

The Okita proposals are thus seen as an imaginative and bold initiative to overcome the current crisis through recycling and to break the vicious circle of lagging economic growth in the developing countries and stagnating world trade. The increased recycling of capital to the developing countries will activate their latent demand and capacity to import much-needed capital goods from the industrialized countries. As a result, the triangular interactions among trade-surplus countries, developing countries, and other industrialized countries will function to reactivate the world economy as a whole.

There are, however, considerable difficulties in the implementation of the proposal for recycling the Japanese surplus. Unlike the recycling of the oil money, which was held by the Governments of the oil-exporting countries, Japan's surplus capital is largely held by the private sector. The private sector has learned from the experiences of the 1970s to be extremely wary of investing in or lending to the high-risk, heavily-indebted developing countries. It is thus essential that the Governments of the trade-surplus countries take the initiative in promoting and underwriting the recycling of the surplus.

Already the Japanese Government has made commitments to provide

---

uncertainty about the "wealth effects" resulting from the loss in financial assets. Both the magnitude of such "losses" and their negative impact on consumption and investment are very difficult to estimate, especially in view of

the fact that at least part of the decline in the values of these assets was in the nature of an overdue "correction". More importantly, the future course of world economic events depends crucially on the policy responses of the Govern-

ments of the leading industrial countries which are yet to be fully articulated.

Notwithstanding these uncertainties, the Organisation for Economic Co-operation and Development (OECD) has revised its pro-

untied funds of $30 billion over three years, 1987-1989. These include $10 billion consisting of, among others, its increased pledges to the World Bank in the form of an access facility in Japan's domestic capital market ($2 billion), contributions to the International Development Association ($2.6 billion), the International Monetary Fund ($3.6 billion) and the Asian Development Bank ($1.3 billion); and $20 billion – also over three years – loan recycling to indebted developing countries in untied loans, presumably either through the Export-Import Bank or through commercial banks with Export-Import Bank guarantee. In addition, the Government has announced its intention of doubling its official development assistance (ODA) in five years, instead of seven years as originally planned.

In order to raise the level of funds to be recycled to that suggested by Professor Okita, a number of new measures will have to be taken by the Japanese Government. These would include concessional interest rates, with subsidies to be financed from ODA, raising funds in capital markets against collateral provided by a government guarantee or subsidy, and involvement of multilateral institutions in the recycling process. In addition, the present low ODA to GNP ratio of 0.29 per cent needs to be raised to, at least, the average of 0.36 per cent of the Development Assistance Committee, if not to the ratio of 0.43 per cent of the Federal Republic of Germany, and the Japanese aid policies need to be further liberalized. The possibility of introducing such measures as the issuance of zero coupon bonds and grants-in-aid for interest payments for heavily indebted countries and the least developed countries also needs to be examined.

jections of the average economic growth in 1988 of its member countries downwards by 0.5 per cent below that for 1987; and the 1989 rate has been projected by another 0.5 percentage points below the 1988 rate.[1] Such a slow-down in the industrial countries would weaken world trade and have a significant negative impact on the growth prospects of the developing world.

2. Slow growth in the world economy

The rate of growth of the world economy, at 2.8 per cent in 1987, slowed down for the third successive year. In the industrial countries as a group the rate of expansion decelerated from 2.7 per cent in 1986 to 2.4 per cent, while in the developing world it decelerated from 4.0 to 3.3 per cent (see table I.1).

A disconcerting feature of the economic performance of the industrial countries was the stagnation of productive investment (see box I.2). Despite continued economic growth during the last four years, productive capacity did not appreciably increase. As a result, inflation continued to be an ever-present concern and inhibited expansionary policies.

The pattern of economic expansion in developed market economies during 1987 also reflected some shifts in the sources of growth in the major economies which were broadly in accordance with the need for reducing their imbalances. In the United States, for example, there was a shift away from domestic demand, which until 1986 had been the main force behind expansion, towards the export sector. The expansion in net exports, however, was not sufficient to compensate for the slow-down in domestic demand. As a result the growth rate at 2.4 per cent was 0.5 per cent below that for 1986.

On the other hand, the economy of Japan was showing some signs of adjustment away from

---

[1] *OECD Economic Outlook,* No. 42 (Paris, December 1987).

its traditional dependence on export markets. During the year the fiscal policy was eased, reinforcing the favourable effects on private consumption and residential construction of the appreciation of the yen and terms-of-trade gains accruing from lower prices of oil and other primary commodities during 1986. As a consequence in 1987 domestic demand grew by 4 per cent, more than offsetting the negative impact of decline in net exports, and resulting in an increase in the rate of growth of the economy form 2.9 per cent in 1986 to 3.2 per cent in 1987. However, in the Federal Republic of Germany the economic performance remained weak as the export-oriented sectors weakened, while the stimulus to domestic demand came too late in the year to make any impact on the economy's growth rate during 1987.

In the developing world an overall growth rate of slightly over 3 per cent in 1987 implies that there was little prospect of any improvement in per capita incomes in a large number of countries (see table I.2). Moreover, when terms-of-trade losses are taken into account, economic performance turns out to be much less satisfactory than that indicated by per capita incomes. Thus, for a large part of the developing world, 1987 was another year of stagnant or falling living standards, especially in Africa and Western Asia.

3. The changing nature of interdependence in the world economy

Global developments in the past few years have strongly underscored both the increase in interdependence in the world economy and its changing nature. The current world economic crisis can be viewed as being partly a result of the failure to accept the interna-

3

Table I.1. World output, 1969-1987[a]

(Annual percentage change)

	Average 1969-1978[b]	1979	1980	1981	1982	1983	1984	1985	1986	1987 (estimated)
World	4.3	3.4	2.1	1.8	0.7	2.6	4.5	3.3	3.2	2.8
Industrial countries	3.4	3.4	1.3	1.5	−0.3	2.7	5.0	3.1	2.7	2.4
Developing countries	6.0	4.3	3.4	1.6	1.6	1.6	4.1	3.3	4.0	3.3
By region										
Africa	5.1	3.3	3.8	2.0	1.0	−1.6	1.4	2.1	0.8	1.5
Asia	5.8	4.5	5.4	5.5	5.2	7.6	8.0	6.4	6.3	6.0
Europe	5.9	3.8	−	−	1.1	1.9	4.0	2.5	3.9	3.0
Middle East	8.2	1.8	−2.5	−2.1	0.3	0.1	0.2	−1.1	1.2	−1.5
Latin America	5.8	6.1	6.1	0.1	−1.0	−2.8	3.6	3.5	4.4	3.6
By analytical criteria										
Fuel exporters	7.8	3.7	1.0	0.8	0.1	−2.0	0.9	0.3	−0.1	−0.6
Non-fuel exporters	5.4	4.5	4.3	2.0	2.4	3.4	5.7	4.7	5.8	4.8
Centrally planned economies[c]	5.9	2.5	4.0	3.4	3.7	4.2	3.3	3.6	4.1	3.6

Source: IMF, *World Economic Outlook* (Washington, D.C., October 1987), which lists countries in the various groups in this table.

[a] Real GDP (or GNP) for industrial and developing countries and real net material product (NMP) for centrally planned economies. Composites for the country groups are averages of percentage changes for individual countries weighted by the average United States dollar value of their respective GDPs (GNPs or NMPs where applicable) over the preceding three years. Because of the uncertainty surrounding the valuation of the composite NMP of the centrally planned economies, they have been assigned — somewhat arbitrarily — a weight of 15 per cent in the calculation of the growth or world output. Excluding China prior to 1978.
[b] Compound annual rates of change. [c] The Union of Soviet Socialist Republics and Eastern Europe.

tional policy implications of this interdependence.

Despite a sharp fall in the dollar against other leading currencies — 35 per cent in real effective terms between early 1985 and the second quarter of 1987 — imbalances in the current accounts of the major industrial countries showed no sign of a turnaround.[2] Towards the end of 1986 and early 1987 there were widespread misgivings in financial markets about the pace of adjustment. Owing to the growing uncertainty in financial markets, the dollar came increasingly under pressure in early 1987. There was serious risk that the fall of the dollar would become disorderly, with damaging con-

[2] IMF, *World Economic Outlook* (Washington, D.C., October 1987), p. 12. By the end of 1987, the dollar's nominal value in terms of the yen was less than half its peak value in February 1985.

sequences for world trade and economic growth.

For much of 1987, as the flow of private capital into the United States dried up, central banks of the major industrial countries, notably the Federal Republic of Germany and Japan, sold deutsche mark and yen worth billions of dollars (by some estimates, around $100 billion in the first nine months of 1987) in attempts to bolster the dollar and to finance the United States fiscal and current account deficits. As a consequence of these interventions, the money supply in the Federal Republic of Germany and Japan significantly increased, engendering fears of inflation. The monetary authorities in the two countries tightened the monetary policy which led to upward pressures on interest rates. This threatened to negate the efforts to shore up the dollar. In the United States the increasing

fear of inflation induced by the continuing depreciation of the dollar had already led to a significant increase in long-term interest rates. With the threat of a general increase in interest rates and uncertainty caused by the continuing loss of ground by the dollar, the onset of a recession, first in the United States and then across the world, began to be perceived as a real possibility. By the autumn of 1987 it was apparent that the objectives of redistributing aggregate demand among leading developed market economies in order to reduce external imbalances were becoming increasingly difficult to achieve.

In the wake of the stock market crash, serious efforts have been under way in the United States to reduce the budget deficit. A package of measures to reduce the deficit by $76 billion over two years was agreed between the

Box I.2. The weak link between profits and investments in developed market economies

The macro-economic policies followed by the leading industrial countries since 1979-1980 were devised largely as a reaction to the inflationary experience of the 1970s. The oil shock of 1973-1974 was followed by high rates of oil price induced inflation, rise of labour costs relative to final product prices and squeeze of profit margins, decline in the rate of investment, and rise in unemployment. In the early 1980s decline in the rate of return on outstanding capital stock was a major policy concern in most developed countries and macro-economic policies were designed to restore the profitability of capital in order to raise the level of investment.

The policy response to the second oil price shock thus had a number of objectives in terms of medium-term strategies:

(i) To manage aggregate demand in such a way as to ensure that the burden of adjustment to oil price rises would fall on labour costs rather than on profit margins; there was widespread reduction in monetary expansion to ensure that only a low rate of price increases was accommodated.

(ii) To reduce budget deficits through cuts in public expenditure and reduce the role of government in production; it was widely believed that government deficits raised interest rates and made private investment less profitable than it otherwise would be.

(iii) To institute structural reforms. It was argued that macro-economic policies needed to be supported by micro-economic reforms — their essence being that production and investment decisions should be guided by market signals.

These reforms were aimed at changes in taxation to strengthen incentives for private initiative in production and investment, removal of obstacles to labour mobility, dismantling of wage indexation, deregulation, privatization, and others. These reforms were expected to improve efficiency, restore business profitability, and thus lead to higher rates of investment and economic growth.

Since the early 1980s control of inflation and "fiscal consolidation" have continued to be the dominant features of economic policy in most of the industrial countries. Restrictive aggregate demand policies were continued even after the oil price increases of 1979-1980 had passed through the economies. The outstanding exception was the United States of America, where a liberal fiscal policy was combined with tight monetary control.

Most of the objectives set out in medium-term policies had been successfully achieved by the mid-1980s. According to an assessment made in 1987 by the Organisation for Economic Co-operation and Development: ". . . inflation is under control in most countries; corporate financial positions are generally good; interest rates have declined markedly in recent years; budget positions have improved in a number of countries; and labour markets show signs of increased flexibility."[a]

However, a major expectation of the macro-economic policies adopted in the early 1980s that increase in profitability would lead to increase in productive investment has generally not been realized (see figure). For example, in the United States, growth of non-residential fixed investment decelerated in 1985, and its level declined in 1986. In 1987, the level of investment was projected to fall further. In Japan, non-residential fixed investment growth, after acceleration in 1985, decelerated in 1986 and in 1987 was projected to stagnate at the 1986 level. Similarly, in the Federal Republic of Germany investment decelerated in 1986 and was projected to decline in 1987. The experience of other leading industrial countries was in general similar. According to OECD projections, in 1987 the contribution of non-residential private investment (in the seven leading industrial countries) to change in real GNP/GDP was zero — against a mere 0.2 per cent in 1986. This contribution has, in fact, consistently

---

[a] *OECD Economic Outlook*, No. 41 (Paris, June 1987).

Major developed market economies. Shares of gross profits and investment in value added in manufacturing industry

(Percentage)

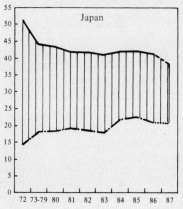

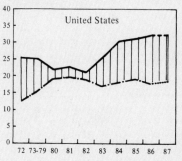

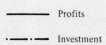

————— Profits

—·—·— Investment

Source: Figure reproduced from UNCTAD, *UNCTAD Bulletin*, No. 236 (October 1987).

(continued overleaf)

(continued from preceding page)

declined over the four-year period 1984-1987.[b]

The above evidence clearly indicates that the economic policies adopted by the leading countries as a group, though they have succeeded in raising profits and controlling inflation, have not led to any significant revival of productive investment. This is a matter of considerable concern for the long-term growth prospects of developed market economies on which the revival of world trade and growth largely depends.

Two explanations for the continuing sluggishness of investment in developed market economies suggest themselves. According to the first, the failure of investment in industrialized countries is attributable to demand management policies. "In the absence of strong demand growth, firms are restricting their investment to that needed for rationalization. . . This serves to increase productivity, but it does not reduce unemployment or add to potential output and growth".[c] There are also other factors affecting the weakness of demand that contribute to the current stagnation of investment. These are uncertainties created by trade imbalances and the threat of protectionism. Both have made investment riskier, thus increasing the required return on investment.

Another way to explain the poor performance of investment in the 1980s is that growth rates achieved by industrialized countries during the 1950s and the 1960s reflected a "once and for all" increase in productivity in Western Europe and Japan as those countries "caught up" with technology in the United States. That process, it is argued, has been completed and the "special factors" of the 1950s and the 1960s cannot be expected to reproduce themselves in the 1980s. The possibility that a similar catching-up operation by developing countries could stimulate world economic growth and favourably affect investment in the industrial countries is suggested by the logic of the emerging interdependence between developed and developing countries.

[b] *Ibid.*

[c] UNCTAD, *Trade and Development Report 1987,* p. 53.

Table I.2. Developing countries. Per capita real GDP, 1969-1987[a]

(Annual percentage change)

	Average 1969-1978[b]	1979	1980	1981	1982	1983	1984	1985	1986	1987 (estimated)
Developing countries	3.4	1.9	1.0	−0.6	−0.9	−0.6	2.0	1.3	1.9	1.3
By region										
Africa	2.2	0.2	0.7	−1.0	−2.0	−4.6	−1.7	−0.6	−2.1	−1.1
Asia	3.5	2.6	3.4	3.6	3.1	5.7	6.1	4.6	4.6	4.3
Europe	4.7	2.8	−0.9	−0.8	0.2	1.1	3.2	1.5	2.8	1.9
Middle East	4.0	−2.1	−6.2	−5.8	−3.8	−2.8	−3.0	−3.8	−2.0	−4.1
Latin America	3.3	3.7	3.7	−1.9	−3.2	−5.0	1.3	1.4	2.2	1.6
By predominant export										
Fuel exporters	3.9	0.2	−2.3	−2.5	−3.4	−4.7	−2.3	−2.3	−3.0	−3.2
Non-fuel exporters	3.3	2.6	2.4	0.2	0.4	1.5	3.9	2.9	4.0	2.9
Primary product exporters	2.8	2.4	2.4	−1.7	−2.0	−2.5	1.6	1.0	3.3	1.9
Agricultural exporters	3.4	2.6	2.4	−2.5	−1.3	−1.8	1.9	1.5	3.8	2.3
Mineral exporters	0.6	1.1	2.4	1.5	−4.9	−5.1	0.5	−1.6	0.1	0.1
Exporters of manufactures	4.2	2.8	2.2	2.3	2.9	5.8	6.6	5.2	5.1	4.4
Service and remittance countries	3.0	2.6	3.0	0.6	1.9	1.5	1.8	2.5	2.5	1.0
By alternative analytical categories										
Oil-exporting countries	4.3	−1.4	−4.6	−4.7	−3.7	−4.1	−3.0	−3.1	−2.2	−3.5
Non-oil-exporting countries	3.3	2.8	2.6	0.7	−	0.6	3.5	2.7	3.1	2.6

Source: IMF, *World Economic Outlook* (Washington, D.C., October 1987), which lists countries in the various groups in this table.

[a] Excluding China prior to 1978. [b] Compound annual rates of change.

Administration and congressional leaders, and the Administration was making strenuous efforts to win wider congressional support for the legislation to give effect to the agreed measures. In the surplus countries there was also greater recognition of the importance of stimulating domestic demand. Both the Federal Republic of Germany and Japan lowered their discount rates. In Japan, in particular, a more balanced pattern of expansion was observable. However, by the end of 1987 it was evident that far more intensive efforts would be necessary for adopting mutually consistent and growth-oriented policies to stimulate the sagging world economy.

The second major aspect of interdependence in the world economy – often not adequately recognized – is that between developed and developing countries. This aspect was highlighted by the lopsided response to the 1986 fall in the prices of oil and primary commodities generally. The collapse of oil prices in 1986 resulted in very substantial gains owing to positive income terms of trade in most of the developed market economies. These gains were increased by continued weakening of commodity prices generally. For the developed countries as a whole these gains amounted to 1 per cent of their collective gross national product (GNP).[3] These benefits were reflected in improvements in business profitability and higher household incomes. Lower oil and commodity prices generally were also a significant factor in keeping the rate of inflation under control.

[3] *OECD Economic Outlook*, No. 41 (Paris, June 1987). For the European OECD members, with the exclusion of the two oil-exporting countries, these gains were equivalent to 2.5 per cent of GNP.

The counterpart of the developed country gains from terms of trade was, of course, the loss suffered by developing countries exporting primary commodities, particularly oil. These losses necessitated cut-backs in imports and thus had a negative influence on output in the developed economies. Less developed countries now account for 20 per cent of world output and 25 per cent of imports, while the exports of goods and services from the OECD countries to developing countries account for about 20 per cent of their collective GNP.

In 1986, oil-exporting developing countries, as a direct consequence of the collapse of oil prices, reduced their imports from developed countries by approximately 20 per cent; other primary commodity exporting developing countries, despite some overall terms-of-trade gains arising from the fall in oil prices, were also obliged to restrain their imports. Overall, the imports of non-OECD countries fell by 6 per cent and the exports of industrial countries experienced a marked slow-down in growth from a rate of 4.3 per cent in 1985 to 2.6 per cent in 1986. As a result, the shrinking developing country markets for industrial country exports had a significant depressive effect on the economic activity of industrial countries (see figure I.1). Thus, reduction in the exports of the developed countries, largely as a result of the reduction in the incomes of oil and other primary commodity producers, offset a significant part of the boost received from improvements in the terms of trade. According to one estimate the decline in the net exports of the OECD countries in volume terms was equivalent to 1 per cent of GNP.[4]

[4] *Ibid.* On the general question of linkages between the developed and developing countries, see also Paul Saunders and Andrew Dean, "The international debt situation and linkages between developing countries and the OECD", *OECD Economic Studies,* No. 7 (Paris, Spring, 1987); and R. Dornbusch, "Policy and performance links between LDC debtors and industrial nations", *Brookings Papers on Economic Activity,* No. 2 (1985).

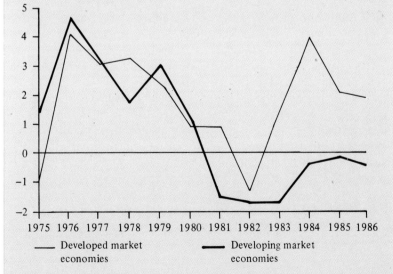

Figure I.1. Real per capita GDP growth rates in developed and developing market economies, 1975-1986

—— Developed market economies   —— Developing market economies

Source: United Nations Department of International Economic and Social Affairs (1986).

With some recovery in oil prices in 1987 no significant terms-of-trade gains to developed economies are likely to have accrued from that source. As the volume of oil exports in 1987 fell below the 1986 level (mainly because of destocking in developed countries) there is a strong probability that the exports of developed countries did not receive any stimulus from that source either.

The position of developing countries dependent on exports of commodities other than oil was unlikely to have improved over that in 1986. Indeed, in 1987 real commodity prices were estimated to fall well below the 1986 levels.[5] With oil prices higher than in 1986 and commodity prices falling relative to the prices of their manufactures imports and little improvement in their access to funds from developed countries, the non-oil primary producers will continue to suffer import compression.

Thus, the impetus to developed country economic activity from the developing countries as a group is unlikely to be strong unless growth in the latter is resumed through the restoration of the flow of resources to developing countires interrupted in the early 1980s. In addition to meeting one of the requirements of long-term growth of the developing world this would, at the same time, give the boost to world aggregate demand needed to counterbalance the deflationary implications of reduction in the fiscal and trade deficits of the United States.

4. Trade and balance of payments

The volume of world trade in 1987 grew at the annual rate of 3.4 per cent as against 4.8 per cent in

1986 (see table I.3). The main influences on world trade during the last two to three years have been the relative trade prices, marked changes in exchange rates, and the shifts in fiscal policies among the major industrial countries. The volume of world trade in 1986 was significantly affected by the decline in oil prices and, to a lesser extent, in non-oil commodity prices. The decline in these prices led to a larger volume of demand from industrial countries through both increases in incomes arising from gains in terms of trade and inventory buildings, particularly of oil. (Exports of fuel exporters increased in 1986 by 11 per cent and declined in 1987 by 2.1 per cent). In contrast, developing countries were forced to restrain their imports which, in 1986, fell by 2.8 per cent.

The depreciation of the dollar during 1986 has had a favourable effect on the volume of world trade. There was some recovery in United States exports without adversely affecting exports from the countries with unchanged or appreciating currencies. The exporters from the surplus countries were able to maintain their exports by accepting reductions in profit margins. The countries whose currencies were linked to the dollar, in general, improved their competitive position and made substantial gains in export performance.

The slow-down in world trade during 1987 is attributed to cuts in the oil imports of industrial countries following reductions in stocks, continued import reductions suffered by oil-exporting countries, and a deceleration in the United States imports.

Oil prices during 1987 made a recovery over the exceptionally low prices prevailing from late 1985 to mid-1986. Prices of non-oil primary commodities also showed some recovery in dollar

terms but these improvements did not match increases in the prices of manufactures, which, on average, were expected to rise by 12 to 13 per cent in 1987. Real commodity prices continued to fall in 1987.

Two encouraging features of the world trade situation in 1986-1987 are worth noting. First, developing countries as a group, in 1986, earned more foreign exchange from the export of manufactures than from primary products. Second, unlike in the past, the expansion in manufactures was not confined to the East Asian industrializing countries; a number of other developing countries also made substantial gains.

Following large terms-of-trade losses, the combined current account position of the developing countries deteriorated in 1986. Their current account deficit increased from $24 billion in 1985 to $47 billion in 1986. The increase in the deficit would have been much larger had the adverse terms of trade not been partly offset by changes in real trade flows. The fuel-exporting countries, with terms-of-trade losses equivalent to $100 billion, were the worst hit. Their current account position deteriorated by $35 billion. Non-fuel exporters continued to record improvement in the current account, their deficit falling from $27 billion in 1985 to $9 billion in 1986. In 1987, both groups were projected to record improvements in their deficits, fuel exporters from a deficit of $38 billion to $12 billion, and non-fuel exporters from a deficit of $7.7 billion.[6]

The combined current account position of the industrial countries improved by $32 billion in 1986. Within the group the United States deficit increased by $25 billion and the surpluses of the Federal Republic of Germany and

---

[5] IMF, *World Economic Outlook* (Washington, D.C., October 1987), p. 12. However, some commodities did record remarkable improvements in 1987 (see box II.2, p. 91).

[6] IMF, *World Economic Outlook* (Washington, D.C., October 1987).

Japan grew by $20 billion and $37 billion respectively. In 1987 and 1988, despite continuing efforts to correct the trade imbalances among the major industrial economies, the deficit of the United States and the surpluses of the Federal Republic of Germany and Japan were projected to persist though some adjustment in the Federal Republic of Germany in the desired direction was expected.[7]

Financial flows between the developed countries continued to

[7] The United States trade deficit for the first 10 months of 1987 was $146 billion, against $138 billion for the corresponding period of 1986.

Table I.3. Summary of world trade volumes and prices, 1969-1987[a]

(Annual percentage change)

	Average 1969-1978[b]	1979	1980	1981	1982	1983	1984	1985	1986	1987 (estimated)
World trade										
Volume	6.7	6.3	1.2	0.8	−2.2	3.0	8.9	3.1	4.8	3.4
Unit value (in US dollar terms)	10.8	18.7	20.1	−1.2	−4.2	−4.8	−2.4	−2.2	4.4	9.9
(in SDR terms)[c]	8.3	15.0	19.3	9.1	2.3	−1.7	1.8	−1.3	−9.7	0.4
Volume of trade										
Exports										
Industrial countries	7.1	7.2	3.9	3.6	−2.1	3.0	9.9	4.3	2.6	2.5
Developing countries	4.6	4.3	−4.2	−6.0	−7.6	3.2	7.1	0.9	8.5	5.9
Fuel exporters	3.1	1.9	−13.5	−15.1	−16.2	−3.2	0.7	−5.7	11.0	−2.1
Non-fuel exporters	6.1	6.7	8.4	5.3	1.2	8.2	11.5	5.1	7.7	8.9
Imports										
Industrial countries	6.8	8.9	−1.6	−2.0	−0.6	4.7	12.6	4.6	8.4	3.5
Developing countries	7.2	2.9	7.4	7.9	−3.9	−2.2	2.3	−0.3	−2.8	1.9
Fuel exporters	15.0	−4.7	13.4	18.6	−1.4	−10.0	−5.6	−12.3	−20.5	−12.0
Non-fuel exporters	4.9	6.4	5.0	3.3	−5.1	1.7	5.8	4.6	4.0	5.9
Unit value of trade (in SDR terms)[c]										
Exports										
Industrial countries	7.6	11.7	12.3	5.8	2.6	−1.0	1.2	−0.2	−1.7	1.0
Developing countries	12.1	25.0	36.5	15.4	1.9	−4.5	3.9	−3.9	−25.9	0.5
Fuel exporters	19.6	39.9	62.0	23.1	3.1	−8.7	2.7	−3.3	−19.3	9.3
Non-fuel exporters	7.3	13.1	12.4	7.2	0.7	−1.0	4.8	−4.3	−12.7	−2.5
Imports										
Industrial countries	8.2	15.0	20.8	7.7	0.7	−2.4	0.9	−1.0	−9.8	1.3
Developing countries	8.0	14.2	17.3	11.4	2.8	−1.1	2.6	−2.5	−11.1	−0.1
Fuel exporters	7.6	10.9	12.4	10.7	3.1	−0.3	2.0	−0.6	−3.6	−0.5
Non-fuel exporters	8.0	15.8	19.3	11.8	2.7	−1.6	2.9	−3.3	−13.7	0.1
Terms of trade										
Industrial countries	−0.5	−2.9	−7.1	−1.8	1.9	1.4	0.3	0.8	9.0	−0.3
Developing countries	3.8	9.5	16.4	3.6	−0.9	−3.5	1.3	−1.4	−16.7	0.6
Fuel exporters	11.2	26.2	44.0	11.2	0.1	−8.5	0.7	−2.7	−47.4	9.9
Non-fuel exporters	−0.7	−2.3	−5.8	−4.1	−2.0	0.6	1.8	−1.1	1.1	−2.5
Memorandum										
World trade prices (in US dollar terms) for major commodity groups										
Manufactures	9.6	13.6	10.4	−3.9	−2.1	−2.8	−3.0	1.2	17.9	12.8
Oil	22.8	46.0	63.6	9.8	−4.1	−11.7	−2.4	−4.8	−49.8	27.6
Non-oil primary commodities	10.3	17.9	5.5	−13.5	−9.9	6.9	4.2	−12.9	−1.1	−1.8

Source: IMF, *World Economic Outlook* (Washington, D.C., October 1987).

[a] Excluding China prior to 1978. [b] Compound annual rates of change. [c] For years prior to 1970, an imputed value of $1.00 has been assigned to the special drawing rights (SDR).

increase rapidly. In 1986, total international lending increased by 70 per cent; in 1985, the rate of increase was 40 per cent. These large increases were accounted for by the rapid structural changes taking place in the domestic and international financial markets and the large current account and fiscal imbalances of the major industrial countries.

By contrast, the flow of funds from the industrial to developing countries continued to stagnate. Net lending by industrial country banks to developing countries was negative as repayment exceeded new borrowing in 1986.[8] Private lending is expected to recover somewhat in 1987-1988 but it will be linked to the restructuring of existing debts. The debt position of many countries has continued to worsen. The total developing country debt in 1987 was projected to increase by nearly $100 billion to an estimated $1,200 billion. In 1988 it was further expected to increase by $37 billion.[9] For many Latin American and African countries, their indebtedness was seriously retarding sustained economic growth and making the process of structural adjustment extremely difficult.

B. IMPACT OF WORLD ECONOMIC DEVELOPMENTS ON THE DEVELOPING ESCAP REGION

The effects of changes in the external environment in the past two years, discussed in the preceding section, have not been uniform,

[8] The estimated net transfer on long-term debt (principal repayments plus interest payments minus disbursements) from developing countries during 1986 was estimated to be around $28 billion. For details, see World Bank, *World Debt Tables: External Debt of Developing Countries* (Washington, D.C., 1987).

[9] IMF, *World Economic Outlook* (Washington, D.C., October 1987).

the elements of change in that environment have had varying significance, extent and sometimes even direction, for different countries and groups of countries. The three factors that had the greatest impact on the region's developing economies were: the continuing depreciation of the dollar *vis-à-vis* other key currencies, the generally adverse trends in primary commodity prices and the lack of any substantial improvements in the capital inflows to the region's developing countries.

1. Trade flows

(a) General

The ESCAP region's exports in 1987 were mainly helped by the continued fall of the dollar in 1987 and the appreciation of the yen by about 22 per cent against it. The currencies of the region generally had a stable relationship with the United States dollar, which enhanced further the competitiveness of their exports on world markets. In the United States market, exports from the region, especially from East and South-East Asia, displaced to some extent more expensive Japanese exports. With the rise in its domestic demand and the progressive opening of its market, Japan also provided an expanding market for exports from developing economies of the region. Both the rise in manufactures exports, which largely benefited newly industrializing economies and some South-East Asian exporters, as well as some improvement in prices of primary commodities, including oil, from the second quarter of 1987 onwards, contributed to growth in export values of commodity-dependent economies of South and South-East Asia and the Pacific islands.

Exchange rate changes in the developing economies of Asia and the Pacific region have played an important part in their export

performance. Thus the depreciation of the regional currencies against the yen and other non-dollar key currencies helped to boost the East Asian newly industrializing economies' exports and create large current account surpluses for them. As a result, the soaring current account surpluses of the Republic of Korea (which reached $5.2 billion for the first seven months of 1987 and is estimated at $8-9 billion for 1987) and Taiwan (a province of the People's Republic of China) (estimated at $18.2 billion for 1987) have increased pressure to appreciate both the won and the new Taiwan dollar. The won appreciated by about 10 per cent against the United States currency between July 1986 – October 1987. In November 1987 the dollar slipped below 800 won, its lowest point in three and a half years. In November 1987, the new Taiwan dollar had appreciated by about 20 per cent compared with the average rate of 1986. The effects of the appreciation of both the won and the new Taiwan dollar started to be felt on the trade performance during the second half of 1987, particularly in the case of Taiwan Province which experienced a stronger deceleration of its export growth during the last quarter of the year. The gains in competitiveness resulting from the currency realignments (including the appreciation of the won and the new Taiwan dollar), on the other hand, helped the exports of South-East Asian economies. In addition, the Indonesian rupiah's devaluation by 31 per cent in 1986 helped accelerate the country's non-oil exports (table I.4).

(i) Exports of manufactures

The manufactures exporters of East Asia, which have shown more flexibility in adjusting to changes in world demand and have been

Table I.4. Selected developing economies in the ESCAP region. Percentage change of nominal exchange rate for the United States dollars and special drawing rights, December 1980-September 1987[a]

	Currency	United States dollars				Special drawing rights			
		December 1980-December 1985	December 1980-December 1985 annual average	December 1985-December 1986	September 1986-September 1987	December 1980-December 1985	December 1980-December 1985 annual average	December 1985-December 1986	September 1986-September 1987
Afghanistan	(Afghani)	10.4	2.1	—	—	−5.0	−1.0	11.4	5.4
Bangladesh	(Taka)	90.8	18.2	−0.6	2.3	64.3	12.9	10.6	7.9
Brunei Darussalam	(Brunei dollar)	0.9	0.2	−0.5	−2.3	...	...	...	—
Burma	(Kyat)	16.1	3.2	−10.2	−5.3	...	...	...	...
China	(Yuan renminbi)	109.2	21.8	16.3	0.2	80.2	16.0	29.4	5.7
Fiji	(Fiji dollar)	41.8	8.4	2.2	9.4	22.0	4.4	13.8	15.4
Hong Kong	(Hong Kong dollar)	52.0	10.4	−0.2	0.0[b]	...	...	...	...
India	(Indian rupee)	53.4	10.7	7.9	3.2	32.1	6.4	20.1	8.9
Indonesia	(Indonesian rupiah)	79.5	15.9	45.9	1.0	54.6	10.9	62.4	6.6
Iran (Islamic Republic of)	(Iranian rial)	16.5	3.3	−10.2	−5.3	—	—	—	—
Lao People's Democratic Republic	(New Kip)	250.0	50.0	—	—	...	...	...	...
Malaysia	(Ringgit)	9.2	1.8	7.3	−3.4	−6.0	−1.2	19.5	1.8
Maldives	(Rufiyaa)	−5.6	−1.1	1.6	41.3	−18.7	−3.7	13.2	49.0
Mongolia	(Tughrik)	26.3	5.3	−16.7	−12.4[b]	...	...	...	...
Nepal	(Nepalese rupee)	72.5	14.5	6.3	2.3	48.6	9.7	18.4	7.9
Pakistan	(Pakistan rupee)	61.4	12.3	7.9	3.1	39.0	7.8	20.2	8.7
Papua New Guinea	(Kina)	57.1	11.4	−5.0	−7.9	35.4	7.1	5.8	−2.9
Philippines	(Philippine peso)	150.4	30.1	7.9	0.7	115.7	23.1	20.1	6.2
Republic of Korea	(Won)	34.9	7.0	−3.2	−8.1	16.2	3.2	7.8	−3.1
Samoa	(Tala)	148.2	29.6	−4.7	−9.3	113.8	22.8	6.1	−4.4
Singapore	(Singapore dollar)	0.6	0.1	3.3	−3.4	−13.4	−2.7	15.0	1.8
Solomon Islands	(Solomon Island dollar)	102.4	20.5	23.1	10.7	74.1	14.8	37.2	16.8
Sri Lanka	(Sri Lanka rupee)	52.3	10.5	4.1	6.3	31.1	6.2	15.9	12.1
Thailand	(Baht)	29.2	5.8	−2.0	−0.9	11.2	2.2	9.2	4.5
Tonga	(Tonga dollar)	−41.9	−8.4	131.1	...	...	...	...	...
Vanuatu	(Vatu)	37.3	7.5	15.9	10.4	18.2	3.6	29.1	16.4
Viet Nam	(New Dong)	618.4	123.7	...	—	...	...	...	—

Sources: ADB, *Key Indicators of Developing Member Countries of ADB,* vol. XLI, No. 5 (July 1986), p. 34; IMF, *International Financial Statistics,* vol. XL, No. 7 (July 1987); United Nations, *Monthly Bulletin of Statistics* (May 1987); and national sources.

a   A positive figure indicates depreciation of a national currency *vis-à-vis the* United States dollars or special drawing rights and a negative figure indicates appreciation.   b   July 1986-July 1987.

11

more successful at diversifying their export markets, were the main beneficiaries of the continuing appreciation of the yen and other key currencies and the consequent increase in the competitiveness of their exports. Total exports of goods from Hong Kong were estimated to rise by 27 per cent in real terms in 1987 compared with 15.2 per cent in 1986. In the case of the Republic of Korea, nominal merchandise exports surged by 28 per cent during the first half of 1987. Exports of goods and services of Taiwan Province were estimated to rise by about 32 per cent in 1987.

The exports of manufactures from South-East Asian economies benefited by the appreciation of both the non-dollar key currencies and the regional currencies of the newly industrializing economies. Along with firmer commodity prices, some South-East Asian economies recorded impressive gains. Thailand, in particular, experienced rapid increases in manufactures exports, which are estimated to rise by about 39 per cent in 1987 compared with 32.8 per cent in 1986. These favourable factors also helped Singapore to accelerate its manufactures exports by an estimated 33 per cent during the first half of 1987 and to attain the high GDP growth rate of 6.8 per cent in 1987 after a three-year long recession. The other economies of South-East Asia — Indonesia, Malaysia and, to a lesser extent, the Philippines — also experienced large growth in their manufactures exports. In Malaysia, manufactures exports grew by 22.6 per cent with total export growth, including oil and primary commodities, projected to rise by 14.7 per cent in nominal terms in 1987.

The strong expansion in manufactures exports in 1987 was not confined to East and South-East Asia. The more diversified econo-mies of South Asia — India and Pakistan — also experienced large increases in exports. Exports from India, which revived in 1986, were estimated to grow during 1987 at a nominal rate of about 15 per cent. The impact of the drought on irrigation and power supply is likely to have adversely affected the export performance of India during the second half of the year. The liberalization programmes undertaken by the Government in the past appear to be having some lagged effect on exports. Pakistan, favoured by better prices for some of its commodities, especially cotton, continued to experience export growth at rate exceeding 10 per cent during 1987, which, however, was below the exceptionally high growth of around 21 per cent in 1986. The other South Asian economy, Sri Lanka, which was also badly affected by adverse climatic conditions also experienced a deterioration in its trade performance in 1987. Lastly, the exports of China have also revived strongly in 1987, rising for the period January to June 1987 by 24.2 per cent from a year earlier (figure I.2).

(ii) Primary commodity exports

While the region's manufactures exports grew rapidly in 1987, its primary commodity exports, which provide the main source of income and foreign exchange in the region's poorer countries continued to arouse concern.[10] The global index of non-fuel primary commodity prices in 1986 was about 30 per cent lower than in 1980. Although the index rose to 77 per cent of its 1980 level by August 1987, the average commodity prices remained well below their

---

10 A detailed analysis of the region's non-fuel primary commodity exports is undertaken in part two of this *Survey*.

cyclical highs. Between 1980-1985, the terms-of-trade for non-fuel primary commodities declined by an annual average of 0.8 per cent for the developing South-East Asian and Pacific island economies and by 1.4 per cent for the South Asian countries. The growth in export volume, however, has more than offset relative price declines to yield higher foreign exchange earnings for the South-East Asian subregion. For the South Asian countries volume growth was insufficient to offset relative price declines, and their foreign exchange earnings fell substantially during 1980-1985.

There was, however, some improvement in commodity prices between December 1986 and August 1987, especially those of agricultural raw materials which increased by about 23.4 per cent. Cotton, jute, timber and rubber prices rose significantly during the first half of the year, although remaining far below their cyclical peaks. While minerals and metals prices also rose by about 20 per cent prices for food and beverages, which are the main exports of the countries of the ESCAP region, continued to stagnate. Prices for tin, an important export item for a number of South-East Asian countries, which had suddenly collapsed in 1985, rose very marginally. Prices for tropical beverages, in particular coffee and tea, continued to decline markedly. Rice prices rose by about 13 per cent but maize and sugar prices continued to stagnate. Prices for vegetable oil-seeds and oils rose only marginally but prices of coconut oil and palm oil firmed somewhat more. The stock market collapse of October 1987 has created considerable uncertainty about continued increases in primary commodity prices. Some prices, notably for industrial raw materials such as aluminium, started to drop

Figure I.2. Selected developing economies in the ESCAP region. Movements in share of manufactures exports, 1980[a], 1983 and 1986[b]

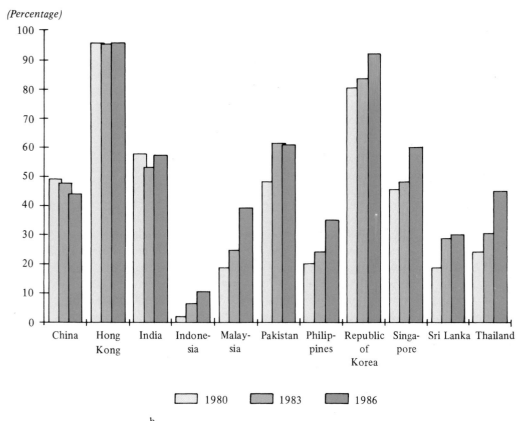

(Percentage)

after the stock market crash of October 1987. On the average, however, prices of primary commodities have been firmer in 1987 than in 1986. The increase in oil prices of about 7 to 8 per cent during first eight months of 1987 benefited the oil exporters of the region, notably Brunei Darussalam and Indonesia.

(b) The subregional pattern[11]

(i) China and East Asia

China's external position, which had weakened substantially in 1984 and 1985, improved considerably in 1987 after a series

---

[11] Trade flows, capital flows and developments in external debt of least developed and Pacific island countries are discussed in chapter III, this *Survey*.

of austerity measures and efforts to strengthen economic management and fiscal policies during 1986. China's foreign trade deficit fell from $8.98 billion to $2.7 billion in the first nine months of 1987, mainly owing to appreciation of the Japanese yen and rising oil prices. Exports rose by 23.9 per cent to $26.5 billion, while imports were down by 3.8 per cent to $29.2 billion. Much of the increase in exports was in light industrial goods, textiles and electrical machinery.

In 1986, the Government tightened monetary control, adopted a more restrictive fiscal policy, and undertook revisions of key prices and a number of pricing measures, including interest and exchange rates. Administrative controls over wages and investment

and selective tightening of foreign exchange allocations and import restrictions, notably on luxury consumer goods were some of the supplementary measures introduced. Moreover, to restore export competitiveness, the authorities allowed China's currency to depreciate.

In Hong Kong, the growth momentum in exports, since the recovery in March 1986, was sustained throughout the first half of 1987. The depreciation of the Hong Kong dollar, in line with the depreciation of the United States dollar under the linked exchange rate system, against most major currencies contributed to this improved performance. Moreover, the rate of depreciation of the Hong Kong dollar against the deutsche mark and yen during

13

the 12 months ending June 1987 was higher than that of the currencies of its major competitors, the Republic of Korea, Singapore, and Taiwan Province, thus enhancing the external competitiveness of Hong Kong's products. In Hong Kong, the value of imports has kept up with the growth of exports. The strong growth in imports during 1986/87 was partly attributable to an increase in retained imports, induced by a buoyant economy, and partly by the continued rapid growth in the re-export trade. For 1987, the merchandise trade balance is expected to be in deficit amounting to $874 million, in view of the rapidly rising value of imports. The strengthening of the yen has also made the imports of capital and intermediate goods from Japan more expensive. The healthy performance of the services sector, however, would offset the negative visible trade balance and bring about a surplus of $0.8 billion.

In the Republic of Korea, where exports picked up sharply in 1986, increasing by more than 14 per cent compared with 3.6 per cent in 1985, a growth rate of 21.6 per cent was expected to be achieved in 1987. Imports rose by only 1.4 per cent in 1986, benefiting from the fall in oil prices and increased import substitution in intermediate goods. In 1986, the trade balance recorded a surplus of $4.2 billion, a marked contrast to the $2.6 billion trade deficit in 1982. The invisible trade balance recorded a deficit of $628 million in 1986, a marked improvement over the previous year, owing to the considerable increases in travel account receipts, as well as to the continuous decline in interest rates.

During the second quarter of 1987, the Republic of Korea began to implement a package of economic measures to slash its

burgeoning trade surplus with the United States, which is the country's biggest export market, along with the appreciation of the won against the United States dollar. Despite these measures, a record trade surplus of nearly $3 billion resulted during the first half of 1987. Merchandise exports reached $20.7 billion, while merchandise imports totalled $17.7 billion. The services balance was also in surplus, at $649 million, owing to decreased interest payments and increased earnings from tourism and overseas construction. Net transfers also recorded $516 million surplus owing to remittances from abroad. This resulted in a current account surplus of $4.1 billion for the first half of this year, compared with $600 million for the same period last year.

(ii) South-East Asia

In Indonesia, export earnings from oil are likely to have revived slightly in 1987 as the 5 per cent cut in oil production adopted by that country in 1986 was expected to be more than offset by the increase in price. The devaluation of the rupiah interacting with the increased demand from Europe and Japan were expected to boost non-oil export earnings by 8.5 per cent. It was estimated that merchandise exports and merchandise imports would amount to $16.1 billion and $12.6 billion respectively, resulting in a trade surplus of $3.5 billion, up from $1.4 billion in 1986. The current account deficit in 1987 was expected to decrease by 26.7 per cent to $3.4 billion owing partly to the fall in the invisible trade deficit.

In Malaysia, the surplus in the merchandise trade account was expected to rise from $3.3 billion in 1986 to $4.7 billion in 1987. In 1986, although export volume rose by 14.5 per cent, the increase

was not strong enough to offset the sharp decline of 18 per cent in export prices, mainly of primary commodities. The terms of trade deteriorated by another 12 per cent on top of the decline of 5 per cent in 1985. In 1987, some recovery in terms of trade was expected owing to an estimated 4 to 5 per cent rise in the average prices of Malaysia's commodity exports. After stagnating in 1985, exports of manufactured products rose sharply by 24.5 per cent in 1986 and a further 12 per cent increase was expected in 1987. This would raise the share of manufactures exports to the record level of 44 per cent of total exports in 1987, owing to the remarkable effort to diversify the sources of Malaysia's export earnings.

In line with the slack in aggregate domestic demand, imports were estimated to fall further in 1987, after a decline of 7.5 per cent in 1985 and 12 per cent in 1986. Significant declines were recorded in imports of crude petroleum and products, machinery, completely-knocked-down parts for passenger car assembly, metal products, fertilizer and rice. Malaysia's improved performance in external trade in 1987, with the stable services account deficit of $3.9 billion, would result in a surplus on the current account amounting to $784 million.

In the Philippines, a merchandise trade deficit of $660 million is predicted for 1987 owing to the higher import bill resulting from the import liberalization scheme adopted in 1986 as well as increased consumer demand in the domestic market. In 1986, merchandise exports rose to $4.5 billion (6.6 per cent), while merchandise imports increased by 2.5 per cent to $5.3 billion, leaving a trade deficit of $0.7 billion. The country's traditional exports, consisting of coconut, sugar and copper concentrates, accounted for about two thirds of total export earnings. The decline in the value of imports was mainly due to reduced demand for capital goods and lower oil prices. A lower trade deficit combined with a positive net services and transfers account resulted in a current account surplus of $0.8 billion. In 1987, the current account is expected to remain in surplus amounting to $410 million, which is lower than last year's surplus as a result of the increased trade deficit.

Exports from Singapore accelerated sharply in 1987 after declining by 1.4 per cent in 1986. Exports were boosted by adjustment measures taken at the beginning of 1986 and the appreciation of the yen and major European currencies against the Singapore dollar. The main impetus to growth in non-oil domestic exports came from strong external demand for disk drives, integrated and printed circuits, radio and television sets and garments. While oil exports continued to post negative growth rates, non-oil exports grew by 33 per cent for the first half of 1987. For the year as a whole, nominal exports are projected to grow at about 15 per cent. Imports also grew in nominal terms, mainly because of the depreciation of the Singapore dollar against the currencies of its major suppliers, except the United States. Income from tourism was expected to rise substantially in 1987. Thus, the projected growth of real exports of goods and services by 9 per cent and of real imports by 6 per cent was expected to improve the current account balance.

In Thailand, growth in total merchandise exports was expected to slow down to about 15 per cent for 1987 from 23 per cent in 1986. The rapid expansion of the economy, large increases in urban incomes, the need to import

larger amounts of raw, semi-processed and capital goods, together with the firming of oil prices, have led to a rapid increase in imports by about 33.3 per cent during the first nine months of 1987. For the first nine months of 1987, the balance-of-trade deficit rose sharply leaving a gap of about 26.8 billion baht (over $1 billion). The current account balance, however, was not expected to deteriorate much as revenues from tourism increased sharply by 26 per cent for the first three quarters of 1987 to an estimated 34.1 billion baht (about $1.3 billion).

(iii) South Asia

In India, performance in foreign trade improved considerably in 1986/87. According to provisional figures, exports grew by 14 per cent in 1986/87, compared with fall of 7.1 per cent in the previous year, while imports

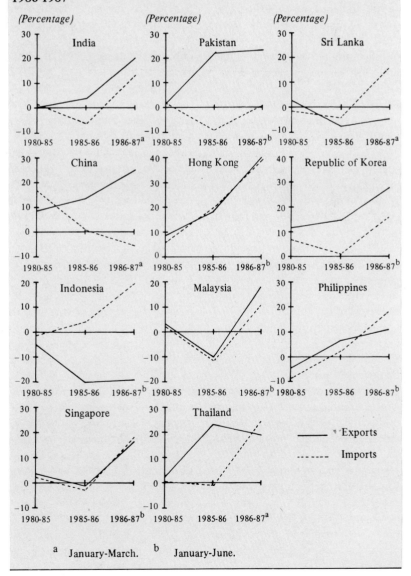

Figure I.3. Selected developing economies in the ESCAP region. Average annual growth rate of exports and imports, 1980-1985, 1985-1986 and 1986-1987

a   January-March.   b   January-June.

15

rose by 1.5 per cent compared with 15.1 per cent in 1985/86. As a result, the trade deficit fell from 4.1 per cent of GNP in 1985/86 to 3.2 per cent in 1986/87. High rates of growth in exports were registered for precious and semi-precious stones (37.5 per cent), leather manufactures (61.3 per cent) and engineering goods (27.5 per cent). As a result of concerted efforts, the level of exports of electronics is likely to go up from Rs 1,510 million in 1984/85 to Rs 2,000 million in 1986/87. The decline in imports in India during 1986/87 was primarily attributable to a sharp fall in the oil import bill, to the tune of Rs 21 billion (44 per cent), as a result of the steep fall in international oil prices.

Between 1981/82 and 1985/86, the invisibles account recorded a yearly surplus of Rs 35 billion to Rs 38 billion mainly owing to tourism and transfer payments which have emerged as an important source of foreign exchange receipts. In 1986/87, earnings from tourism are expected to go up considerably in view of the significant increase in tourist arrivals in the country. Negative factors on the balance of payments are the increase in debt-service payments and some slackening in the flow of remittances from Indians working abroad.

In Pakistan, in 1986/87 exports surpassed the plan target for the first time despite the fall in the world prices of rice and raw cotton. The merchandise exports, which averaged around $2.5 billion during the first half of the 1980s, increased to $3.0 billion in 1985/86 and are estimated to increase further to $3.5 billion in 1986/87. Exports of manufactured goods are expected to increase by nearly 42 per cent during 1986/87. Major gains were made in the exports of cotton and synthetic textiles. The rapid growth of exports

was accompanied by significant changes in the composition of exports. From July 1985 to March 1986, the share of primary goods declined from 35 to 27 per cent, while that of semi-manufactures and manufactured goods increased from 16 and 49 per cent to 20 and 53 per cent respectively. During 1986/87, exports proceeds are estimated to increase by 17.7 per cent in dollar terms and imports are expected to fall by 2.5 per cent over the previous year. The trade deficit is, therefore, likely to decline to $2.4 billion. Workers' remittances are estimated at $2.3 billion, lower by 6 per cent than the target. As a result, the current account deficit is expected to decline from over $1.1 billion (3.3 per cent of GNP) in 1985/86 to $0.9 billion (2.4 per cent of GNP) in 1986/87.

In Sri Lanka, the performance of the external trade sector continued to be unfavourable in 1986. The value of exports decreased by 8 per cent. However, imports also declined by 4.3 per cent, resulting in a contraction in the trade deficit by about 3 per cent as compared with the deficit in 1985. In common with other primary producing exporters, Sri Lanka suffered a heavy drop in the earnings from agricultural exports as a result of the fall in agricultural commodity prices. Industrial exports earned 11 per cent more in terms of rupees in 1986, but in terms of special drawing rights the earnings were lower by 7 per cent. The current account balance of Sri Lanka remained under pressure in 1986. The gross foreign exchange earnings from tourism in 1986 at Rs 2,000 million (SDR 61 million) were the lowest since 1980. When compared with the peak level of earnings of SDR 133 million in 1982, the earnings in 1986 showed a decrease of 54 per cent.

2. Capital flows

The marked decline in total net resource flows to developing countries throughout 1982-1985 continued in 1986, when measured at constant 1985 prices and exchange rates, with a decline in volume of some 15 per cent in 1986 from the 1985 level. This fundamental underlying downward trend during 1982-1986 was dominated by sharp cuts in export credits and private flows. Disbursements of official development finance from all sources, including both concessional aid and non-concessional development loans, also fell by about 4 per cent in volume terms. At the same time, disbursements to developing countries by multilateral agencies appear to have fallen in volume terms in 1986, despite the increase in fast-disbursing adjustment lending by the World Bank. For the capital-importing developing countries together, the net transfer of financial resources resulting from net capital flows minus international payments of interest and profit was negative in 1986 for the third consecutive year, primarily on account of private credit flows.[12] Negative transfers from developing countries amounted to $50 billion in 1985 and 1986 and are expected to continue for the next few years.

A welcome development for Asia, however, has been the increase in its share of private capital flows to developing countries in 1985-1986 to 55 per cent, compared with 19 per cent in 1981. Asia has replaced the western hemisphere (20 per cent in 1985-1986, compared with 70 per cent in 1981) as the main recipient.[13]

---

[12] United Nations, *World Economic Survey 1987* (United Nations publication, Sales No. E.87.II.C.1), p. 72.

[13] OECD, *Financing and External Debt of Developing Countries, 1986 Survey* (Paris, May 1987), p. 27.

The current dominance of Asia covers bank lending, bonds and foreign direct investment. Total flows to Asia increased from $29 billion in 1984 to $31 billion in 1985 and $33 billion in 1986, and the increase was due to both official and private flows. Nominal gains in official development assistance (ODA) in 1985-1986 are considerably lower if amounts are adjusted for constant prices and exchange rates. Within Asia, the share of China and India together in ODA receipts remained modest (22 per cent during 1984-1986) but was much higher in private flows (48 per cent).

(a) Bank lending

Net international bank lending grew by $160 billion in 1986, some 50 per cent more than in 1985 and a figure comparable to the historical high recorded in 1980-1981. However, the bulk of the expansion ($142 billion) was accounted for by new lending to countries within the Bank for International Settlements reporting area. Private bank lending to developing countries fell in 1986 to one half of its level in 1985. For the great majority of developing countries, the continued low level of bank lending is a reflection largely of the interaction between the large overhang of debt and the persistent worsening of the terms of trade. Moreover, the near totality of international bank lending to developing countries in 1986 and early 1987 consisted of lending to a few creditworthy Asian countries. In 1986, Asian countries received some $2.7 billion of new lending and increased their deposits by $11.7 billion. The reasons for their reduced loan demand in 1986 were several and varied. While China sharply curtailed its borrowing from foreign banks in 1986, following a large uptake of loans in 1985, its net creditor

position declined by $1.5 billion to an outstanding level of only $0.5 billion by the end of 1986. The Republic of Korea's large current account surpluses have induced it to repay loans with the aim of reducing its outstanding debt over the next five years. Debt repayments by the Republic of Korea led to a $2.3 billion fall on outstanding claims on the country, which more than offset a $1.7 billion contraction in deposits. For similar reasons, Taiwan Province developed a net creditor position of over $29 billion by the end of 1986.[14] Several creditworthy countries in Asia, such as Malaysia and Thailand, cut net borrowing from international banks.

During the decade ending in 1981, net export credits to developing countries had become an important source of financing, reaching $18 billion in 1981. These credits fell, on a net basis, throughout 1982-1986, down to an estimated $2 billion in 1986, which represents an even sharper decline than for bank lending. The reasons for this weakness include debt crises and loss of creditworthiness, cuts in imports and increased recourse to financial markets. In some cases the development of barter trade reduced the demand for export credits. The fall in commodity prices also played a role, e.g., in leading to cuts in new mining projects.[15]

New gross external bond offerings rose by 35 per cent in 1986, reaching $226.4 billion. The concentration of external bond offerings in favour of borrowers from the OECD area remained extremely high, as indicated by a share of nearly 94 per cent in 1986. In a major turnaround, develop-

ing country borrowing on external bond markets fell significantly in 1986 to $4.4 billion from $7.9 billion in 1985. As a result, the share of the developing countries in total bond issues more than halved, from 4.7 per cent in 1985 to 1.9 per cent in 1986, the lowest figure in the present decade. Among developing countries, those from the ESCAP region were the predominant borrowers on external bond markets. The aggregate volume of borrowing on external bond markets by countries of the ESCAP region amounted to $6.9 billion in 1985 and $3.2 billion in 1986. As far as individual countries and areas are concerned, in 1986, only China, Hong Kong and the Republic of Korea were in a position to raise significant amounts in floating bond issues.[16] At $600 million, aggregate borrowing on external bond markets by developing countries was very modest in the first quarter of 1987, confirming the slowdown that had become apparent in the final quarter of 1986.[17]

(b) Direct foreign investment

There has been a renewed and growing interest in foreign direct investment, both as a possible substitute for international bank lending, and as a complement to the ODA, whose future growth prospects continue to be dim. At present, the contribution of foreign direct investment to total external resource inflows is moderate when considered for the developing ESCAP region as a whole, amounting to about 14 per cent of the total.[18] The

---

[14] OECD, *Financial Market Trends* (Paris, May 1987), pp. 46-47.

[15] OECD, *Financing and External Debt of Developing Countries, 1986 Survey* (Paris, May 1987), p. 20-21.

[16] OECD, *Financial Market Trends* (Paris, May 1987), pp. 96.

[17] *Ibid.*, p. 63.

[18] ESCAP/UNCTC Joint Unit on Transnational Corporations, *Transnational Corporations and External Financial Flows of Developing Economies in Asia and the Pacific* (Bangkok, 1986), p. 28.

economies of East and South-East Asia receive the lion's share of foreign investment flows to the region. The disparity in the shares of different economies within the East and South-East Asian region is also worth noting. Hong Kong, Malaysia, the Republic of Korea, Singapore and Thailand have attracted a great deal of foreign investment compared with Indonesia and the Philippines. Resources mobilized through foreign investment have been extremely low in all of the South Asian countries. In some South Asian countries, other private sector flows, particularly export credits, have been more important than foreign investment in external finance received (table I.5).

3. Developments in external debt

The decline in net resource flows contributed to the deceleration in the underlying growth in the external debt of developing countries as a group during 1985-1986. The fall in the value of the dollar *vis-à-vis* other key currencies, however, had the effect of boosting the dollar value of non-dollar debt stocks. Thus, total external debt of developing countries increased by $83 billion in 1985, only $32 billion of that amount was due to increased new borrowing and the rest represented the "exchange rate effect". This valuation effect was even more overwhelming in 1986 during which changes in the value of the United States dollar accounted for more than three fourths of the $95 billion total estimated increase in the debt of developing countries.

In recent years, growth in external debt has accelerated in several developing countries of the ESCAP region. This is partly due to the fact that these countries were less affected by debt-

servicing difficulties and so they were in a better position to borrow from the international capital markets that were looking for new borrowers. In contrast to the rapid increase in external debt, exports and GNP in United States dollar terms grew much more slowly, thereby aggravating the debt-servicing situation in some ESCAP countries.

According to OECD data,[19] the external debt of 15 ESCAP developing countries and areas — Bangladesh, Burma, China, Hong Kong, India, Indonesia, Malaysia, Nepal, Pakistan, the Philippines, the Republic of Korea, Singapore, Sri Lanka, Thailand and Taiwan Province — increased by 15.3 per cent in 1985, against 9.8 per cent in 1984 and 11.7 per cent in 1983. These countries and areas experienced much faster growth in their external debt relative to all developing countries. Their external debt situation, assessed by various external debt indicators, worsened in 1985. Both the external debt outstanding and debt-service payment increased significantly. According to OECD data, the debt outstanding to GNP ratio increased from 26 per cent in 1984 to 31 per cent in 1985. The ratio of debt outstanding to exports jumped from 124 to 149 per cent during the same period. According to World Bank data, the debt-service ratio increased from 11 to 16 per cent and the interest-service ratio increased from 8 to 9 per cent. However, it should be noted that these ratios are still lower than the averages of all developing countries, implying that the debt situation in the ESCAP

region is relatively better than in other regions.[20]

The Republic of Korea was the largest debtor in the ESCAP region, its debt outstanding being $57.5 billion at the end of 1985. Its huge debt, however, does not invoke serious concern since its exports have been increasing rapidly in recent years.

Indonesia was the second largest debtor among the developing countries of the ESCAP region, its debt reaching $37.1 billion at the end of 1985. Its 1985 debt-service payments increased by $0.76 billion, while export earnings decreased owing mainly to the lower oil prices, thus pushing up the debt-service ratio to 20 per cent.

The external debt of the Philippines reached $28 billion at the end of 1985. The ratio of debt outstanding to GNP at 88 per cent and that of debt outstanding to exports at 361 per cent in 1985 were quite high. The debt-service ratio rose from 13.9 per cent in 1984 to 15.8 per cent in 1985, in spite of the fact that close to $1 billion bilateral official loans by the Paris Club were rescheduled in 1984.[21] Over $5.8 billion of commercial debts were also rescheduled in 1985. Nevertheless, the country's debt situation continued to cause anxiety owing to depressed export earnings. The external debt of the Philippines was estimated to rise to $29 billion by the end of 1987, owing mainly to the decline of the United States

---

[19] The OECD coverage of external debt is broader and therefore data are higher than World Bank data. See Jungsoo Lee and I.P. David, "A survey of the external debt situation in Asian developing countries, 1985", *Statistical Report*, Series No. 9 (Manila, Asian Development Bank, April 1987).

[20] *Ibid.*, pp. 10-12.

[21] The Paris Club is the name given to an *ad hoc* Group of Creditor Governments — all of them industrialized countries — which meets in Paris at meetings organized and chaired by the French Treasury. The club originated in 1956 when Argentina requested that bilateral negotiations be replaced with multilateral meetings of its creditors. Since then it has become the major forum for rescheduling official debt.

Table I.5. Selected developing countries in the ESCAP region. Balance of payments, 1982-1987

(Millions of US dollars)

	Year	Trade balance	Other goods, service and income balance	Private transfer	Current account balance	Official transfer	Direct and portfolio investment	Other long-term capital	Basic balance	Short-term capital	Errors[a] and omissions	Overall balance	Change in reserves (– = increase)
Bangladesh	1982	–1 452.6	–346.8	394.4	–1 405.0	749.2	—	609.9	–45.9	–121.1	123.2	–43.8	43.9
	1983	–1 206.8	–271.1	649.6	–828.3	768.5	1.7	474.4	416.3	–51.4	–42.9	322.0	–322.0
	1984	–1 408.3	–338.2	473.3	–1 273.2	730.1	1.0	546.5	4.4	12.3	–45.7	–29.0	28.8
	1985	–1 287.0	–352.1	449.4	–1 189.7	650.2	–7.2	464.3	–82.4	–31.3	–9.2	–122.9	122.9
	1986	–1 373.7	–395.9	520.7	–1 248.9	612.2	2.5	763.4	129.2	–9.6	–81.2	38.4	–38.6
	1987 I	–183.2	–57.1	181.2	–59.1	117.5	2.1	98.9	159.4	–14.5	–17.7	127.2	–127.2
Burma	1982	–490.2	–74.7	7.1	–557.8	59.1	—	328.9	–169.8	11.3	11.7	–146.8	146.7
	1983	–353.0	–73.2	8.1	–418.1	74.1	—	213.4	–130.6	32.2	74.0	–24.4	24.5
	1984	–200.4	–85.3	7.2	–278.5	60.7	—	193.5	–24.3	0.2	8.3	–15.8	15.7
	1985	–202.1	–83.9	5.8	–280.2	74.7	—	132.4	–73.1	16.4	34.1	–22.6	22.6
China	1982	4 249	1 088	530	5 867	–44	427	–18	6 232	98	8	6 338	–6 338
	1983	1 990	1 986	436	4 412	75	563	609	5 659	–28	–846	4 785	–4 785
	1984	14	2 053	305	2 372	137	1 207	401	4 117	–411	–1 889	1 817	–1 816
	1985	–13 123	1 463	171	–11 489	72	1 795	2 644	–6 978	2 270	70	–4 638	4 638
	1986	–9 140	1 727	255	–7 158	124	3 032	4 515	513	–2 295	–224	–2 006	2 006
India	1982	–4 820	–620	2 599	–2 841	318	—	1 116	–1 408	–659	173	–1 894	1 894
	1983	–4 098	–879	2 650	–2 327	411	—	1 536	–379	519	–895	–755	755
	1984	–4 025	–1 089	2 278	–2 836	492	—	2 769	425	275	207	907	–908
	1985	–5 616	–1 337	2 456	–4 497	320	—	3 341	–836	–60	1 040	144	–145
	1986 I	–1 481	–573	499	–1 555	158	—	1 301	–96	–97	178	–15	15
Indonesia	1982	1 893	–7 351	—	–5 458	134	540	4 556	–228	526	–2 177	–1 879	1 879
	1983	963	–7 415	10	–6 442	104	660	4 663	–1 015	731	455	171	–172
	1984	5 707	–7 730	53	–1 970	114	212	2 855	1 211	476	–747	940	–941
	1985,b	5 822	–7 833	61	–1 950	110	238	2 054	452	–98	174	528	–528
	1986	1 615	–5 122	53	–3 454	86	507	1 975	–886	969	–421	–338	338
Malaysia	1982	–753	–2 816	–53	–3 622	21	3 201	404	5	140	–535	–390	390
	1983	432	–3 920	–35	–3 523	26	2 671	1 296	470	–113	–398	–41	42
	1984	2 981	–4 614	–63	–1 696	24	1 800	1 343	1 471	–123	–1 005	343	–343
	1985	3 577	–4 284	–46	–753	19	1 030	552	849	350	5	1 204	–1 204
	1986	3 369	–3 661	–19	–311	14	1 129	99	932	33	62	1 027	–1 027

(continued overleaf)

Table I.5 (continued)

Year	Trade balance	Other goods, service and income balance	Private transfer	Current account balance	Official transfer	Direct and portfolio investment	Other long-term capital	Basic balance	Short-term capital	Errors[a] and omissions	Overall balance	Change in reserves (— = increase)
Nepal												
1982	−318.7	90.8	34.0	−193.9	108.6	—	60.5	−24.8	2.1	27.1	4.4	−4.2
1983	−366.8	88.7	39.1	−239.0	93.4	—	62.0	−83.6	45.4	−21.2	−59.4	59.4
1984	−272.8	59.9	34.8	−178.1	82.9	—	71.9	−23.3	−11.8	−9.6	−44.7	44.7
1985	−288.6	45.3	36.4	−206.9	80.6	—	90.3	−36.0	−29.5	32.9	−32.6	32.6
1986	−297.2	75.3	39.5	−182.4	69.5	—	69.3	−43.5	5.0	65.8	27.3	−27.3
Pakistan												
1982	−3 403	−552	2 793	−1 162	360	66	458	−278	6	103	−169	170
1983	−2 715	−635	3 116	−234	258	31	401	456	94	296	846	−846
1984	−3 754	−768	2 942	−1 580	384	69	353	−774	−110	127	−757	756
1985	−3 230	−914	2 710	−1 434	354	252	343	−485	4	235	−246	246
1986	−2 819	−991	2 635	−1 175	476	200	447	−52	−137	315	126	−125
Philippines												
1982	−2 646	−1 040	322	−3 364	152	17	1 548	−1 647	1 281	−264	−630	629
1983	−2 485	−738	237	−2 986	235	112	1 044	−1 595	−1 550	1 227	−1 918	1 918
1984	−679	−975	118	−1 536	268	6	285	−977	474	895	392	−392
1985	−482	111	172	−199	207	−9	3 051	3 050	−2 741	−284	25	−25
1986	−202	783	235	816	206	114	1 674	2 810	−1 671	204	1 343	−1 343
1987 I	−182	−38	65	−155	37	31	121	34	180	−183	31	−31
Republic of Korea												
1982	−2 594	−555	447	−2 702	52	−61	1 858	−853	2 159	−1 233	73	−74
1983	−1 763	−435	566	−1 632	26	131	1 660	185	524	−880	−171	171
1984	−1 036	−877	516	−1 397	25	406	2 606	1 640	−189	−924	527	−527
1985	−19	−1 446	555	−910	23	1 182	1 113	1 408	−333	−917	158	−158
1986	4 206	−628	1 028	4 606	11	626	−3 197	2 046	−1 422	−459	165	−165
1987 I	1 423	294	238	1 955	—	−38	−1 080	837	−1 080	170	−73	73
Singapore												
1982	−6 762	5 670	−101	−1 193	−13	1 272	671	738	365	−173	930	−931
1983	−5 823	5 427	−170	−566	−14	802	239	461	1 422	−1 099	784	−784
1984	−4 071	3 909	−193	−355	−11	812	−125	321	893	−62	1 152	−1 152
1985	−3 014	3 170	−159	−3	−12	1 276	−710	552	−42	1 920	2 430	−2 431
1986	−2 328	2 964	−143	493	−14	634	−180	933	−1 711	871	93	−93
Sri Lanka												
1982	−780.4	−194.0	263.8	−710.6	161.6	63.6	454.9	−30.5	−18.1	99.7	51.1	−51.2
1983	−664.4	−246.4	274.5	−636.3	170.1	37.8	370.9	−57.5	36.0	−2.9	−24.4	24.5
1984	−237.1	−241.1	276.5	−201.7	202.6	32.6	337.1	370.6	−20.2	−111.8	238.6	−238.6
1985	−522.6	−338.5	265.5	−595.6	177.2	24.8	304.4	−89.2	17.7	12.6	−58.9	59.0
1986	−555.4	−327.4	294.1	−588.7	176.9	29.2	313.2	−69.4	−1.6	7.5	−63.5	63.5

(continued overleaf)

Table I.5 *(continued)*

Year	Trade balance	Other goods, service and income balance	Private transfer	Current account balance	Official transfer	Direct and portfolio investment	Other long-term capital	Basic balance	Short-term capital	Errors[a] and omissions	Overall balance	Change in reserves (- = increase)
Thailand												
1982	-731	-456	75	-1 112	108	257	978	232	58	-411	-121	120
1983	-2 861	-290	153	-2 998	124	456	844	-1 574	662	723	-189	188
1984	-1 898	-386	59	-2 225	115	555	1 231	-324	767	-13	430	-432
1985	-1 332	-370	47	-1 655	118	1 057	558	78	-99	249	228	-228
1986	306	-303	62	65	158	224	-178	269	-230	893	932	-932

Source: IMF, *International Financial Statistics*, vol. XL, No. 10 (October 1987).

a Including counterparts to monetization/demonetization of gold, special drawing rights allocations, and valuation changes. Including exceptional financing and liabilities constituting foreign authorities reserves.   b January-September.

I January-March.

dollar against the deutsche mark and the yen in which a considerable portion of the country's foreign debt is denominated. Interest payments alone have been sapping almost half of total export revenue. In an effort to trim the debt burden, the Government adopted a debt-to-equity conversion scheme allowing foreign traders to sell Philippine foreign currency obligations at a slight loss to investors. These obligations, called Philippine investment notes, which are convertible into equity in firms taken over by government banks, are also designed to channel foreign investment into the country (see box I.3). The debt-service burden is expected to ease off slightly in 1987 with the debt-rescheduling

---

Box I.3. The role of debt-equity swaps in the solution of the debt problem

In recent years, a number of debtor developing countries in Latin America, notably Argentina, Brazil, Chile and Mexico, have adopted mechanisms for converting debt into equity. In the ESCAP region, the Philippines has adopted such measures. Although similar in objectives, the debt-equity swap programmes of various countries differ as to the types of debt used, the effective exchange rate for the swap, the equity investments allowed, and the restrictions placed on profit remittances and capital repatriations.

The basic modality of a debt-equity swap is for a corporation or individual to purchase debt in the secondary market at a discount, redeem that paper with the debtor country for local currency and use the currency to make an investment in a local operation. Since the paper is purchased at a discount but is converted into local currency for its full value at the market foreign exchange rate (although a portion of the local currency proceeds of the operation is usually retained by the Government for its own account), the buyer of the paper is effectively getting a subsidy to make the investment. That subsidy comes not from the debtor country itself, which is able to retire its debt at its full foreign currency face value, but from the original creditor, who has disposed of the asset at a loss. However, the debtor country does give some incentives for investment by the purchaser of the debt.

Under the Philippine scheme, preferred investments are granted superior treatment with respect to both the discount from face value at which debts are converted to local currency and the restrictions placed on profit remittances and capital repatriation. While in most countries the programmes are restricted to foreign individuals and corporations, the Philippine programme also allows domestic residents to participate in debt conversions. Under the debt conversion scheme in the Philippines, American Express (United States of America) exchanged $10 million in the Philippine public sector loans for 40 per cent interest in the International Corporate Bank of Manila.

Although debt-equity swaps can make some contribution to reducing external debt levels and to increasing the flows of foreign direct investment, their beneficial economic impact and their future potential are often overestimated. On balance, debt conversions will be beneficial to a debtor country only if they result in a net inflow of capital. The balance-of-payments effect of swaps depends on a number of factors. On current account, fixed interest payments are replaced by variable profit outflows. Whether profit remittances are smaller or larger than savings on interest will depend on the profitability of the investment and the share of profit that is reinvested. It is worth noting that during 1970-1983 in the Philippines, aggregate inflow of foreign direct investment amounted to $1,144 million, whereas outflow of foreign direct investment income was $1,641 million, or about 40 per cent higher.[a] Furthermore, international banks may be less willing to extend new credits to countries that have been purchasing existing debt at a discount.

The impact of debt-equity swaps on reducing the level of external debt has been generally very small in most countries, including the Philippines. Up to September 1986, the value of developing country debt retired through such means is estimated to have been around $3 billion. This is less than 1 per cent of the total value of the stock of the developing country debt. Moreover, market prices of developing country debt have been falling, particularly since January 1987. Secondary market prices of the international debt of the Philippines fell from the range of 72-76 per cent of face value in January 1987 to 65-67 per cent in August 1987 and 57-60 per cent in October 1987.[b] Even if debt-equity conversions or swaps were to increase markedly they would be unlikely to be of sufficient magnitude to reduce the volume of outstanding debt very significantly. The secondary market can be nurtured by improving the informational efficiency and by creating new financial instruments that enhance is liquidity. This process is under way and as a result the secondary market can be expected to make some contribution towards resolving the internationl debt problem, mainly through resuming financial flows to developing debtor countries. But it cannot reasonably be expected to resolve the whole problem. On the contrary, there is some danger that it may breed complacency among leading creditor Governments and international institutions about the debt problem and over-emphasis of the role of a market solution without undertaking other broader initiatives to solve the debt problem.

---

[a] ESCAP/UNCTC Joint Unit on Transnational Corporations, *Transnational Corporations and External Financial Flows of Developing Economies in Asia and the Pacific* (United Nations, 1986), p. 35.

[b] Jaime de Piniés and George Anayiotos, *The Secondary Market and the International Debt Problem*, Department of International Economic and Social Affairs, Working Paper No. 7 (United Nations, November 1987), pp. 15-16.

package covering loans of $13.2 billion being worked out in March 1987. The debt is payable over 17 years from 1987 with a grace period of seven and a half years and interest rate of 0.875 over LIBOR (London Interbank Offered Rate).

Until recently, Malaysia's external debt situation was relatively comfortable compared with other highly indebted countries in the region. However, its debt-service ratio increased from 7.8 per cent in 1984 to 22.3 per cent in 1985, (see table I.6). This sudden increase was partly caused by the decline in its exports of goods and services and partly by the increase in its debt-service payments. The debt-service ratio was projected to decline to less than 20 per cent in 1986, but it would still be much higher than the level in 1984.

China's debt has increased rapidly in recent years, by 35 per cent in 1984 and 49 per cent in 1985. However, its $19.5 billion debt at the end of 1985 was only 65 per cent of its exports and 7 per cent of its GNP. While international banks are the major sources of the country's debt, it

Table I.6. Selected developing countries in the ESCAP region. Debt-service payments, 1982-1987

(Millions of US dollars)

		1982	1983	1984	1985	1986[a]	1987[a]
India	A	1 137.3	1 282.1	1 464.2	1 885.1	3 636.3	3 712.0
	B	470.3	567.1	680.2	800.8	1 262.2	1 304.6
	C	667.0	715.0	784.0	1 084.3	2 374.1	2 407.4
	D	8.9	9.5	10.7	13.3	...	...
Indonesia	A	2 246.3	2 548.2	3 251.0	4 015.1	4 930.6	5 407.8
	B	1 144.7	1 255.1	1 623.6	1 655.2	2 142.1	2 218.6
	C	1 101.6	1 293.1	1 627.4	2 360.0	2 788.6	3 189.2
	D	10.6	12.8	14.7	20.1	...	...
Malaysia	A	793.5	954.1	1 479.6	3 969.3	2 859.9	3 019.8
	B	536.6	668.5	966.5	1 129.9	1 499.0	1 433.5
	C	256.9	285.6	513.1	2 839.4	1 360.9	1 586.3
	D	5.5	5.9	7.8	22.3	...	...
Pakistan	A	575.8	1 066.0	937.4	1 071.7	1 070.1	1 163.5
	B	251.5	307.8	317.5	305.3	352.2	351.6
	C	324.3	758.2	619.9	766.4	718.0	811.9
	D	17.6	28.0	27.1	29.5	...	...
Philippines	A	1 091.2	1 298.4	1 115.3	1 257.0	2 980.2	3 296.5
	B	547.9	656.7	780.3	831.1	1 314.8	1 302.1
	C	543.3	641.7	335.0	425.9	1 665.4	1 994.3
	D	13.6	16.0	13.9	15.8	...	...
Republic of Korea	A	3 844.5	4 147.3	4 671.3	5 030.1	7 317.8	7 548.7
	B	1 947.4	1 889.7	2 068.6	2 151.0	2 800.6	2 655.0
	C	1 897.1	2 257.6	2 602.7	2 879.1	4 517.2	4 893.8
	D	13.6	13.6	13.9	15.2	...	...
Sri Lanka	A	142.3	167.0	201.7	226.3	288.1	324.6
	B	69.0	92.2	102.7	107.8	102.6	99.2
	C	73.4	74.8	99.0	118.5	185.5	225.4
	D	10.6	11.9	11.2	13.9	...	...
Thailand	A	784.6	939.1	1 251.2	1 499.1	2 609.8	2 278.7
	B	476.5	521.5	562.3	602.8	1 023.9	949.5
	C	308.1	417.5	688.8	896.3	1 585.9	1 329.2
	D	8.3	10.2	12.0	14.7	...	...

Source: World Bank, *World Debt Tables: External Debt of Developing Countries,* 1986-87 edition (Washington, D.C., 1987).

Notes: A Total debt-service payments.
B Interest.
C Repayment of principal.
D Debt-service ratio.

[a] 1986, 1987 figures are projections.

reduced its commercial bank debts by $1.7 billion in the first half of 1986.[22]

While Thailand has the lowest level of external debt among the South-East Asian debtor countries its debt-service ratio has consistently increased during 1982-1985, reaching 14.7 per cent in 1985. The external debt situation is likely to have improved in 1986 as Thailand recorded an external current account surplus owing to the lower oil prices and increased exports.

India's external debt increased gradually during 1981-1984, but accelerated by 20.7 per cent in 1985. Although its debt outstanding was only 20 per cent of GNP, it was over 2.5 times its exports and the debt-service ratio was 13.3 per cent in 1985. The adverse impact of commercial borrowings on the overall debt-service ratio can be seen from the fact that the debt-service ratio for the external assistance remained between 6 and 7 per cent

---

[22] Bank for International Settlements, *The Maturity Distribution of International Bank Lending* (Basle, Switzerland, 1986).

during the period 1982-1983 to 1985-1986, while the overall debt-service ratio for commercial borrowings and external assistance put together increased considerably. The debt-service burden is expected to increase even further in the coming years. Repayments of instalments to the International Monetary Fund (IMF) which have started in 1985-1986 with SDR 250 million, will increase progressively to SDR 909 million by 1988-1989.

The debt situation in Pakistan has worsened in recent years. The debt-service ratio reached 29.5 per cent in 1985, from 27.1 per cent in 1984, and debt outstanding reached 3.9 times its exports.

The external debt situation of Sri Lanka deteriorated in 1985 owing mainly to the decline in export earnings. Its debt outstanding increased from 191 per cent of exports in 1984 to 241 per cent in 1985.

Debt pressures intensified in 1986 as world growth slowed and commodity prices fell further. The decline in oil prices markedly affected oil-exporting debtor countries. The fall in export prices has been so sharp that ratios of

total outstanding debt to exports — the most widely used measure of the degree of indebtedness — have risen despite sizeable increases in export volumes; their average level in 1986 was more than 70 per cent higher than in 1981 for a group of highly indebted countries, and more than 90 per cent higher for low-income countries. Ratios of debt service to exports have changed little and declines in nominal interest rates have not been accompanied by corresponding movements of real interest rates. In 1987, new actions and initiatives have emerged, both public and private, aimed at introducing more leeway into the treatment of debt problems, reflecting the more sober assessment which is now widely shared regarding the immediate prospects for growing out of debt problems. The interruption of debt servicing by a number of countries (notably Brazil and Côte d'Ivoire), together with the steps taken by some United States and other banks in the late spring of 1987 to set aside major new reserves against developing country loans, is a manifestation of the increased pressures and uncertainties.

II. MACRO-ECONOMIC PERFORMANCE OF THE DEVELOPING ESCAP ECONOMIES

A. OVERVIEW

The developing countries of the Asian and Pacific region continued to achieve satisfactory growth in 1987 despite growing uncertainties in the global economy and the costly effects of unfavourable weather in many countries. Performance varied widely, however, and the region's robust aggregate growth stemmed mainly from the much stronger performance of East Asia's newly industrializing economies and China, which pulled up the lower average growth elsewhere in the region. Thus, despite slower growth in some countries, the real GDP growth rate of the overall ESCAP developing region was expected, from available data, to have risen from 4.2 per cent in 1986 to 6 per cent in 1987. The region's growth prospects for 1988 are likely to be adversely affected by recessionary trends in the world economy, reducing average growth to 5.6 per cent.

Notwithstanding the increasing uncertainties in the global economy, the developing countries of the ESCAP region pursued their efforts to adjust their economies to the changing international environment and to achieve continuing growth with varying degrees of success. The region's East Asian newly industrializing economies, which had regained double-digit growth rates in 1986 as their export competitiveness improved with the rise of the yen, strengthened

their performance further in 1987 and achieved a remarkable average of 11.7 per cent growth, with Hong Kong and the Republic of Korea expanding more than 12 per cent.

The performance of the South-East Asian economies, which in 1985 and 1986 had dropped to its lowest average during the 1980s, owing largely to primary commodity-related problems, recovered considerably in 1987. Their overall performance was notably lifted by the growth resumption in the Philippines and Singapore, whose expansion rates of 4.9 and 8.0 per cent, respectively, in 1987 were their highest in more than five years. The increasingly robust performance of the Thai economy, which grew by nearly 6 per cent in 1987, was second only to that of Singapore which was recovering from a prolonged recession.

The region's largest developing economy, China, recovered to a near double-digit growth rate in 1987. It had decelerated its growth pace through fiscal measures in 1986 in response to problems of overheating and inflationary pressures experienced during 1984-1986, when measures for opening up the economy had unleashed pent-up aggregate demand. The corrective measures introduced in the latter half of 1986 were gradually relaxed in 1987, and the economy regained its momentum with 9.5 per cent growth, compared with 7.8 per cent in 1986.

A major set-back to the region's growth performance in 1987 was caused by unfavourable weather conditions, which affected virtually the entire ESCAP region, but particularly South and South-East Asia. In several countries of the region, including Burma, China, Indonesia, the Lao People's Democratic Republic and the Philippines, the effect of unfavourable weather might not be fully reflected in the aggregate growth of 1987 figures. The impact has, however, been felt very unevenly across countries mainly because agricultural production in some countries had become more "weather proof", owing to increased irrigation and improved cropping cycles. Although the full effect of the adverse climatic conditions of 1987 is not yet fully assessed, some countries whose economic prospects appeared reasonably optimistic at the start of the year have experienced a dramatic fall in their growth performance in 1987.

The performance of the major South Asian economies was adversely affected by both drought (northern India, Pakistan and Sri Lanka) and floods (Bangladesh and eastern India). India's GDP growth, which has shown a strong upward trend in recent years, slowed to 2.4 per cent in 1987 and was only half of that in 1986. This was the major contributor to South Asia's growth deceleration from 5.1 to 3.2 per cent. Drought had a delayed effect on Pakistan and its GDP growth rate, the highest in South Asia, improved slightly to 7.7 per cent in 1987, while Bangladesh managed to maintain the growth rate of about 4.5 per cent achieved in 1986. Sri Lanka and Nepal were also hard hit by drought, and their GDP growth rates in 1987, at 2.5 and 2.3 per cent respectively, were considerably lower than in 1986.

The growth performance of the least developed and Pacific island economies weakened perceptibly in 1987 and is the major cause of concern in the growth picture of the developing Asian and Pacific region.[1] With the inclusion of Burma, accorded least developed status by the General Assembly in 1987, the number of such disadvantaged countries in this region has risen to 11. In 1987 the performance of three major ones, Bangladesh, Burma and Nepal, were affected by adverse weather and low commodity prices, though Burma's growth recovered from 3.7 per cent in 1986 to 5.0 per cent in 1987.

Disparities in the growth performance of various Asian and Pacific subregions and country groups (see box I.4) stemmed largely from two factors. The first was how well the countries were placed to take advantage of the changed international economic environment. The East Asian newly industrializing economies, with a strong industrial base and able to compete with the manufactures of Japan and other developed countries whose currencies had appreciated considerably *vis-à-vis* the dollar, benefited a great deal from the dollar's continuing fall, in spite of some pressure to appreciate their own currencies. China and some South-East Asian countries, especially Singapore and Thailand, also benefited considerably from

these changes. The second group of countries growing more rapidly in 1987 were those that had already undertaken strong measures to restructure their economies. These included the Philippines, Singapore, and to an extent, China.

The prospects for the region's growth in 1988 were generally subdued as towards the end of 1987 the international economic environment became much more uncertain. World trade and output growth entered a period of heightened uncertainty after the October 1987 stock market collapse. Econometric forecasts estimate world GNP growth rate to be 1-1.5 percentage points lower compared with earlier forecasts for 1988. For developing countries of the ESCAP region this would imply a sizeable slowdown in export growth, which fuelled expansion in the major East and South-East Asian economies. Fortunately, however, there has been no clear evidence so far of a large negative impact of the stock market crash on the performance of the United States of America and other developed economies Nevertheless the earlier optimism concerning the region's growth outlook does not seem valid and regional growth is expected to slow down substantially in 1988.

Although the direct impact of the stock market crash will be marginal for a number of countries of the region, as domestic stock markets did not fall so sharply,[2] its effects are likely to be felt largely through a slowing down in world output and trade. This could result in a reduction in the GNP growth rate forecasts of the region made by the Link model before the stock market crash of October 1987 by 0.8-1.0 per cent in 1988.[3] The economies of the region likely to be particularly affected by the world trade slowdown would be mainly the East

Asian newly industrializing economies, especially Hong Kong, but also South-East Asian economies such as Malaysia, Singapore and Thailand. Finally, the optimism about a sustained general rise in primary commodities prices also received a set-back from the stock market crash. A sustained marked increase in primary commodity prices now appears unlikely in 1988. This will obviously hurt the growth prospects of the commodity exporters of the region.

All the above uncertainties make growth projections for 1988 very tentative and hazardous. Assuming that the recessionary impact of the above factors is not excessive, growth for the ESCAP region in 1988 is estimated at about 5.6 per cent in 1988. The slowdown in growth is expected to be particularly marked in East Asia, which is projected to grow by 7.4 per cent in 1988. A slight decline in growth is projected in South-East Asia as growth in the economies of Singapore and Thailand is foreseen to decelerate. Finally, if normal weather conditions prevail next year, the eco-

[1] For a detailed discussion of the performance of these economies, see Chapter III, this *Survey*.

[2] This is the case in South Asia and also in the Republic of Korea and Taiwan (a province of the People's Republic of China). However, in economies such as Hong Kong, Singapore and Thailand, the decline in the domestic stock market might be felt. From historical experience, real private consumption expenditures declined, for instance, by 1.9 per cent in 1974, following the 1973 stock market fall in Hong Kong. Real investment declined by 1.5 per cent. In Singapore, the GDP growth rate might lose about 0.5 per cent owing to the wealth effect.

[3] Most of the forecasts made for 1988 are on the basis of an econometric model for the world economy, under Project LINK which the Nobel Laureate Professor Lawrence R. Klein has constructed with the collaboration of the United Nations. ESCAP is responsible for making projections for the Asian and Pacific region under Project LINK.

Box I.4. Disparities in growth performance

The overall GDP growth rate of developing ESCAP region which reached 6 per cent in 1987 hides substantial disparities in economic performance in the region. If the three newly industrializing economies and China were excluded, the region's GDP growth rate would be a little over 3 per cent and the per capita GDP growth rate would be nearly 1.5 per cent. GDP growth in South-East Asian and South Asian countries was estimated at 4.3 and 3.2 per cent, respectively, with per capita GDP growth of 2.4 and 1.3 per cent, respectively.

A more disaggregated analysis carried out on a per capita income growth basis, which more accurately reflects changes in welfare, shows how varied the growth picture is in the ESCAP region. In a sample of 17 countries, in 1987 per capita income declined in three countries and grew by less than 2 per cent in five countries. Thus, about half the countries considered had per capita growth rates far too low for much hope of significantly improved living standards within a generation. For assessing growth trends, it is more appropriate to look at average growth rates over time. Thus, during 1985-1987, the average per capita growth rate of the developing countries of the ESCAP region was 3.3 per cent, compared with 4 per cent in 1987. While the number of countries with negative per capita growth rates remained unchanged, the number of countries with per capita growth rates below 5 per cent was higher in 1985-1987 on average than during 1987 (see table).

It is interesting to note that all the South-East Asian countries listed in the table, except Thailand, had an average annual per capita growth rate of below 2 per cent during 1985-1987, while three major South Asian economies, India, Pakistan and Sri Lanka, had an average per capita growth rate above 2 per cent. The two major South Asian least developed countries, Bangladesh and Nepal, however, had per capita income growth significantly lower than 2 per cent. The general trend is in contrast to the pattern of growth rates prevailing in earlier years, especially in the 1970s. The reasons for the weaker performance of the South-East Asian economies in the 1980s has been due largely to their greater dependence on primary commodity exports. The deterioration in the performance of South Asian economies in 1987, on the other hand, has been due to the more adverse effects of unfavourable weather conditions.

A greater convergence of growth rates among the region's developing countries is likely in the medium term. Past differences in economic performance between South Asian, on the one hand, and of East and South-East Asian countries, on the other, have been based on the differential emphasis placed on domestic and external sources of growth. In the 1980s, both groups of countries have tried to adopt a more diversified approach to ensure continued growth in a changing and uncertain international economic environment. This has been particularly evident in 1986 and 1987 as the South Asian economies were forced to pay more attention to export growth, in response to declining foreign exchange receipts. The East and South-East Asian countries complemented their export-led growth with a recovery in domestic demand, mainly to cushion themselves from the uncertainties of the external economic environment.

Selected developing economies of the ESCAP region. Distribution by per capita GDP growth rates, average 1985-1987 and 1987.

Average 1985-1987	*1987*
Below 0 per cent	**Below 0 per cent**
Iran (Islamic Republic of)	Iran (Islamic Republic of)
Malaysia	Malaysia
Philippines	Nepal
0-1.9 per cent	**0-1.9 per cent**
Bangladesh	Bangladesh
Fiji	Fiji
Indonesia	India
Nepal	Indonesia
Singapore	Sri Lanka
2.0-4.9 per cent	**2.0-4.9 per cent**
Burma	Burma
India	Philippines
Pakistan	Thailand
Sri Lanka	
Thailand	
Viet Nam	
Above 5 per cent	**5.0-9.9 per cent**
China	China
Hong Kong	Pakistan
Republic of Korea	Singapore
	Viet Nam
	10 and above
	Hong Kong
	Republic of Korea

Sources: National sources; Population Division, ESCAP; *Statistical Yearbook for Asia and the Pacific 1985* (United Nations publication, Sales No.E/F.86.II.F.24); secretariat estimates based on results from the UNDP/ESCAP Interlinked Country Model Project.

nomies of South Asia should experience some recovery.

The forecasts of world and regional growth will be more pessimistic if the recession in the United States is avoided but its trade and fiscal deficits continue unabated. This is likely to lead to a strong resurgence of protectionist tendencies in the United States and to hurt the developing countries even more. Protectionism would also increase pressures on the East Asian newly industrializing economies to revalue their currencies.

B. EAST AND SOUTH-EAST ASIA

1. East Asian newly industrializing economies and the People's Republic of China

Newly industrializing economies

The factors that aided the recovery of the newly industrializing economies of East Asia in 1986 propelled their growth more strongly in 1987, helping them achieve double-digit growth rates. Some overheating of the economies, exchange rate appreciation and the uncertainties in the business expectations after the October 1987 stock market crash slowed down growth in the last quarter of the year. However, prospects for 1988 remain generally optimistic, although GDP growth rates are likely to decelerate from the exceptional levels of 1987, they are still expected to range between 6.5 and 7.5 per cent for the East Asian subregion as a whole.

The Hong Kong economy has displayed more flexibility and resilience in 1987 than was expected. Although production was running nearly at full capacity towards the end of 1986 and the labour market was very tight, significant in-

creases in output were achieved in 1987 so as to meet strong domestic and external demand. This was achieved without inflationary pressures getting beyond manageable limits. On a year-to-year basis, inflation was running at 5.8 per cent in June 1987, while an average inflation rate of about 6 per cent might be expected in 1987, up from 2.8 per cent in 1986 (see figure I.4).

The shortage of labour was compensated for by productivity increases which allowed increases in the levels of export quota utilizations. For textiles and clothing, for instance, as of 31 August 1987, quota utilization levels were 67.8 per cent for the United States market compared with 63.2 per cent for the corresponding period of 1986. However, increased labour demand pushed the wage index in nominal terms in manufacturing by 8.3 per cent during the 12 months ending March 1987, while in construction wages increased by 15.8 per cent in May 1987 compared to that a year ago.

With rapidly rising incomes in the export sector for two years in a row, domestic demand continued to grow rapidly. Owing to large increases in household incomes, further stimulated by a half per cent decrease in the standard staff income tax and the strong increases in property and stock prices, private consumption is projected to grow by 11 per cent in 1987, up from 9.5 per cent in 1986. Investment demand also recovered with the return of confidence in the economy along with the rise in exports and the lowering of the corporate profits tax. Overall, real gross fixed capital formation was expected to rise by 15.5 per cent in 1987, double the 1986 rate of increase.

The rapid growth in both domestic and external demand is expected to be dampened substantially in 1988, with the wealth ef-

fects of the October stock market crash likely to exercise a considerable negative effect on consumption and investment expenditures. On the external market, slower growth in export markets and protectionist legislation, affecting in particular textile exports, are also likely to reduce the growth rate of real exports to about 11-12 per cent in 1988 compared with the 27 per cent estimated for 1987.

The strong recovery of the economy of the Republic of Korea continued to strengthen during the first half of 1987, fuelled by mark-

---

Figure I.4. Selected developing economies in the ESCAP region. Movements in consumer price indices, 1985-1987[a]

(Percentage)

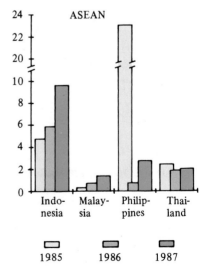

[a] First half of 1987.

Table I.7. Selected developing ESCAP economies in East and South-East Asia. Average annual growth rates and relative shares of gross domestic product at constant prices, 1983, 1984, 1985, 1986 and 1987 (estimated)

	Total	Average annual growth rates			Sectoral shares[a]		
		Agriculture	Industry	Services	Agriculture	Industry	Services
China[b]							
1983	9.8	9.6	8.8[c]	...	44.3	41.4[c]	14.2[d]
1984	13.5	14.5	13.6	...	44.1	40.6	15.3
1985	12.3	6.4	17.5	...	41.4	41.5	17.0
1986	7.4	...	...	...	...	...	...
1987[e]	9.5	...	...	...	...	...	...
Hong Kong[f]							
1983	6.5	...	...	...	0.6	31.7	73.8
1984	9.5	...	...	...	0.6	32.0	72.5
1985	0.6	...	...	...	0.5	29.5	74.7
1986	11.0	...	...	...	...	...	...
1987[e]	12.1	...	...	...	...	...	...
Indonesia							
1983	4.2	4.8	3.0	4.6	24.0	37.0	39.0
1984	6.1	5.5	7.3	5.4	23.9	37.4	38.7
1985	1.9	3.4	−0.5	3.3	24.2	36.6	39.2
1986	3.1	...	...	...	...	...	...
1987[e]	3.2	...	...	...	...	...	...
Malaysia							
1983	6.2	−0.6	10.4	6.5	21.1	36.3	40.7
1984	7.8	2.8	11.4	7.9	20.1	37.5	40.7
1985	−1.0	2.5	−3.4	1.5	20.8	36.6	41.8
1986	1.2	2.8	5.0	−1.0	21.2	38.1	41.0
1987	2.0	2.1	2.8	1.2	21.4	38.6	40.8
Philippines							
1983	0.9	−2.4	0.8	2.9	24.8	36.0	39.1
1984	−6.0	2.4	−10.3	−7.4	27.0	34.3	38.6
1985	−4.4	3.5	−10.2	−4.4	29.3	32.3	38.5
1986	1.1	3.4	−2.8	2.3	30.0	31.0	39.0
1987[e]	4.9	...	...	...	...	...	...
Republic of Korea							
1983	10.9	6.5	14.3	8.9	15.6	42.3	42.2
1984	8.6	0.2	13.4	8.1	14.4	44.1	42.0
1985	5.4	4.8	5.0	7.7	14.3	44.0	42.9
1986	11.9	4.4	15.1	11.4	13.3	45.2	42.7
1987[e]	12.1	...	...	...	...	...	...
Singapore							
1983	7.9	1.7	9.2	8.4	0.9	31.4	74.8
1984	8.2	3.8	10.9	8.8	0.9	32.2	75.2
1985	−1.8	−12.4	−7.1	3.5	0.8	30.5	79.3
1986	1.8	−11.5	−1.4	4.6	0.7	29.5	81.5
1987[e]	8.0	...	...	...	...	...	...
Thailand							
1983	5.9	3.8	19.5	6.5	23.7	29.1	47.1
1984	5.5	3.3	8.0	5.1	23.2	29.8	46.9
1985	3.2	3.2	2.0	4.0	23.2	29.4	47.3
1986	3.4	1.6	9.3	4.2	22.8	31.1	47.7
1987[e]	6.1	...	...	...	...	...	...

Sources: National sources.

[a] The sectoral shares may not add up to 100 per cent owing to import duties and imputed bank service charge. [b] National income and the sectoral shares were calculated on current price basis. [c] Excludes construction. [d] Comprises construction, transportation and commerce. [e] Link Project forecasts. [f] Calculated on current price basis.

edly rapid export growth and the increased competitiveness of exports following substantial appreciation of the Japanese yen. Sustained domestic and external demand resulted in fairly large increases in imports which were reinforced by the acceleration in the won appreciation.

Domestic demand in 1987 was characterized by higher growth in consumption expenditures, which rose at an annual rate of 6.9 and 8.0 per cent respectively in the first two quarters. This was about 1.5 per cent faster than the corresponding figures in 1986. Gross fixed capital formation expanded very rapidly during the first quarter by 16.5 per cent before slowing down to 13.5 per cent in the second quarter over the corresponding period in the previous year. For 1987, real consumer expenditures should accelerate to 7.6 per cent up from 6.7 per cent in 1986, while fixed capital formation might grow slightly slower at about 13.5 per cent, just below the 15 per cent recorded in 1986.

The high growth of the economy for two consecutive years, some increases in primary commodity prices, including oil, as well as higher import prices from Japan have fuelled inflationary pressures, particularly during the first half of the year. However, the inflation rate increased only moderately, with the consumer price index increase of only about 4 per cent in 1987 compared with 2.3 per cent in 1986. The success in keeping inflation under control can be attributed to fiscal and monetary policies adopted during the period.

During 1987, the unemployment rate in the economy of the Republic of Korea was one of the lowest it had ever recorded, falling from 4.3 per cent in January 1987 to 2.6 per cent in June and 2.8 per cent in July. At the same time, there was a significant in-crease in labour participation rates, from 52 per cent in January 1987 to 60 per cent in July.

The prospects for the Korean economy for 1988 will depend primarily on the strength of foreign demand and the ability to keep inflation under control. It will also depend on the smoothness of the political transition process and on meeting the demands for a more equitable pattern of development. The export growth in the Republic of Korea will be considerably slower owing to mounting pressures to appreciate the won and the slower growth in the world economy.

People's Republic of China

After a slow-down in its economy in 1986, the national income of China in 1987 was expected to have grown by 10.5 per cent. The main targets of the 1987 annual plan have been fulfilled, with the value of gross output of agriculture and industry expected to grow by 12.6 per cent. The value of total industrial output increased faster than agriculture, but the growth of light and heavy industries was balanced, both expanding by more than 14 per cent during the first half of 1987.

In the agricultural sector, grain output in 1987 was expected to be about 400 million tons; cotton and oil crops were well harvested. The output of summer crops totalled nearly 96 million tons, 2.4 million tons less than the output of 1986, owing to the fall in the acreage for summer crops and poor weather conditions. Since 1985, when the volume of grain production fell by 7 per cent, domestic food supply has been increasingly falling short of domestic demand and thus tending to create heavy pressure on prices and resulting in heavy imports of food and feed grain. It has also resulted in declin-ing production of pork, the meat staple, the shortage of which led in late 1987 to the introduction of pork rationing in major cities. The decline in grain production was partly in response to changes in procurement prices which reduced the profitability of grain production relative to cash crops, such as cotton, causing a decline in acreage devoted to grain. Another adverse influence on yields was the difficulty experienced by farmers in securing adequate access to chemical fertilizers and pesticides, total supplies of which increased very slowly, resulting in the large increase in prices of these products. Moreover, in recent years, there has been some weakening of investment in agriculture.

Growing concern about record grain imports, a below-target grain harvest and falling investment in agriculture have led to adoption of measures to raise the profitability of grain production with a view to achieving the target of at least 400 million tons in 1987. These measures have included a rise in the average price of grain paid to farmers by reducing the target for state procurement at quota prices from 79 million tons to 61.5 million tons, and raising the proportion procured at the higher negotiated or market prices,[4] and by raising quota prices in some provinces. Among other incentives provided to boost agricultural output are the linking of the availability of fertilizer at lower prices to the state procurement quota, as well as a variety of other measures with a view to increasing investment in infrastructure, conservation, and research, and efforts to channel part of the profits of rural industry into agriculture.

The amount of investment in fixed assets in state-owned units

---

[4] For information on price reforms in China, see the box on "Increasing use of market prices in China", *Survey,* 1986, p. 46.

increased by 21 per cent during the first half of 1987, compared with the same period in the previous year. The investment in capital construction increased by 19.3 per cent, while investments for technological transformation increased by nearly 25 per cent. By June 1987, the proportion of small state-owned enterprises that had carried out management reforms was nearly 38 per cent, as against 8 per cent by the end of 1986. Over 50 per cent of small state-owned commercial enterprises also implemented the system of collective management, leasing and the individual contract system while retaining state ownership. Several large and medium-sized industrial enterprises have implemented the contract responsibility system.

Foreign exchange reserves rose by $2 billion in the first half of 1987 reaching $12.6 billion at the end of June 1987, mainly owing to rise in exports. Foreign borrowings increased in 1987 as China sought funds for modernization projects (see box I.5).

One of the major problems of economic management in China in 1987 was the building up of inflationary pressure, which was aggravated by the rapid rise in consumption funds and investment in capital construction projects outside the state plan. In the first six months of 1987, the retail sales price index was 6 per cent higher than during the corresponding period in 1986. Prices of vegetables, meat, poultry, eggs and aquatic products rose markedly in large cities.

According to the projections for 1988, the value of gross output of agriculture, industry and national income will rise by 4, 12.6 and 10.7 per cent respectively. Light industry will grow by 13 per cent, whereas heavy industry will grow by 12 per cent. The investment in fixed assets will be controlled, as a result of which its growth rate will drop by 3 to 4 per cent. The value of exports and imports is projected to increase by 11 and 8 per cent respectively in 1988. Economic reforms in 1988, among others, will be focused on enterprise management, supply of raw materials and allocation of foreign exchange.

2. South-East Asia

For 1987, the economic growth of the South-East Asia (ASEAN countries) as a whole is expected at around 4 per cent, compared with 2.2 per cent in 1986. The higher growth rates of the Philippines, Singapore and Thailand, compared to those of Brunei Darussalam, Indonesia and Malaysia were largely the reflection of continuing weakness in oil and other commodity prices.

The economies of the ASEAN countries, with the exception of Singapore, are largely dependent on the production and export of primary commodities. In 1987, the production of major commodities, except for palm oil and crude petroleum, is likely to have increased owing to stable prices and a slight rise in external demand. Performance of the manufacturing sector in these countries improved in 1987 mainly owing to increased export competitiveness arising from relative depreciation of their currencies *vis-à-vis* the currencies of their major competitors such as the yen, the Korean won and the Taiwanese dollar. The construction sector in the South-East Asian countries as a whole remained sluggish in 1987. The glut in office space in both Malaysia and Singapore adversely affected the sector. In Indonesia and the Philippines, growth in this sector was estimated to have risen at a lower rate because of the slowdown in the rest of the economy and the reduction in government expenditure. For Thailand, the growth of the construction sector picked up compared with the previous year owing to significant expansion in economic activity.

The rate of inflation for the South-East Asian countries decelerated markedly in 1986, rising to less than 2 per cent compared with 5.7 per cent in 1985 as a result of lower oil prices, lower interest rates and sluggish domestic demand. Singapore recorded the lowest rate, at 1.4 per cent and Indonesia the highest, at more than 8.5 per cent. The overall rate of inflation in this subregion was expected to increase to 3.4 per cent in 1987 in line with the pickup in economic activities.

During the period 1974-1985, the Brunei Darussalam economy grew in real terms by nearly 3 per cent per annum. However, the economy experienced a declining trend during the period 1979-1985 owing to the drop in oil prices after 1981 and the sluggish domestic demand. During this period, GDP in real terms declined by 4.2 per cent per annum. Moreover, owing to the decline in oil prices and production, the share of the oil and gas sector in total GDP declined from 87.5 per cent in 1974 to 71.3 per cent in 1985.

The growth of real GDP in Indonesia slowed considerably during 1985/86, following two years of accelerating growth after the recession of 1982. The slow-down was attributable to the stagnation of the oil sector and a deceleration in the growth of agricultural output, marginally offset by a small increase in the growth of manufacturing. In 1987, GDP was estimated to have grown by about 3 per cent as a result of recovery in oil export revenue with the firming up of prices to $18 a barrel and increased non-oil/liquefied natural gas exports.

Agricultural output, accounting for about one fourth of GDP

in 1986, increased by a yearly average of 2.5 per cent during 1985/86, compared with 3.5 per cent during 1983/84, largely reflecting a decline in the expansion of rice production after several years of rapid gains. In recent years, agricultural policy has aimed at achieving self-sufficiency in rice, enhancing agricultural exports, and creating employment opportunities.

The manufacturing sector expanded steadily in the past few years. Value added in the sector rose at an average of about 6 per cent during 1984/85 in real terms. In 1986, real growth of manufacturing is expected to be about 5.5 per cent. Among the industries that appear to have expanded markedly in 1986, important ones

---

Box I.5. Changing patterns of resource inflows to China

Until 1985, China made relatively little net use of foreign capital. During the period 1981-1984, the country enjoyed a sizeable current account surplus resulting from the success in export promotion during the early years of "opening up" the economy. Medium- and long-term borrowing, mainly from international institutions, and foreign direct investment in China were largely offset by Chinese aid to other countries, direct investment abroad by China, and short-term capital movements (including errors and omissions) during this period.

However, reflecting the sharp rise in imports which led to the deterioration in the balance of payments on current account in 1985, the capital account recorded a net inflow of more than $8 billion in that year. Medium- and long-term borrowing rose to over $3 billion from $0.7 billion in 1984. The large increase mainly reflected borrowing from foreign banks, which rose to $2.1 billion net from almost nil in 1984. China made nine bond issues equivalent to $0.8 billion, compared with $0.1 billion (one issue) in 1984.

A noteworthy feature of resource inflows in 1985 was a sharp rise in net short-term capital borrowing to nealry $4 billion, out of which $2.5 billion was from foreign banks. Moreover, foreign direct investment in China increased by 32 per cent in 1985. This followed substantial increases recorded in 1982-1984 owing to the liberalization of regulation on foreign investment and the introduction of incentives for joint ventures operating in special economic zones and 14 coastal cities. On an approval basis, foreign direct investment rose by 110 per cent to $5.5 billion with nearly 3,000 projects in 1985. The cumulative total of foreign direct investment for the period 1979-1985 reached $12 billion with 6,200 projects.

In 1986, foreign borrowing in China rose sharply, reaching $4.83 billion. In total, the country has taken on $20.6 billion in foreign loans from 1979 to 1986, of which only $7.6 billion has been in the form of long-term, low-interest official loans.

Along with the growth in foreign resource inflows, the total external debt of China (including short-term debt) approximately doubled between the end of 1983 and the end of 1985, both in absolute terms and as a ratio of GDP, although the ratio, at 7.5 per cent, was still relatively small. At the same time, the maturity structure of the country's debt worsened with short-term debt rising to 45 per cent of total external debt. At the end of 1985, bilateral loans and loans from multilateral institutions (mainly the World Bank) accounted for 24 per cent of total debt (27.5 per cent in 1984); suppliers' credits and other trade credits, 19 per cent (30 per cent in 1984); foreign commercial banks, 48 per cent (37 per cent in 1984); and bond issues, 5 per cent (0.5 per cent in 1984). Balance-of-payments developments during the first half of 1986 indicated a further increase in external debt of $2.8 billion. Debt-service payments amounted to $2.1 billion in 1985, or 7.2 per cent of exports of goods and services.[a]

Following the sharp increase in external debt in 1984 and 1985, measures were taken to strengthen debt management in China. In April

---

[a] Calculated from OECD, *Statistics of External Indebtedness* (Paris, 1985); OECD/Bank of International Settlements, *Statistics on External Indebtedness: Bank and Trade Related Non-Bank External Claims on Individual Borrowing Countries and Territories*, (Paris and Basle, July 1986); OECD, *Financing and External Debt of Developing Countries 1986 Survey* (Paris 1987).

1986, the State Administration of Exchange Control (SAEC), a unit within the People's Bank, was designated by the State Council as the sole agency responsible for monitoring external debt. Subsequently, SAEC established reporting channels for all borrowing units. Efforts are continuing to improve the coverage of external debt statistics. Limits on total external borrowing and on short-term debt are determined so as to be consistent with a viable medium-term balance of payments on the current account. Approval procedures have been revised to ensure that external borrowing remains within these limits. All commercial borrowing, including placement of bonds abroad, has been made subject to prior approval by SAEC.

All entities are now required to report their borrowing to SAEC. Central government agencies, financial institutions, local governments, municipalities, joint ventures and foreign-owned enterprises submit reports to SAEC, through their supervising agencies which indicate *inter alia*: (a) amount of debt outstanding; (b) actual and prospective draw-down schedule; and (c) actual and future debt-service schedule. This has been the reaction to the unrestrained borrowing undertaken by various institutions in the earlier period of "opening up" and decentralized decision making in the economy.

More recently, the Government has been considering three further measures with a view to ensuring effective use of foreign loans: control over their overall amount and more careful assessment of the ability to apply as well as repay the loans; concentration of foreign loans in the production and construction sectors; and mandatory tying of a portion of the resultant earnings to repayment.[b]

---

[b] *China Newsletter*, No. 68 (May-June 1987).

are plywood, textiles, cement, and steel. Following the policy to encourage plywood exports (including the prohibition of log exports in 1980), domestic output of plywood rose steadily from around 2 million cubic metres in 1982 to over 5 million cubic metres in 1985-1986. During this period, the share of exports rose in total production from one fifth to four fifths, and Indonesia became the world's largest producer and exporter of hard wood and plywood. Despite sluggish domestic demand, the textile industry is estimated to have expanded sharply because of the increase in exports.

The inflation rate increased in late 1986 and early 1987, after several years of steady decline. The rise in the consumer price index was broadly based, but was particularly pronounced for food and clothing. In the case of foodstuffs, an important factor was a sharp increase in the domestic market price for rice in October 1986 owing to less buoyant growth in domestic production. Increases in other prices largely reflected the feed through of the September 1986 devaluation.

The economy of Malaysia, which has been severely affected during the last few years by low non-oil primary commodity prices, and since 1985, by sharp fall in oil prices, revived in 1986 with the real GDP growing by 1 per cent, and in 1987 by 1.5 per cent. The recovery in 1986 originated in some revival in primary commodity prices, while in 1987 it stemmed largely from the export-oriented manufacturing industries.

The output of the agricultural sector, despite better commodity prices, was adversely affected by the decline in the production of palm oil in 1987, although the production of rubber expanded to 1.6 million tons in 1987 and accounted for nearly 36

per cent of world natural rubber production. In 1986, for the first time in this decade, rubber production in Malaysia recorded an increase, estimated at about 4.8 per cent, reflecting mainly increased smallholder output.

The manufacturing sector, which stepped up its output by 7.5 per cent in 1986, continued to maintain a steady pace of output expansion in 1987. Underlying this steady increase in output were firmer overseas sales orders, which have recovered markedly since March 1986. This has prompted export-oriented manufacturing industries, such as electrical machinery and electronics, as well as textiles, to increase their output significantly.

Construction activity weakened further in 1987. For the third consecutive year, real value added in the construction sector declined, reflecting an increasing oversupply of office space, continued weak demand for residential housing, except for low-income housing and restraint in government development spending.

The country's low rate of inflation continued in 1987 owing to effective enforcement of various price control legislations, the moderation in import price increases, as well as the tight budgetary policy. In line with the moderate growth in the Malaysian economy, the employment situation in 1987 was expected to have remained weak as in 1986. The growth in the labour force was estimated to have expanded at a rate of 2.8 per cent in 1987, compared with 2.9 per cent in 1986. Total employment, however, was expected to have grown by only 2.1 per cent compared with an increase of 1.8 per cent in 1986.

In the Philippines, after two years of steep contraction and a year of slow recovery, real GNP was estimated to have grown by 4.5 per cent in 1987. The Philippines

was in the midst of economic crisis for nearly three years. During this period, steps were taken to reduce a large external imbalance and to restore price stability. These gains, however, were accompanied by a substantial decline in output and a large fall in per capita real income. The impressive performance in 1987 was attributable to expansion in domestic demand as well as revival of investors' confidence as a result of the increase in real income, the decline in interest rates, the stable local currency and the low rate of inflation.

In 1987, the output of the agricultural sector, which accounts for around one fourth of GDP, over one half of total employment, and one third of merchandise exports, was adversely affected by a serious drought. Output of rice, corn, sugar and coconut declined by nearly 1.5 per cent in the first half of 1987. For 1987 as a whole, the agricultural sector was estimated to have grown by less than 1.5 per cent.

Growth in the industrial output at 8.3 per cent in the first half of 1987 was largely due to the upturn in domestic demand. During the first half of 1987, manufacturing, construction and mining grew by nearly 7, 14 and 15.4 per cent respectively. Output from mining and quarrying represents only about 2 per cent of GNP. However, the subsector is an important source of export earnings — over 10 per cent of merchandise export earnings — with gold and copper production accounting for about three fourths of total value added.

The manufacturing sector accounts for about one quarter of GNP, and manufactures exports represent over one half of total merchandise exports, although the sector is largely oriented towards production for the domestic market. Export-oriented manufactures, especially electrical equipment and garments, grew rapidly during the late 1970s and early 1980s, but their contribution to total value added is still relatively small since they depend largely on imported inputs. In 1985, the electrical products and garments industries still accounted for under 11 per cent of total value added in the manufacturing sector.

The high inflation rates of the early 1980s were brought down by the end of 1985, with the consumer price index rising by only 5.7 per cent and wholesale prices actually declining by about 1 per cent. In 1986, inflation in terms of consumer prices eased further to 0.8 per cent, mainly owing to reduction in oil prices and stabilization of the exchange rate of the Philippine peso. In 1987, the boost in domestic demand generated a faster growth in money supply and consequently revived inflationary pressures. Consumer prices were expected to rise by 6 per cent and wholesale prices by 1 per cent in 1987.

Since commodity prices are unlikely to recover much, exports are not expected to contribute much to economic growth. Thus the prospects for sustained economic growth in the Philippines in 1988 will hinge largely on strong revival of private sector investment. If investors' confidence in the economy is restored and investment strongly revived, GNP can be expected to grow at a rate of over 5 per cent in 1988. As economic activity gains momentum, the current account is expected to post a deficit of about $710 million in 1988.

After recovery from the severe recession of 1985 and the registering of a 1.8 per cent growth rate of real GDP in 1986, the growth rate of the economy of Singapore accelerated to over 6 per cent in 1987, reflecting substantial strengthening of domestic as well as external demand.

In 1986, the gross capital formation declined by 12 per cent, while private consumption recovered somewhat with 3 per cent growth. In 1987, gross capital formation grew by 3 per cent and trade expanded rapidly in consequence of the implementation of the Government's integrated policy package designed to restore the competitiveness of Singapore through measures to cut production costs and stimulate domestic demand.

The rise in labour productivity and the easing of the exchange rate improved considerably the rate of return on capital and Singapore's international competitiveness. While the recovery at first was narrowly based and concentrated mainly in the electronics industry, all sectors except construction recorded progressively higher growth rates.

Singapore's recent economic growth was accompanied by remarkable price stability. Following an increase of only 0.5 per cent in the previous year, consumer prices fell by 1.4 per cent during 1986, mainly owing to poorer petroleum prices. During the first half of 1987, the rate of inflation was zero, partly because of low commodity prices and partly owing to wage restraint and other cost-cutting measures.

Trade, particularly in non-oil exports, will continue to remain the main source of growth in the Singapore economy, although domestic spending and tourism contributed substantially to growth in 1987. However, the recent plunge in the stock market is likely to affect adversely the economic activity in 1988 as companies find it difficult to raise equity capital and consumer expenditure declines owing to the wealth effect. Nevertheless, if Singapore maintains its competitive edge by keeping labour costs down in the face of a very tight labour market and avoiding the danger of an overheated econo-

my, the growth rate in 1988 is likely to be in the range of 5 to 6 per cent. The rate of inflation may accelerate but would remain less than 4 per cent.

The economy of Thailand continued to be South-East Asia's fastest growing economy for the second consecutive year in 1987. After lacklustre growth performance of 3.5 per cent in 1986, the growth rate of GDP in 1987 was expected to reach 6 per cent, in spite of the adverse effects on agriculture of drought during the first half of the year and of floods in the third quarter of 1987. Growth in the agricultural sector was not likely to exceed 4 per cent for the year, with crops such as maize, soybean, first crop paddy and kenaf being worst hit by bad weather conditions.

Growth in manufacturing, transport and public utilities was spurred by low oil prices and interest rates reducing operating and production costs. Growth in industry was expected to be around 9 per cent in 1987, slightly lower than in 1986. On the demand side, the growth was stimulated by some increase in rural income owing to firmer farm prices, rapidly rising urban incomes, tax reforms which boosted purchasing power and an accommodating monetary policy. Easier access to credit at lower cost stimulated the construction sector, which resumed positive growth in 1987. The service sector benefited greatly from the "Visit Thailand Year" campaign and the large increase in tourist arrivals (up by at least 20 per cent for the first half of 1987).

Although Thailand achieved high export growth, the balance of trade deficit rose sharply in 1987 owing to the unprecedented increase in imports. However, the balance of payments surplus was favourably affected by the boom in tourism and large inflows of foreign investment.

Inflation remains low with the GDP deflator expected to rise in the range of about 2.5-3.0 per cent for 1987. The consumer price index rose by 1.8, 2.1 and 2.7 per cent respectively for the first three quarters of the year. Most of the rise in prices is due to firmer prices for most agricultural products, in particular rice, and some increase in import prices.

The manufacturing sector, led by the export-oriented industries, is projected to be the main source of growth in 1988. With the appreciation of the currencies of other newly industrializing economies, the Thai economy should remain very competitive and foreign investment inflows should continue to provide a strong stimulus to manufacturing growth. While industrial growth is projected at 7 to 8 per cent, the agricultural sector may not grow rapidly in 1988 partly because of the overhang of the 1987 drought. In 1988, inflation may accelerate largely owing to higher agricultural product prices following the 1987 drought. Overall, the economy is expected to grow at a slightly lower rate in 1988 than in 1987.

C. SOUTH ASIA

There is increasing evidence that the medium-term growth performance of two of the larger South Asian economies, India and Pakistan, has improved significantly in the 1980s. Following the introduction of wide-ranging economic reforms in 1977-1978, Sri Lanka achieved a sustained period of economic growth, exceeding 5 per cent per annum in each year until 1986. However, in recent years, economic performance in Sri Lanka has been severely affected by a combination of underlying structural weaknesses, adverse external factors and civil conflicts. In 1987, the economic performance of South Asian countries, parti-cularly Bangladesh, India and Sri Lanka, was adversely influenced by weather conditions (see box I.6).

In Bangladesh in 1986/87 the rate of growth of GDP, at 4.5 per cent, was well below the target rate of 5.2 per cent. This was largely due to the depressed export prices for the country's principal commodity exports and the sluggish performance in the industrial sector. Heavy rains and floods during July-September 1987 caused extensive damage to the economy and thus adversely affected the growth prospects for 1987/88. Economic growth in Bangladesh, averaging about 4.4 per cent per year so far in the 1980s, seems satisfactory when compared with low-income countries generally. In 1986/87, the agricultural sector grew by less than 2 per cent mainly owing to the fall in the output of jute, and in food grains, which necessitated imports of food grains of about 500,000 tons. In 1986/87, the jute crop, at 900,000 tons, was the lowest for several years and was 42 per cent below the 1.5 million tons recorded in 1985/86. The jute acreage in 1986/87, at around 600,000 hectares, was 40 per cent lower on the 1985/86 level.

The growth of the industrial sector, estimated at around 2 per cent, was much below the planned target of 10 per cent. The deterioration of industrial performance was largely attributable to disruption of power supplies, labour disputes and, to flood-induced supply shortages of raw materials which particularly affected agrobased industries such as foodstuffs and tobacco.

Despite slow growth of the economy, there was impressive growth in export earnings in 1986/87, estimated at over $1 billion, 25 per cent over 1985/86. The increase in export earnings occurred, despite the serious set-back in jute exports largely as a result of buoyant non-traditional exports as well as the favourable impact of exchange rate alignments. Earnings from garment exports increased by more than 100 per cent to $226 million, while shrimp exports rose by 24 per cent. Among non-traditional exports, garments and frozen seafood have grown rapidly in the last few years. However, it is worth noting that while Bangladesh has achieved impressive growth rates of garment exports, it holds less than 0.3 per cent of the developing countries' share of such exports to the industrial countries.

In contrast, export receipts from raw jute amounting to nearly $80 million were 30 per cent down over the previous year, mainly owing to a fall in jute prices. At the same time, exports of jute manufactures fell by more than 8 per cent in volume terms in the first nine months of 1986/87 over the same period of the preceding year. The Bangladesh market share in jute products has fallen markedly in recent years as exports from India and Thailand, which, excluding China, are the only other significant suppliers of jute manufactures to world markets, were much higher than in 1985/86. In the period July-December 1986, exports of jute goods from India and Thailand were up by 38 and 17 per cent respectively.

It is estimated that the value of imports in 1986/87 rose by 9 per cent over 1985/86, largely · as a result of food imports. The trade deficit in 1986/87 increased by more than 10 per cent. In 1987/88, the trade deficit was expected to widen, mainly owing to the higher import bill resulting from food grain imports, higher oil prices as well as depressed markets for the main exports, jute, tea and leather. While pledges of external aid worth nearly $2

Box I.6. The impact of unfavourable weather on the developing economies

Despite considerable progress in agricultural development in recent years, the performance of the agricultural sector in the region remains a considerable "gamble on the monsoon". This was illustrated by the prevalence of adverse climatic conditions in 1987 virtually throughout the developing ESCAP region. Mainly drought, but in some countries floods or a combination of the two disasters, have severely curtailed agricultural production in most countries of the region, adversely affecting their overall economic growth and causing serious strains on economic management, especially owing to inflationary pressures and balance-of-payments difficulties.

Although the impact of unfavourable weather across countries has not been uniform, the region has shown an improved capacity to cope with the calamity. While a few decades earlier wide-ranging drought would have caused famine in some parts of the region, its present damage has been limited to lower economic growth. Although the effect of the drought was only partly felt in 1987 and will continue to reverberate to some extent into future years, agricultural production has exhibited much more resistance to adverse weather, at least in some countries, as a result of irrigation and higher input intensity. Increased irrigation facilities and better cropping patterns have resulted in reducing agriculture's vulnerability to the caprices of the monsoon. Some countries, such as India, have launched special programmes for compensatory production, the key elements of which consist of the use of varieties of rice and other crops which mature quickly, supplemented by farming practices to conserve moisture and increased nutrient supply.

The South Asian economies have been particularly hard hit by drought and/or floods, and with the exception of Pakistan, where a much larger proportion of land is irrigated, their rate of economic growth in 1987/88 will be considerably lower than that which could have been expected under normal monsoon conditions. The growth rate of India, for instance, is projected to be about 3 per cent below the forecasts made before the drought.

The extent of the drought was particular severe in India, where the summer monsoon (mainly in June/July) measured from the all-India rainfall index, has been the worst since 1950.[a] The drought has affected virtually the whole of India except the eastern region and some areas of the north-east (such as Bihar and West Bengal) which have, however, been plagued by severe floods. The States producing a large surplus of food grains, such as Punjab, Haryana and Uttar Pradesh, have all suffered badly from the monsoon failure. It is estimated that, compared with a good crop year such as 1983/84, about 60 per cent of the area sown was affected by drought in 1987/88. Although the country has faced a number of droughts during the past, e.g. in 1965-1967, 1973-1975, 1979-1980 and 1982-1983, the present drought is the most severe and widespread with 17 out of 24 States in its grip.

It is not easy to estimate the exact extent of the losses in agricultural outputs (and incomes) in India. Among other things, the outcome of the rabi (winter) crop is not yet known although early indications point towards rather good winter rains (September 1987-February 1988) and a normal rabi crop, which would put estimates for the output loss of food grains between 18 million and 40 million tons, compared with potential normal monsoon output of 160 million tons. Estimates around 25-30 million tons are considered most likely. Losses for other crops are estimated at about 25 per cent for sugar-cane, 40 per cent for cotton and 50-70 per cent for oil-seeds. Agricultural incomes could fall by as much as 24 per cent, about 9 per cent of national income.[b] Other estimates put the decline in agricultural GDP at about 7 per cent.[c]

---

[a] Prannoy Roy, *The 1987 Monsoon and Its Impact on the Indian Economy* (mimeographed), UNDP/ESCAP, Seminar on an Interlinked Country Model System, November 1987, Bangkok.

[b] Arun Kumar, *Consequences of the 1987 Monsoon Failure*, a preliminary assessment, EPW, 26 September 1987.

The repercussions of the 1987 drought on the economy are likely to be far reaching although, perhaps, not as serious as in previous droughts in view of the sizeable stocks of food grains accumulated in the past. Besides the serious slow-down in its growth rate, per capita income will at best stagnate; inflation, on which India has had a good record in recent years, may revive and reach double-digit levels; the budgetary resources of the Government will come under increased strain owing to drought relief expenditures; the balance of payments is also likely to worsen significantly. The drought will also have far-reaching impact on the growth performance of other sectors, particularly industry as domestic demand weakens as a consequence of falling incomes.

Among other effects the drought has had on the economy are: the sizeable shortage of power, which can have adverse effects on the utilization of industrial capacity; the increase in budget deficits owing to famine relief measures and curtailment of some public expenditures; and imposition of additional taxation measures announced in September 1987. The drought will also necessitate the import of agricultural commodities of about $600 million, which will largely be financed with assistance from the World Bank, Japan and the European Economic Community. The balance of payments is, however, likely to remain under pressure. Finally, and perhaps more importantly, the fall in agricultural incomes will reduce agricultural and industrial demand and is likely to result in increasing poverty. While it is estimated that about 40 per cent of the population, or nearly 300 million people, will have their incomes affected, the consequences will be particularly serious for landless farmers and for marginal and small farmer families on non-irrigated land.

The Indian economy is by no means the only economy badly hit by drought in 1987. Growth in Sri Lanka is estimated to decline to only 2.5 per cent in 1987, compared with 4.3 per cent in 1986, while in Nepal, growth performance will also be badly hit. Bangladesh, on the other hand, has

---

[c] Prannoy Roy, *op. cit.*

been dramatically affected by floods, which could cause up to 2 per cent reduction in its growth rate. Losses of food grain output are estimated at 3 million tons, necessitating the import of some 3.5 million tons of food grains, mainly wheat. The flood damage has been estimated at about $1 billion. The Government is diverting funds from urban and other low priority projects to repair bridges, roads and other infrastructure destroyed by floods. It has also launched a recovery plan to generate employment and restore purchasing power.

Although adverse weather has plagued agriculture nearly all over the ESCAP region, drought and/or floods have particularly affected China, Fiji, Indonesia, the Lao People's Democratic Republic, Thailand and Viet Nam.

In Indonesia and Thailand, the consequences of severe drought have, to some extent, been offset by strong manufacturing sector growth, while the impact of the drought will in part manifest itself in lower agricultural production in 1988. In Thailand, severe drought has increased income growth differentials between regions in the country, depending on the importance of agriculture, the productivity of land and the extent of irrigation.

In Thailand, the effect of the drought has resulted in a further decline in the sector's output by 1 per cent in 1987 following a decline of 0.7 per cent in 1986. Rice production, particularly in the north and north-east – the poorest areas of the country – will be seriously affected in terms of both areas cultivated and areas damaged. A decline in production of about 9 per cent for the main crop is estimated for 1987, while the 1986 production was already low at 6.1 per cent below the 1985 level. The consequences on rice production, a major export of the country, are thus serious. The second crop will also be badly curtailed and could fall by a half compared with 1986, with an adverse effect on growth in 1988. The output of maize, a major crop, was also seriously affected, while that of other major crops, such as cassava, sugar-cane and cotton, are not expected to suffer significantly.

billion have been made for 1987/88, up 5.4 per cent on 1986/87, $1.3 billion (17 per cent above the 1986/87 level) would be disbursed.

Domestic savings at 3.2 per cent of GDP in 1985/86 remain among the lowest in the world. Remittances from Bangladeshis working abroad rose from $441 million in 1984/85 to $555 million in 1985/86, permitting national savings to rise. Over the longer term, however, the importance of remittances as a share of domestic investment is expected to fall, requiring that domestic savings rise if investment is not to fall.

The rate of inflation, which was below 10 per cent in 1985/86, rose to 11 per cent in 1986/87, mainly owing to increases in prices of food grains and other food items.

In India, although the rate of growth of real GDP decelerated marginally in the second year (1986/87) of the seventh five-year plan, the average rate of growth in the first two years of the plan was very close to the targeted growth rate of 5 per cent (see figure I.5).

The real GDP was expected to grow between 4.5 and 5 per cent during 1986-1987, compared with 5.1 per cent for 1985/86. The setback in the performance was primarily caused by the poor monsoon. Food grain production during 1986/87 was likely to have fallen short of the 150.5 million tons achieved in 1985-1986 by about 0.5 to 1.5 million tons. Despite three successive years of drought of increasing intensity, Indian agriculture has shown some degree of resilience and maintained an average production level of over 148 million tons of food grains during the three years ending 1986/87, which was 10 million tons more than the average annual production recorded during the sixth plan period, 1980-1985.

The industrial output recorded a robust performance, growing at more than 8 per cent during two years 1985/86 and 1986/87. Although the manufacturing subsector has shown the most significant acceleration, other subsectors have also performed well. There have been fewer bottle-necks in the

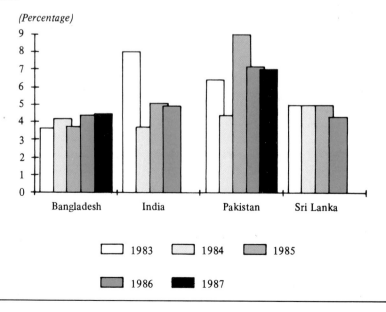

Figure I.5. Selected South Asian economies. Growth rates in GDP, 1983-1987

(Percentage)

industrial infrastructure subsectors for the third year running, with high growth in the three major components: electricity generation, railway movement and coal production.

Although the share of the agricultural sector in GDP has recorded a fall from 41.4 per cent in 1980/81 to about 37 per cent in 1985/86, the share of manufacturing has stagnated at around 22 per cent, while the share of the tertiary sector (transport, communication, trade, financial services, real estate, public administration and other services) has increased rapidly. A major area of concern is the increase in the problem of sick industries resulting from uneconomic scales of operation and old technology. It is estimated that 120,000 industrial units involving institutional credit of Rs 43 billion were sick as at the end of December 1985; 83 per cent of these units were considered to be nonviable. In view of the adverse implications of this problem, Government has initiated measures, both legislative and administrative, to identify and prevent it.[5]

In recent years, the output of the electronics industry, a major growth industry, has grown at the rapid rate of around 40 per cent per annum during the two years 1984-1985 and 1985-1986. Its remarkable growth was accompanied by a significant increase in productivity and fall in the prices of electronic items, e.g. the prices of computers declined by over 50 per cent and of television sets by around 10 per cent. During 1986-1987, the industry expected to reach a level of output of Rs 36,850 million, a growth of about 28 per cent over 1985-1986.

Balance-of-payments pressure in India seems to have eased during

⁵ Government of India, *Economic Survey 1986-87*, pp. 40-41.

1986-1987. India's foreign exchange reserves improved marginally by 3.5 per cent during 1986-1987. However, the overall trend shows deceleration in the growth of reserves over the past two years ending March 1987. The overall foreign exchange reserves position was equivalent to over four months' import requirements.

Net external assistance (net of debt-servicing) received by India is estimated to increase by about 43 per cent to Rs 22,410 million in 1986-1987 against Rs 15,710 million in 1985-1986. In recent years, India has had greater recourse to external borrowings subject to the maintenance of a safe debt-service capability. Approvals for external commercial borrowings amounted to Rs 72,580 million in the sixth plan, Rs 17,000 million in 1985-1986 and Rs 6,490 million during the first six months of 1986/87. Reliance on the inflow of capital from abroad has increased from 1.5 per cent of GDP in 1984/85 to 1.8 per cent in 1985/86.

For the third year in succession, in 1986/87 the GDP in Pakistan grew at a rate exceeding 7 per cent with relative price stability. During 1986/87, per capita income increased by nearly 3 per cent at constant factor cost. Agricultural output increased by nearly 6 per cent during 1986/87, mainly because of increases of over 20 per cent in rice, 9 per cent in cotton, 7 per cent in sugar-cane and 10 per cent in maize. The value added in manufacturing, which is the second largest sector of the economy and accounts for one fifth of GDP, increased by 7.4 per cent in 1986/87, against 7.8 per cent in 1985/86. Services as a whole registered an increase of 6.8 per cent.

Rapid growth in recent years has led to significant structural changes in Pakistan's economy. For example, the share of agricul-

ture in the GDP has declined from 30.5 per cent in 1979/80 to 25.5 per cent in 1986/87, while the relative contribution of manufacturing and mining has risen from 17.6 per cent in 1979-1980 to 20.5 per cent in 1986/87. Changes in sectoral employment have been relatively less sharp, with agriculture still absorbing more than half of the labour force. Agriculture's role in industrialization and exports is also reflected by the fact that around one half of manufacturing output and four fifths of the country's exports are agro-based.

During 1986/87, for the second year in succession, Pakistan's balance of payments continued to improve. The foreign aid commitment increased by 21 per cent from $2,150 million in 1985-1986 to an estimated $2,606 million during 1986/87, while the disbursements of $1,531 million remained almost at the 1985/86 level.

The growth in 1986/87 was accompanied by remarkable price stability. Appropriate monetary policy, increased production, liberal imports, derationing of wheat and rice and decontrol of edible oil and cement have resulted in slowing down the inflation rate in terms of consumer prices to 3.5 per cent in the first nine months of 1986/87.

A continuing weakness in Pakistan's economic performance has been in domestic resource mobilization efforts, which need to be considerably strengthened. Both the public and private savings have been inordinately low. Although in 1986/87 the estimated investment/GDP ratio rose to 17.2 per cent from 16.7 per cent in 1985/86, about one third of the required investment continues to be financed through foreign capital. Unless the currently low rates of domestic savings are stepped up, Pakistan's debt burdens are likely to exceed manageable levels.

In Sri Lanka, the GDP growth rate in real terms slowed down to 2.5 per cent in 1987 compared with 4.5 per cent, mainly as a result of a major drought, in late 1986. The rate of inflation rose significantly, from near price stability in 1985 to 6 per cent in 1986 and over 8 per cent in 1987.

Almost all subsectors of agriculture, but especially paddy and coconuts, have been adversely affected by a serious drought. Hence, agricultural output is expected to decline by about 5 per cent in 1987 compared with the growth of 2.6 per cent in 1986.

Value added in manufacturing continued to grow, rising at an estimated average annual rate of 7.5 per cent during 1985-1986 and the same rate of growth was expected for 1987. In 1986, output in the construction sector remained virtually flat during the past three years, reflecting the near completion of the major headworks of the Mahaweli project. In 1987, the construction sector was expected to expand at about 5 per cent largely owing to downstream development in Mahaweli, road development, flood protection and building construction activities. The service sector was expected to grow by more than 5 per cent in 1987. However, in recent years, the tourist industry has declined significantly; by 1986, total tourist arrivals had fallen by more than two fifths from their peak 1982 level.

The external sector imbalance which has been a recurrent feature of the Sri Lankan economy has become a major constraint on economic performance in recent years. The external current deficit more than doubled in 1985 and then narrowed only slightly in 1986, remaining over 9 per cent of GDP, as domestic supply-demand imbalances continued and the external environment deteriorated. Although the special drawing rights value of Sri Lanka's export earn-ings declined by about 15 per cent during the first half of 1987, the flow of imports continued more or less at the same level as in 1986, largely through utilization of foreign aid and the country's international reserves. During the period May 1986-May 1987, external reserves of Sri Lanka declined by 18 per cent.

Sri Lanka's domestic saving rate recovered only slightly in 1986, to just over 14 per cent, a little below the average for the period 1978-1983. Much of the variation in savings was due to movements in the terms of trade. The decline in tea prices during 1985/86 eroded the financial position of the publicly-owned plantations, whose savings are included with those of the private sector, and also led to sharply lower export tax receipts. Gross fixed capital formation as a percentage of GDP has fallen every year since 1982, from 30.5 to 23.6 per cent in 1986. This was mainly due to weakening of business confidence and the completion of important components of the Mahaweli programme contributing to a decline in investment activities by private enterprises and public corporations. While a substantial portion of Sri Lanka's total investment is financed by foreign savings, the resource gap narrowed sharply from 15.2 per cent of GDP in 1982 to 9.3 per cent in 1986.

In 1988, a greater expansion of economic activities, particularly in manufacturing, tourism, coastal fishing and construction, was expected mainly as a result of the favourable impact of the peace accord.

D. OTHER DEVELOPING ECONOMIES

The performance of the economy of the Islamic Republic of Iran, in which oil plays a predominant role, has been adversely affected by falling oil prices and difficulties in its oil shipments arising out of the continuing Gulf war. As a result GDP is estimated to have stagnated in 1984/85, to have fallen by about 1 per cent in 1985/86 and then to have slumped by about 8 per cent in 1986/87 as a result of the impact of the oil price drop as well as war-time conditions. The country has also suffered from the falling value of the United States dollar since 1985 since oil exports are generally denominated in United States dollars.

The agricultural sector showed some hopeful signs of improvement in recent years. There has been a rapid rise in cereal output as a result of increased incentives. Sugar output has also shown strong growth, with increases in the output of both sugar-beet and cane. However, climatic changes in 1986/87 also adversely affected the Islamic Republic of Iran, with severe flooding in some areas.

The modern industrial sector in the Islamic Republic of Iran, which produces a wide range of manufactures, including fertilizer, sugar, cement, textiles, machine tools and petrochemicals, has suffered heavily owing to shortages of physical and human inputs. There have been chronic shortages of electric power as power stations have been a prime target in the war, and their maintenance and repair has not been adequate. Delay in the completion of major power schemes has also contributed to the shortage. The traditional sector in the Islamic Republic of Iran, comprising carpet-making, metalware, ceramics, jewellery and other crafts, is a major employer within industry as a whole. While the handicraft industry has maintained remarkable resilience in both the major towns and many villages, carpet production has increasingly faced severe international competition from traditional producers of hand-woven rugs and carpets.

In 1983/84 the value of the export of carpets fell to $69 million from $149 million in 1981/82 and a peak of $425 million in 1980/81.

Since 1983 there has been a declining trend in export earnings, mainly owing to the fall in the volume and price of oil. Only a small volume of refined products is exported, amounting to approximately 39,000 barrels per day in 1985, compared with 94,000 barrels per day in 1981. During the first half of the 1980s export earnings from other primary commodities also declined. In 1985, oil accounted for 98 per cent of all exports.

In the early 1980s there has been a major shift in the type of goods imported. The share of capital goods in total imports declined from 30 per cent in 1979 to 15 per cent in 1982. There was also a sharp cut in imports of consumer goods. However, the value of imports of food and live animals rose rapidly throughout the early 1980s, from $1.5 billion in 1980/81 to $2.4 billion in 1983/84.

The current account of the Islamic Republic of Iran has mainly followed oil income developments. Thus, increased oil volume in 1985 and drastic import cuts returned the balance of trade to surplus. However, with the fall in oil prices and the lower volume available for export in 1986, export earnings plummeted and thus a large trade deficit was incurred.

The national income of Mongolia increased by 5.6 per cent in 1986. Industrial and agricultural output grew by 8.0 per cent and 12 per cent respectively.[6] Labour productivity in industry was up by 5.8 per cent, in construction by 3.8 per cent, and in transport by 6.9 per cent. In 1986, national income in real terms was 2.5 times the level in 1960.[7]

Agriculture accounts for 25 per cent of national income, and about 60 per cent of the country's exports.[8] Recently the country has become self-sufficient in grain. In 1985, 890,000 tons of grain were harvested and the per capita grain production reached 450 kg, exceeding the world average.[9] Livestock breeding accounts for 70 per cent of the gross agricultural output. Mongolia is among the world's leading countries in terms of per capita head of cattle and meat production: there are approximately 16 livestock per person.

The share of industry in national income rose from 14.6 per cent in 1960 to 32.6 per cent in 1986. There has been a considerable growth in the productive capacities designed to strengthen the energy and raw materials base of the national economy and to ensure a better supply of food and consumer goods. The sectoral pattern of industry has been undergoing qualitative changes. The degree of processing agricultural raw materials has been on the rise. One of the most developed national economic branches of Mongolia is light industry. It accounts for about 35 per cent of the export earnings of the country, about 40 per cent of the aggregate industrial and agricultural output.

In 1986, the volume of foreign trade increased by 3.2 per cent over the previous year.[10] The volume of foreign trade is equivalent to about one third of Mongolia's real national income. In the eighth five-year plan (1986-1990), the volume of foreign trade is targeted to increase by 20-25 per cent as compared with the seventh five-year plan. Mongolia meets almost 90 per cent of its requirements of investment goods and 60 per cent of consumer goods through imports. Mongolia's main trade partner is the Soviet Union, accounting for 80 to 90 per cent of the country's foreign trade. From a traditional supplier of animal husbandry products and raw materials, Mongolia is diversifying and becoming an exporter of semi-processed and finished industrial goods. Mongolia exports, among others, hides and finished leather goods, camel wool and goat fleece, non-ferrous metals, timber, clothes, knitted goods, meat and meat products. Foodstuffs, manufactured consumer goods, buses, cars, household electrical goods, machine tools, agricultural machines and spare parts predominate in Mongolia's imports.

In 1987, the national income was expected to grow by not less than 5 per cent over 1986, and the output of the agricultural and industrial sectors by 3 and 5.3 per cent, respectively. The total volume of capital investments in 1987 was targeted to grow by 5.3 per cent over the preceding year.

The national income of Viet Nam in 1986 increased by 4 per cent over 1985. However, food production remains a matter of great concern. Almost stagnant agricultural output in 1986 resulted in decline in per capita food production from 304 kgs in 1985 to 301 kgs in 1986. In the first half of 1987, output of rice and subsidiary crops was adversely affected by hailstorms and drought.

In 1986, livestock production grew by 2.2 per cent. Industrial output was estimated to be

[6] Council for Mutual Economic Assistance, *Economic Co-operation of the CMEA Member Countries,* No. 4, 1987, p. 105.

[7] *National Report of the Mongolia People's Republic,* p. 6.

[8] *News from Mongolia,* No. 13, 1986.

[9] *Ibid.,* No. 8, 1986.

[10] CMEA, *Economic Co-operation of the CMEA Member Countries,* No. 4, 1987, p. 105.

up nearly 8 per cent on the year for the first six months of 1987, with investment in the productive sector growing rather slowly at 4.0 per cent. Investment appears to have been directed away from industry as agriculture's share rose to 29 per cent from 24.5 per cent in 1986 (including forestry and

---

Box I.7. Foreign investment code of Viet Nam[a]

Beset by severe balance-of-payments constraints which have caused a slow-down in its economic growth, the Government of Viet Nam has been making persistent efforts to attract foreign capital inflows. Towards this end, it promulgated a new Investment Code on 1 January 1988, superseding the Investment Code of 18 April 1977. The new Code, which has substantially modified the previous Code, reflects a flexible and pragmatic approach by the Government aimed at facilitating and speeding up foreign investment inflows from developed as well as developing countries. The policy towards foreign investment in developing countries generally centres on five major issues: definition of foreign capital; permissible and priority areas for investment; foreign ownership (and control); performance requirements; and investment incentives.

The definition of foreign capital in the Code is broad. A foreign partner can contribute capital in the form of foreign currency; plants, buildings, equipment, machineries, tools, components and spare parts; and patents, technical know-how and technical services.

All regions and almost all sectors, including public utilities, are open for foreign investment. However, the Code delineates priority areas for foreign investment, including production for export and for import substitution. A detailed list of industries and sectors in which foreign investment is encouraged will be published by the State organization responsible for management of foreign investment.

The policy with respect to foreign ownership and control has three major facets: foreign ownership, employment of national personnel and foreign control at the enterprise level. One of the major revisions in the Code relates to the maximum

share of foreign capital that is permitted. This share has been raised from 49 to 100 per cent foreign ownership and management. Moreover, there is no upper limit for the sum of capital that a foreign investor can invest in Viet Nam. The Code retains the minimum requirement of 30 per cent foreign ownership of capital in a joint venture operating in Viet Nam. Foreign investors can enter into various forms of agreement with host country partners such as joint ventures, production-sharing agreements, technical assistance agreements, etc. While the duration of the venture with foreign capital cannot, in principle, exceed 20 years, it may be extended for a longer period in special cases. The Code stipulates that priority should be given to Vietnamese nationals in the recruitment of personnel for enterprises with foreign capital. However, employment of expatriate personnel is allowed when Vietnamese personnel of sufficient calibre are not available.

The major performance requirements for foreign enterprises in most developing countries generally take the form of export obligations, utilization and processing of domestic raw materials and natural resources and employment generation. The Vietnamese Code does not specify such performance obligations of enterprises receiving foreign financial or technological participation and *inter alia* seems less restrictive. Regarding export obligations, foreign enterprises are not required to export a minimum amount of their output. Nevertheless, the guiding principle is that they have to meet their own foreign exchange needs.

The Code contains provisions guaranteeing: (a) repatriation of income, profit, interest as well as capital invested; and (b) protection of foreign investment against nationalization. The Code accords liberal fiscal incentives to stimulate foreign investment. The corporate income tax levied on foreign enterprises has been reduced from the range of 30 to 50 per cent in the old Code to 15 to 25 per cent in

the new Code. It must be noted that the current range of corporate income tax on foreign enterprises is quite low compared with the norm of 30 to 40 per cent in other developing countries of the ESCAP region.

The State organization for management of foreign investment is empowered to grant tax holidays exempting foreign enterprises from payment of income tax for up to two years starting from the first year in which a profit is made. Foreign enterprises may also be allowed a 50 per cent reduction in income tax for a maximum period of two successive years. Further incentives in the form of reduction of income tax up to 10 per cent of earned profits and extension of the period of income tax exemption may be granted at the discretion of the State organization for management of foreign investment. While foreign enterprises are liable to pay tax from 5 to 10 per cent on repatriation of profits, reduction of, or exemption from, this tax may be permitted. Furthermore, the State organization for management of foreign investment has the discretion to grant further incentives including exemption from, or reduction of, export and import duties in spheres where foreign investment is particularly encouraged.

As alluded to in the Code, a State organization for management of foreign investment has been set up to deal with matters pertaining to foreign investment. The major functions of this body include the formulation of investment priorities and the range of incentives, the screening and processing of investment applications, and granting of incentives.

The Code provides that further regulations will be enacted with a view to facilitating investment inflows from overseas Vietnamese residents. Cognizant of the fact that the foreign exchange arrangement is an important factor influencing foreign investment inflows, the Government is in the process of deciding on a single foreign exchange rate that will be applied to all business transactions.

[a] Based on an unofficial English translation of the Code provided to the secretariat by the Government of Viet Nam.

water conservancy). Performance was particularly disappointing in textiles, sugar, paper, soap and detergent owing to shortage of raw materials.

In 1986, exports and imports estimated at $641 million and $1,590 million, respectively, resulted in a trade deficit of $949 million. The rate of inflation was estimated at 700 per cent for 1987.

Several reforms were introduced in 1986 and early 1987, especially in the field of wages and distribution of goods. A number of measures were initiated with a veiw to encouraging overseas Vietnamese to remit funds to Viet Nam in order to augment the much-needed foreign exchange inflows (see box I.7, p. 41). Substantial tariff reductions have been announced for imports of investment goods used in most economic activities, including agriculture, industry, fisheries and public health. These reductions are to bring the cost of such goods into line with the price on the free market. Renewed attention is being paid to improving the quality of goods entering the state wholesale sector.

III. LEAST DEVELOPED AND PACIFIC ISLAND ECONOMIES

As far as can be judged from the limited data available,[1] the recent rate of growth of per capita income in most of the region's least developed countries fell, stagnated or rose very slowly. In most cases, per capita growth has been considerably lower than 2 per cent, while some of the smaller Pacific island economies have had declining per capita incomes. In Vanuatu, per capita income has declined for two successive years; the per capita income of Kiribati fell by 9 per cent in 1985.

The vulnerability of the agricultural sector illustrates the severity of the food security problems in the least developed countries. The low growth rates of food production and above-average population growth rates in the majority of the region's least developed countries make it ne-

cessary for them to spend a large amount of their foreign exchange receipts for food grain imports. In 1985, for instance, in Afghanistan, Bangladesh, Bhutan, Nepal, Samoa and Vanuatu, the rate of population growth exceeded that of food production; only Burma and the Lao People's Democratic Republic were able to achieve overall food self-sufficiency.

A disquieting aspect of the lack of food self-sufficiency in the least developed countries is widespread malnutrition, which is most serious among vulnerable groups in rural areas where the majority of the people live. The problem is not simply one of augmenting aggregate food supply but also of improving its distribution and generating effective demand.

The flow of official development assistance (ODA) to the least developed countries of the ESCAP region has not registered any satisfactory increase over the first half of the decade. The net ODA flow from DAC member countries to these countries declined marginally from $1.88 billion in 1985 to $1.84 billion in 1986, expressed in constant prices with adjusted exchange rates (see box I.8).

The developing Pacific island countries have generally registered a poor economic performance in recent years, with real GDP growth reaching 3 per cent or less for most island countries in 1986, the latest year for which data are

available. This was largely the result of external factors. These included unfavourable prices for the major export commodities of the subregion, notably vegetable oil products, and the adverse impact of natural disaster (on the Solomon Islands). The relatively unfavourable economic performance in Australia and New Zealand also contributed to poorer earnings from tourism in some islands, including Vanuatu. The adverse external circumstances created pressures on the fiscal and external balances, resulting in a more restrained rate of public spending and aggregate demand in several countries.

A. LEAST DEVELOPED COUNTRIES

1. Macro-economic performance

With the inclusion of Burma in the category of least developed countries, the number of this group of countries in the Asian and Pacific region stood at 11[2] out of a total of 41, as of December 1987. However, in terms of population the region's least developed countries account for about half of the total population of the least developed countries of the world. This indicates that the problem of underdevelopment re-

---

[1] Any discussion on current economic developments and recent growth performance in the least developed and Pacific island economies of the ESCAP region must be prefaced by cautioning the reader on the reliability of the available macro-economic data for most of the countries discussed in this chapter. With few exceptions, these countries are still in the process of developing the basic data series that are prerequisites for the compilation of the national accounts and related macro-economic aggregates. As such, it would be advisable to treat the data published and the accompanying analysis as providing only broad indications of the level and pace of economic activity in the countries concerned.

[2] Afghanistan, Bangladesh, Bhutan, Burma, Kiribati, the Lao People's Democratic Republic, Maldives, Nepal, Samoa, Tuvalu and Vanuatu.

Box I.8. Development assistance to the ESCAP least developed countries

The prospects of the least developed countries of the ESCAP region attaining the aid target of the Substantial New Programme of Action for the 1980s for the Least Developed Countries appear, with a few exceptions, to be getting more distant. Neither of the two alternative official development assistance (ODA) targets set out in the Programme have even a remote chance of being fulfilled before the Programme for the 1980s is concluded.

The first of these two targets, requiring all bilateral donors to provide, by 1985 or as soon as possible thereafter, 0.15 per cent of their gross national product (GNP) as ODA to the least developed countries, was fulfilled in 1985, by 6 out of 18 members of the Development Assistance Committee (DAC), while the DAC countries as a group achieved a little over half that target,

i.e., 0.08 per cent of their combined GNPs.[a]

The average annual flow of ODA to the eight ESCAP least developed countries during 1976-1980 was estimated at $1.4 billion. The 1981-1986 average flows for the same eight countries, according to data available (see table) can be estimated at $1.8 billion at current prices and exchange rates,[b] an increase of 28.6 per cent.[b]

---

[a] Development Assistance Committee, *DAC Chairman's Report for 1987 (DAC/(87)14), table 2, p. 12.*

[b] For Afghanistan and the Lao People's Democratic Republic, the 1986 flows are assumed at $259.7 million and $115.9 million respectively, which are averages during 1981-1985, see *Survey,* 1986, p. 49.

Net disbursement of ODA to the present 11 least developed countries of the ESCAP region in current dollar terms fluctuated between the lowest of $1.61 billion in 1983 to $2.25 billion in 1986 over the period 1980-1986. In terms of constant prices and exchange rates, the lowest and the highest values of $1.58 and $1.88 billion are estimated in 1983 and in 1985 respectively. Price and exchange rate changes in recent years have greatly distorted financial flow data. It is interesting to observe that the $2.25 billion current dollar aid flow to the 11 countries in 1986, representing a 19.7 per cent rise over 1985, reduces to $1.84 billion in constant dollar and exchange rate terms, a decrease of 2.1 per cent over the 1985 flow of $1.88 billion. Per capita real aid receipts for the group of 11 countries have stagnated at $10-$11 over the period.

Net disbursement of official development assistance[a] to the ESCAP least developed countries, 1980-1986

(Millions of US dollars)

	1980	1981	1982	1983	1984	1985	1986
Afghanistan	30.8	2.6	8.9	15.7	7.3	18.3	6.0
Bangladesh	1 212.3	1 047.6	1 220.2	970.4	1 186.6	1 142.0	1 373.4
Bhutan	8.3	9.8	11.3	12.9	17.6	21.3	31.7
Burma	308.7	283.4	319.0	302.0	274.9	355.7	416.1
Kiribati	19.2	15.3	15.1	16.8	12.0	12.1	13.4
Lao People's Democratic Republic	40.8	35.0	38.3	29.7	34.2	37.0	46.7
Maldives	6.3	6.6	3.9	7.4	6.2	10.5	16.0
Nepal	156.3	171.8	200.6	201.7	199.2	237.8	296.3
Samoa	25.7	25.0	22.9	26.7	20.3	19.1	23.1
Tuvalu	4.9	5.4	6.3	4.2	5.5	3.4	4.4
Vanuatu	44.0	30.5	26.0	26.9	24.5	21.8	24.4
Total[b]	1 857.3	1 633.0	1 872.5	1 614.4	1 788.3	1 879.0	2 251.3
Total[c]	1 728.8	1 576.7	1 846.3	1 579.9	1 807.8	1 879.0	1 835.7
Per capita flows[d]	11.0	9.8	11.2	9.3	10.4	10.6	10.2

Sources: Organisation for Economic Co-operation and Development, *Geographical Distribution of Financial Flows to Developing Countries,* various issues.

[a] Net disbursement from members of the Development Assistance Committee of the OECD and multilateral agencies. [b] Total in current United States dollars. [c] Total in constant prices and adjusted exchange rates. [d] Per capita real flows in United States dollars for all ESCAP least developed countries.

in the 1980s

This rather disappointing record of aid flows to the least developed countries of the region is in line with the continuing crisis in capital flows since 1982, characterized by declines in most major components to virtually all groups of developing countries.[c]

The flow of ODA in current dollar terms to Bangladesh, the largest aid recipient among the least developed countries of the region, remained stagnant at around $1.2 billion for most of the 1980-1986 period. However, there was a sharp downturn in 1983. On the other hand, for the other two large recipients, Burma and Nepal, a general rising trend is discernible despite year-to-year fluctuations, and for both countries ODA flows in current prices in the mid-1980s are much higher than the levels attained by them earlier in the decade. No firm trend is noticeable for Maldives. Its aid receipts came mainly from the OPEC members in western Asia and their aid flows have declined sharply since 1982. In 1985 and 1986, the current dollar aid flow to Maldives showed sharp upturns again, large proportions of which are, however, price and exchange rate effects. Bhutan is the only country in the group that displayed an uninterrupted increase in the ODA flow, which rose from $8.3 million in 1980 to $31.7 million in 1986.

Afghanistan's receipt of ODA from members of the Development Assistance Committee of OECD and multilateral agencies declined sharply after 1980. Similarly, the ODA flows to the Lao People's Democratic Republic from these sources showed no significant improvement during 1980-1986.[d]

Aid flows to the four least developed Pacific island countries over the recent past have been very disappointing. For Kiribati, Samoa, Tuvalu and Vanuatu, the levels of ODA in current dollar terms in the 1985-1986 period were much lower than in the early 1980s.

---

[c] UNCTAD, *Review of International Monetary and financial Questions related to Trade and Development* (TD/B/C. 3/215), p. 8.

[d] See footnote b.

---

presented by the existence of such countries is no less serious than in any other developing region and that the flattering image of Asia as having largely rid itself of its past inheritance of backwardness is greatly exaggerated.

In spite of continuing difficulties in both the external environment and domestic developments, the rate of growth of output in a number of the region's least developed countries increased in 1986 and 1987 (see table I.8). The GDP of Afghanistan grew at the rate of 3.3 per cent in 1986/87 compared with that of 0.1 per cent in the previous year, owing to increased production in the agricultural and industrial sectors. For 1987/88, GDP was estimated to have increased by 4.5 per cent. However, the economy continued to suffer because of continuing political problems. The first five-year socio-economic plan (1986-1991), approved by the Government in February 1986, envisages economic growth of 25 per cent (compared with an official estimate of only 2 per cent average annual growth rate since 1978), with the industrial production set to increase by 38 per cent and agricultural production by 14-16 per cent. Despite recent improvements in economic performance, the prospects of these targets being achieved do not look bright.

The economy of Bangladesh achieved an annual growth rate of 4 per cent in the first two years of the third five-year plan (1985/86-1989/90), as compared with the overall target of 5.4 per cent annual growth rate for the plan period.[3] Reflecting the widespread feeling that the statistical base of such estimates

---

[3] For a more detailed account of the macro-economic performance of Bangladesh economy, see pp. 35-37, this *Survey*.

---

needs to be strengthened, the National Income Commission was set up to assess the contribution of different sectors to the national economy and to ensure proper and systematic collection of data and methodology for the preparation of reliable estimates of national accounts.

In Bhutan, GDP growth rate increased by 9.2 per cent in 1986, compared with the growth rate of 3.3 per cent in the previous year. This was due to the inclusion of hydroelectricity generated by the Chukha project which started in September 1986. Consequently, the average annual growth rate of output during 1981-1986 period reached 6.3 per cent. The sixth five-year plan (1987-1992), which was launched in July 1987, envisaged at total outlay of Nu 9,485 million, of which development expenditure and current expenditure will account for 63 and 37 per cent respectively. A major plan objective is to pursue further the decentralization process which was initiated during the fifth plan period.

The annual average growth rate of GDP achieved by Burma during the fourth four-year plan period (1982/83-1985/86) was 5.0 per cent. This comparatively favourable economic growth rate was attributed to the improvement in the planning process and greater participation of the people in plan implementation. However, the GDP growth in 1986/87 slowed down to 3.6 per cent as a result of lower output in the agricultural sector because of drought conditions brought about by the late onset and early withdrawal of the monsoon.

In the Lao People's Democratic Republic, the annual growth rate of output averaged over 5 per cent between 1982 and 1985 with large fluctuations; the growth of the economy has been on an upward trend since 1984 as a result of continuing good harvests. The economy continued to improve in 1986, benefiting from favourable weather, improved incentives and easing of import constraints. During the first plan period (1981-1985), official information indicated the achievement of self-sufficiency in food production

Table I.8. Selected least developed economies in the ESCAP region. Growth rates and relative share of components of GDP at constant prices, 1982-1987

	Total	Growth rates			Sectoral rates[a]		
		Agriculture	Industry	Services	Agriculture	Industry	Services
Afghanistan							
1982	2.0	0.5	3.2	7.7	61.7	25.4	13.0
1983	4.8	2.2	11.8	3.8	60.1	27.0	12.8
1984	2.0	−0.4	4.0	9.5	58.6	27.6	13.8
1985	0.1	−0.6	6.5	−10.1	58.3	29.4	12.4
1986	3.3	1.6	6.3	4.3	57.3	30.2	12.5
1987[b]	4.5	2.2	6.5	8.8	56.1	24.2	19.7
Bangladesh							
1982	0.8	0.9	3.1	−0.2	48.8	15.2	36.0
1983	3.6	4.6	0.6	3.5	49.2	14.8	35.9
1984	4.2	1.6	8.3	6.1	48.0	15.4	36.6
1985	3.7	1.0	6.2	6.3	46.7	15.8	37.5
1986	4.4	3.4	2.3	6.6	46.3	15.4	38.3
1987[b]	4.5	1.6	7.9	6.6	45.0	15.9	39.1
Bhutan							
1982	10.8	11.5	18.3	5.5	49.2	18.9	33.8
1983	6.1	18.3	5.4	3.9	49.7	18.8	33.2
1984	2.6	5.4	−3.7	5.3	50.2	17.6	34.0
1985	3.3	6.7	−10.2	5.6	51.9	15.3	34.8
1986	9.2	9.4	21.0	2.4	52.0	17.0	32.7
Burma							
1982	5.6	6.0	6.6	4.9	37.8	15.5	46.7
1983	4.4	4.9	4.0	4.1	38.0	15.4	46.6
1984	5.6	4.4	9.4	5.2	37.6	16.0	46.4
1985	6.2	2.5	4.7	5.6	36.9	16.0	47.0
1986	3.6	3.0	6.2	3.3	36.7	16.4	46.8
1987	5.0	5.5	9.0	3.2	36.9	17.1	46.0
Lao People's Democratic Republic							
1982	2.0	−0.4	23.2	3.2	76.1	9.5	14.4
1983	−2.1	−4.9	7.0	6.9	73.9	10.4	15.7
1984	14.5	19.0	4.6	0.2	76.8	9.5	13.7
1985[b]	7.2	7.1	15.9	1.4	76.8	10.2	13.0
Maldives							
1982	7.5	−5.3	14.8	18.1	35.5	15.5	49.3
1983	4.4	6.3	4.5	3.2	35.8	15.5	48.6
1984	13.9	15.8	8.6	14.2	36.4	14.8	48.8
1985	15.3	20.9	4.2	14.5	38.2	13.4	48.4
1986	4.2	3.6	8.2	3.6	38.0	13.9	48.1
Nepal							
1982	3.8	4.6	———— 2.6 ————		60.3	———— 39.7 ————	
1983	−3.0	−1.1	———— −5.8 ————		61.5	———— 38.5 ————	
1984	7.8	9.5	———— 4.9 ————		62.5	———— 37.5 ————	
1985	3.0	2.4	———— 4.0 ————		62.1	———— 37.9 ————	
1986	4.0	4.4	———— 3.4 ————		62.3	———— 37.6 ————	
1987	2.3	1.0	———— 4.4 ————		61.6	———— 38.4 ————	

Sources: National sources; and ADB, *Key Indicators of Developing Member Countries of ADB,* vol. XLI, No. 5 (July 1986).

[a] The sectoral shares might not add up to 100 per cent owing to import duties and imputed bank service charge. [b] Estimated.

and higher literacy rate. The second five-year plan (1986-1991), which was adopted in November 1986, has the main objectives of sustaining self-sufficiency in food production and developing natural resources, especially hydropower and timber.

In Maldives, real GDP increased at an annual average rate of 15 per cent during 1984-1985 compared with a 6 per cent annual increase in 1982-1983. This strong performance was associated with a substantial increase in the fish catch, owing to a rise in the number of mechanized fishing vessels and improved fuel distribution system for those vessels. Tourist arrivals also increased rapidly, reflecting the expansion of new resorts and related facilities. In 1986, however, economic activity slowed down markedly as a result of unfavourable weather conditions which hampered fisheries activity. During 1987, the country was hit by three unexpected high tidal waves, causing heavy damage to the assets and crops in the low-lying islands.

In Nepal, GDP growth fell to 2.3 per cent in 1986/87. During the sixth plan period (1981-1985), the annual average growth rate of GDP was 4.1 per cent in real terms as compared with the target of 4.3 per cent. However, this masks the highly volatile year-to-year performance, which ranged from the negative rate of 3.0 per cent in 1982/83 to 8 per cent in 1983/84. The GDP growth rate during 1984/85 was reported at 3 per cent, owing to sluggish agricultural and industrial production. It improved slightly as a result of the expansion in the agricultural and industrial production in 1985/86.

The four least developed island countries of the Pacific, Kiribati, Samoa, Tuvalu and Vanuatu, have also experienced slow economic growth owing to stagnant agricultural production and decline in the export prices of their commodities. Apart from serious structural problems, these countries suffer from geographical disadvantages as they are located far away from the main international shipping routes. These economies are also susceptible to frequent natural disasters.[4]

In Kiribati, with the termination of phosphate mining in 1979, the Government began to focus its attention on increasing the output of coconuts and fishing. However, despite the Government's incentives to producers, copra production has been volatile because of export price fluctuations and weather conditions. In contrast, commercial fishing expanded sharply and its share of GDP almost tripled between 1979 and 1984. On the other hand, progress in developing other resources has been minimal. Both copra and fisheries are exported in unprocessed form. With the establishment of an exclusive economic zone of over 3 million sq km in the Pacific, fishing offers the best overall prospects for the country.

During the 1982-1986 period, Samoa had a rather slow growth rate of GDP, ranging from −1.1 to 2.2 per cent. The market value of its exports of agricultural and forestry products diminished and the price of its most important product, copra, fell from $1,050 per ton in 1984 to an all-time low of $390 in 1985.

In Vanuatu, the annual average GDP growth rate in real terms was 2.0 per cent between 1982 and 1986. However, the economy was adversely affected by major cyclones in 1985 and 1987, which caused widespread damage to agricultural crops, including copra, the main export and foreign exchange earner. Manufacturing con-

---

[4] For greater details on some of these economies, see the following section on Pacific island countries.

tributed less than 5 per cent. Tourism and financial services are important sources of revenue.

2. Sectoral performance

(a) Agriculture

Agriculture constitutes the largest component of GDP in most of the least developed countries of the region. This sector contributes well over 50 per cent of the total GDP (except in Bangladesh, Burma and Maldives), provides employment for 80 per cent of the labour force and accounts for over half of the exports. However, the performance of these countries in the agricultural sector has been mixed and output growth has fluctuated frequently owing largely to weather conditions, with slow growth as the main feature in most countries in the 1980s.

During 1987, agricultural output grew at a slow pace in the majority of the least developed countries. In Afghanistan, the rate of growth of agricultural output continued to be modest, partly as a result of a reduction of total area under cultivation by 18,000 hectares in 1986/87, compared with the previous year. Production of cereals and raw cotton correspondingly declined.

In Bangladesh, the rate of growth of the agricultural sector in 1987 was only 1.6 per cent owing mainly to the lower production of jute, which fell by over 20 per cent from the previous year's production level. Successive floods and heavy rain caused extensive damage to the economy estimated at about $1,000 million. In Bhutan, the fifth plan (1981-1987) target of self-sufficiency in food production could not be achieved. The country's demand for rice was met largely by imports from India. However, there was a continuing progress in the production of cash crops such as potatoes, apples and oranges. In Nepal, agricultural output grew at the rate of 1 per cent in 1986/87 because of unfavourable weather conditions and also on account of the deterioration of jute prices in the previous year. Production of cereals was adversely affected owing to drought in late 1986 and floods in early 1987.

In the Lao People's Democratic Republic, a poor harvest was expected, particularly in the mountain area in the middle of 1987 on account of the late arrival and weak intensity of monsoon rains. However, Burma achieved a rate of growth of agricultural output of over 5.5 per cent in 1987, which was above the 4 per cent annual growth target envisaged by the Substantial New Programme of Action for the 1980s for the Least Developed Countries. Measures were taken in Burma to raise agricultural output through widespread adoption of improved methods of cultivation, including distribution of agricultural inputs and implements,

and an increase in the area under cultivation.

The agricultural sector in small South Pacific island least developed countries, Kiribati, Samoa and Vanuatu, were badly affected by weather and other unfavourable conditions in 1986/87. Severe cyclones caused significant damage to Vanuatu in early 1987. Moreover, the steep drop in prices in coconut products adversely affected these economies.

In Tuvalu, agriculture is essentially of the subsistence type and the resources are extremely limited. The country has only one export crop, copra. A crop development programme has been launched with the aim of achieving self-sufficiency in food production and introducing new crops with import substitution and export potential. The prospects for fishing are also good, as the country possesses a vast exclusive economic zone.

Owing to the continued problems in the agricultural sector, inadequate food supply and resultant malnutrition remain a serious concern in the majority of the region's least developed countries. The per capita protein and calorie intake in general are far below the normative requirement levels (see table I.9).

(b) Industry

In most of the least developed countries, the manufacturing sector consists mainly of processing primary commodities and producing consumer goods. Food, beverages, tobacco and textiles account for two thirds of the total manufacturing activities in many of these countries. As a result, this sector is closely linked with the agricultural sector which provides both raw materials as well as markets for the industrial products. The generally weak performance in the agricultural sector has adversely affected industrial growth as well as overall economic performance in these countries.

In Afghanistan, the output of the industrial sector grew by over 6 per cent between 1985 and 1987. During this period the pro-

Table I.9. Selected least developed economies in the ESCAP region. Daily per capita protein and calorie supplies, selected years

	Protein (grams)			Calorie[a] (calories)			Normative[b] requirement
	1975	1980	1985	1975	1980	1985	
Afghanistan	...	...	...	2 010	2 220	2 180	...
Bangladesh	39	39	41[c]	1 760	1 820	1 870[b]	2 310
Burma	57	62	63	2 220	2 360	2 510	2 160
Kiribati	58	67	68[c]	2 160	2 670	2 520	...
Lao People's Democratic Republic	49	56	61	1 840	2 100	2 320	2 220
Maldives	62	54	55[c]	1 750	1 980	1 950	2 210
Nepal	49	51	51	2 030	1 960	2 000	2 200
Samoa	54	58	...	2 260	2 400	2 300	2 280
Vanuatu	65	66	63[c]	2 400	2 420	2 290	2 160

Source: FAO Basic Data Unit, Statistics Division, 9 January 1987.

[a] Figures are rounded to the nearest ten. [b] *Survey,* 1985, p. 75. [c] 1984 estimate.

duction of natural gas increased and measures were taken to optimize the use of the existing capacity of the plants and to bring additional plants into operation. Greater emphasis was given to agro-based industries. A new investment law was promulgated to encourage private investment. A central office has been set up to expand the activities of the private sector in the economy, including providing technical and economic advice to private entrepreneurs.

The industrial sector in Bangladesh, which progressed well in 1983/84 and 1984/85 with growth rates of 8.3 and 6.2 per cent, decelerated to 2.3 per cent in 1985/86. However, it was estimated to pick up again to 8 per cent in 1986/87. The fluctuations were mainly on account of uneven development of the jute manufactures and garment markets. The latter suffered severely from the export restrictions imposed by developed countries in early 1986. In early 1986, the industrial policy was thoroughly reviewed in the light of past experience and a new industrial policy was introduced to accelerate industrialization in the country. A high-powered committee was established with a view to facilitating industrial investments and entrusting greater responsibility to the principal development institutions. In June 1987, the Industrial Enterprises Bill was passed which empowered the Government to transform nationalized corporations into holding companies which would then sell shares to the public to widen the ownership base. Workers' representatives would be elected on the Board of Directors of these enterprises to safeguard the interests of workers.

In Bhutan, industrial output of other than forest-based products consists of a small range of consumer goods (soap, liquor) and a few intermediate goods (cement).

More than two thirds of the total industrial output and employment (excluding construction) are accounted for by the three major enterprises: the Penden Cement Authority, the Army Welfare Project (distilleries) and the Bhutan Fruit Products Company.

In Burma, the average annual rate of growth in the manufacturing sector recorded for the fourth four-year plan (1982/83-1985/86) was 6.1 per cent and a high rate of growth of 9 per cent was achieved in 1986/87 (see box I.9). This was attributed to the measures taken to enable factories and plants to run at their full capacity and to ensure the availability of raw materials and spare parts — both domesitic and imported. Efforts to improve the supervision and co-ordination of implementation of the on-going projects have also contributed to industrial growth.

In the Lao People's Democratic Republic, the industrial sector which is comprised of a number of state industrial enterprises, mostly located in and around Vientiane, achieved a growth rate of 16 per cent in 1985. This was in contrast to the deceleration experienced in the past, particularly in 1983 and 1984, owing to lack of adequate raw materials, equipment, spare parts, qualified expertise and markets. In order to revitalize this sector, the Government introduced major reforms in 1985 involving increased prices to reflect actual production costs and increased wages. Moreover, the managers of several public enterprises were given greater freedom to make their own production and marketing decisions. Priority is being given to the processing of agro-industries aimed at meeting the growing internal demand for daily consumption goods and for exports.

The manufacturing sector in Maldives accounts for about 5 per cent of GDP because of the limited

size of the domestic market and a lack of raw materials. The major activities in this sector are boat-building and handicrafts, production of consumer goods such as soft drinks and breads and manufacturing of garments for exports. The value added in this sector increased by 11 per cent per year in 1982-1986, with the garment sector being the main contributor to the rapid growth.

The industrial growth in Nepal was fairly stable at the rate of 4 per cent during the 1984/85-1986/87 period, after a decline in output by 6 per cent in 1983/84. During the sixth five-year plan (1980-1985) period, Nepal became self-sufficient in a variety of consumer products and confectionary. In order to promote industrialization, emphasis is given to the adequate supply of raw materials and to the increase in efficiency and capacity utilization of existing industries. In October 1987, the New Industrial Policy was promulgated with the objective of further accelerating the pace of industrialization in the country and meeting the basic needs of the people by the year 2000.

3. Foreign trade

The importance of the foreign trade sector varies considerably among the least developed countries of the ESCAP region. Thus, while Bangladesh, Bhutan and the Lao People's Democratic Republic and Nepal have a relatively small ratio of exports to GDP, the degree of openness is significantly higher in the island economies, Maldives, Samoa and Vanuatu. In all countries, however, merchandise exports are highly concentrated on a few primary commodities, and there is considerable instability in earnings owing to fluctuations in world prices. Foreign exchange earnings from non-merchandise exports are significant in a number of least developed countries, form tourism in Bhutan, Maldives, Nepal and Vanuatu and from private transfers (workers' remittances) in Bangladesh and Samoa. Neighbouring countries are important trading partners for the land-locked least developed countries (India for Bhutan and

---

Box I.9. Inclusion of Burma in the least developed category

The United Nations General Assembly at its forty-second session held in 1987 unanimously approved the inclusion of Burma in the category of least developed countries. There are thus 41 least developed countries, of which 11 are in the Asian and Pacific region. However, in terms of the total population of all the least developed countries in the world, about half is in this region.[a]

With an area of 676,580 square kilometres (261,228 square miles) Burma is bounded on the east by Thailand and the Lao People's Democratic Republic, the north and north-

east by China and the west by Bangladesh and India. The population of Burma is 37.12 million (1985/86), with a growth rate of about 2 per cent per annum, and the density is about 54.59 per square kilometre. The per capita GDP at current market prices in 1982/83 was $175 and by 1985/86, it increased very slightly to $179. The

---

[a] The total population of all the 41 least developed countries was estimated at 359 million, of which the population of the 11 Asian and Pacific least developed countries accounted for 172 million (1984).

average annual real GDP growth since 1970 has remained at a low level, about 2.5 per cent.

Agriculture (including livestock, fishery and forestry) contributes nearly half of the total GDP and accounts for 66 per cent of the labour force in the country. Traditionally, the economy is dominated by rice, which is the main staple food, the major export commodity, and a primary source of fiscal revenue. It accounts for approximately one third of the agricultural output and 40 per cent of total exports. However, lack of adequate infrastructural support,

Least developed countries of the ESCAP region: selected indicators

	Population total (million) 1984	Population growth rates (percentage per annum) 1980-1984	Per capita GDP (real product) (percentage) 1984	Annual average growth rates per capita (real product) (percentage) 1980-1984	Share of agriculture in GDP (percentage) 1984	Share of manufacturing in GDP (percentage) 1984	Adult literacy rate (percentage) 1985	Year of inclusion in the list of the least developed countries
Afghanistan	17.7	2.6	210	0.1	59	28	24	1971
Bangladesh	96.7	2.2	145	1.6	48	9	33	1975
Bhutan	1.4	2.0	122	4.9	50	4	–	1971
Burma	36.2	–	180	6.0[a]	37[a]	10[a]	53[b]	1987
Kiribati	0.1	...	460	...	...	–	–	1986
Lao People's Democratic Republic	3.7	2.2	203	1.0	60	7	84	1971
Maldives	0.2	3.0	432	5.8	29	5	–	1971
Nepal	16.1	2.4	155	2.0	56	4	26	1971
Samoa	0.2	0.6	619	−2.5	51	6	–	1971
Tuvalu	0.01	–	491	–	–	–	–	1986
Vanuatu	0.1	2.8	683	0.2	–	–	–	1985
ESCAP least developed countries	172.4		...	...	...	...		
All least developed countries	359.3	2.6	206	−0.2	45	9	32	
All developing countries	2 471.7	2.4	870	−1.3	17	18	58	
Developed market economies	787.7	0.6	10 106	1.4	...		...	
Socialist countries of Eastern Europe	390.7	0.9	2 606	2.5	...	...	...	

Sources: UNCTAD, *The Least Developed Countries 1986 Report* (TD/B/1120); *World Bank Atlas, 1986;* and national sources.

[a] *Key Indicators of Developed Member Countries of ADB,* July 1987. [b] Committee on Development Planning, twenty-third session, New York, 21-24 April 1987, *Identification of the Least Developed among the Developing Countries: the Cases of Burma and Zambia,* 10 March 1987.

Nepal; Thailand and Viet Nam for the Lao People's Democratic Republic; and the Union of Soviet Socialist Republics for Afghanistan) under bilateral trade and transit agreements or barter arrangements. Generally food grain and fuel account for a significant part of the import bill of these countries. But

in particular irrigation facilities, insufficient milling and storage capacity, together with transport difficulties, have hampered production as well as domestic distribution and exports. Apart from agriculture, forestry is a major component of the Burmese economy, with teak and other hard-woods providing about a quarter of total export earnings.

Burma is well endowed with energy resources; crude oil, natural gas, and hydropower. Although oil production has decreased in recent years, this is due to technical constraints rather than an exhaustion of reserves. Natural gas output and coal production are expanding rapidly, and concomitantly, electric power generation grew by 19, 23 and 12 per cent respectively in the last three fiscal years (1984/85-1986/87).

The share of manufacturing in GDP was only 4.7 in 1985/86. However, with primary processing activities included, it accounted for about 10 per cent of GDP at current market prices. Employment in the manufacturing sector is estimated at 8.5 per cent of the total labour force, which is about the average for other least developed countries.

Burma is a centrally planned economy, and about two fifths of the GDP originates in the public sector. The planning process in Burma gained momentum with the launching of the 20-year long-term plan (1973/74-1993/94). The main objectives of this plan are: (a) to raise the per capita output to twice the level prevailing in 1973/74; and (b) to transform Burma from a predominantly agricultural economy to an agriculture-based industrial economy. Within the framework of this long-term plan, a series of four-year plans have been implemented. The fifth four-year plan (1986/87-1989/90) is at present in its second year of implementation.

Burma's foreign trade is mainly with Asian countries: Japan, Singapore and China are its main trading partners. The European Economic Community ranks second in importance. Besides rice and teak, other important agricultural exports include pulses and beans, jute, rubber, and animal feedstuffs as well as metals and ores such as tin, tungsten, lead, zinc, copper and nickel.

As has occurred for other primary commodity exports, demand for the major export commodities of Burma has declined and there has been a significant fall in prices. Average export prices of rice as well as of metals and ores have fallen during 1981/82-1985/86, with the overall level of prices of the country's exports declining by about 30 per cent during the period.

In 1986/87, external factors largely outside its control continued to affect the country's economic development. The world demand for its major exports, particularly rice, slackened and the terms of trade further declined. This resulted in a 62 per cent import cut in 1986/87 as compared with the level in 1981/82. These drastic cuts affected all the sectors of the economy and consequently the implementation of the development projects. Despite these adverse developments, GDP for 1986/87 was estimated to have increase by 3.7 per cent as against the target of 3.6 per cent. With the exception of livestock and fisheries, growth rates in major sectors exceeded the target. Mining and forestry sectors made considerable gains during the year.

As a result of reduced earnings from traditional exports, the foreign exchange position of Burma has come under considerable strain. The country's international reserves fell from $239 million in 1981 to $40 million in 1985. The debt-service ratio rose from a level of 15.9 per cent in 1970 to over 50 per cent in 1985. As a result, efforts were made by the Government to curtail further commercial borrowings as well as to seek loans on concessional terms. Burma has a good reputation in meeting its international debt obligations.

The transport network of Burma has remained virtually unchanged for the past two decades or so. Expenditure on road maintenance and construction is rather low and the poor conditions of roads make them a relatively slow and hazardous mode of transport. Moreover, vehicle operating costs are high. Road transport services increased by about 4.8 per cent annually during the period from 1970/71 to 1985/86. In fact, the formal transport sector has also been supplemented by traditional non-powered facilities. This indicates the need to improve transport services by expanding modern transport facilities.

Medical care is free in Burma. A basic objective of Burmese health planning is to extend health services throughout the country. Nevertheless, diseases such as malaria, tuberculosis and leprosy still pose a threat in certain parts of the country. The average annual per capita expenditure on health is estimated at less than $2.

The literacy rate is estimated at 53 per cent. However, the proportion of people with more than four years of education who could meaningfully contribute to developmental activities is less than 20 per cent. Only 17 per cent of the total population has access to safe drinking water and the sewerage system serves only one third of the urban population or about 10 per cent of the total population.

Despite abundant natural resources, Burma remains underdeveloped and economic progress has not matched its potential. The difficulties encountered in its efforts towards development are long term and structural in nature; resources for development have to be generated from a relatively low capital and technological base, and heavy dependence has to be placed on a limited range of primary commodities for export. The crisis that is affecting the world economy has had serious repercussions on the development efforts of the least developed countries, including Burma. With its inclusion in the least developed group, Burma stands to benefit from the special measures extended to it by the international community within the context of the Substantial New Programme of Action for the 1980s for the Least Developed Countries.

again exceptions can be noted: Burma is a significant exporter of rice, while Afghanistan and the Lao People's Democratic Republic have substantial foreign exchange earnings from energy exports.

The weak foreign trade position of the least developed countries of the region is reflected not only in the narrow composition of their exports but also in the virtual stagnation or deterioration of export earnings in real terms. For instance, in Afghanistan the value of exports, after achieving the all-time high of $729 million in 1983, declined to $557 million in 1985, and in 1986 the level declined slightly further. In Bangladesh, the value of exports decreased in 1986 compared with the preceding year. Burma experienced a continual decline in exports from $393 million in 1982 to $300 million in 1986. Bhutan's exports, which remained more or less stagnant during 1983-1984, achieved steady gains in 1985 and 1986. Kiribati showed a sharp

fall in its exports, from $25 million in 1979 to $4 million in 1983; it reached $11 million in 1984 to slump again to $4 million in 1985. Export growth in Maldives continued to rise from $13 million in 1983 to $25 million in 1986. In Nepal, the exports, which had risen up to 1985 declined in 1986. Similarly, Samoa and Vanuatu experienced a decline in exports in 1986 compared with 1985 (see table I.10).

In Afghanistan, the value of exports in 1985 and 1986 declined mainly owing to the decrease in export volume of wool and fruits. The value of imports also declined as certain essential consumer items such as sugar, cement, wheat and clothes began to be imported as grants from the USSR. The share of the USSR in the exports of Afghanistan was over 70 per cent in 1986. Natural gas has featured prominently as the major export item, accounting for more than 48 per cent of the total export and about 8 per cent of the earnings of the State.

In Bangladesh, in 1985/86, for the first time export receipts reached one billion dollars. The export receipts increased by 7.3 per cent over the figure in 1984/85. Significant contributions came from the non-traditional exports, namely ready-made garments, frozen food, leather and vegetables. The share of the non-traditional exports accounted for 60 per cent in 1985/86, compared with 43 per cent in 1984/85. However, the value of overall exports declined by 12 per cent in 1986/87. In order to improve the competitiveness of exports and encourage export expansion and diversification, the Government introduced various incentive measures, including: (a) exchange rate adjustment to make exports competitive; (b) access to reduced or tax-free imports of intermediate and capital goods used in export industries by a variety of measures; (c) cash premium on export sales; and (d) liberal and subsidized access to credit. An export

Table I.10. **Selected least developed economies in the ESCAP region. Balance of trade, 1983-1986**
(Millions of US dollars)

	Exports (f.o.b)				Imports (c.i.f.)				Balance of trade			
	1983	1984	1985	1986	1983	1984	1985	1986	1983	1984	1985	1986
Afghanistan	729	633	557	552	1 064	1 390	1 194	1 404	−335	−757	−637	−852
Bangladesh[b]	725	932	1 000	880	2 166	2 827	2 760	2 703	−1 441	−1 895	−1 760	−1 823
Bhutan	16	18	22	26	72	71	75	89	56	53	53	63
Burma	378	378	331	300	268	240	283	306	110	138	48	−6
Kiribati[a]	4	11	4	...	18	18	15	...	−14	−7	−11	...
Lao People's Democratic Republic	43	44	61	70	135	149	110	113	−92	−105	−49	−43
Maldives	13	18	23	25	57	53	53	64	−44	−35	−30	−39
Nepal	94	128	160	142	464	416	453	459	−370	−288	−293	−317
Samoa	18	19	16	11	49	51	51	47	−31	−32	−35	−36
Vanuatu[c]	18	32	19	9	43	48	50	46	−25	−16	−31	−37

Sources: IMF, *International Financial Statistics,* vol. XL, No. 5 (May 1987); IMF, *International Financial Statistics Yearbook 1986;* and national sources.

[a] Domestic export earnings beginning from 1980 decline significantly owing to the exhaustion of phosphate in Banaba Island by the end of 1979; imports are at c.i.f. values. [b] For fiscal years 1983/84 to 1986/87. [c] Domestic origin only.

processing zone was set up near Chittagong Port, the first phase of which was completed, with the necessary back-up facilities, in June 1985.

Although value of imports declined by an average of 2.2 per cent during 1984/85–1986/87, food imports figured prominently. The volume of food grain imports increased from 1.19 million tons in 1985/86 to 1.77 million tons in 1986/87. Imports of capital goods also increased as public sector investment and disbursement of project aid picked up significantly in 1986/87.

The exports of the Lao People's Democratic Republic increased from $61 million in 1985 to about $70 million in 1986; over half of this export trade was with the convertible currency area. The value of imports also increased from $110 million in 1985 to $113 million in 1986, of which about 60 per cent were from the non-convertible area. The exports were dominated by the sale of hydro-electricity to Thailand from the Nam Ngum Dam, which provided a significant portion of the country's hard currency earnings. In turn, about one fourth of its imports, mainly of consumer goods, comes from Thailand. The deficit is met from foreign grants and credits. However, the country has significant potential for exports of minerals, hydropower, and forestry products. New opportunities are being sought to increase performance of the export sector. Forestry and minerals have better prospects for trade, but the basic infrastructure and internal security are lacking. The second five-year plan envisages a doubling of foreign trade by 1990.

The main export earning activities of Maldives are fishing, tourism, garment production and international shipping, although the significance of the latter has declined in recent years. Domestic exports increased during 1984-1985 at an average annual rate of 28 per cent, reflecting a buoyant expansion of fish exports. In 1986, however, domestic exports increased modestly. While garment exports recorded an increase, exports of fish remained virtually unchanged at the 1985 level, because of the stagnant fish catch and weak export prices. However, with the establishment of a new cannery in November 1986, the prospects appeared better for 1987 and beyond. The private sector has been encouraged to be involved in garment production and exports.

Between 1982/83 and 1984/85 the value of Nepal's exports had increased by 70 per cent as a result of the increase in the export of ready-made garments, carpets and pulses. However, they declined in 1986/87, as exports of ready-made garments and hides and skins suffered a set-back. During the same period, exports to India increased, mainly owing to the increase in exports of ginger, rice and bran oil. In 1986/87, the value of total imports increased marginally compared with the previous year. As the increase in exports could not keep pace with the increase in imports, the trade gap continued to widen. Although in 1985/86, the total trade deficit declined by about 4 per cent compared with 1984, it increased in 1986/87 by 14 per cent.

B. THE PACIFIC ISLAND SUBREGION

Economic performance in the developing Pacific island economies during 1985-1987 continued to be conditioned by the persistent volatility in the external trade environment, adverse weather conditions and other unfavourable developments of a non-economic nature. These factors contributed directly to corresponding changes in domestic consumption and investment demand, government revenue, external resource inflows and hence a "stop-and-go" pattern of overall economic growth.

Most Pacific island countries for which the relevant estimates are available suffered a reversal of economic fortunes in 1986 (see figure I.6). Real GDP, which registered a further decline of 8.6 per cent in the Solomon Islands, exhibited a slow-down of various magnitudes in Papua New Guinea, Samoa and Vanuatu. Fiji, however, recovered strongly from a decline of 4.8 per cent in its real GDP in 1985 to expand by over 9 per cent in 1986.

The prospects for improved growth performance were generally good in the Pacific island subregion during 1987-1988. The prospects of further expansion for 1988 were predicated considerably on the possibility of improvement in world commodity prices, on national policy responses and economic management, and on technical and economic assistance from the international community (see box I.10). Prospects for individual island countries are likely

---

Figure I.6. Selected Pacific island economies in the ESCAP region. Percentage change in real GDP, 1984-1986

(Percentage)

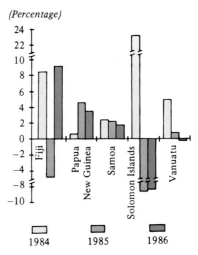

1984	1985	1986

to differ according to the nature of their past economic difficulties. The process of economic rehabilitation, stabilization and recovery in some countries such as Fiji, Solomon Islands and Vanuatu is likely to be a comparatively longer-term one. However, others, such as Papua New Guinea and Samoa, could reasonably expect a sustained rate of real GDP growth in 1987.

The Solomon Islands, which had registered a drop of almost 9 per cent in real GDP largely owing to falling export prices and lower merchandise earnings during 1985, experienced some abatement in

---

Box I.10. International assistance for private sector development in the Pacific through international business joint ventures

In their pursuit of diversifying their economies in order to overcome the instability and stagnation associated with the dependence on a few primary commodities, many Pacific island economies are fostering greater private sector development. This has long been recognized as an urgent need and given due emphasis by Governments in the Pacific island subregion by introducing a variety of business incentives and other promotion measures. Given the many serious problems facing the island economies, private-sector business development has to be a long-term goal whose achievement is considerably aided by several schemes of international assistance currently in operation – particularly through training and strengthening and acquisition of technical and business skills in co-operation with overseas equity partners. Three important sources of international aid provide such assistance.

Australia's (South Pacific) Joint Venture Scheme has provided, or committed, since its inception in 1976 approximately $A 6 million through the Australian International Development Assistance Bureau in support of local equity participation by Pacific island bodies or firms in both the public and private sectors in joint business undertakings with Australian partners;[a] the latter normally hold at least a quarter of the equity investment in the projects. To be eligible for aid, all assisted ventures should be commercially viable and development-

ally worth while. The funds are not used to assist the joint ventures themselves or the Australian partners; they are only available to facilitate the acquisition of project equity by the local counterparts.

The financial assistance is transferred as a grant to island Governments, or is treated as a grant-in-aid if made available to public sector bodies. For private-sector local partners, JVS funds are to be on-lent through a local institution, usually a development bank or the economic development board, under its normal terms although some concessionary elements may be involved (e.g. less demanding lending and repayment conditions). The amount of repaid loans, however, remains in the participating island and thus finance under the Joint Venture Scheme constitutes a *de facto* revolving fund available to meet additional local needs for development finance.

The available information indicates that support under the Scheme has been extended to 10 projects, covering banking and finance (2 projects); agro-business activities such as forestry, agriculture and cattle-raising (3 projects); transport (1 project); and manufacture, including wood veneer products, cement and leather work, and wine-making (4 projects). Of these joint ventures, nine remain operational. In terms of geographical distribution, three assisted projects each were located in Samoa and Vanuatu, while there were two in Fiji and one each in Kiribati and the Solomon Islands.

A similar aid programme, the Pacific Islands Industrial Development Scheme, was initiated by New Zealand in November 1976. The Scheme, administered by the Department of Trade and Industry, offers financial incentives and assistance for New Zealand entrepreneurs to establish approved manufacturing or agro-based proces-

sing ventures .with local business partners of the South Pacific Forum.[b] Among other qualifying conditions, for assistance under the Scheme business projects and joint ventures must have a minimum New Zealand share holding of 20 per cent, and a minimum combined New Zealand/island share holding of 75 per cent.

Currently, financial assistance under the Scheme is obtainable for a number of purposes.[c] Grants may be provided for up to 50 per cent of the cost of approved feasibility studies; of training local employees either in the islands or in New Zealand; and of transfer of key employees, and plant and equipment owned by New Zealand shareholders to the island location. In addition, interest-free loans may be provided for up to 30 per cent of qualifying capital expenditure in large business joint ventures. The maximum size of such loans is $NZ 75,000 although larger amounts would be considered in exceptional circumstances. These loans will be converted to grants if the business is still operational after 5 years from the time of loan disbursement. Lastly, there are smaller grants of up to $NZ 25,000 for approved capital expenditure or working capital costs or job creation measures. The value of the qualifying capital assets or costs must not exceed $NZ 50,000, and the

---

[a] Details and issues relating to external development assistance by Australia are extensively discussed in the *Report of the Committee to Review the Australian Overseas Aid Program* (Canberra, Australian Government Publishing Service, March 1984), particularly ch. 4-8.

---

[b] Forum members are the Cook Islands, Fiji, Kiribati, Nauru, Niue, Papua New Guinea, Samoa, Solomon Islands, Tonga, Tuvalu and Vanuatu, with the Federated States of Micronesia and the Republic of the Marshall Islands attaining full membership in 1987.

[c] Further details can be found in Department of Trade and Industry, New Zealand, *Pacific Island Industrial Development Scheme* (Wellington, October 1985), pp. 4-8.

its externally-induced economic difficulties in 1986, but growth was negated by the devastation, and subsequent floodings and silting, caused by cyclone Namu in May 1986.[5] The set-backs, together

new jobs must be maintained for at least six months for grant qualification.

As of March 1986, assistance under the Scheme of $NZ 1.93 million was made to 228 proposals; of these, one third related to feasibility study grants, 42 per cent to other types of grants, and 15 per cent to suspensory loans. Most of the established projects, totalling some 78 in number, received more than one type of assistance; about 20 projects, of which 19 were joint ventures, were no longer operating.

In terms of geographical distribution, projects were set up in seven countries with Fiji accounting for 27 per cent of the established ventures, followed by Samoa (24 per cent), and Cook Islands and Tonga (17 and 14 per cent respectively). Businesses assisted by the Scheme covered a wide range of activities, from food processing, wood works, building materials and accessories to various kinds of manufactured goods. There were an estimated 935 jobs directly created with assistance under the Scheme.

Lastly, the Centre for Development of Industry set up by the European Economic Community (EEC) under the Lomé Convention also provides technical and financial assistance for the joint promotion of industrial development in the region as part of its assistance to the African, Caribbean and Pacific (ACP) countries. Under this scheme, assistance is obtainable for the promotion of, and negotiations concerning contractual agreements on and/or finance for, joint ACP-EEC ventures. The Centre also assists the conduct of feasibility studies, as well as the rehabilitation or upgrading of existing industrial activities and the training of key technicians and supervisors in EEC or ACP countries. The Centre, however, does not participate directly in any financial investment in the joint venture.

with exchange rate depreciation, exerted a severe squeeze on social and economic well-being. Real GDP declined by another 8.6 per cent during the year, while real per capita income fell significantly, from $SI 272 in the boom year of 1984 to $SI 139 two years later.

Earnings from two of the Solomon Islands' traditional major exports, copra and palm oil products, fell to one third of the already depressed level recorded in the previous year. Copra production dropped by almost 30 per cent and export earnings to just one quarter of the previous year's total. Palm oil production, however, was more severely hit by the cyclone. Total oil production and export for 1986, at 14,500 tons, was the lowest since 1980, which, coupled with lower export prices, reduced earnings from palm oil products by over one half in 1986.

However, total export earnings, expanded strongly by about $SI 11 million, or 10.6 per cent, over the 1985 level (see table I.11). This was attributable to two factors: first, there was a depreciation of about 19 per cent in the local currency relative to the United States dollar; second, significant increases in earnings were registered by forestry and fishery products, which reached $SI 88.6 million in 1986, compared with $SI 56.7 million a year earlier. Higher forestry and fishery export receipts, in turn, were largely the result of increased harvests: log export volumes expanded by over one half, and fishery export quantities by 31 per cent. At the same time, world prices for these commodities, particularly for forestry pro-

ducts, also picked up somewhat during 1986.

Rising demand for public services owing to a high rate of population growth,[6] sustained wage costs in real terms, a higher debt-service burden, the localization of public service positions and cyclone damage combined to cause a 31 per cent rise in public sector expenditure in 1986, compared with an increase of 27 per cent in the previous year (see figure I.7). Domestic prices went up by 13.6 per cent, or over two fifths higher than the 1985 level (see table I.12), largely as a result of higher landed prices of imported goods owing to the 24 per cent depreciation of the local currency on a trade-weighted basis.

There was a slow-down in nominal import demand, which grew by almost 23 per cent in 1985 but by only 13.4 per cent a year later. Given the lower exchange rate, this represented a considerable compression in real terms. Receipts from the transfer account were boosted by sizeable inflows from cyclone relief and assistance, and STABEX (system of stabilization of export earnings) transfers. Net transfers consequently reached $52 million, which substantially negated the combined deficit in the trade and services account. The large increases in loan capital receipts improved the overall balance-of-payments situation. The debt-service burden, however, remained relatively modest, at just about 10 per cent of export earnings and 7 per cent of the monetized component of GDP.

Given the serious set-backs borne by the Solomon Islands over 1985-1986, the prospects of im-

---

[5] The cyclone damage was estimated at about $SI 20 million, or 10 per cent of the current value of GDP during 1986. Further details relating to the extent of such damage can be found in Central Bank of Solomon Islands, *Annual Report 1986*, pp. 10-11.

[6] Data from the national census of November 1986 indicated an average annual rate of population growth of 3.5 per cent in the Solomon Islands during 1976-1986. Central Bank of Solomon Islands, *Annual Report 1986*, p. 9.

Table I.11. Selected Pacific island economies. Major components of external transactions, 1983-1987[a]

(Million units of local currency)

		1983	1984	1985	1986	1987
Fiji						
1.	Exports	245	280	271	312	64
	Of which: Sugar	112	110	112	134	25
	Gold	17	20	22	39	10
	Travel receipts (gross)	136	163	169	185	31
2.	Merchandise imports	493	487	508	497	124
3.	Current accounts balance	−64	−27	−14	−8	−20
4.	Exchange rate ($US/$F)	0.98	0.92	0.87	0.88	0.89
Papua New Guinea[b]						
1.	Exports	687	822	926	1 004	435
	Of which: Gold	201	183	319	401	197
	Copper	161	135	164	156	75
	Coffee	95	111	117	208	49
2.	Merchandise imports	815	867	873	950	513
3.	Current accounts balance	−309	−209	−197	−183	−218
4.	Exchange rate ($US/kina)	1.20	1.12	1.00	1.03	...
Samoa[b]						
1.	Exports	27	34	36	23	11
	Of which: Coconut oil and cream	12	23	19	10	5
	Taro	2	3	5	4	3
	Private remittances	31	38	53	63	37
2.	Merchandise imports	75	93	115	105	59
3.	Current accounts balance	−18	−23	−21	−11	−9
4.	Exchange rate ($US/$WS)	0.65	0.54	0.45	0.45	0.47
Solomon Islands						
1.	Exports	71	119	104	115	22
	Of which: Logs and timber	20	30	25	36	9
	Fish	29	29	32	53	6
	Copra	8	32	23	6	2
2.	Merchandise imports	85	100	122	140	...
3.	Current accounts balance	−7	9	−28	−22	...
4.	Exchange rate ($US/$SI)	0.87	0.79	0.68	0.57	...
Vanuatu[b]						
1.	Exports[c]	1.78	3.22	1.98	0.93	0.57
	Of which: Copra	1.31	2.73	1.39	0.44	0.31
	Meat	0.19	0.14	0.20	0.13	0.10
	Travel receipts (gross)	2.20	2.36	2.00	1.52	0.77
2.	Merchandise imports	4.30	4.81	5.29	4.85	1.46[a]
3.	Current accounts balance	0.96	2.52	0.75	−0.31	−0.32[a]
4.	Exchange rate[d]	1.00	1.00	0.94	0.94	0.90

Sources: Official national sources.

[a] First quarter only for 1987 data; figures may not add up owing to rounding. [b] First-half data for 1987; Vanuatu data are in billion vatu. [c] Domestic origin only. [d] United States dollar per 100 vatu.

proved economic performance and a return to positive growth in real GDP were reasonably good, particularly in 1988. The economy displayed a remarkable degree of resilience during 1986 despite the great strains and constraints on, and the subsequent adjustments in, its economic activities and operations necessitated by lower export earnings (in foreign currency terms), substantial damage and considerable increases in prices owing directly or indirectly to cyclone Namu, and the tighter monetary stance to sustain, among other things, the domestic and external financial balance.

The set-backs to export earnings of some major commodities would partly be offset by the improved performance of other commodities. Higher copra prices were expected to raise domestic out-

Figure I.7. Selected Pacific island economies in the ESCAP region. Percentage change in total and development expenditure, 1984-1987

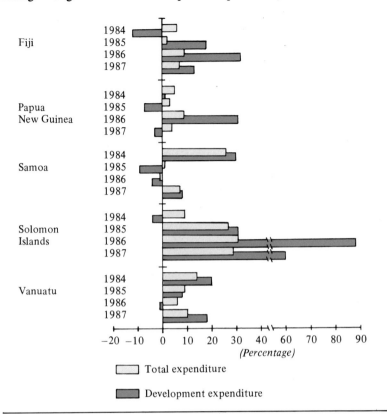

put and hence earnings considerably, although copra would remain a comparatively minor source of foreign exchange in 1987. On the other hand, receipts from a major export, fishery products, would tend to be lower than the level attained during an extraordinary good year in 1986. The planned addition of two purse seiners, which would enlarge the fishing fleet capacity by a quarter, would contribute significantly to higher export volume and earnings in 1988. On balance, domestic demand and the external balance-of-payments position would tend to weaken somewhat.

Vanuatu, one of the four least developed countries in the Pacific island subregion, also suffered a considerable economic setback caused by adverse factors of an exogenous origin. Real GDP remained virtually unchanged bet-

ween 1984 and 1986 (figure I.6, p. 53). The process of recovery was constrained measurably by another natural disaster, one of the worst cyclones in recent memory, in February 1987; cyclone damage to physical buildings, facilities and infrastructures, estimated to reach 11.4 billion vatu or 90 per cent of nominal GDP in 1986, was expected to have a far-reaching long-term impact on the country's capital development programme.

Real GDP had expanded by only 0.4 per cent in 1985, largely as a result of the losses caused by two cyclones on the agricultural and tourism sectors. The damage to coconut palms and copra driers, and hence physical production of copra, was aggravated by a sharp drop in export prices. Earnings from this commodity consequently fell by over one half. At the

same time, the volume of tourist arrivals was additionally constricted by the economic downturn in Australia, the major source of Vanuatu's tourists; gross travel receipts were then reduced by about 15 per cent (table I.11, p. 56).

These adverse developments, however, were largely negated by three stabilizing forces. Rural income and hence demand were effectively sustained through high domestic support prices from the Vanuatu Commodities Marketing Board.[7] Second, there was higher government spending which, after being discounted by the current inflation rate, represented a real increase of almost 8 per cent in 1985. Lastly, the subsistence sector recovered strongly from the devastation of the two cyclones. These factors contributed to the higher value added registered during the year by commercial, financial and government services, among other sectors.

Such economic resiliency apparently was inadequate to propel the Vanuatu economy on the recovery path in 1986 when real GDP fell by about 1 per cent. Among other reasons, copra export earnings were lower than the 1985 level by over two thirds. Although receipts from cocoa exports went up by almost one half owing to a record harvest, this commodity is only a minor export with a relative share of one fifth of domestic export value in 1986, and only 5 per cent during 1984-1985. As a whole, merchandise export receipts, at 930 million vatu in 1986, were less than one half of the previous year's total. Another major source of foreign exchange

---

[7] In fact, the domestic prices paid to copra producers during 1985 averaged 19 per cent higher than in the previous year. Central Bank of Vanuatu, *Quarterly Economic Review – December 1986,* p. 198.

Table I.12. Selected Pacific island economies. Major components of public finance, and percentage change in the consumer price indices, 1983-1987

(Million units of local currency)

		1983	1984	1985	1986	1987[a]
Fiji						
1.	Budget balance[b]	−44	−44	−44	−67	−80
	Revenue	293	330	338	348	363
	Recurrent expenditure	280	324	323	337	355
	Development expenditure	57	50	59	78	88
2.	Changes in consumer prices (%)	6.7	5.3	4.4	1.2	3.2
Papua New Guinea						
1.	Budget balance[b]	−77	−46	−44	−82	−21
	Revenue[c]	632	700	749	749	844
	Recurrent expenditure	627	662	687	730	768
	Development expenditure[d]	82	83	77	101	98
2.	Changes in consumer prices (%)	7.9	7.5	3.7	5.5	3.7
Samoa						
1.	Budget balance[b]	−9	−14	−2	8	−2
	Revenue[c]	65	79	93	100	96
	Recurrent expenditure	29	35	41	42	44
	Development expenditure[d]	44	57	51	50	54
2.	Changes in consumer prices (%)	16.4	11.9	9.1	5.7	2.5
Solomon Islands						
1.	Budget deficit[b]	−13	−8	−15	−17	−29
	Revenue[c]	40	52	59	82	97
	Recurrent expenditure	39	46	58	66	73
	Development expenditure[d]	15	13	17	32	53
2.	Changes in consumer prices (%)	6.8	11.0	9.6	13.6	12.0
Vanuatu[e]						
1.	Budget deficit[b]	−0.06	0.45	−0.04	−0.72	0.21
	Revenue[c]	4.49	5.62	5.58	5.25	6.76
	Recurrent expenditure	2.42	2.62	2.87	3.23	3.34
	Development expenditure[f]	2.12	2.55	2.75	2.73	3.21
2.	Changes in consumer prices (%)	1.7	5.5	1.1	4.8	14.0

Sources: Official national sources.

[a] First half of 1987 only consumer prices. [b] Revised and provisional outturn for 1986 and budget estimates for 1987; figures may not add up owing to rounding. [c] Including foreign budgetary grant-in-aid. [d] Including the allocation for maintenance works, and net lending. [e] Figures in billion vatu. [f] From the development fund; including technical assistance from external sources.

and urban sector employment, tourism, was also adversely affected with the volume of arrivals falling by another 29 per cent and tourism receipts by a further 24 per cent in 1986.

The external balance also became unfavourable in 1986 for the first time in recent years. Lower import spending, by 444 million vatu or 8 per cent was insufficient to offset reduced merchandise export earnings; the trade deficit went up by 13 per cent to 4.03 billion vatu. The balance on services and investment income, and transfer accounts showed a smaller surplus on account of falling travel receipts, and a lower level of official aid in both cash and kind. Consequently, the balance on current accounts deteriorated from a surplus of 752 million vatu in 1985 to a deficit of 313 million vatu a year later. The smaller amount of capital inflows resulted in a basic payments deficit of 46 million vatu.[8]

---

[8] However, movements in net foreign assets of the Vanuatu authorities and commercial banks registered an overall payments surplus of 1.46 billion vatu. This amount reflected a substantial revaluation of assets as a result of two devaluations of the vatu in February and October 1986.

Generally, Vanuatu's external financial position was reasonably good as a result of a cautious borrowing policy. Post-independence external debt, for example, rose from 3.7 per cent of GDP in 1983 to 6.2 per cent in 1986. All external obligations, however, were contracted on soft terms and the service ratios were manageable at 1.3 and 2.9 per cent of total exports of goods and services during these respective years. Furthermore, in 1986 there was a gradual increase in gross official reserves which were adequate to cover the relatively high level of the equivalent of 6.3 months of imports for home consumption.

The process of economic recovery in Vanuatu became more difficult after February 1987 when cyclone Uma caused extensive destruction and damage to the capital city and facilities and infrastructures in the southern islands; the agricultural sector and tourist facilities were less affected. The rehabilitation of physical assets would take several years and a large amount of real resources which would be difficult to raise without international assistance.

In spite of a smaller volume, during the first half of 1987 copra export earnings were equivalent to 70 per cent of the previous year's total, largely as a result of a doubling in prices received for the crop. Their impact on producers' income and consumption, however, was partly negated by the continuing low-support prices so as to conserve and build up the marketing authority reserves: domestic copra prices had remained largely around the same level between June of 1986 and 1987. The volume of tourist arrivals also declined significantly, although travel receipts in the first half of 1987 as a whole were only marginally below those recorded for the corresponding previous year period.

From the available indicators, it would appear that the overall economic performance of Vanuatu would be more resilient and better than could be expected, given the difficult circumstances facing the country in 1987. There was, to begin with, a higher level of building and construction activities with the associated rise in urban employment. These activities were expected to gather much pace following the successful donors meeting on rehabilitation aid to Vanuatu in the middle of the year. A recovery in the tourism sector was also projected as a result of improved air transport links and travel services. Moreover, the upturn in commodity earnings would continue with the continuing pick-up of copra prices in the third quarter, and with possibly higher export volumes. Other things being equal, the Vanuatu economy could possibly perform better than in 1986 with real GDP registering some positive gain during 1987.

The Fiji economy, in sharp contrast to that of the Solomon Islands and Vanuatu, recovered very strongly from the cyclone-affected performance of 1985 to grow by 9.1 per cent during 1986 (figure I.6, p. 53). The major stimuli, export earnings from sugar and tourism, made themselves increasingly felt in the second half of the year. Generally, however, the secular growth rate of real GDP tended to be modest, averaging about 2.3 per cent annually during the 1980s, compared with an annual average population growth rate of about 2 per cent.[9] Comparatively, Fiji's ability to sustain a marginal improvement in real income per head of population during the same period was a notable achievement within the Pacific island subregion.

_____

[9] Central Planning Office, *Fiji's Ninth Development Plan 1986-1990* (Suva, November 1985), p. 25.

Sugar production, at the record level of 502,000 tons, was over two fifths higher than the 1985 level although its export volume fell by 21 per cent, partly as a result of the rebuilding of sugar stocks previously run down to meet contractual commitments. Receipts from sugar exports went up by almost two fifths to reach $F 134 million, or 43 per cent of merchandise trade receipts, owing to a significant pick-up in unit prices, averaging 57 per cent in 1986.

The number of tourist arrivals in 1986 was also at a record high of almost 258,000, or 13 per cent up on the previous year's total. Gross tourism receipts, however, expanded by about one tenth to reach $F 185 million (table I.11, p. 56).

The upward trend in gold production, making this commodity the second most important export item, continued into 1986 with shipment quantities totalling 2.9 tons; this represented a 56 per cent increase over the 1985 level. Boosted by higher prices, gold export value reached $F 38.6 million, or just over 12 per cent of merchandise trade receipts. Fishery exports likewise benefited considerably from higher catches. The volume and value of canned tuna exports were both up by almost one half. Total domestic exports of fishery products amounted to over $F 18 million, compared with less than $F 12 million in 1985.

The net result of these upward movements in commodity exports was an increase of just over 15 per cent to $F 312 million in earnings during 1986. The increase was somewhat lower in foreign currency terms, as the local currency unit depreciated by about 5 per cent against its currency basket. Higher export volumes and income contributed to the recovery of manufacturing pro-

59

duction, which rose by 20 per cent over the 1985 level. Much of this expansion, however, was attributable to the larger volume of processed sugar-cane; non-sugar manufacturing went up by just under 8.8 per cent and construction by almost 11 per cent.

These favourable developments contributed to the improved current accounts balance and the declining trend in inflation in Fiji during 1986. The merchandise trade deficit fell by 11 per cent owing to almost equally to higher export receipts (by $F 41 million) and lower import expenditure, by 2.4 per cent to $F 497 million. The surplus on the services account, at $F 134 million, was 17 per cent lower than the previous year's level owing to the lower value of service exports, including re-insurance money receivables, and lower import spending itself. Nevertheless, Fiji registered a small surplus of $F 7.6 million on current accounts. This represented a significant reversal of the earlier trend: the current accounts deficits, at $F 71.6 million or 15 per cent of GDP in 1981, steadily declined to $F 14.5 million or 1.2 per cent of GDP in 1985; the small surplus was equal to 0.6 per cent of GDP in 1986.

Inflation also continued on a declining trend in Fiji (see figure I.8). Apart from the demand-restraining forces noted earlier, supply factors were also exerting a stabilizing influence on consumer prices. The net result was an increase of 1.2 per cent in consumer prices in 1986. This rate of inflation was the lowest within the Pacific island subregion, and was among the lowest elsewhere among the developing economies of the ESCAP region.

The Fiji economy continued to expand during the first four months of 1987. The available data indicated buoyant domestic demand which represented the lagged response to the previous year's strong economic performance. There were higher earnings on the major commodities and services exports.[10] Rising effective demand, however, generated some upward pressures on consumer prices which, by the end of the first quarter, had increased by 1.9 per cent compared with 1985 as a whole.

The Fiji economy entered a downturn phase following the events and developments since May 1987. The late start for the sugar-cane harvest and crushing, and the prolonged drought, are expected to result in considerably lower

___

[10] Provisionally and on a quarterly basis, sugar export value expanded by almost 180 per cent in the March quarter of 1987; the export value for gold and fishery products went up by one third and over one half respectively. Gross tourist receipts rose by about 30 per cent.

output compared with the initial forecast. Tourism receipts are also expected to be lower. There was some capital outflow, with gross foreign reserves amounting to $F 120 million at the end of June 1987, compared with $F 189 million in net foreign assets in 1986.

Several policy measures were introduced for domestic economic and financial stabilization. There were several restraints on public spending to contain the budget deficit. The two devaluations of the local currency (in June and October 1987) reduced its exchange value by about 33 per cent relative to the United States dollar. These adjustments were to discourage capital outflows and imports, to promote commodity and services exports. To minimize further external leakages, monetary policy and exchange controls were tightened during June and August 1987. The measures taken included

___

Figure I.8. Selected Pacific island economies in the ESCAP region. Changes in consumer prices, 1984-1987[a]

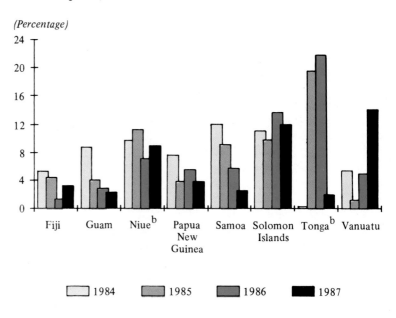

(Percentage)

a First half 1987 over first half 1986.   b First quarter 1987 over first quarter 1986.

the imposition of a higher minimum lending rate from the Reserve Bank and statutory reserve deposit ratio, the rationing of emigrant transfers and remittances, the suspension of overseas portfolio investments, and the relaxation of regulatory ceilings on interest rates on bank deposits and loans.

Consumer prices picked up somewhat in the middle of 1987, largely owing to rising prices for foodstuffs. Inflationary pressures, however, were expected to be felt more strongly following the two devaluations of the local currency. The annualized rate of inflation reached 3.2 per cent during the first half of 1987, compared with 1.2 per cent for 1986 as a whole.

After undergoing a comprehensive economic adjustment and stabilization programme supported by IMF in 1983-1985, real GDP growth in Samoa totalled 4.2 per cent over 1984-1985, compared with a decline of 0.6 per cent during the previous biennium, and the rate of inflation recorded a significant fall. Although inflation has also continued to decline, the rate of growth in real GDP has slowed down to 1.5 per cent in 1986 (figure I.6, p. 53).

Samoa's merchandise export earnings fell by almost 35 per cent in 1986, largely owing to a severe contraction in the export value of processed and semi-processed agricultural products (table I.11, p. 56). Falling prices reduced the receipt from coconut oil exports by 42 per cent, in spite of an increase of 15 per cent in volume. Taro export earnings were also 15 per cent lower, while earnings from forestry products and coconut cream remained by and large stagnant. Other minor export items, including fruit juice and such manufactured goods as beer and cigarettes, also brought back less foreign exchange during the year.

Poorer export performance and the continuing restraint on public spending, among other factors, caused imports to fall by 9 per cent, or almost $WS 10 million, in 1986 compared with the rise of 24 per cent a year earlier. The trade deficit of $WS 82 million was largely covered by a substantial inflow of private remittances and, to a less extent, by tourism receipts. Overseas Samoans had become in the early 1980s the most important source of foreign exchange, sending home in 1986 a total of $WS 63.5 million, which was almost one fifth higher than the 1985 level. The number of tourists, at 49,280 persons, went up by 12 per cent and net tourist receipts rose by 31 per cent to $WS 15.5 million (or two thirds of merchandise trade earnings). There was also a large inflow of international aid and other official transfers, to reach $WS 35.1 million from $WS 25.7 million in 1985. The net result was a surplus of almost $WS 25 million in the overall balance of payments while international reserves went up by two thirds to $WS 53.7 million, equivalent to five months of imports of goods and services.

Despite the comfortable balance-of-payments situation, the Samoan economy suffered from a number of structural weaknesses.[11] The economic base remained relatively undiversified, with coconut production accounting for an average of 56 per cent of merchandise trade receipts during 1983-1986; the proportion rose to over two thirds with the addition of cocoa beans. Merchandise exports covered on average less than one third of imports, and the export/import ratio declined from 36 per cent during

---

[11] Central Bank of Samoa, *Annual Report 1986*, pp. 3-4 and p. 9.

1983-1984 to 26 per cent during 1985-1986.

The largest economy in the Pacific island subregion, Papua New Guinea, experienced a slow-down in 1986 with real GDP growing by an estimated 3.3 per cent (figure I.6, p. 53). As in the previous year, however, economic performance in 1986 was also dominated by the strong positive contribution from mineral exports. Earnings from these products, which formed 56 per cent of total export value, went up by 15 per cent. Most of the increase in export earnings came from gold; boosted by a rise of around 15 per cent each in export prices and volume (to 36.5 tons), gold receipts increased by a quarter over the previous year total (table I.12, p. 58). By comparison, exports earnings from copper fell by 5 per cent as a result of lower export unit values of around 9 per cent, notwithstanding a modest increase in copper shipments. The country has become one of the major gold producers and this commodity accounted for 71 per cent of its mineral export receipts in 1986.

Agricultural exports receipts were stagnant during the year, with the exception of coffee earnings, which expanded by 78 per cent to 208 million kina, on account of both price and volume increases. In sharp contrast, earnings from other traditional export commodities declined sharply. This was due to substantial falls in the prices of vegetable oil products (coconut and palm oil), tea, and to a less extent, cocoa. Copra export shipments also fell marginally while those of other commodities remained stagnant.

The export values of minor products from the fishery and forestry sectors in particular, rose only marginally. The net result was an 8 per cent increase in total merchandise trade receipts in

1986 compared with 13 per cent in 1985.

The fiscal policy stance was moderately expansionary (table I.11, p. 56 and figure I.7, p. 57). Public spending, at 831 million kina in 1986, went up by 9 per cent compared with an increase of 2.2 per cent the previous year. The immediate impact of the fiscal stimulus apparently was constrained owing to several factors. There were tight limits on recurrent outlays imposed by the Government. In addition, the impact was also dissipated through external leakages. Merchandise import spending, in particular, went up by almost 9 per cent in 1986. Part of this large expansion reflected a certain amount of pent-up demand and commercial restocking and higher public sector spending on capital works; the value of merchandise imports, for example, was almost stagnant in 1985. Taking into account capital movements, there was a negligible addition to Papua New Guinea's net reserves; at 461 million kina, this was sufficient to cover about six months of merchandise import expenditure.

In spite of the relatively less robust economic performance in 1986, formal employment and consumer prices continued to rise. Private sector employment outside the mining sector expanded in 1986 by 3 per cent, concentrating mostly in rural production, transport, retail trade and financial services. Mining sector employment rose by 17 per cent owing to an upsurge in capital spending at Ok Tedi and, to a less extent, higher labour intake at the Bougainville mine.

The increase in minimum wages, the sharp appreciation of the yen and increased import duties contributed to the increase in consumer prices, which went up sharply, particularly during the first three quarters of 1986 (figure I.8, p. 60). For the full year, it stood at 5.5 per cent which was almost one half higher than the 1985 rate (of 3.5 per cent), notwithstanding the restraining and stabilizing influence of lower imported energy costs and more subdued aggregate demand.

Papua New Guinea was likely to have another year of relatively strong real GDP growth during 1987. The major impetus would continue to come from the export sector although the performance of domestic sectors could exert a restraining influence on the pace of economic growth. Export earnings would likely improve considerably, particularly those from mineral commodities, especially gold, the prices of which went up by 16 per cent in 1986, and accelerated further to an average of over $460 dollars per troy ounce during the second and third quarters of 1987, or over 22 per cent higher than in 1986. Copper prices also firmed up during the same period to average almost one fifth higher than the 1986 level. At the same time, mineral production would increase, especially with the commissioning at the Ok Tedi gold/ copper mine of the first stage of copper concentrate processing facilities in late 1986 and of facilities at the Bougainville copper/gold mine to recover precious metals from the ores that were discarded previously as waste. However, prospects of export earnings from non-mineral commodities were poor.

The 1987 budget provided for a net reduction, in real terms, of around 3.5 per cent in public spending. This policy stance continued to reflect official commitment to lowering recurrent expenses, and to redirecting and concentrating fiscal resources in areas and sectors, economic and infrastructure especially, that would contribute most to generating production activities, income and hence revenue. At the same time, additional fiscal resources would help lower the budget deficit which was only one quarter of the 1986 total.

IV. SELECTED ISSUES OF SOCIAL AND ECONOMIC POLICY

A. SOCIAL SECURITY

1. Social protection

Development economists in the past have implicitly treated social security as a luxury which poor countries cannot afford in the initial stages of development and should postpone until significant per capita income increases have taken place. This view has, however, been changing in recent years owing to the growing inadequacy of the two safety nets that the developing countries had relied on. First, the traditional family or tribal structure, which provided an "informal" social security system, has considerably weakened over time in most developing economies, especially in the urban areas. Second, economic growth, which was supposed to provide a safety net through its trickle-down effect, is now considered a much less reliable ally of the poor and the disadvantaged than earlier.

As a result, there have been increasing pressures for establishing formal social security structures along the lines prevalent in many developed countries. The growth of per capita real income and the need for institutionalized savings have also accelerated the interest in establishing social security arrangements in developing countries. In many centrally planned economies the emphasis has been not so much on the formal social security system as on guaranteed employment at real wages that provide exchange entitlements adequate to avoid extreme poverty.[1]

This section examines the rationales for establishing social security structures of different kinds and their relevance to the developing ESCAP region. It also looks at the scope and coverage of these arrangements and the likely problems to be encountered in establishing and maintaining them.

The concept of social security is open to a wide variety of definitions ranging from some form of paternalism on the part of an employer towards the employee to the "cradle to grave" kind of social protection prevalent in many developed welfare States. Its social function consists largely of protecting the population against major risks associated with the conduct of daily economic activity and in contributing to the health and well-being of the population. A more formal and comprehensive definition of social security provided by the International Labour Organisation (ILO) runs as follows: "The protection which society provides for its members, through a series of public measures, against the economic and social distress that otherwise would be caused by the stoppage or substantial reduction of earnings resulting from sickness, maternity, employment injury, unemployment, invalidity, old age and death; the provision of medical care; and the provision of subsidies for families with children".[2]

In most developing countries the formal social security system is still in its infancy and has only limited coverage. However, informal social security systems do exist and provide a safety net to people in distress. These operate mainly through the joint family system, community solidarity, and even through landlord-tenant and farmer-moneylender relationships. These informal arrangements are embedded in a set of social obligations that are mutually understood, accepted and reciprocated, but seldom spelled out as a formal contract.

There is a growing view that these traditional arrangements are being eroded under the impact of modernization, which brings with it monetization and commercialization of the economy.[3] However, it seems too early to predict the demise of these informal relationships — although systema-

[1] See Amartya Sen, *Poverty and Famine: An Essay on Entitlement and Development* (Oxford, Clarendon Press, 1981).

[2] ILO, *Introduction to Social Security* (Geneva, 1984), p. 3.

[3] For some evidence on the continuing resilience of traditional relationships in the rural areas of India, see G.K. Karanth, "New technology and traditional rural institutions: case of *Jajmani* relations in Karnataka", *Economic and Political Weekly,* vol. XXII, No. 51 (Bombay, 19 December 1987), pp. 2217-2224.

tic studies of the impact of development on such arrangements are lacking and are badly needed for formulating policies to fill the vacuum created by the erosion of such relationships.[4] There are obvious ways in which the informal support systems come under stress during the process of development. Resettlement and urbanization result in the breaking of traditional ties. The increasing participation of women in the work-force reduces their ability to care for older parents and parents-in-law. The reduction in the size of the family itself reduces its capability as a social support mechanism.

In spite of these developments, formal social security arrangements have hardly been able to replace the traditional arrangements and cover only a small proportion of the labour force. The evolution of formal social security systems in most countries started with the coverage of the most organized or patronized sections of the labour force (the armed forces, the civil service, employees in public utilities). There is almost no coverage for agricultural workers, landless labourers, self-employed and part-time or seasonal workers. These groups also form "poor risks" for social insurance schemes.

The social security schemes in developing countries have to be selective not only in terms of whom to cover but also in terms of what risks to cover. In most developing countries the coverage

relates mainly to the liability of the industrial employers in large-scale industries in respect of paid leave in case of sickness and maternity and for providing medical and cash benefits in the event of work-connected accidents or the contracting of occupational diseases. Even these benefits are of limited nature and avoidance and non-compliance by employers in paying benefits are widespread. This has led many countries to convert the employers' liability schemes into social insurance schemes, which, by sharing of risks and pooling of financial resources by employers, employees and the Government, are able to achieve a higher degree of compliance and larger benefits to the employees.

A brief survey of the social security programmes in the ESCAP region shows its main features. First, all the countries (see table I.13) have some schemes for the long-term contingency covering old age, surviving dependants and invalidity cases. This is identical with the restrictive definition of social security used by some developed countries. Most of these countries also have programmes covering work injury.

Unemployment schemes exist only in a few developing countries with numerous restrictions. However, some innovative attempts for guaranteeing employment have been made (see box I.11). Lastly, there is practically no scheme for family allowances, with the exception of the centrally planned economies. This too, indicates that the extended family, rather than the employers or the public, continues to be the main source of support in time of need. Here, the process of urbanization and the ensuing dissolution of large families into two-generation cell families will probably entail the emergence of pension schemes for old age and dependants.

Table I.14 provides information on the type of social security schemes based on different sources of funding for work-related injury and old age, survivors and invalidity insurance schemes. There are basically four sources of funding: employers' liability schemes; social insurance systems; statutory provident funds; and non-contributory schemes. The following section examines these different types of insurance and their functioning in the ESCAP region.

The employers' liability method is extensively used for work injury, sickness and maternity leave coverage.[5] There is a legal obligation for employers to give paid leave in respect of sickness and maternity and to provide medical benefits in the event of work-connected accidents or in the case of occupational diseases. These schemes are easier to implement than a unified system of protection, since they depend on the nature of the work and are therefore limited in many ways.

First, they apply only to that part of the work-force facing job accidents. In Afghanistan, Indonesia, the Republic of Korea and Sri Lanka, the coverage is limited to employees in construction, transport, mining and occupations using machinery. There are some limits to participation through earning ceilings, for example in India, Singapore and Sri Lanka.

Other limitations result from the definition of the contingency itself, the inadequacy of medical care in case of severe injury and the form of financial compensation. In many schemes, the interpretation of work-injury is so narrow that its benefits are out of reach of most workers. For instance, pen-

---

[4] The United Nations University has launched such a study to examine the components of the systems and networks constituted by such informal support systems, especially in regard to the problems of the aged. See A. Hashimoto, "Cross-cultural research design: methodology of the United Nations University project on social support systems for the aged", a paper presented at the Seminar on Research on Aging in Asia and the Pacific, held in Singapore in September 1987.

[5] K. Thompson, "Survey of social security in developing countries in Asia and the Pacific" (Bangkok, ILO, 1986), p. 7 (mimeographed).

Table I.13. Social security programmes, by type

	Type of social security programme				
	Old age survivors and invalidity	Sickness and maternity[a] (medical care)[b]	Work injury	Unemployment	Family allowance
Afghanistan	X[c]	X[d]	X	...	...
Burma	X[c]	X[o]	X	...	...
China	X	X[o]	X	...	...
Fiji	X	...	X	...	...
Hong Kong	X	X	X	X	...
India	X	X[o]	X	X[e]	...
Indonesia	X	X[o]	X	...	...
Iran (Islamic Republic of)	X	X[o]	X	X[f]	X[g]
Kiribati	X	...	X	...	...
Malaysia	X	...	X	...	...
Nepal	X	...	X	...	...
Pakistan	X	X[o]	...	...	...
Papua New Guinea	X	...	X	...	...
Philippines	X	X[o]	X	...	...
Singapore	X	...	X	...	...
Solomon Islands	X	...	X	X[f]	...
Sri Lanka	X	...	X	...	...
Taiwan (a province of the People's Republic of China)	X	X[o]	X	...	...
Thailand	X[c]	X[h]	X	...	X[h]
Trust Territory of Pacific Islands	X	...	...	...	...
Western Samoa	X	...	X	...	...

Source: United States, Department of Health and Human Services, *Social Security Programs Throughout the World – 1985,* Research Report No. 60 (Washington, D.C., 1986).

[a] Sickness and maternity refers to cash benefits for sickness and maternity. Countries must provide both benefits to be included. [b] An "o" denotes that medical care and/or hospitalization coverage are provided in addition to sickness and maternity benefits. [c] Special system for public employees only. [d] Larger employers are required to maintain own medical facilities. [e] 4 States – Kerala, West Bengal, Punjab and Maharashtra have instituted temporary unemployment programmes. [f] Dismissal indemnity to be paid by employers. [g] Employment related system. [h] Regulation never came into force.

sions and survivors benefits would be preferable in case of serious disablement or death of the provider but employers' liability schemes are generally based on lump-sum cash benefits.[6]

In Burma, India, Indonesia, Malaysia, Nepal, Pakistan, the Republic of Korea, Sri Lanka and

[6] *Ibid.,* p. 9.

Thailand, the legal obligation to have a liability scheme exists only for enterprises with a minimum number of employees, from 5 to 10 or more. This is intended to reduce the financial burden and risk borne by employers. However, the trend towards a transformation of employers' liability schemes into a social insurance system is noticeable in Indonesia

and the Philippines and indicates growing concern for wider coverage of the population.

With regard to the quality of the benefits derived from the various schemes, there is considerable variation among developing countries within the ESCAP region. For example, sick leave in Burma, India, Pakistan and the Philippines is for 26 weeks, 91 days, 121 days

Box I.11. Guaranteeing employment to the rural poor: the Maharashtra Scheme[a]

Although most developing countries are not yet able to provide an unemployment insurance scheme especially in the rural areas, the Maharashtra State in India has taken an innovative initial step in this direction. The Employment Guarantee Scheme (EGS) was started in Maharashtra in 1972-73 with two objectives in view, namely, to create job opportunities for the rural poor and to promote capital formation in the countryside. These two objectives were considered equally important. Thus, the work guarantee provided by EGS is only for unskilled manual labour and the Scheme is restricted to certain types of work and to certain locations.

The focus of the Scheme on providing jobs for unskilled manual labour and the importance it attaches to rural capital formation have meant reliance on labour-intensive public works for employment creation. A sample of these would include minor irrigation works, soil conservation and land development projects, road construction, tree planting, and work associated with building of minor irrigation tanks and improving drainage and water distribution channels.

The Scheme has taken considerable care to ensure that its activities do not lead to a drain of labour away from agriculture or from other essential rural services. The stress has therefore been on providing supplemental employment that do not compete with normal agricultural work or with labour required by other government projects in rural areas. Indeed, a stipulation exists which prohibits expenditure of EGS funds until budgetary resources on other government rural projects have been used up.

In the light of the above, a fair degree of co-ordination and planning is required to prepare a manpower budget for the Scheme. Since the objective is to generate employment opportunities in excess of the labour that would normally be absorbed in agricultural production and in government rural projects, the preparation of an EGS budget involves three steps. These are: (a) estimation of employment needs of unskilled labour net of the requirement in agriculture and related activities; (b) assessment of the employment likely to be provided by existing and planned government rural projects; and (c) estimation of the additional employment required to be created under EGS.

The Scheme has been found useful and has been made a permanent scheme of the Maharashtra state government. Regular provisions are made for it in the state budget, and from 1975-76 onwards special taxes were levied to raise revenue for the Employment Guarantee Fund. The Maharashtra state government makes a further annual contribution to the Fund in amounts that match the total net receipts realized each year from the special taxes.

Notable achievements have been made by the Scheme both in terms of the resources committed to it as well as in generating employment. Thus, during the five-year period from 1980-81 to 1984-85, total expenditures under EGS increased from Rs 1.22 billion to Rs 2 billion. Similarly, the state's budgetary provisions for it over the same period rose from Rs 1.11 billion to Rs 1.56 billion. The total man days of employment created under the Scheme from its inception up to 1985 is estimated to be 1.58 billion while the average number of participants went up from about 478,000 in 1982-83 to roughly 600,000 in 1984-85. Further, it is of considerable significance to note that of the beneficiaries, a fairly large percentage, amounting to 35 to 48 per cent, represented the poorest of the poor of rural society. It has also been pointed out that the Scheme has a particular appeal to female workers, and estimates indicate that on average, about 40 per cent of the additional employment created by EGS has been taken up by women.

The Employment Guarantee Scheme of the state of Maharashtra therefore provides an interesting case where local initiative and resources have been successfully marshalled to meet a pressing social and economic need to provide, in a limited manner, some form of job security in the rural areas.

[a] Based on C. Dinesh, "Guaranteeing employment to the unskilled: assessing the Maharashtra experiment", *Ceres 114*, pp. 24-26.

---

and 120 days respectively, with provision for extended periods. In China, Hong Kong, Indonesia, the Islamic Republic of Iran, Pakistan, the Philippines and Taiwan (a province of the People's Republic of China), sickness benefits represent from 50 to 100 per cent of earnings for a period varying with the length of service.[7] There is generally a trade-off between benefit coverage of the population and the rate of compensation. In employers' liability schemes, benefits tend to be higher, since the coverage is narrow and the probability of incidence is limited. In generalized social insurance systems, the cash benefits tend to be lower, but a greater proportion of the population is covered. In the latter case, the more general access to benefits can be interpreted as a greater degree of social protection.

The medical care and health service delivery system was analysed in the *Survey, 1986*.[8] It was indicated that social security schemes do not play a major role in financing health care services in most developing countries of the

---

[7] United States, Department of Health and Human Services, *Social Security Programmes throughout the World, 1985* (Washington, D.C., 1986).

[8] *Survey*, 1986, pp. 110-139.

Table I.14. Social security contingencies covered and type of statutory general schemes of income protection in selected ESCAP countries[a]

Economy (1)	Employment injury (2)	Sickness (3)	Maternity (4)	Old age (5)	Invalidity (6)	Survivorship (7)
Bangladesh	EL	EL	EL	b	b	b
Burma	EL/SI	EL/SI	SI	...	...	...
China[c]	EL/SI	EL/SI	EL/SI	SI	SI	SI
Fiji	EL	d	EL	NPF	NPF	NPF
Hong Kong	EL	EL	EL	NC[e]	NC[e]	...
India	EL/SI	EL/SI	EL/SI	NPF	NPF	NPF[f]
Indonesia	EL/SI	d	EL	NPF[g]	NPF[g]	NPF[g]
Iran (Islamic Republic of)[h]	EL/SI	EL/SI	EL/SI	SI	SI	SI
Kiribati	EL	...	...	NPF	NPF	NPF
Malaysia	EL/SI	EL[i]	EL[i]	NPF	SI/NPF	SI/NI
Nepal	EL	EL	EL	NPF	NPF	NPF
Pakistan	EL/SI	EL/SI	EL/SI[j]	SI	SI	SI
Papua New Guinea	EL	...	...	NPF	NPF	NPF
Philippines	EL/SI	EL/SI	EL/SI[j]	SI	SI	SI
Republic of Korea	EL/SI	d	EL[k]	l	l	l
Samoa	SI	EL	...	NPF[m]	NPF	NPF
Singapore	EL	EL	EL[n]	NPF	NPF	NPF
Solomon Islands	EL	EL	EL[n]	NPF	NPF	NPF
Sri Lanka	EL	d	EL	NPF	NPF	NPF
Thailand	EL/SI	EL	EL	...	...	...

Source: K. Thompson, *Survey of Social Security in Developing Countries in Asia and the Pacific* (Bangkok, ILO, 1986), pp. 29-31.

Notes: EL = Employers' liability. SI = Social insurance. NPF = National provident fund. NC = Non-contributory.

[a] In addition, medical care is provided under social insurance arrangements in Burma, India, the Islamic Republic of Iran, Pakistan, the Philippines, and the Republic of Korea.   [b] There is a statutory provident fund which applies only to workers in the tea plantations.   [c] The social security programmes shown are for employed persons in state-run enterprises (different from collectively owned enterprises). There are separate systems for employees of government and party organizations, mass organizations and cultural educational public health and scientific institutions. Medical services are provided in employers' clinics or hospitals at the expense of the employer. Fees include treatment by doctor, surgery, maternity care, midwifery, bed and full cost of ordinary medicines. Employees pay registration fees for both out-patient and in-patient care, and also fees for nourishment and tonic medicines.   [d] Collective agreements generally provide for periods of certified sick leave with pay.   [e] Persons aged 70 and over who satisfy certain conditions mainly concerned with residence in Hong Kong qualify for old-age allowance. Severely disabled persons are entitled to disability allowance. Both types of allowance are non-means tested.   [f] In addition to the provident fund benefits, there is the Family Pension Scheme for survivors, the Gratuity Fund for termination of employment by superannuation, resignation, retirement or death and a deposit-linked insurance scheme for additional payments on death in certain circumstances.   [g] Indonesia also has a special scheme for employees of central and provincial governments paying lump-sum benefits in respect of old age and death, as well as a compulsory savings and insurance scheme for the same employees.   [h] Family allowances are also payable (on an employment-related basis).   [i] These provisions apply to employees earning up to $M 500 per month.   [j] Limited to four confinements after March 1973.   [k] Under the medical insurance system in the Republic of Korea, a maternity grant is payable in respect of the confinement of an insured person or the wife of an insured person. Medical insurance benefit is not payable for the third and subsequent children from January 1983, except where illness results from the delivery.   [l] Legislation for a national welfare pension scheme was enacted in 1973 but has not been implemented.   [m] In Samoa, provident fund pensions are payable compulsorily with the right to commute 25 per cent of the pension, unless the total amount credited is below the prescribed figure, when it is paid out as a lump sum or a pension as desired by the member.   [n] Entitlement is limited to three confinements since 1968.

region, with the noticeable exception of the Republic of Korea. The issue relates to the choice between private/individualized and public schemes of medical care. In the case of health systems funded directly by beneficiaries as practised in India and Pakistan, there are deficiencies in terms of trained personnel, equipment and buildings owing to a lack of financial resources.

2. Role of social security schemes in savings mobilization

Interest in social security schemes also arises from their role in mobilizing savings. However, in order to generate savings, the social security schemes should be funded or capitalized, or of the "save-as-you-earn" type, rather than the "pay-as-you-go" type which is commonly used in developed countries. The "save-as-you-earn" type is financed via capitalization and accumulates payments, made by current economically active population during their working lives, in a trust fund, out of which lump-sum or annuity payments are made to the members of the fund. The capacity of the fund to generate savings depends on a number of factors, including the demographic profile of members, the nature of risk coverage provided, the impact of the economic environment, such as inflation which erodes the real value of reserves and recession and unemployment which adversely affect the contribution as well as the administrative costs of operating the fund.

The extent to which social security schemes compete with other forms of savings and result in lower (or even negative) net savings depends on the other savings instruments available and the saving habits of the people. In view of the special nature of social security payments, especially its illiquidity, it is unlikely that an increase in such payments will be offset by a decline in other forms of savings. The net savings are likely to be substantially positive. Some analysts, however, believe that social security programmes are not an effective means of mobilizing savings in the long term and that their savings mobilization potential is generally short-lived.[9] The evidence cited, however, is from Latin America, where the macro-economic environment is substantially different from that in the ESCAP region. In the developing ESCAP region, Singapore has the highest ratio of social security receipts to GDP, 11 per cent, which compares favourably with the ratios of developed market economies. However, during the recent recession, Singapore had to lower the social security contributions considerably.

According to available information, 11 countries are using the provident fund method for financial support in cases of old age, invalidity and death of the breadwinner. The scheme in Malaysia had 4.8 million active members in 1986. Sri Lanka had 2.5 million in 1985 and Singapore about 943,000 in 1984. In India, the Employees Provident Fund had approximately 13.2 million members in 1986, out of which 700,000 were coal miners and 500,000 were tea plantation workers in Assam.[10]

The main features of these schemes are that their benefits depend largely on the length of service, the stability and location of employment, and the amount of earnings. In India, Indonesia, Malaysia, Nepal, the Republic of Korea and Singapore, lump sum payments are mainly used for housing,[11] for financing small enterprises and to pay educational expenses. In Fiji and Malaysia, a formula is added to the provident fund to raise the benefits in case of death to allow for the length of membership in the fund.[12]

In a number of countries, there are circumstances in which all or part of the current credit may be withdrawn prior to retirement age, including the purchase of approved housing accommodation (Malaysia and Singapore), while the Employees' Provident Fund in India allows non-refundable advances for such purposes as the financing of life insurance, purchase of a house or land for the purpose of constructing a dwelling and the marriage of daughters. In Nepal, government employees may apply for real estate loans from the fund up to a value of five years' salary, the repayment term being 25 years at 12 per cent per annum.

Capitalized social security funds can also play an important role in determining the allocation of investment funds in the economy. There are a number of ways in which this can be achieved. In the case of larger economies, social insurance schemes can contribute to the widening of the capital markets by ensuring a constant demand for assets. Second, the surpluses can be invested in important national development projects or social infrastructure (schools, hospitals, roads) or in government securities to finance such projects. Finally, surpluses can be returned to the schemes' affiliates through the lowering of contribution levels, increased benefits and subsidized loans or other purposes.

[9] See C. Wallich, *Savings Mobilization through Social Security, The Experience of Chile during 1916-1977*, World Bank Staff Working Papers, No. 553 (Washington, D.C., 1983).

[10] K. Thompson, *op.cit.,* fn. 10, p. 14.

[11] *ASEAN Economic Bulletin*, vol. 3, No. 1 (July 1986), p. 15.

[12] K. Thompson, *op. cit.*, p. 15.

In most developing countries of the region the investment policy of social security institutions is regulated by Government, but the extent of government influence varies widely. In Malaysia, for example, the Employees Provident Fund is required to invest at least 70 per cent of its surplus funds in government securities (in practice, this proportion reached 94 per cent in 1975); the rest must be invested in high-quality, approved assets.

In India and the Philippines, on the other hand, investment is authorized in a wide variety of assets. In the case of the Philippines, such a policy reduced the potential contribution which the social security scheme's surpluses could have made to development. In addition to salary loans and educational loans, real estate and mortgage loans represented a very large proportion of total loans and investment over the period 1965-1975, encouraging private real estate investment, while a housing programme for the low-income group was interrupted.

The cases of Singapore and Sri Lanka provide an interesting comparison. In both countries, state influence on the allocation patterns of funds is strong: all surpluses must be invested in government securities. However, in Sri Lanka, these funds were used to finance up to one third of the Government's net cash deficit, since they were used for the country's welfare system of extensive social services. It could therefore be said that there was no direct contribution to financial, industrial or agricultural development.

By contrast, in Singapore, a programme of mass housing and urban renewal was begun in 1968, in which the Central Provident Fund participated directly. An overt effort was made to rehouse the lower-income population by allowing affiliates of the Fund to borrow against their contributions in order to finance housing purchases. By acting as a financing agent for public housing schemes, the Fund contributed to the development of the social infrastructure of Singapore and made possible a general sharing of capital wealth generated in the economy.

B. URBANIZATION AND HOUSING PROBLEMS

1. Trends in urbanization in the ESCAP region

In spite of high population growth rates in many of the large cities of the ESCAP region, the overall pace of urbanization over the past quarter century has not been rapid in comparison with the other developing regions of the world. The rate of urbanization is, however, projected to increase between now and the end of the century. Between 1960 and 1985, the total urban population of Asia[13] grew at an annual rate of 3.0 per cent, doubling in a period of 23 years.[14]

There have been declines in the rate of growth of urban and rural populations in Asia in the recent past. The annual growth rate of the urban population declined from 3.24 per cent during the 1960s to 3.03 per cent in the 1970s, while the growth rate of the rural population declined from 2.03 to 1.71 per cent in these two periods. As a consequence, the proportion of the population living in urban areas increased from 21.1 per cent in 1960 to 23.2 per cent in 1970, to 25.6 per cent in 1980, and to a further 26.9 per cent in 1985.

---

[13] Excluding countries west of the Islamic Republic of Iran.

[14] Calculated from *The Prospects of World Urbanization, revised as of 1984-85* (United Nations publication, Sales No. E.87.XIII.3).

Trends in the pace of urbanization depend on not only the absolute rate of growth of the urban population but also the relative rates of growth of urban and rural populations. The difference between the urban and rural population growth rates is a useful measure for reflecting the pace of urbanization. Its usefulness is apparent if, for example, the rate of urbanization of India is compared with that of the Republic of Korea. During 1985-1990, the absolute annual rate of urban growth in India is projected to be higher (3.58 per cent) than in the Republic of Korea (3.36 per cent), yet the relative rate of growth of urbanization in the Republic of Korea is much higher (5.37 per cent) than in India (2.54 per cent) because the former's rural population is declining by 2.0 per cent per annum whereas that of India is expanding by 1.0 per cent (see table I.15).

Although the growth in overall urbanization has not been very rapid, the abnormal growth of a few cities and urban agglomerations does present a serious challenge to planners in the developing ESCAP region. For example, there are five urban agglomerations with a population of over 10 million, namely, Tokyo/Yokohama, Shanghai, Calcutta, Seoul and Greater Bombay (see figure I.9). By 1990, 40.1 per cent of the urban population of East Asia and 38.6 per cent in South Asia will reside in cities with a population of over 1 million. In both subregions, cities in the 1 to 2 million category are expanding most rapidly. The populaiton in cities of 4 million and over is also growing rapidly.

The ESCAP region contains another 11 "mega-cities" exceeding 5 million population.[15] Half of the world's 20 largest urban agglomerations are located in Asia.

---

[15] *Ibid.*, table A-9.

Table I.15. Measures of urbanization in selected countries and areas of the ESCAP region, 1980-1990, and per capita GNP, 1985

	Population mid-1985 (million)	GNP per capita 1985 ($)	Urban population as percentage of total population 1985	Urban population 1985 (thousand)	Rural population 1985 (thousand)	Average growth rate of urban population[a]		Average growth rate of rural population[a]		Tempo of urbanization difference between urban and rural growth rate
						1980–1985	1985–1990	1980–1985	1985–1990	(1) – (2)
							(1)		(2)	(2)
Afghanistan	16.52	189[b]	18.5	3 056	13 462	3.92	8.05	-0.13	4.02	4.03
Australia	15.70	10 830	85.5	13 415	2 283	1.25	1.26	1.74	1.19	0.07
Bangladesh	101.15	150	11.9	12 008	89 139	5.35	5.38	2.41	2.21	3.17
Bhutan	1.20	160	4.5	64	1 353	4.95	5.32	1.90	1.86	3.46
Burma	37.15	190	23.9	8 879	28 273	1.94	2.46	1.94	1.71	0.75
China	1 059.52	310	20.6	218 575	840 945	1.44	1.95	1.18	0.97	0.98
Hong Kong	5.55	6 230	92.4	5 129	419	2.12	1.81	-0.26	-0.02	1.84
India	758.93	270	25.5	193 612	565 315	3.64	3.58	1.39	1.04	2.54
Indonesia	166.44	530	25.3	42 164	124 276	4.59	4.30	1.13	0.79	3.51
Iran (Islamic Republic of)	44.63	...	51.9	23 166	21 465	4.01	3.89	1.74	1.48	2.41
Japan	120.74	11 300	76.5	92 347	28 395	0.74	0.62	0.41	0.17	0.45
Lao People's Democratic Republic	3.60	80[c]	15.9	653	3 464	5.52	5.64	1.66	1.76	3.88
Malaysia	15.56	2 000	38.2	5 946	9 611	4.65	4.15	1.20	0.75	3.40
Mongolia	1.90	...	50.7	968	939	2.61	2.93	2.88	2.54	0.39
Nepal	16.48	160	7.7	1 270	15 213	6.95	6.67	1.99	1.86	4.80
New Zealand	3.32	7 010	83.7	2 778	540	1.02	0.97	0.44	0.29	0.68
Pakistan	100.38	380	29.8	29 899	70 482	4.25	3.65	2.57	1.60	2.06
Papua New Guinea	3.51	680	14.2	500	3 011	4.35	4.46	2.30	2.02	2.44
Philippines	54.50	580	39.6	21 597	32 900	3.59	3.57	1.67	1.32	2.25
Republic of Korea	41.26	2 150	65.4	26 961	14 297	4.36	3.36	-2.80	-2.00	5.37
Singapore	2.56	7 420	100.0	2 559	...	1.16	1.09	...	–	...
Sri Lanka	16.21	380	21.1	3 419	12 786	1.35	1.73	1.91	1.41	0.32
Thailand	51.41	800	19.8	10 173	41 239	4.67	4.30	1.39	0.88	3.41
Viet Nam	59.71	...	20.3	12 118	47 595	2.98	3.56	1.69	1.64	1.92

Sources: World Bank, *World Development Report 1987*; and United Nations, Department of International Economic and Social Affairs, *The Prospects of World Urbanization*, revised as of 1984-85, Population Studies No. 101 (United Nations publication, Sales No. E.87.XIII.3).

a Percentage per year.   b GDP per capita.   c 1984.

Figure I.9. Population of ten largest urban agglomerations in Asia, 1985 and 2000

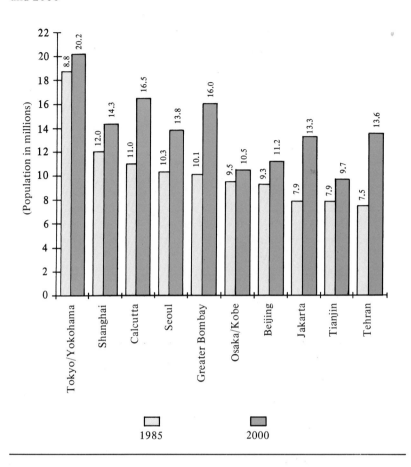

(Population in millions)

City	1985	2000
Tokyo/Yokohama	18.8	20.2
Shanghai	12.0	14.3
Calcutta	11.0	16.5
Seoul	10.3	13.8
Greater Bombay	10.1	16.0
Osaka/Kobe	9.5	10.5
Beijing	9.3	11.2
Jakarta	7.9	13.3
Tianjin	7.9	9.7
Tehran	7.5	13.6

☐ 1985   ■ 2000

Rates of population growth in Asia's largest urban agglomerations vary widely. China's largest cities of Shanghai, Beijing and Tianjin are projected to grow at rates between 1.2 and 1.4 per cent to the year 2000, but the pace of urbanization in China is likely to have increased since these projections were prepared. Other urban agglomerations in the developing ESCAP region, however, are projected to expand more rapidly during the remainder of the century. The average annual rate of growth of Jakarta would be 3.4 per cent, Calcutta 2.7 per cent, Greater Bombay 3.1 per cent, and Tehran 3.9 per cent.

2. Housing problems

One of the more serious social consequences of urban growth and its concentration in a few big cities is the emergence of slums and squatter settlements in urban areas. It is estimated that up to 30 per cent of the urban population in the ESCAP region is living in slums.[16] The problems in slums and squatter settlements are of serious concern and have been highlighted recently in the United Nations Centre for Human Settlements (Habitat) *Global Report*.[17] The following brief survey shows the widespread nature of the problem in the developing ESCAP region.

In Bombay, whose total population was estimated at 10.1 million in 1985, some 3.5 million slum dwellers live on about 8,000 acres of land. It was also estimated that some 100,000 people live on the pavement.[18] In Calcutta, where about one third of the city's 8.3 million people live in overcrowded settlements comprising single-storey huts of temporary construction, the number of pavement dwellers was estimated at 600,000.[19] In Greater Bangkok, an estimated one million people, or nearly 18.6 per cent of the population, were estimated to live in slums in 1984.[20] Similar figures were also reported from the Philippines, where one third of the city population dwell in slums and squatter settlements, while in Jakarta the proportion of slum dwellers was estimated at one quarter of urban households.[21]

In Colombo, more than half of the city's population in 1985 was estimated to be living in substandard accommodation.[22] In Hong Kong, despite a considerable effort to remove and resettle squatters, it was estimated that in 1982 their numbers had increased when compared with the situation in 1976.[23] In Dhaka, 24 per cent

16 UNCHS, *Human Settlement Policy Issues in the ESCAP Region* (Nairobi) (HS/33/84/E).

17 UNCHS, *Global Report on Human Settlements* (Oxford University Press, 1987).

18 *Ibid.*, p. 80.

19 Department of International Economic and Social Affairs, *Population Growth and Policies in Mega-Cities: Calcutta,* Population Policy Paper No. 1 (United Nations, New York, 1986) (ST/ESA/SER.R/61).

20 Shlomo Angel and Sopon Pornchokchai, *Bangkok Slum Lands: The Policy Implications of Recent Findings,* Working Paper No. 4, The Bangkok Land Management Study (April 1987).

21 Trinidat S. Osteira, "Recent trends in urbanization in the ASEAN region: implications for health programmes", *South-East Asian Affairs* (Singapore, 1987), p. 81.

22 UNCHS, *Global Report...*, p. 81.

23 *Ibid.*, p. 82.

of the population was estimated to be living in slums.[24]

The living conditions of the urban poor are much worse than those of the average urban inhabitants, who themselves are deprived of the basic amenities. For example, less than a third of the urban population in Bangladesh, India, Indonesia and Nepal are provided with a satisfactory sanitation system. 26 to 38 per cent of the urban population is served with community water supply in Afghanistan, Bangladesh, Burma and Indonesia. In India, Pakistan, Sri Lanka and Thailand, the figures are 65 to 77 per cent.

3. Changing attitudes towards urban slums

A basic cause of the origin and growth of slums and squatter settlements in the large cities of the region is the lack of adequate facilities relating to the supply, control, and planning of urban land. Housing opportunities for low-income urban dwellers have been decreasing in the inner-city areas of many countries in the ESCAP region. This has resulted in changing attitudes of public authorities towards slum dwellers, which varies from benign neglect and tolerance to eviction and slum clearance. In the 1970s, many Governments adopted more supportive "innovative approaches" emphasizing on-site upgrading and tenure regularization of slum areas. They were a response to the simmering unrest and social tensions created by the earlier approach of slum clearance and involuntary resettlement. However, in recent years, as the land price increased sharply in the metropolitan areas, landowners of slums and squatter settlements became increasingly aware of the more lucrative possibilities of land use. This awareness has tempted many landowners, both private and public, to resort to massive evictions and involuntary resettlement of squatters, and to abandon the previous policy of improving the conditions of the present residents of the squatter-occupied settlements.

This has been evident from the sharp rise in land prices in recent years. For example, the residential land price in Kuala Lumpur increased at an average annual rate of 50 per cent during 1980-1983, while the rate of inflation was around 6 per cent. In Bangkok, the price of land along major roads, lanes, and vacant parcels, increased in real terms on an average of 17, 7 and 12 per cent per year respectively, between 1977 and 1986. During the height of the Bangkok property boom from 1977 to 1981, the price of centrally-located land increased more than 50 per cent per year.[25]

Simultaneously, a number of mass evictions have taken place in a number of large cities in the region. For example, in 1987, some 20,000 dwellers were evicted from their existing slum settlements in Calcutta and their dwellings demolished completely, while an old public housing area in Seoul was demolished under the Urban Redevelopment Act, affecting nearly 100 families. In Bangkok, during a period of two years 1985-1986, more than 5,000 households have been evicted, and an additional 1,500 are being demolished.[26]

The current trend towards more "efficient" land use of converted slums and squatter settlements, involving eviction, is not simply a reversion to the earlier approach of slum clearance. It represents a new trend towards the formalization and commercialization of the urban land and housing market, which is now being increasingly dominated by large corporations and developers. It has replaced a number of informal housing arrangements which benefited the urban poor, such as unauthorized occupation of government land, cheap land rental, and subdivision of housing units for sublease. For example, in Dhaka, while the poor living in *bustees,* old tenements, etc., constitute 70 per cent of the city's population and are confined to only 20 per cent of the land, the middle- and the upper-income groups form only 30 per cent of the population but occupy 80 per cent of the residential land of the city. Such distorted structures of residential patterns are prevalent in many other metropolises in the region. At the same time, land currently occupied by low-income people is under increasing pressure from the government and corporate sectors for conversion to more profitable uses, without providing the slum dwellers adequate alternative opportunities for resettlement.

4. Policy responses

With a view to meeting the urgent housing needs of the region, the United Nations Centre for Human Settlements (Habitat) has set a target annual construction rate of 10 dwelling units per 1,000 population.[27]

Budget and land constraints together with the impact of recession, which limited social expenditures in many countries, have prevented most countries of the region from reaching this target, which only Hong Kong and Singapore have been able to

[24] Centre for Urban Studies, *Slums in Dhaka City* (Dhaka, University of Dhaka, June 1983).

[25] David E. Dowall, "The Bangkok land and housing market study" (1987) (mimeographed).

[26] Shlomo Angel and Sopon Pornchokchai, *op. cit.*

[27] UNCHS, *Global Report. . .* , p. 14.

achieve. The shortage of public resources, however, has induced a change in the attitude of Governments towards substandard housing and slums. Self-help construction arrangements, improvement of urban services and upgrading of the housing units are now encouraged, to the extent possible, as an alternative to the eviction of families and destruction of these slums.[28]

National housing programmes have included the establishment of new financial institutions and of an integrated urban development approach. In centrally planned economies, with the State as traditional main provider of housing finance, private and co-operative sectors are increasingly involved in housing investment.

A number of countries in the region have undertaken special programmes for assisting housing development programmes for the poor. Thus, in Indonesia, the Kampung Improvement Scheme has become one of the main national shelter programmes addressed to the needs of the disadvantaged. In Malaysia, the special low-cost housing programme aims to construct 80,000 houses through incentives to the private sector.

In the Republic of Korea, the Housing Construction Promotion Act has provided the basic framework for government efforts to promote low-income housing. Through a World Bank project, the private sector in the Philippines is participating in the construction of low-income housing. Sri Lanka has established a permanent process for the provision of shelter for the poor known as the Million Houses Programme. It provides small loans for construction and rehabilitation of shelter and essential services.

In the short-term, government policies contribute in various ways to the improvement of housing finance and credit schemes, especially for the low-income population. In some States of India and Malaysia, housing programmes allocate a certain proportion of housing units to low-income groups. In India, Nepal and Papua New Guinea, housing finance institutions have been established with a three-tier system covering the national, regional and local levels. Such institutions are strengthened in Thailand, where the Government carefully reviews the loan system and housing subsidies.

In China and Viet Nam, reforms in the urban housing system have led to a larger share of personal investment in urban and rural housing projects and have encouraged individual families to buy houses. Building materials in China are provided at subsidized prices with tax exemption granted for buildings purchased.[29]

In Indonesia, the National Urban Development Strategy provides for the establishment of a municipal development fund to be administered by the National Urban Development Co-ordination Board. Other financial arrangement include mortgage schemes for the purchase of complete and sub-core houses.

The Million Houses Programme of Sri Lanka has adopted an institutional approach based on the principle of minimum intervention, maximal support by the State and maximal involvement of the builder families. It is claimed that through this approach the number of houses built is triple the number that would have been built through conventional sources of finance.

The preceding brief survey highlights the necessity of an integrated approach to housing policies. Such an approach includes three main components: first, the institutional aspect, which consists of reform of land tenure, rent control and public and private schemes of financing; second, the physical aspect, which includes housing improvement as well as the extension of basic services to the urban poor; lastly, the economic aspect, which involves the augmentation of the incomes of the low-income groups through various employment schemes.

The success or failure of different resettlement programmes is linked to the capacity to develop such an integrated approach to human settlements.

C. SMALL-SCALE INDUSTRIES

Interest in small-scale industries in the developing world has stemmed largely from their potential for increasing employment opportunities. It has been reinforced by the disappointing impact of increases in manufacturing output on employment. Interest in small-scale industry was further enhanced after the disillusionment with the growth-oriented development strategies in the 1960s and the increased concern for equity.[30]

However, over the past decade and a half experience with respect to the role of small-scale industries in development has been rather mixed. The ESCAP region, in fact, presents a very variegated picture concerning small-scale production, with respect to both its relative size in the manufacturing industry and the policies adopted.

[28] Alan Gilbert, "Self-help housing and State intervention: illustrated reflection on the Petty Commodity Production debate" in David Drakais-Smith, ed., *Urbanization in the Developing World* (London, Croom Helm, 1986), pp. 175-194.

[29] E. Carlson, *op. cit.*

[30] ILO, *Employment, Incomes and Equality: A Strategy for Increasing Productive Employment in Kenya* (Geneva, 1972).

Moreover, definitions of the sector vary from country to country and, indeed, within countries.

A comprehensive assessment of the subject can only be undertaken as a major project which falls well beyond the scope of the present *Survey*.[31] This section therefore, focuses on six economies – India, Indonesia, Malaysia, Thailand, the Republic of Korea, and Hong Kong – as the basis for discussing the policy issues relating to the small-scale manufacturing sector in the ESCAP region. Of all countries in the region, India has perhaps the most wide-ranging policy experience in promoting small-scale industries. Indonesia, Malaysia and Thailand have substantial small-scale sectors and have active policies to support them. In the Republic of Korea, such support is limited and selective, but the small-scale sector has an important role in the country's export-oriented economy. In Hong Kong, the sector has enormous importance but it has no clear small industry policy. Taken together, these countries provide a good cross-section of the ESCAP region's small-scale production sector.

1. A cross-section view

This section presents an overview of trends in growth of the small-scale industries, their relative importance in the industrial sector, problems they have encountered and policies that have been adopted for their development.

The small industry sector in India includes all units whose investment in plant and machinery is less than Rs 1 million. These

industries have been given a distinct place under the heading "Village and Small Industries (VSI)" in the national development plans. Village and small industries comprises two subsectors. One consists of traditional cottage and village activities such as the production of khadi, coir and handicrafts, etc. This subsector is distinguished by its wide geographical distribution, household-based production, and rather semi-urban and rural nature. The other is the modern small-scale industry subsector, which is characterized by a relatively high technological level, product sophistication and urban orientation.

The 1970s and 1980s have seen a tremendous growth in village and small industries. Over the period 1973/74-1985/86, the number of small-scale industry units rose from 312,000 to 1.3 million and employment increased from 3.9 million to 9.6 million persons.[32] However, employment has not grown as much as output and exports, mainly because of technological improvements and higher productivity achieved over the years. The small-scale industry subsector also decisively improved its export performance. It now accounts for 22.5 per cent of the total exports of India.[33] The village and small industry sector as a whole employs about 29 million persons. Half of the manufacturing sector's output is generated by this sector.[34]

After independence, modern small-scale production was first established in industries producing soap, detergents, leather goods,

etc., but more recently small-scale activity has extended into such sophisticated fields as electrical goods, electronics and electro-medical devices. Small-scale leather manufacture is export-oriented and provides employment to a large number of people belonging particularly to the weaker sections of the community. The export performance in the production of coir, handicrafts, silk, handloom cloth, etc., has also made considerable progress. The output of the khadi and village industries, traditionally aimed at the local market, has been increasingly exported.

As noted earlier, the Government of India has an explicit policy aimed at promoting the development of village and small industries. Among its other objectives, the small industry movement aims at uplifting the weaker sections of the population and redressing regional imbalances.

In order to implement its small-scale industry promotion policy, the Government has adopted a wide range of support programmes. One such programme reserves products for exclusive production in the small-scale sector. Introduced in 1956/57, the list has been enlarged to 163 from 47 items included initially.

In the field of finance, the state governments have set aside special funds to provide medium- and long-term finance to small-scale industries administered through the state financial corporation, state small industry corporations, and the National Small Industry Corporation. The Government, through the Reserve Bank of India, has also implemented a credit guarantee scheme to provide the sharing of possible losses between private lending institutions. The Government also encourages commercial banks and other credit institutions to join in the effort to provide loans to small industries.

[31] For a recent comprehensive review of the problems of small-scale manufacturing enterprises, see I.M.D. Little, Dipak Mazumdar and John M. Page, *Small Scale Manufacturing Enterprises: A Comparative Study of India and Other Countries* (New York, Oxford University Press, 1987).

[32] India, *Economic Survey 1986-87* (New Delhi, Ministry of Finance, 1987), p. 43.

[33] *Ibid.*

[34] ESCAP, *Small Industry Bulletin for Asia and the Pacific*, No. 21 (United Nations publication, Sales No. E.86.II.F.25), p. 42.

Other schemes include the provision of consultancy services, aid in marketing, modernization of production as well as encouragement of subcontracting between small units and medium/large units. The Government also encourages public sector undertakings to engage in subcontracting arrangements with small-scale units. In addition, a comprehensive industrial estate programme has been launched which provides electricity to small factories at subsidized rates.

The degree of success of the village and small industry schemes and programmes is not easy to estimate. Sick industries continue to cause concern, and lack of reliable statistics has hindered systematic analysis of the problems in the subsector.

In Indonesia, small-scale industry is defined in a number of different ways. The Jakarta-based Bank Indonesia characterizes small-scale enterprises as having a net worth not in excess of Rp 20 million and current assets not exceeding Rp 10 million. The Department of Industry has used three criteria to define a small industrial enterprise: (i) investment in plant and equipment not more than $120,000, (ii) investment per worker not more than $1,000, and (iii) ownership by an Indonesian citizen. The Indonesian Central Bureau of Statistics includes in the sector units employing between 5 and 19 persons. Enterprises with four or less employees are categorized as part of the cottage and household sector.

According to a 1979 survey of industrial establishments, the small-scale and cottage sector (1-19 employees) accounted for 99 per cent of all manufacturing enterprises, over 80 per cent of total industrial employment and 22 per cent of value added in the country's manufacturing industry.[35] Small-scale and cottage units are largely found in industries producing food, beverages, tobacco, textiles and apparel, leather and leather goods, and furniture and other wood products. Subcontracting between small-scale units and medium/large enterprises is still rare in the manufacturing industry of Indonesia.

Because of the importance of the small-scale and cottage sector for employment and its wide geographical dispersion in the country, the Indonesian Government extends it strong support. Most of the Government's efforts are focused on financial and technical assistance.

The primary source of financial credit for the cottage and small-scale industries of Indonesia is Kredit Investasi Kecil (KIK), a scheme for loans for plant and equipment, and Kredit Modal Kerja Permanen (KMKP), a similar loan scheme for working capital. There are other programmes, such as the Mini Kredit (a programme for financing equipment and working capital with a ceiling of $160 only), and the Kredit Candak Kulak, a working capital loan programme with a lending ceiling of $24 for tiny businesses. These financial credit schemes are generally administered by the Central Bank, funded by the Government and supplemented by external sources. According to the World Bank, while the Mini Kredit and the Kredit Candak Kulak play some role in the development of Indonesia's small industrial enterprises, the KIK/KMKP programmes have become increasingly important in meeting the financial needs of these enterprises since 1974.

In Malaysia, small-scale industry consists of establishments having 5 to 49 employees. Enterprises with less than 5 persons are referred to as tiny-scale (or traditional) establishments. These are generally artisan-type units, owned and managed by craftsmen.

Official surveys indicate that 42 per cent of all manufacturing establishments are tiny-scale and 45 per cent are small-scale. In the industrial sector as a whole (manufacturing, mining, construction), 87 per cent of the enterprises employ less than 50 workers. Of the manufacturing employment, tiny-scale accounts for 3 per cent and the small-scale for nearly 20 per cent of the work-force. Furthermore, tiny- and small-scale enterprises contribute 14 per cent of the manufacturing value added. In the industrial sector as a whole, the small- and tiny-scale enterprises combined account for 31 per cent of employment and 20 per cent of value added.

Large enterprises, defined as those employing more than 200 employees, account for nearly 41 per cent of the labour force and 46 per cent of the value added in the industrial sector, but only for 2.6 per cent of industrial establishments. The rest of the employment and value added in the industrial sector is accounted for by the medium-scale, that is units employing 50 to 199 workers.

Since the 1970s, the Malaysian Government has actively promoted the development of small-scale industries. As stated in the fourth plan, "Small-scale industries played an important role in the development of entrepreneurship, creation of employment, mobilization of individual savings for investment, broadening of the industrial base for the Bumiputra and the provision of inputs and supportive services for larger-scale industries".[36]

[35] Biro Pusat Statistik, *Statistik Indonesia, Statistical Yearbook of Indonesia 1986* (Jakarta, 1986), pp. 292-295.

[36] Malaysia, *Fourth Malaysia Plan 1981-1985* (Kuala Lumpur, 1981), p. 297.

Box I.12. The rise and decline of small-scale tube-well industry in Pakistan

The case of the Pakistan tube-well industry in Punjab throws interesting light on both the strengths and weaknesses of small-scale manufacturing activity. A sector which had earlier shown remarkable dynamism, when confronted with a sudden collapse of its market in the mid-1970s, went into decline. A field survey conducted in 1982-1983 showed that in the course of its growth the artisanal type of enterprise reaches a stage when it confronts a barrier blocking its further expansion and technological improvement.

The story goes back to the early 1960s. As the installation of tube-wells in the private agriculture of Punjab gained momentum, a large number of artisan-type units established production of slow-speed diesel engines and low-capacity water pumps. A survey conducted in 1969 estimated the size of the small-scale sector at 444 enterprises employing 6,000 workers.[a] Nearly 66 per cent of these units were estimated to employ less than 10 workers.

Two features of the phenomenon attracted particular attention: the ease with which these units were able to acquire the new technology, and their entry into an oligopolistic industry dominated by a few large firms. Both these features called for an explanation.

A detailed study of the industry sought to answer these questions.[b]

On the acquisition of the new technology, the study identified two factors which complemented each other. First, although the new technology was distinctly more advanced than the production methods familiar to the artisanal units, it was not too remote to be inaccessible on the basis of existing skills. For instance, production of most tube-well components needed no more than simple equipment, the operation of which required no formal training and was thus within the competence of a labour force with metal-working experience, which was in abundant supply.

Further, the assembly nature of the product provided considerable scope for vertical specialization within both the small-scale sector, and the engineering industry generally. By giving the small enterprise the choice to buy or make various components in-house, the possibility of vertical specialization reduced both the technological and capital requirements of entry into tube-well production. The components which were beyond the production capacity of small enterprises could be purchased from larger engineering enterprises or commercial importers. Thus, though unable to enjoy economies of scale, the small enterprises could benefit from economies of specialization available within the industry.[c]

Two considerations have been offered to explain the second feature of the development – the entry into an oligopolistic industry. The first of these relates to the opportunities for expansion available to large enterprises in the buoyant industrial environment of the early 1960s. This period saw not only the expansion of the private agriculture demand for tube-wells but also a variety of investment opportunities in related markets. The entry of small firms

into the private agriculture market did not pose a threat to large enterprises, as it inevitably would have done in static markets. Second, small units, with access to relatively simple equipment only, chose to establish themselves in the large, low-price, low-quality segment of the market. The large firms continued to cater for the upper segment of the market and expanded in related but more protected markets. This horizontal specialization, together with the small firms' comparative advantage in the fabrication of relatively low-quality products, provided favourable conditions for the coexistence of both types of enterprises.

Decline of the small sector

From around 1974 there was a substantial decline in the private agricultural market for tube-wells. The average annual rate of tube-well installation in Pakistan, which was 14,700 during the period from 1970/71 to 1974/75, fell to an annual average of 7,400 in the subsequent four years. Correspondingly, the small-scale tube-well sector contracted. In 1982-1983, it was difficult to find enterprises that had successfully adapted by switching production to superior or even similar products, such as the tube-well.[d] More generally, over the entire period 1960-1983 the small artisan unit, having once upgraded its technological and production base, was unable to go beyond the level of tube-well production.

It was observed that on the basis of their technological and financial resources these artisan units could achieve technical upgrading and expansion only within certain definite limits. Beyond that point expansion

---

[a] See F.C. Child and H. Kaneda, "Links to the Green Revolution: a study of small-scale agriculturally-related industry in Pakistan Punjab", *Economic Development and Cultural Change*, vol. 23, No. 2 (January 1975).

[b] Khalid Aftab and Eric Rahim, "The tube-well industry in Pakistan Punjab: entry, survival and the role of small-scale engineering units", *Economic Bulletin for Asia and the Pacific*, vol. XXXVI, No. 1 (June 1985).

---

[c] *Ibid.*

---

[d] Khalid Aftab and Eric Rahim, "Barriers to the growth of informal sector firms: a case study", 1987 (forthcoming).

The main purpose of government agencies assisting and coordinating the development of small-scale industries is to provide financial aid. The loans are at well below market interest rates. For instance, Bank Pembanguaan Malaysia Berhad (BPMB) lends at between 0 and 2 per cent interest rate, Majlis Amanah Rakyat (MARA) at 5 to 7.5 per cent and the commercial banks of the Coordinating Council for Development of Small-Scale Industries at between 7.5 to 8.5 per cent.

required (i) a range of skills that were qualitatively different from those possessed by these firms and which are necessarily acquired through formal training, and (ii) a certain minimum volume of funds which was well beyond their resources. The educational and social background of the owner, and the very nature of the artisanal enterprise, proved a serious barrier to the acquisition of qualitatively different skills. Further, the intensely competitive nature of the product market environment left little room for internal generation of investment funds. The size and the economic position of the enterprise also restricted its ability to absorb requisite resources through the market — for the ability to acquire resources is determined by the potential of the firm as perceived by the market. It is this perceived potential which is ultimately limited by the essentially artisanal character of the firm.

The story offers a number of lessons, two of which are noted here. The expansionary phase of the industry's development supports the view that there is no necessary conflict between the simultaneous development of large- and small-scale industries. Large and small firms can specialize on the basis of their comparative advantages not only across industries but also, where the market situation permits, within industries. The second phase of the industry suggests that even competitive factor markets need not treat large and small firms equally. In particular, small enterprises of artisanal origin suffer from certain disadvantages, which cannot be explained in terms of identifiable distortions of policies affecting them. Their main disadvantage is in terms of their inability to upgrade their technology and it could be removed through active human resource development policies in their favour.

In Thailand, three different definitions of small-scale enterprises are used. First, the Small Industry Finance Office defines small units as those having fixed assets of 2 million baht or less. Second, the Division of Industrial Service uses a definition based on the characteristics rather than the size of enterprises. Accordingly, small enterprises are defined as units that are owner-managed and in which business functions are not clearly departmentalized. Finally, most of the empirical studies of the small-scale sector and industrial structure distinguish four types of enterprises — handicraft and cottage, having 1-9 employees, small-scale, with 10-49 workers, medium-scale, with 50-199 employees, and large-scale, employing 200 or more persons.

According to the last definition, cottage and small-sized firms account for nearly 95 per cent of the total number of enterprises in the manufacturing sector. They employ nearly 40 per cent of the labour force and account for 16 per cent of value added in the manufacturing industry.[37]

Smaller enterprises are generally concentrated in the Greater Bangkok area and, to a lesser extent, in central Thailand. This is due to the proximity of a large market and infrastructure facilities in the capital.

Small-scale industries have developed into a significant sector of the Thai economy. However, Government policy measures directly aimed at the promotion of the sector have been rather limited in scope. Nevertheless, various public agencies provide such services as the supervision of the industrial service institutes, handicraft promotion and planning, enhancing industrial productivity and assistance to cottage and textile industries.

Two industrial service institutes — one in Bangkok and the other in Chiang Mai — were set up with international support a decade ago. Their task is to provide technical assistance and advisory services to small-scale industries. Financial assistance is organized by the Small Industry Finance Office. Loans of less than baht 500,000 are selectively given to small enterprises by the Krung Thai Bank at below market interest rates. The total amount of credit provided is usually between baht 20 million and 46 million a year. There is, however, no separate agency in Thailand to co-ordinate the activities of various bodies providing assistance to small-scale industries.

In the Republic of Korea, small and medium industries are usually treated as part of the same sector. The small- and medium-scale sector includes enterprises having less than 300 employees. However, in one survey (1984) a distinction was made between small (5-49 employees) and medium-size firms (50-299 employees). According to this survey, 81 per cent of all manufacturing establishments were small and 17 per cent fell in the medium category. Based on this definition, small enterprises accounted for 22 per cent of the employment and 11 per cent of the value added of the manufacturing sector. The corresponding shares of the medium-scale sector were 33 and 25 per cent.[38] The main products of small- and medium-sized enterprises include fabricated metal products, machinery and equipment, textiles, apparel, and leather goods.

Despite the adoption of some measures favouring small-scale production, the Republic of Korea's industrial policy during the 1970s

---

[37] Saen Sanguanruang and others, *Development of Small and Medium Scale Manufacturing Enterprises in Thailand*, vol. 1, Main Report (1978), pp. 12, 16 and 17.

[38] Republic of Korea, National Bureau of Statistics, Economic Planning Board, *Korea Statistical Yearbook 1986* (Seoul, 1986), pp. 164-167.

tended to favour large enterprises, such as those in the heavy and chemical industries, and lately it has favoured the electronics sector as well. Assistance given to the small-scale sector has been highly selective and influenced by considerations related to export expansion.

In the beginning of the 1960s, the Small Industry Division was established in the Ministry of Commerce and Industry and several measures were introduced to encourage the formation of small industry co-operatives and to increase their export-orientation. Furthermore, small industry centres were set up to provide consultancy services and management courses. Since 1964/65, financial assistance has been provided for small enterprises on a more selective basis.

Within the general context of a policy aimed at "structural modernization", the Government encourages specialization of small enterprises and subcontracting between large and small units. The measures adopted include the establishment of specialized industrial estates and co-operatives to bring together small-scale units of the same type operating in related industries. The Government also annually selects 100 small-sized enterprises with good export-growth potential for intensive promotion and the award of incentives. With the exception of the favoured enterprises, the small-scale industries are usually charged market rates for services and credit.

Hong Kong classifies small-scale enterprises as those having less than 50 employees. These establishments are largely found in industries producing textiles and clothing, plastic goods, watches and clocks, and electrical and electronic products.

In 1985, 92 per cent of all manufacturing enterprises were small-scale; of these, nearly 67 per cent had less than 10 employees. The small-scale sector as a whole accounted for 40 per cent of the manufacturing sector's employment, and for 32 per cent of gross output.[39] Over the last decade both the number of establishments and total employment of small enterprises have increased significantly.

The Hong Kong Government does not extend any direct assistance to industry; there is no specific policy on small industry, and no government or non-governmental agency is engaged in promoting small enterprises. However, Hong Kong has a loose system of support for encouraging exports. This includes, for example, facilities for exports and promoting goods in overseas markets. Because of the small industry's high stake in exports — in several cases only indirectly as a supplier to large exporting industries — they of course benefit from the Government's trade promotion efforts.

2. Some general policy issues

The preceding brief account of policies adopted in the six economies of the ESCAP region allows some degree of generalization. First, the small-scale sector in all six economies accounts for a large proportion of the industrial labour force. In fact, the actual volume of the labour force employed in the small-scale sector is usually underestimated as a large number of unregistered enterprises are often not covered in official surveys. In many countries the employment-generating potential of small-scale production provides the principal justification for the official support that the sector receives.

Second, the small-scale sector

is seldom found to be a homogeneous group. In most countries it includes three distinct types: (i) cottage and household establishments producing traditional types of products using traditional methods — for instance, handicrafts, khadi cloth, hand-knitted carpets, and others; (ii) enterprises making modern products, such as electrical and electronic goods, using modern techniques; and (iii) an intermediate type of enterprise which has a traditional background and has graduated into the production of non-traditional products — simple metal products such as water pumps, slow-speed diesel engine components, and repair and maintenance of motor vehicles. These various types of enterprises vary significantly in their levels of technology and face different problems.

Third, small enterprises operate in certain definite types of industries and certain types of markets. In these sectors and markets, they enjoy a comparative advantage which is based on certain technical factors and market situations. The technical conditions favourable to small-scale production are the absence of economies of scale and the technical separability of vertical processes of production (see box I.12, p. 76). This technical separability is found in engineering and metal fabricating industries where the final product is made of different components that can be independently manufactured. These and similar technical features also provide the appropriate conditions for subcontracting arrangements between large and small firms.

The most usual type of market condition favourable to small-scale production is provided by market fragmentation, which may be the result of geographical dispersion of demand, or product differentiation based on product quality, design, etc., and consumer

---

[39] *Hong Kong Annual Digest of Statistics,* 1986 edition (Hong Kong Census and Statistics Department), p. 48.

78

tastes. Where markets are large and homogeneous or distant, small firms can only reach them through co-operatives and larger distribution and export enterprises. The latter type of arrangements sometimes emerges through the market; when appropriate arrangements do not evolve through the market, government assistance becomes necessary.

Another area in which markets do not always produce the desired results relate to the transfer of technology to small enterprises. Small firms often lack the necessary financial resources and managerial expertise to acquire new and unfamiliar technologies. Thus, in a number of countries (India and the Republic of Korea, for instance) a network of officially-supported small industry technical institutes, extension services, etc., have been established to bring new methods of production and improved managerial practices to small enterprises.

In general, policy will be more successful where it is based on close observation of the technical and market conditions that favour small-scale production and where it is aimed at rectifying market failures.

Part Two

INTERNATIONAL TRADE
IN PRIMARY COMMODITIES

I. GENERAL PERSPECTIVE ON ISSUES AND POLICIES

A. THEME AND CONTENTS OF THE STUDY

Trade in primary commodities has provided the life blood to most economies of the Asian and Pacific region and has been their main link with the world economy. Although founded during a period of colonial domination of the region, such trade has proved most valuable in generating the external and domestic financial resources needed for development. During the past two decades, however, extremely important developments have taken place in the volume, value, structure and direction of such trade, raising serious questions about the role of trade in primary commodities in the economic development of the developing countries of the region.

The fortunes of developing countries dependent on trade in primary commodities have fluctuated widely during this period, with sudden and short booms alternating with long periods of stagnation and decline. The perceptions about the long-term trends in terms of trade between primary commodities and manufactured goods largely governed the debate on "inward- and outward-looking" development strategies in the 1950s and 1960s. In the 1970s, the increasing concerns about the depletion of natural resources and the limits of growth in developed countries coincided with the quadrupling of oil prices and suddenly engendered optimism among the producers of primary commodities. It lulled the disquiet and fears of developing countries about perennial dependency on primary commodities and provided them a breathing space (of which they did not always fully avail themselves) in which to diversify their economies.

A confluence of events in the early 1980s brought the virtual collapse of the prices of a wide range of primary commodities, which has served to revert the attention to the problems of international trade in primary commodities. The failure of prices of primary commodities to recover appreciably since 1980-1982 has led to the strengthening of apprehensions — not yet fully supported by incontrovertible empirical evidence — that an irreversible secularly declining trend in the demand for primary commodities has set in. The current pessimism among the producers of primary commodities contrasts with the euphoria which characterized the prospects of primary commodities, especially oil, over a decade ago. Indeed it has been argued that the present "commodity crisis" is partly a legacy of the somewhat misplaced perception of and policy responses to the commodity boom of the 1970s. However, since the early 1980s a number of new developments have taken place altering the basic configuration of supply and demand which have further limited the contribution of primary commodities as an important source of the foreign exchange earnings of developing countries.

The problems of trade in primary commodities are, of course, part of the general weakening of the stimulus provided by international trade to the development of developing countries, reflected in the slowing down in the rate of growth of total exports of goods and services from 9 per cent per annum in the years 1963-1973 to 3.0 per cent in the years 1973-1986. Since 1980, the growth in world trade has barely kept pace with the growth of output in the world economy. Moreover, even the strong, though transient, upsurge of world trade in 1984 which accompanied the recovery in growth in the United States of America was centred around growth in manufactures.[1]

A more pressing need for a study of trade in primary commodities is the growing threat of protectionism which is being faced by producers of primary commodities, especially agricultural products, in a number of developed country markets. In recent years two parallel trends have become noticeable in agricultural production. First, a number of countries in the developed world, especially the United States, the members of the European Economic Community (EEC) and Japan, have adopted policies of either protecting or

---

[1] See *Survey*, 1985, p. 2.

subsidizing their agriculture, which have contributed to growing agricultural surpluses in these countries and are creating downward pressures on prices in commodity markets. Second, there has been a parallel development in developing countries, especially those of the ESCAP region, which have increased their agricultural production largely through the adoption of new agricultural inputs, multiple cropping and investment in irrigation facilities. These countries have not only succeeded in achieving self-sufficiency in food and in keeping the Malthusian spectre at bay but some have even become significant exporters of food grains and many others are vying to attain that status.

Both these developments have resulted in a situation of excess supply in many agricultural products in the international market and have depressed their prices. In the case of non-agricultural primary commodities, technological factors, rather than protectionist measures, have been more important, reducing effective demand and creating excess supply. A major adjustment is, therefore, needed in the world-wide production of primary commodities which would lead to a more balanced pattern of international specialization, reflecting more closely the underlying elements of comparative advantage and the need for increasing the export opportunities for developing countries.

The issues relating to international trade in primary commodities, especially agriculture, have begun to receive the belated attention of developed countries. In their most recent sequence of meetings at the ministerial level (Organisation for Economic Co-operation and Development (OECD) in May) and at the Summit level (in June 1987), have agreed to negotiate at the Uruguay Round of GATT (General Agreement on Tariffs and Trade) to phase out agricultural subsidies and other measures affecting agricultural trade. The outcome of these negotiations is uncertain and it will be a long time before the benefits of any agreement accrue to developing countries which depend so much on commodity trade for their economic growth and development. The continuing instability of prices and export earnings from trade in primary commodities and the declining trends in the long-term demand for a number of commodities are issues which require urgent policy action at the national, regional and international levels. Recognizing the critical importance of these issues for the development of the developing countries in the ESCAP region, as well as for two of the developed market economies of the region, Australia and New Zealand, which have a vital stake in these issues, the Commission at its forty-third session urged the secretariat to undertake a study on the subject.

It seems, therefore, necessary and opportune to undertake a detailed study of the issues and problems which affect trade in primary commodities and to evaluate their likely role in the future development strategies of the countries of the region. The purpose of this *Survey* is to highlight the issues and policies, both domestic and international, which have given rise to current concerns about primary commodities in this region and to suggest, where necessary, the possibilities of remedial policy actions at the national, regional and international levels.

In 1985 the *Survey* devoted its attention to the problems of trade and development, in general. Although the problems of trade in primary commodities were also addressed in that *Survey,* the treatment was more general and the focus was not on the differences but on the similarities of constraints faced by different categories of exports. This *Survey* attempts to highlight the critical importance of commodity trade in the structural transformation of the developing economies of the ESCAP region.

The present *Survey* is structured in the following way. The remaining sections of this chapter discuss some of the important general features of and developments in trade in primary commodities and their implications for national and international policies. Chapter II examines the changing role and structure of primary production in the domestic economies of the ESCAP region. Chapter III analyses the patterns of commodity trade flows in terms of both exports and imports in the ESCAP region. In addition to the commodity structure of trade, it looks into the geographical pattern of trade flows. Chapter IV examines fluctuations in and trends of prices of primary commodities of export interest and their impact on the economies of the region. Chapter V looks into the issues concerning market access barriers and other developments affecting trade in primary commodities of interest to the region. Chapter VI seeks to assess future prospects and policy options available at the national regional/subregional and international levels in the light of past initiatives and efforts and based on the findings of the preceding chapters.

Before proceeding further, it is necessary to define the scope of the commodities covered in this study. However, defining a primary commodity is far from easy. A commonly used definition is to include the products obtained from the use of natural resources, such as land, sea and mines and subjected to a minimum degree of processing,[2] a proviso which often leads to controversy. Although for most commodities accepted conventions exist to define the stage at which they cease to be primary commodities, for some commodities this stage is defined with a degree of arbitrariness. The problem is not an academic one either. In a world riddled with protectionist legislation which protects domestic processing industries the definitional boundaries are often used to strengthen trade barriers. For example, new-process, scientifically graded rubber exported under the Standard Malaysian Rubber Scheme is often treated as a semi-manufacture for tariff purposes by developed countries and smelted tin or copper is treated as a manufactured product by some countries.

In this study, the SITC (Standard International Trade Classification) is followed to define the primary products. In much of the discussion in the text attention is concentrated on non-fuel primary products, since trade in oil and other fuels has assumed a quite distinctive role in international trade discussions in recent years. Many of the general findings of this study, however, are equally applicable to oil and related primary commodities.

B. DISTINGUISHING FEATURES OF TRADE IN PRIMARY COMMODITIES

Trade in primary commodities has a number of distinctive characteristics which require separate analysis from the other major component of merchandise

[2] For other possible definitions of primary commodities, see J.F.W. Rowe, *Primary Commodities in International Trade* (Cambridge University Press, 1965) and C.P. Brown, *Primary Commodity Control* (Kuala Lumpur, Oxford University Press, 1975).

trade, trade in manufactures. Indeed, there are some striking asymmetries between the two categories of trade; failure to recognize this often oversimplifies discussions on international trade policies. Many of the distinctive characteristics derive from the physical nature of commodities — such as greater perishability and bulkiness — but the more significant differences are rooted in the institutional arrangements governing their production, distribution and exchange. These asymmetries go a long way toward explaining why the incidence of "market failure" and the need for government intervention is so high in the case of trade in primary commodities relative to trade in manufactures.

In general, production and trade of primary commodities, unlike manufactures, are location-specific.[3] This is illustrated by substantial differences in the types of commodities traded by different country groups and individual countries. Climate and the natural environment have largely determined the patterns of commodity production. The North-South division of the globe, based on a natural boundary with a large part of the developing world being located within the tropics and most of the developed world in the temperate and subtropical zones, has ordained the pattern of specialization in primary production (see box II.1).

Trade in primary commodities produced by the developed countries has been relatively free of trade barriers compared with other trade between developed and developing countries. Similarly, the developing countries have historically sold their produce to de-

[3] See Paul S. Armington, "A theory of demand for products distinguished by place of production", *International Monetary Fund Staff Papers*, vol. 16 (March 1969), pp. 159-178.

veloped country markets without any hindrance since there was generally no competition with their domestic production. The above dichotomy, however, was neat only in theory. In fact there was often substantial overlap since some of the large developed countries extend into the tropics while some of the large developing countries extend into the temperate zones. However, technological progress and discoveries have continually eroded this special feature of commodity trade.

Asymmetry in trade in primary commodities arises in major part from the inflexibilities in the production structure of commodities, which often leads to a high degree of specialization by individual developing countries with limited resources. Switching from one product to another or even adjusting the rate of output is virtually impossible in the short run in the case of primary commodities, unlike that in most manufactures. This makes for the high dependence of individual countries on a few products for their exports, low elasticities of supply and consequent instability in their export receipts. Although many developed countries also have substantial exports of primary commodities, they are not heavily dependent on them — with some significant exceptions such as Australia, Canada and New Zealand, whose production structures are, nevertheless, more flexible and diversified.

An important difference between primary commodities and manufactures is in the microeconomic adjustment of output in response to changes in prices. Since land and other fixed assets have a large share in total costs and have few readily available alternative uses, mobility of resources into or out of the production of a primary commodity is more difficult, particularly in the case of tree and plantation crops. The objective of maintaining employment, irrespective of family or hired labour, also transforms wages partially or wholly into fixed costs. Thus faced with falling prices production is carried out much beyond the optimal point for primary commodities compared with manufactures.

The structure of primary commodity markets is qualitatively different from that of manufactured goods. This is partly derived from the degree of homogeneity of non-processed primary commodities. At a certain level, most primary commodities are com-

Box II.1. Historical evolution of primary commodity trade

Primary commodity trade has played a major historical role in the development of the North-South economic relationships. In particular, the commodity trade between Europe and the developing countries of the ESCAP region has played a key role in the evolution of the pattern of international specialization that exists in the world today.

Since very ancient times, the countries of the South Asian sub-region and China have been known as the main producers and exporters of primary commodities. Long before the advent of large European merchant companies in the seventeenth and eighteenth centuries, the Greeks and Romans were well acquainted with Indian merchandise and direct commerce developed between Europe and the western seaports of India.[a] From Ptolemy's map, the Greeks are considered to have travelled as far as the South-East Asian peninsula in search of gold and ivory.

With the spread of Islam and the maritime supremacy of the Arabs, direct contacts with Europe were interrupted but trade continued to develop via three routes: the first north via the Don and Volga towards the Baltic Sea and the Hanse towns of northern Germany; the second in the centre via the Persian Gulf and the Middle East ending by sea in Genoa, Venice or Constantinople, and finally the southern route via the Red Sea, the Nile and Alexandria. Because of the necessary long overland journeys, only less bulky merchandise could be transported and the "East" became known as the land of silks, spices and precious stones.[b]

At the same time regional trade developed rapidly in Asia between the east coast of India and the western shores of Sumatra, Java, Bali and the Malaysian peninsula. Chinese traders had traded with Malaysia since pre-Christian times and had settled in Malacca by 1400 A.D., while Arab traders were based in Sumatra.

However, Europe's trade with the Asian and Pacific region really started to expand significantly with the rise of the merchant class in Europe and the emergence of some European nation-states as the foremost maritime powers in the world.[c] The fifteenth century saw some significant improvements in shipbuilding and navigation techniques, as the overland trading routes to India became increasingly threatened and the attraction of the "riches" of India grew stronger. The main breakthrough came with the discovery of the Cape of Good Hope route by Vasco da Gama in 1498. The trade in spices from India and the islands of Sumatra and Java was the major commodity trade at that time. A century later, the British and the Dutch created their East Indian companies and intensified their trade in the region.

The spice trade was practically a monopoly of the Dutch throughout the seventeenth century. Other main commodities traded both within the region and with Europe were indigo, raw silk, calicoes, textiles, saltpetre, rice, gangetic opium, porcelain, ebony as well as tea, tobacco, sugar and cotton.

The development of trade was also accompanied by the expansion of European colonialism all over Asia; trade also became monopolized by European powers, and Asian traders – particularly Indian traders –

were driven out. The Dutch traded mainly with Indonesia but were also established in Gujarat (India), Bengal and Sri Lanka (then Ceylon).[d] Large Asian cities such as Calcutta, Dhaka, Goa, Madras, Canton and Bombay are associated with the expansion of commodity trade during this period.

As trade with South-East Asia and the Far East, in particular China, developed, other major trading settlements were established such as Penang in 1786. While "China trade" involved tea, porcelain and silk, while the South-East Asia trade involved mainly tin, coconut oil, gambier, nutmeg, pepper and cloves. This trade was partly financed through the imports of European cloth, woolens and cottons as well as other manufactured goods.

The so-called "China trade" was further boosted by the founding of the free port of Singapore in 1819 by Sir Stamford Raffles. Very rapidly Singapore became a centre for regional entrepôt trade, with commodities from all over East and South-East Asia being brought there by Chinese merchants and other "country" vessels for trans-shipment to India or Europe. The abolition of the East India Company's monopoly on British "China trade" in 1813 played a major role in the rapid growth of the port of Singapore. Officers of the East India Company could no longer trade on their own account and received a fixed salary. However, this restriction was applied only to shipments to and from China's ports and not on those destined for or coming from ports in South-East Asia. Hence, trans-shipment to East India ships in Singapore became very profitable. Regional trade between India and East Asia, mainly China, was already very important at that time, as was com-

[a] Hugh Murray, *History of British India* (London, T. Nelson and Sons, 1860).

[b] A.L.A. Morton, *People's History of England* (London, Lawrence & Wishart, 1951).

[c] R.H. Tawney, *Religion and the Rise of Capitalism* (London, Pelican Books, 1948).

[d] Maurice Dobb, *Studies in the Development of Capitalism* (London, George Routledge & Sons, Ltd., 1946).

pletely homogeneous. There may, of course, be quality differences, such as between different varieties of rice, cotton or different grades of iron ore, or differences in consumer preferences for different types of mangoes, pineapples or wheat. However, these can be produced, by and large, by any producer, given climatic and other production constraints. On the other hand, most manufactured goods have a high degree of product differentiation — increasingly reflected in designer clothes and other high fashion goods. As a result, much of the primary production is carried out under conditions of perfect competition with costs being the main determinant of prices, while the market for manufactured goods is generally non-competitive to some extent. These differences manifest themselves in the ability of individual firms in manufacturing to protect themselves from falling demand and prices for a particular category of goods (such as cigarettes), whereas the effect is more generalized on the primary producers (such as tobacco).

The weak bargaining power at the micro level of commodities also is reflected in the vulnerability of most primary-producing developing economies at the macro-economic level. Although there is generally no presumption that cyclical fluctuations discriminate against or in favour of primary-producing countries, the macro-economic consequences of these fluctuations are highly asymmetric.[4]

The fact that primary commodities trade is much more susceptible to instability than trade in manufactures produces asymmetric macro-economic effects. Thus while commodity price increases cause inflationary pressures in developed countries because of real wage resistance and lead to restrictive macro-economic policies causing a contraction of aggregate demand, the fall in commodity prices does not lead to an expansion of aggregate demand in developed market economies. First, since the demand for primary commodities, as raw materials, is partly a derived demand as their prices can be delinked with final product prices with little impact of fall of input prices on demand for final products. Second, as has been evidenced by the experience in 1980, the fall in commodity prices, despite causing a substantial reduction in the rate of inflation in developed market economies, has not led to a reversal of the restrictive monetary policies of those economies and of the contractionary fiscal stance in Europe and Japan. On the other hand, the developing countries, in view of their worsening foreign exchange earnings position, are "frequently compelled to sell competitively on a falling market ... in the face of a limited number of financially strong buyers in developed countries who postpone purchases in the expectation of lower prices".[5] The external financial difficulties of the developing countries since the early 1980s, which have been caused by lower inflows of capital and the increasing debt-servicing burden, have further underscored this asymmetry.

Another asymmetrical effect at the macro-economic level related to the cyclical nature of primary commodity trade, arises through the emergence of balance-of-payments difficulties during both commodity booms and recessions. It is evident that non-oil commodity producing countries have

modity trade with South-East Asia. Rice, rattans and spices were increasingly important commodity exports within the region.

Throughout the nineteenth century, numerous new commodities were discovered and traded, for instance, antimony from Borneo and Guttapercha or "Jelutong", a type of rubber, from Borneo, Sumatra and the Malaysian peninsula. Demand for rubber expended rapidly, in particular for producing telegraph cables in Europe. Coffee was also produced on a large scale in Malaysia, but the Asian coffee market collapsed towards the end of the nineteenth century (1894) as Brazilian coffee flooded the market. However, a few seedlings of rubber brought from Brazil some years earlier in 1876 resulted in a major transformation in South-East Asian commodity-producing economies, making rubber a major export commodity for Malaysia and Indonesia, particularly from the beginning of the twentieth century. Another important commodity, palm oil, had been first planted in Java in 1859. However, commercial-scale production and trade of palm oil started only in 1910, first in Sumatra and soon afterwards in Malaya.[e]

This brief account of the evolution of commodity production and trade in the Asian and Pacific region provides a perspective on its historical importance. Not only has the region the longest tradition in commodity trade across national frontiers but throughout the centuries it has consistently shown a remarkable capacity for introducing new primary products and exports. While the importance of some traditional commodities is declining, the trade continues to thrive on the introduction of new and exotic primary commodities.

_____

[e] Sjovald Cunyngham-Brown, *The Traders* (London, Newman Neame, 1971).

_____

[4] See D.M.G. Newberry and J.E. Stiglitz, *The Theory of Commodity Price Stabilization — A Study in the Economics of Risk* (Oxford University Press, 1981); and S.M. Ravi Kanbur, "How to analyse commodity price stabilisation?: a review article", *Oxford Economic Papers,* vol. 36, No. 3 (November 1984), pp. 336-358.

_____

[5] D. Avramovic, "Commodity problem: what next?" *World Development,* vol. 15, No. 5 (Oxford, Pergamon Journals Ltd., May 1987), pp. 645-655.

suffered large balance-of-payments deficits during the commodity booms of the 1970s when the favourable effects on balance of payments were largely negated by the much steeper rise in oil prices, and during the continuing commodity slumps of the 1980s when the fall in primary commodity prices was not offset by that in oil prices.[6] However, some developing countries, mainly those in the western hemisphere, did benefit from the recycling of large surpluses of major oil-exporting countries in the 1970s. During the slump in commodity prices since 1980, the balance-of-payments surpluses have accrued largely to some developed countries. Unfortunately, these surpluses have been used largely to finance the large current account deficit of the United States, rather than the deficits of the developing countries (see box I.1, part I, p. 2).

There is also an asymmetry between trade in primary commodities and trade in manufactures in terms of the trade barriers and regulations imposed on them by developed and developing countries. While the developed countries give significantly greater protection to their primary sector than to their manufacturing sector, the reverse is the case for developing countries — where the primary sector is often taxed rather than subsidized. The asymmetry goes even further. In many developed countries, agriculture is highly

protected and it was explicitly excluded from the discipline of GATT from the very beginning. Conversely, many developing countries have not only followed a policy of protecting industry but have often done so at the expense of neglecting their agriculture sector. This asymmetry is at the heart of the difficulty which developing countries are faced with in accepting demands for "reciprocity" in GATT negotiations on agriculture.

C. CHANGING PERCEPTIONS ABOUT TRADE IN PRIMARY COMMODITIES

During the post Second World War period, perceptions about the prospects of primary commodities in the world economy have undergone considerable changes. Before 1970 the world view of the prospects of primary commodities was broadly in accord with Prebisch's hypothesis of a secular trend in declining terms of trade of primary commodities.[7] The predictions of the classical economists about a rise in price of food relative to manufactures did not come about as the rise in productivity of temperate agriculture offset diminishing returns to land while Engel effects moderated food demand.

However, around 1970, a number of major developments significantly changed perceptions about the adequacy of resources to sustain the demand for primary commodities in the growing world economy. The commodity boom of 1973-1979 resulted in an annual rate of growth in the prices of non-fuel primary commodities of 7.8

per cent in terms of dollars and 6.7 per cent in terms of special drawing rights. In real terms, however, the prices declined at an average of 2.6 per cent per annum. Moreover, the rise in nominal prices was concentrated in tropical beverages (tea, coffee and cocoa), which grew by an average of 22.8 per cent per annum, with much slower growth in the prices of agricultural raw materials (7.5 per cent) and mineral ores and metals (5.7 per cent). Food prices declined at the rate of 2.9 per cent per annum, notwithstanding a yearly increase of 4.4 per cent in the prices of vegetable oil-seeds and oils (see table II.1).

Although the nominal prices of primary commodities increased substantially during the 1970s, the fluctuations in the prices were much larger. According to an International Monetary Fund (IMF) estimate, during 1972 to 1982 the price instability of non-fuel primary commodity prices was more than threefold that from 1957 to 1971.[8] This was especially true of raw materials, whose prices fluctuated much more sharply in response to changes in industrial production after 1971. The sharp rise in prices in 1972-1974 was followed by an almost equally sharp fall in 1974-1975 and a recovery in later 1975 and in 1976 and again, after a sharp fall, by a sharp rise in 1978 accompanying the second oil shock. These fluctuations were fed by changing expectations concerning inflation far more than by changes in real demand.[9]

Expectations about emerging

[6] The oil-exporting countries did, of course, accumulate large current account surpluses during the 1970s. Their problems characterized by the "Dutch disease" consisted mainly of the reduced competitiveness, created through a rise in exchange rate consequent on the windfall gains in export revenues, of non-oil exports; see, for instance, W.M. Corden and J.P. Neary, "Booming sector and de-industrialization in a small open economy", *Economic Journal* (December 1982), pp. 825-848.

[7] For a comprehensive review of the literature, see David Evans, "The long-run determinants of North-South terms of trade and some recent empirical evidence", *World Development,* vol. 15, No. 5 (Oxford, Pergamon Journals Ltd., May 1987), pp. 657-671.

[8] See K.Y. Chu and T.K. Morrison, "The 1981-82 recession and non-oil primary commodity prices", *International Monetary Fund Staff Papers,* vol. 31, No. 1 (March 1984), p. 94.

[9] N. Kaldor, "The role of commodity prices in economic recovery", *Lloyds Bank Review* (July 1983).

Table II.1. Trends[a] in prices of various groups of non-fuel primary commodities, selected periods

(Annual percentage rate of change)

Commodity	1973–1979	1980–1986[b]	1962–1980
Food and beverages	9.1	−4.5	9.3
Food	−2.9	−11.4	8.0
of which:			
Vegetable oil-seeds and oils	4.4	−5.2	7.2
Tropical beverages	22.8	1.3	10.0
Agricultural raw materials	7.5	−5.0	7.4
Minerals, ores and metals	5.7	−6.1	6.9
All non-fuel primary commodities:			
in current dollars	7.8	−4.8	8.2
in terms of special drawing rights	6.7	−2.0	6.5
in real terms[c]	−2.6	−3.9	1.3

Source: UNCTAD, *Revitalizing Development, Growth and International Trade: Assessment and Policy Options* (United Nations publication, Sales No. E.87.II.D.7), annex table 16.

[a] The growth rate for each period has been calculated using the following formula: Log p = a + bt, where p is the price index and t is time. [b] For 1986, commodity prices are an average of the first 9 months and the deflator is that of the first half of the year. [c] Nominal price index deflated by the United Nations index of export unit value of manufactured goods exported by developed market-economy countries (1980=100).

shortages in resource-based primary commodities played an important role in the commodity boom, which was triggered by oil price increases in the early 1970s (see figure II.1). In the 1960s, the prices of primary commodities remained subdued and there were no signs of any significant upturn in them. Indeed oil prices were declining

and the formation of the Organization of the Petroleum Exporting Countries (OPEC) in 1960 was mainly to resist the downward pressure on prices resulting from overproduction by the major oil companies.[10] Non-oil primary commodities, after experiencing a transitory boom in the early 1950s as a result of the Korean conflict, were also declining between 1963 and 1972.

However, with the change in the status of the United States from a substantial self-sufficiency in oil supplies to substantial import dependence around 1970 and the well-publicized apocalyptic findings of such studies as Forester's *World Dynamics*[11] and Meadows' *The Limits of Growth*,[12] the perceptions about primary commodities dramatically changed. Continuing economic growth in the developed countries and population growth in the developing countries raised the spectre of serious raw materials and food shortages in the foreseeable future. These factors began to dominate the formation of price expectation and were reinforced by such factors as holding stocks off the market, the upsurge in economic activity in industrial countries in 1972-1973 and the rise in interest rates in 1969-1970 and 1972-1973. These developments culminated in the sharp increase in 1973 in prices of oil, which also gave rise to similar — though considerably less steep — increases in the prices of other commodities.

The sharp increase in the prices of oil and other primary commodi-

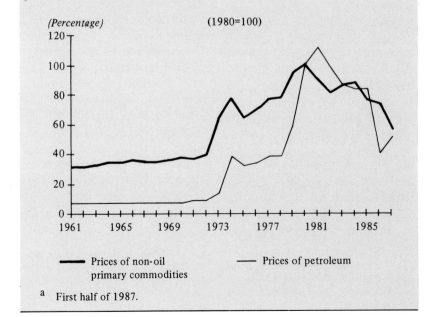

Figure II.1. Movements in the price indices of petroleum and non-oil primary commodities, 1961-1987[a]

(Percentage)   (1980=100)

— Prices of non-oil primary commodities

— Prices of petroleum

[a] First half of 1987.

[10] See P. Dasgupta and G.M. Heal, *Economic Theory and Exhaustible Resources* (Oxford University Press, 1979), pp. 438-455.

[11] J.W. Forrester, *World Dynamics* (Wright Allen Press, 1971).

[12] D.H. Meadows and others, *The Limits of Growth* (New York, Universe Books, 1971).

ties in early 1973 changed the perceptions about the profitability of producing primary commodities. This led to an expansion in their outputs and in the case of oil and minerals in the increase in exploration and production capacity. The area under cultivation of a number of these commodities (sugar, coffee, tea, rice and cotton, for example) increased substantially in the 1970s in response to high prices as compared with the 1960s.

Since 1980, however, the prices of primary commodities have been on a downward trend and have failed to recover or even stabilize at a lower level, except for a brief period between 1983 and 1984. By early 1987, real commodity prices had fallen to a level 40 per cent below those in 1980.[13] The pendulum has swung back beyond the 1970 position and the world is again faced with commodity pessimism as in the 1950s and 1960s. Indeed, there seems to be continuing downward pressures in most commodity markets and it seems unlikely that the current perceptions about the long-term prospects of primary commodities will change soon. Indeed, one analyst has compared the current commodity crisis with that of the great depression of the late 1920s for having "had the strongest and longest lasting negative impact on nominal commodity prices".[14]

The predominant perception about commodity prices is that of "glut" rather than "scarcity". According to the World Bank, until 1990 supplies are likely to be abundant and demand rather weak. Even by 1990, real prices are not likely to recover to the levels prevailing in 1985. While some strengthening is expected in the first half of the 1990s, the World Bank predicts this not to last beyond 1995 "due to continuing productivity increases, the long-term declining trends in the prices of most commodities should reassert themselves".[15] However, in 1987 there was a limited improvement in commodity prices, especially in minerals and metals (see box II.2), which called for some reassessment of these predictions.

D. STRUCTURAL CHANGES IN PRIMARY COMMODITY TRADE: 1970-1986

The annual value of world non-fuel commodity exports has risen from about $103.9 billion in 1970 to $399.8 billion in 1985, or by about 10 per cent per annum. However as a percentage of total world exports, their share has declined from 37.5 to about 26.7 per cent.

For developing countries, the share of non-oil export earnings has fallen from one half to less than one fifth of their total export earnings between 1970 and 1985 mainly owing to increases from petroleum and manufacture exports. The developed market economies, which accounted for about 55.8 per cent of the world's non-oil primary commodity exports during 1966-1967, increased their share to 62.8 per cent in 1983-1984. The share of developing countries correspondingly fell from 33.9 to 30.9 per cent, while that of East European socialist countries also fell from 8.6 to 5.3 per cent.[16]

In terms of imports of non-oil primary commodities, however, the share of developed market economies declined from 72 to 67 per cent, while that of developing countries correspondingly increased from 18 to 23 per cent during the decade. The largest change in primary commodity trade shares occurred in the case of European countries, which increased their export shares from 26.5 to 33.2 per cent and reduced their import shares from 49.0 to 39.4 per cent during 1966-1967 to 1983-1984.

The most noticeable change in the composition of non-oil primary commodity trade during the last two decades has been a marked increase in the share of food items (from 56 per cent in 1966-1967 to 62 per cent in 1983-1984). This increase has been mainly at the expense of agricultural raw materials which have fallen from 20 to 15 per cent, while the share of minerals and metals has remained unchanged. These changes reflect partly relative price movements — the prices of food rising most and those of minerals and metals rising the least — and partly the effect of differential rates of increase in the degree of local processing.

Significant changes have also occurred in the direction of trade in primary commodities (see table II.2) of developing countries during the last decade. The market share of developed market economies in the primary commodity exports of developing countries declined from 70.8 per cent in 1973-1974 to 60.0 per cent in 1983-1984, while their share in primary commodity imports remained almost unchanged. The absorption of developing countries food exports in developed market economies

[13] IMF, *Annual Report 1987* (Washington, D.C., 1987).

[14] E.R. Grilli and M.C. Yang, "Long-term movements of non-fuel commodity prices: 1900-1983" (Washington, D.C., World Bank, 1986).

[15] World Bank, *Price Prospects for Major Primary Commodities,* Report No. 814, vol. 1 (Washington, D.C., October 1986), p. 35.

[16] Figures in this section are based on UNCTAD, *Revitalizing Development, Growth and International Trade: Assessment and Policy Options* (United Nations publication, Sales No.E.87.II.D.7).

declined markedly from 70.0 per cent in 1973-1974 to 56.1 per cent in 1983-1984, reflecting largely the impact of their recent policies to increase output and reduce imports of agricultural products. The largest fall was in cereals and oils and oil-seeds, in which shares of developing country exports to developed market economies fell from 37.0 to 12.4 per cent and from 81.3 to 46.8 per cent, respectively, between 1973-1974 and 1983-1984. The importance of developed market economies for exports from developing countries of agricultural raw materials and mineral ores and metals has declined to a lesser extent.

There has been a considerable increase in the importance of South-South trade in primary commodities. The share of the developing countries' exports of primary

---

Box II.2.   The rise in commodity prices in 1987

There was some cause for optimism and hope among commodity producers as prices of many primary commodities began to rise in 1987 after reaching in 1986 their lowest levels in many years. The overall index of commodity prices rose by 9.6 per cent between December 1986 and August 1987. Prices of agricultural raw materials (19.2 per cent) and metals (23.9 per cent) recorded the highest rise during the period. Prices of food products registered a rise of 4.9 per cent but those of beverages fell by 17.7 per cent. However, the overall index based on 1980 stood at 77.6 in August (see table below) and despite increases from the very low levels of the past year, almost all prices, with the exception of some metals and minerals, were still below their cyclical highs. The prices in 1987 were also lower than their levels during the short-lived boom that the commodity market experienced in 1983-1984.

The upturn in 1987 did not strongly indicate a basic change in the downward trend in prices observed since 1980. Most forecasters predicted that the trend would continue into the 1990s. Apart from the sharp depreciation of the United States dollar since 1985, there was little change in the world economic situation which could explain the upturn in the prices in 1987 or which could be expected to lead to a sustained upward trend. The October 1987 stock market crash caused further uncertainties for the world economy and the weakening of commodity markets. The depreciation of the dollar failed to arrest the fall of commodity prices in 1985 and 1986. It may, however, have had its belated effects in 1987. The unevenness in the rise of commodity prices suggested that the explanations perhaps lay in micro-economic or structural causes specific to particular commodity markets.

The strongest rise in prices was in the case of some metals and minerals, especially copper, aluminium and nickel which experienced a fall in reserves and decline in production capacity, sharply pushing up their prices. The recovery in copper prices which had been depressed for years was indeed phenomenal, almost doubling during the year. Nickel prices also rose sharply during 1987 but began falling in early 1988. Aluminium prices rose more steadily during the year but showed some signs of weakening again towards the end of the year. On the other hand, supply overhang since the market collapse in 1985 kept the tin prices depressed. Iron ore prices remained similarly depressed.

Among raw materials, cotton made strong gains in prices in 1987, after significant cuts in production and inventories occurred in 1986-1987 following the steady decline in prices that took place between 1984 and 1986. There was an increase in rubber demand following strong performance of the auto industry, the increasing scare about the Acquired Immune Deficiency Syndrome (AIDS) and a rise in the cost of synthetic rubber following some recovery in oil prices. Demand was also favourably affected owing to strong construction activities in Japan.

Food, beverages and edible oil prices, except for palm oil, generally remained soft. Prices of wheat rose somewhat in expectation of lower production in the Union of Soviet Socialist Republics and that country's large purchase recently from the United States of America. The USSR crop estimate was subsequently revised upwards, stocks remained high and the upward drift in prices was halted. Corn prices fell further from their 1986 level. Production shortfall in Australia, Burma, Indonesia, Pakistan and Thailand was the main cause of the recovery of rice prices, which had bottomed out in the first quarter of 1987. Sugar prices, after recovering somewhat in the first quarter of 1987, stabilized and even declined later in response to expectations of higher production in several countries. Coffee and cocoa prices fell in response to larger supplies and difficulties in reaching agreements on the extension of their commodity agreements.

Recent evolution of commodity prices

(Index 1980 = 100 and percentages)

Item	December 1986	August 1987	Percentage change
Food	61.6	64.6	4.9
Beverages	83.7	68.9	−17.7
Agricultural raw materials	85.5	101.9	19.2
Metals	66.1	81.9	23.9
Global index	70.8	77.6	9.6

Source: F.G. Adams and J. Vial, "Factor influencing recent commodity price movements", paper presented at the Regional Seminar on an Interlinked Country Model System, sixth session, 17-20 November 1987, Bangkok.

Table II.2. Commodity exports and imports of developing countries by destination and origin, selected periods

Commodity group	Destination of exports (Percentage of exports to the world)				Origin of imports (Percentage of imports from the world)				Composition of commodity trade among developing countries (Percentage)	
	Developed market economy countries		Developing countries		Developed market economy countries		Developing countries			
	1973–1974[a]	1983–1984	1973–1974	1983–1984	1973–1974	1983–1984	1973–1974	1983–1984	1973–1974	1983–1984
I. Food and beverages of which:	70.0	56.1	19.4	26.5	62.1	60.9	27.6	30.9	60.4	67.7
Cereals[b]	37.0	12.4	51.7	58.2	76.5	75.4	17.4	22.5	14.1	14.0
Tropical beverages[c]	83.6	78.7	8.2	16.0	6.9	6.9	84.4	80.7	5.6	3.8
Oils and oil-seeds[d]	81.3	46.8	14.6	43.5	68.2	53.6	25.3	40.8	5.4	12.1
II. Agricultural raw materials	61.5	56.9	22.9	31.1	46.9	50.1	45.6	38.8	27.1	20.7
III. Mineral ores and metals	81.6	76.5	10.1	15.7	63.1	62.7	32.9	30.4	12.5	11.6
Total non-fuel primary commodities	70.8	60.0	18.1	25.3	59.4	59.3	31.6	32.2	100.0	100.0

Source: UNCTAD, *Revitalizing Development, Growth and International Trade: Assessment and Policy Options* (United Nations publication, Sales No. E.87.II.D.7), annex table 20.

[a] Use of hyphen between dates representing years, e.g., 1973-1974, signifies the full period involved, including the initial and final years.   [b] SITC 041 to 045.   [c] Coffee, cocoa and tea: SITC 071 + 072 + 074.   [d] SITC 22 + 4.

commodities destined for other developing countries has increased from 18.1 to 25.3 per cent during the last decade, with oils and oil-seeds and agricultural raw materials showing the highest increase. However, the developing countries have not been able to significantly increase their share in the imports of primary commodities from other developing countries, which has remained unchanged at around 32 per cent over the last decade. Nevertheless, with increasing industrialization and the higher raw material use intensity of industrial production as well as the higher income elasticities of demand for food in developing countries, the importance of commodity trade among these countries can be expected to rise, if adequate supplies can be ensured.

E. FACTORS AFFECTING SLOW GROWTH IN PRIMARY COMMODITY TRADE

Aggregative analysis of primary commodities is useful only in iden-

tifying the general trends and is not very helpful in revealing the policy options available to different countries and for different commodities.[17]   Only a detailed and disaggregated analysis can uncover the complexity of underlying forces at work in commodity markets. However, there are certain common factors affecting all primary commodities and producing countries, which can be identified at an aggregate level and can be helpful in formulating policy options at a disaggregated level.

The recent trends in primary commodity trade — the declining prices and earnings, increased instability, falling shares of developing countries, decreasing importance of developed market economies for developing countries' primary com-

[17] For a recent analysis of primary commodity exports from developing countries see M.E. Bond, "An econometric study of primary commodity exports from developing country regions to the world", *International Monetary Fund Staff Papers*, vol. 34, No. 2 (June 1987) pp. 191-227.

modity exports and the emerging importance of South-South trade — can be explained in terms of broad developments by three main factors: demand, supply and technological changes. The last factor affects the other two but it may be better for analytical and policy purposes to consider each of them separately.

1. Demand factors

The major determinant of demand for primary commodities is the rate of growth of the world economy. For more than a decade and a half, especially since 1980, the rate of growth of the world economy has slowed down perceptibly. The growth of world GDP, which averaged above 5 per cent per annum during 1963-1972, slowed down to 3.6 per cent during the rest of the 1970s and fell to below 2 per cent during 1980-1986. The period has also been marked by two severe recessions, in 1975 and in 1981-1982. Moreover, the spread of growth, especially during the 1980s, has been very uneven, among both developed and developing countries. These factors have undoubtedly exercised a considerable depressing effect on the demand for primary commodities in recent years (see figure II.2).

A second major factor affecting the demand for primary commodities is the structural shift in many developed market economies away from the manufacturing sector, which is the most intensive user of primary commodities as raw materials. The growth elasticity of industrial production in developed market economies fell from 1.1 during 1960-1972 to 0.7 during 1973-1984. The sector mainly responsible for GDP growth in the period from 1973 to 1984 was services. In recent years a striking phenomenon in many European countries has been the emergence of agriculture as the fastest growing sector — a somewhat unusual evolution in the post-industrial society. Thus the agricultural

sector in Europe grew at the rate of 3 per cent per annum during 1980-1985, almost double its average rate of GDP growth during the period. In many countries, the rate of agricultural growth was several times more rapid than GDP growth.[18] This development is, of course, related to the growing protectionism and subsidization of agriculture in Europe and other developed market economies, which is discussed below.

Not only is the manufacturing sector expanding less rapidly than other sectors in developed market economies, available evidence also suggests that growth within manufacturing industries is concentrated in those industries which are less raw material intensive. In the period from 1973 to 1984, the relatively more raw-material-intensive industries such as textiles, wearing apparel and leather, wood

and furniture and basic metals, recorded zero or negative growth, whereas the high growth industries such as those producing industrial robots, computers, consumer electronics and telecommunication were those where relatively little raw materials are used. These developments have led some observers to believe that the raw materials economy has become "uncoupled" from the industrial economy.[19]

In recent years, some of the raw-material-intensive industries have been relocated to developing countries in view of their lower labour costs. To the extent that the income elasticity of consumption of raw materials is higher in developing countries this should have some offsetting influence on the decline in the demand for raw materials. However, since many

[18] See *The Economist*, 3-9 October 1987, p. 82.

[19] See Peter F. Drucker, "The changed world economy", *Foreign Affairs*, vol. 64, No. 4 (Spring 1986), pp. 771-775.

Figure II.2. Major developed market economies. Share of commodity imports from developing economies and growth of GDP, selected periods

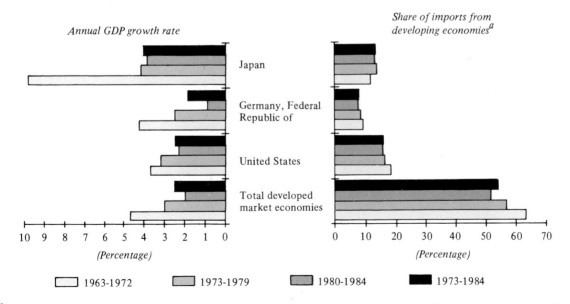

| | 1963-1972 | 1973-1979 | 1980-1984 | 1973-1984 |

[a] Commodity imports from developing economies into selected developed market economies as a percentage of total world commodity imports from developing economies.

of these industries change their location frequently in search of cheap labour and tax concessions, this makes for higher instability in the pattern of consumption of raw materials. Nevertheless, this source of strengthening the demand for primary commodities needs to be tapped further and taken greater advantage of by developing countries, perhaps, in collaboration with developed market economies and transnational corporations.

2. Protectionism

A major impediment to the growth in international demand for primary commodities has been the emergence of a new wave of protectionism in many developed market economies. This has taken two main forms: (a) measures to assist domestic production against competitive imports of agricultural commodities, and (b) measures to raise border prices of imports through (i) tariff barriers, (ii) import quotas, and (iii) non-tariff barriers. Huge amounts have been spent by developed market economies to subsidize a wide range of primary commodities, in particular agriculture. For example, in the four-year period ending 1985, the United States and EEC are estimated to have spent about $60 billion each on agricultural support programmes, while Japan spent $51 billion during 1980-1983.[20] These budgetary expenditure are in addition to costs of income transfers from consumers to producers through higher domestic prices.

The effect of these fiscal measures on developing countries is twofold, affecting both demand and suppply of primary commodities. They reduce the demand for developing countries exports and often lead to export surpluses which compete with the latter in third countries. Both these effects contribute to sharp declines in prices. Subsidized exports from developed countries have affected developing country exports of meat, sugar, wheat, rice, cotton and edible oils in recent years.[21]

Tariffs are an important barrier to trade for a number of primary commodities and are considerably high on coffee, tea, processed meat and fish, fresh and preserved vegetables and fruits, sugar, spun silk, yarn and woven fabrics, processed aluminium and copper. Import quotas have been placed on a number of commodities, particularly those which compete with domestic production and include such commodities as sugar, oilseeds, grains, meat and raw silk.

Non-tariff measures are widely prevalent against imports of primary commodities into developed market economies. Meat, dairy products, sugar, tobacco, mushrooms and fruits and vegetables are among the commodities most severely affected by such measures as import quotas (global and bilateral), seasonal tariffs and quotas, discretionary import licensing, health and sanitary regulations as well as outright prohibition. There is, however, considerable scope for developing countries to overcome many of these barriers through quality control, following the specifications of developed countries and understanding their genuine concerns about health and environment.

3. Increasing pressures on supply of primary commodities

The current "commodity crisis" is perceived by some as mainly a problem of supply glut or supply bias created largely by the inability of developing countries to adjust supplies to the changing patterns of world demand. The preoccupation of developing countries with expanding supplies, and maintaining market shares and foreign exchange earnings from their primary commodity exports has often proved counter-productive and has led to even greater declines in prices and increased dependence on primary commodities. However, as was pointed out earlier, the increase in the supply of commodities, especially agricultural products, is largely the creation of developed countries. Nevertheless, it is well-known that in recent years the developing countries, especially in the ESCAP region, have also been able to expand outputs of primary commodities at a rate much higher than can be absorbed at existing levels of domestic demand. However, there is considerable room for expansion of this demand through growth and redistribution of income. Indeed, since the growth in the demand for most primary commodities either significantly decelerated in the 1980s, compared with the 1970s, or became negative, any increase in the rate of growth of production was likely to have increased downward pressure on prices. A qualitative difference in the supply pressure created in the 1980s and that which occurred in earlier periods is that the current supply pressures are not the result of random factors, such as good harvests, but of systematic increases brought about either by policy-induced factors or by technological changes.

An analysis of aggregate data shown in table II.3 confirms, in

---

[20] See *Economic Report of the President* (Washington, D.C., United States Government Printing Office, 1986), p. 30 for the United States, Commission of the European Countries, *The Agricultural Situation in the Country, 1985 Report* (Brussels, Luxembourg, 1986) for EEC and S.J. Anjaria and others, *Trade Policy Issues and Developments,* Occasional Paper No. 38 (Washington, D.C., IMF, July 1985).

[21] For a more detailed discussion of these policies and their impact on ESCAP developing countries, see chapter V.

Table II.3. Rates of change in prices, world exports, production and consumption of various categories of primary commodities of interest to developing countries, 1980-1984

(Percentage per annum)

Commodity	Prices[a]	Exports[b] Growth rate	Exports[b] Change in rate[c]	Production Growth rate	Production Change in rate[c]	Consumption Growth rate	Consumption Change in rate[c]	Percentage share of developing countries in world exports (1983-1984)
Group I: Commodities whose rate of growth of production increased in comparison with 1973-1979								
Food								
Sugar	−34.0	0.8	−2.5	3.9	0.5	2.7	−0.9	75
Rice	−15.0	−2.0	−8.0	4.3	1.8	2.9	0.7	49
Fish and products	−6.1	2.3	−3.6	3.6	1.5	...	...	41
Tea	10.7	2.4	−0.5	4.3	0.1	3.4	−0.5	76
Wheat	−10.8	3.7	1.8	4.1	0.8	2.7	0.1	8
Agricultural raw materials								
Cotton	−3.2	−2.5	−2.7	4.3	4.3	1.6	0.4	40
Rubber	−8.3	2.7	1.9	2.8	1.0	3.1	1.2	97
Sisal	−6.4	−4.6	6.4	−4.9	4.0	−5.3	4.4	97
Minerals, ores and metals								
Copper ore	−9.8	0.6	0.5	1.1	0.3	1.2	0.6	68
Group II: Commodities whose rate of growth of production decreased in comparison with 1973-1979								
Food								
Cocoa	−1.5	2.6	5.7	−1.0	−2.4	3.4	4.8	75
Coffee	−1.1	3.5	4.2	0.8	−0.9	1.7	1.5	92
Maize	−5.6	−4.5	−12.0	−0.2	−5.2	−1.0	−5.7	15
Bovine meat	−4.0	−0.3	−5.6	2.0	−1.0	1.3	−4.5	14
Bananas	0.4	−1.3	−2.2	0.6	−2.4	−0.5	−2.8	90
Vegetable oil-seeds and oils	3.4	2.7	−4.7	3.4	−1.2	...	...	...
Agricultural raw materials								
Jute	12.5	−3.5	5.5	−2.9	−5.6	−2.6	−2.5	87
Minerals, ores and metals								
Refined copper	−9.5	1.7	0.4	0.6	−0.7	0.3	−2.7	55
Tin ore	−6.9	−2.4	1.9	−6.1	−7.4	−6.0	−7.8	62
Aluminium	−5.5	16.1	3.2	−1.1	−3.7	1.3	−1.8	11
Phosphate rock	−9.5	−1.6	−1.7	1.5	−2.9	...	...	59
Tin metal	−6.9	15.1	−16.0	−5.2	−6.2	−1.3	−0.1	85
Alumina	−2.7	−1.7	−6.1	−0.8	−3.6	−0.6	−3.3	29
Bauxite	−2.7	−3.0	−4.3	−1.1	−3.5	−1.3	−3.8	83
Iron ore	−3.3	−2.4	−2.0	−2.7	−4.2	−2.9	−4.5	62

Source: UNCTAD, *Revitalizing Development, Growth and International Trade: Assessment and Policy Options* (United Nations publication, Sales No. E.87.II.D.7), table II.9.

Note: The growth rates have been calculated as in table II.1.

[a] World free market prices, except for copper ore, alumina and bauxite, which are unit values of exports from developing countries.   [b] Including re-exports.   [c] Difference between the rates of change in 1980-1984 and 1973-1979.

general, the tendency of prices of commodities, the annual rate of growth of world production of which in 1980-1984 period exceeded that in 1973-1979, to have fallen much more sharply than those the growth rates of which were lower in the latter periods. The commodities in the first group are sugar, rice, fish and fish products, tea and wheat in the food group, cotton, rubber and sisal in agricultural raw materials and copper ore among minerals.[22] Consumption and stocks also generally rose for these commodities.

The commodities for which output growth rates during 1980-1984 were smaller than in 1973-1979 were cocoa, coffee, maize, bovine meat, bananas, vegetable oils and oil-seeds and jute among agricultural produce and a variety of minerals and metals, for which prices rose or fell less sharply than in the first group. However, the relationship between the degree of price falls and the increase in growth rates of output is not a simple one and needs more detailed and rigorous econometric analysis. It does seem, however, to support the conjecture that supply increases are the main factor affecting fall in the prices of most agricultural commodities. Minerals and metals generally tend to adjust to demand conditions much better.

There are a number of reasons why developing countries have not been successful in adjusting supplies to changes in demand, apart from the usual explanation in terms of low elasticities of supply at the micro-economic level. Much of the

supply pressure generated in the early 1980s was in the nature of lingering perceptions about commodity scarcities generated in the 1970s, which was discussed in section B. Both developed and developing countries undertook large investments to increase production capacity, especially in mining. The expectations about high prices brought many marginal producers into the market, while hopes for continuing growth in developed market economies raised expectations of higher demand for commodities. Both these expectations largely failed to materialize in the early 1980s.

An overwhelming reason for many developing countries to expand supplies of primary commodities for exports since 1980 has been to overcome the balance-of-payments problems caused by declining commodity prices. In order to meet their foreign exchange needs for imports and debt servicing, they had to increase the volume of exports in the face of falling prices. Many countries have attempted to achieve this through devaluation of their currencies. When this is done for the same commodity or same set of commodities by a large number of competing exporters, it results in the "fallacy of composition", not unlike the case of exports of manufactures, and leads to not only a fall in prices but also restrictive action by importing developed market economies.

Other sources of supply pressures come from the fact that most primary-producing economies, especially in Asia, consist of small independent producers who seldom have a co-ordinated response to changes in market demand. The small farmers, because of the high initial costs of their investment in plantation crops such as rubber and palm oil, find it difficult to switch to other crops or activities or to withhold their output from

the market. They can also absorb some of the decline in prices as the ratio of fixed labour costs is generally low.

4. Technological factors

Among the long-term factors affecting the prospects of primary commodities, technological development is, perhaps, the most important factor affecting the growth of export earnings from primary commodities. In general, however, the effects of technological change act on factors affecting both demand and supply. Most of the recent technological developments affecting the demand for primary commodities are related to raw materials, especially metals and minerals.

Technological substitution is not a new problem for primary commodities. Steel per unit of final output has been showing a historically declining trend. Low-cost synthetic substitutes have been increasingly eroding the demand for such important export crops as rubber, cotton, sugar, jute and wool for decades. While some of these commodities (such as cotton, wool and rubber) have staged a come-back, mainly based on rising health and environmental concerns created by the use of synthetic materials, the general trend is unmistakably unfavourable and indeed disquieting. The rapid and somewhat mind-boggling technological advancements are likely to have much greater adverse effects on the use of primary products in the future than has been the case so far.[23] Most metal industries — notably copper, aluminium, zinc, lead, nickel and tin — are likely to face continuing weak-

---

[22] However, tea and cotton are exceptions in that the increase in their output growth rates did not lead to steep price declines in 1980-1984. The price of tea rose strongly despite a small increase in the growth rate of world output, while in the case of cotton the price decline was moderate despite a large increase in growth rate of output.

[23] See for example, E.O. Larson, M.H. Ross and R.H. Williams, "Beyond the Era of Materials", *Scientific American*, vol. 254, No. 6 (June 1986), pp. 34-41.

ness in demand due to declines in the intensity of their use.

Technological improvements in production are likely to exert downward pressure on prices — but not necessarily on export earnings — in agriculture. The green revolution has yet to be consummated in many developing countries of the region and breakthroughs in biotechnology continue unabated. The shortening of the agricultural production cycle and the virtual elimination of the need for growing plants in the field — such as has been recently achieved in the case of vanilla by growing cells from plants in fermentation vats or laboratory flasks[24] — are likely to continue to reduce costs and increase supplies.

However, the technological concerns should not be exaggerated. The "frontier" technologies are not likely to have an immediate or medium-term impact on most developing countries. Neither is technology transfer likely to be possible without complementary progress in human resources development. The need in the large majority of developing countries is for more sober and pragmatic efforts which will upgrade rather than replace existing technologies.

F. IMPLICATIONS FOR DEVELOPMENT STRATEGIES

A major objective of development during the last three decades has been the reduction of dependence on the primary sector. This has been motivated by a number of considerations, including raising of per capita incomes, protection against declining terms of trade, avoidance of external dependency and the many social and economic benefits that accompany diversification of the economy. Historical evidence on growth in both developed and developing countries

has amply demonstrated the association of the declining share of the primary sector and the corresponding rise in manufacturing and other non-primary sectors and the rise in income and living standards.[25]

In retrospect, it does seem, however, that the "pioneers of development" underestimated the difficulties of transformation from traditional agriculture to modern industry. A number of important transitional problems, such as demographic changes, human resource development, rural-urban migration, environmental deterioration and infrastructural difficulties, were totally ignored, at worst, or inadequately taken into account, at best. But, it appears from hindsight that the most important error in many countries was to treat the primary sector, especially agriculture, as a passive sector whose basic role was to give without any need to receive. Such a cavalier attitude resulted in agricultural stagnation and in transforming many agricultural surplus and exporting countries into deficit and importing countries in the 1950s and 1960s.

Both domestic and external factors were instrumental in changing the policies of developing countries towards the primary sector, particularly agriculture. Infrastructural investments, especially irrigation, and the availability of productivity-raising inputs at fair prices considerably reversed the tendency of terms of trade to move against agriculture. The rising prices of food grains in the early 1970s made the import bill of food deficit countries an unbearable burden. In addition there was a decline in concessional food assist-

ance. These factors led to growing concern about food security and the need for developing countries to attain a high degree of self-sufficiency in food.[26]

By the 1980s in many developing countries, even outside the newly industrialized countries, the value of exports of manufactures had exceeded that of primary products. However, because of both increasing protectionism in developed market economies and increasing competition among developing countries in exports of manufactures, there is an increasing need for the expansion of commodity exports. The development of the primary sector in the current circumstances seems essential for their overall development not only to generate external financial and investment resources but also to provide the basis for further economic growth and industrial advances.

The primary commodities could provide a basis for renewed and integrated industrialization efforts through processing industries with forward and/or backward linkages.[27] Although during the last two decades the degree of processing of locally-produced primary products has generally increased, there remains a considerable scope for increasing it further to maximize the value added.[28] For developing coun-

---

[24] *Development Forum,* September 1987, p. 11.

[25] See S. Kuznets, *Modern Economic Growth* (New Haven, Yale University Press, 1966); and H. Chenery and L. Taylor, "Development patterns: among countries and over time", *Review of Economics and Statistics,* vol. L, No. 4 (November 1968), pp. 391-416.

[26] See chapter II for the evolution of the policies in the ESCAP region.

[27] See F.G. Adams and J.R. Behrman, "The linkage effects of raw material processing in economic development: a survey of modelling and other approaches", *Journal of Policy Modelling,* vol. 3, No. 3 (October 1981), pp. 375-397.

[28] It is significant that the Tokyo Declaration of 1986 Economic Government of developed countries contains a commitment to support the effort of developing countries heavily dependent on the export of primary commodities "for further processing of their products and for diversifying their economies".

tries, since 1970 both the rates of growth of local processing and their share of processed and manufactured imports by developed countries have decelerated. Further, in many countries processing remains limited to the first stages of transformation. With the expansion in export processing zones and export-oriented strategies in general, there has also been an increase in exports of certain manufactured goods, such as those based on iron and cotton, from those developing countries importing such raw materials rather than producing it themselves.

The models of development, on which the development strategies (whether emphasizing import-substitution or export promotion) of many developing countries are based, have generally assigned a passive role to the primary sector. It is that of an accessory to achieving industrial growth. What happens to it or to those who earn their livelihood in it, is not considered of primary importance. The current commodity crisis seems to have some effect on development theory as evidenced by attempts to correct this bias.[29]

An implication of the prevailing commodity situation for development strategies which has not received adequate attention is the possibility of taking advantage of the currently low level of prices of many primary commodities for pursuing basic-needs-oriented development strategies. The demand for materials required for housing, water, nutrition and health care, as well as rural infrastructure, is likely to remain insatiable in most developing countries for the next few decades and the availability of cheap raw materials in the current situation should provide an opportunity for meeting these needs at relatively low social cost.

---

[29] See, for example, I. Adelman, "Beyond export-led growth", *World Development* (September 1984); and A.P. Thirlwall, "Model of growth and development on Kaldorian Lines, *Oxford Economic Papers,* vol. 2, No. 2, (July 1986).

II. CHANGING ROLE OF THE PRIMARY SECTOR IN THE DEVELOPING ESCAP REGION

A. SIGNIFICANCE OF THE CONTRIBUTION OF THE PRIMARY SECTOR

1. Overview

The developing countries of the ESCAP region, with only a few exceptions, continue to depend on the production of primary commodities as one of the main sources of their income, employment and export earnings. The degree of this dependence has, however, varied considerably across countries and has generally diminished in recent years. For the region as a whole, it is lower and has declined faster than that for other developing regions. This lower and decreasing dependence on primary commodity production is largely a reflection of the region's poorer endowment of natural resources and the relatively higher population pressure on land, which necessitates a more serious pursuit of other economic activities. The aggregate situation, however, hides considerable differences across the region.

The availability of natural resources and land, however, varies a great deal in the region. Japan, the Republic of Korea and Taiwan (a province of the People's Republic of China), are extreme examples of economies of the region which during the process of their development have been forced to diversify out of commodity production owing to the scarcity of natural resources. Australia and

New Zealand stand at the other end of the spectrum for the opposite reason (Hong Kong and Singapore never had significant primary activities). It is worth noting that both groups have the highest per capita incomes, which goes to show that there is no *a priori* reason for primary production to be strongly associated with low levels of per capita incomes.

Most countries of the region lie somewhere between these two extremes. In large developing countries of the region, such as China and India, primary commodity exports form a relatively small proportion of total output and do not affect changes in overall economic performance significantly. In medium-sized countries such as Indonesia, Pakistan, the Philippines and Thailand, the effect of changes in primary commodity trade is greater and serious policy dilemmas about whether to promote the primary or the industrial sector often confront their policy makers.

The smaller and more open economies, such as Malaysia and Sri Lanka, as well as those in the Pacific islands, and the least developed countries have a much greater, and in some cases even rising, dependence on primary commodities — many on one or two main crops or minerals — for generating income, employment and exports. Many of these countries, import significant amounts of food grains as well as essential manufactures and indus-

trial raw materials, which have to be paid for by the export of the few primary commodities they produce. As a result of declining terms of trade, many of these economies have had to increase their relative dependence on primary commodities in order to earn the same level of income and exports. The current concern about primary commodities in the region relates much more strongly to this particular group of countries, whose opportunities for diversification remain limited. For the poorer and least developed countries this concern is enhanced by the diminishing prospects for capital inflows to assist such diversification.

In the 1980s, in contrast to the previous decade, the economic performance of various groups of countries has varied inversely with the degree of their export dependence on primary commodities. Exports, imports, investment and real GDP have grown more slowly in country groups with a higher proportion of primary exports to GDP. The relative resilience of the economies of the ESCAP region, especially if the least developed and Pacific island economies are excluded, is thus largely explained in terms of their lower dependence on primary commodity exports, whose prices have fallen steeply during this period. In the 1970s, when commodity prices were more buoyant, these differences were not so marked (except in the case of oil-exporting economies, whose per capita incomes rose sharply).

Empirical evidence, based on both the historical experience of contemporary developed economies and the more recent experience of developing countries, suggests that the share of primary producing sectors in income, exports and employment falls steadily in a growing economy.[1] The contemporary experience of the Asian and Pacific developing region indicates, *inter alia,* that the steepest fall has occurred in the proportion of GDP contributed by the primary sector while the proportion of employment provided by the primary sector remained relatively stable. The proportion of primary exports generally fell but the extent of the decline varied widely among countries, with the smallest decline occurring in the least developed and Pacific island economies.

2. The share of primary sectors in gross domestic product

The majority of countries in the developing ESCAP region derive less than a third of their GDP from primary producing sectors, while in most of the least developed countries this proportion is still more than a half. More significantly, the proportion in many countries has declined by 20 to 50 per cent during the last two

decades (see figure II.3). Thus, for example, in the Republic of Korea the proportion of GDP contributed by the primary sector fell from 28.9 per cent in 1970 to 14.4 per cent in 1984, in India, from 47.4 per cent in 1970 to 30.7 per cent in 1984, in Pakistan, from 39 per cent in 1970 to 25.8 per cent in 1986, and in Sri Lanka

from 35.6 per cent in 1970 to 25.3 per cent in 1986. In South-East Asia, the reduction in primary commodity dependence has been slower, except in Thailand, where the contribution to GDP declined from 32 per cent in 1970 to 23.2 per cent in 1982, while in Indonesia the proportion fell from 58 per cent in 1970 to 41 per cent in

Figure II.3. Changes in share of primary commodities in GDP of selected developing economies of the ESCAP region

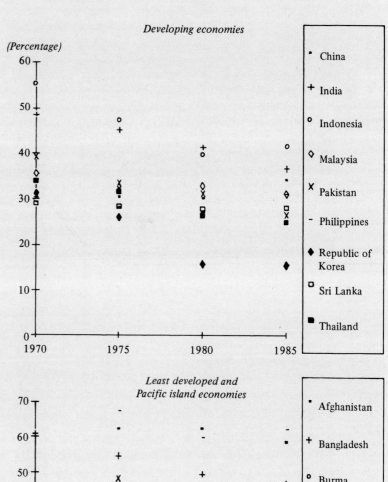

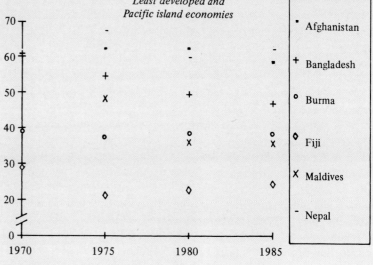

---

[1] Three factors are generally cited for the falling proportion of the contribution of primary sectors (especially agriculture) to GDP in a developing economy. First, the elasticity of demand for food and other agricultural products, which is generally low compared with manufactures. Second, the increasing reliance of agriculture and mining on industrial inputs, which accompanies technological progress. Third, the demand for off-farm marketing services, such as distribution, storage and processing, which is more income-elastic than the agricultural products.

1984 and in Malaysia from 38.9 to 32.4 per cent between 1970 and 1986; in the Philippines, it rose marginally from 29.2 to 29.4 per cent during the same period. In many other countries, especially those in the least developed and Pacific island countries, the proportions have been more stable or have generally fallen much more slowly.

3. Share in the labour force

In contrast to the general decline in the primary sector's contribution to GDP, there has been a much less marked decrease in the proportion of the labour force employed in the sector. In the majority of countries of the region, between half to three fourths of the labour force continues to be employed in the primary sector. The decline in the proportion of the labour force employed in the primary sector has been generally significant. Among the countries where significant declines have taken place since 1970 are China (from 81 to 61 per cent in 1986), Malaysia (from 55 to 28 per cent in 1986) and the Republic of Korea[2] (from 51 to 39.2 per cent in 1985). India, Pakistan, the Philippines and Thailand have also recorded similar, but less significant, declines.

The explanation for the slower decline in the proportion of the labour force employed in the primary sector (mainly agriculture) in the developing countries of

the region compared with those experienced by the contemporary developed countries, including Japan,[3] lies largely in the differences in initial conditions relating their respective demographic, technological and external economic environments. The increase in the rate of population growth, brought about largely by declines in mortality rates unattainable in earlier decades, preceded rather than followed the rise in agricultural productivity, with resulting absorption of the bulk of incremental labour force in agriculture. This has diminished the possibility of mobilizing the surplus from the agricultural sector to finance non-agricultural investment. Moreover, the pattern of industrial investment adopted in many developing countries has not only been capital-intensive but has resulted in increasing the dualism in the economy and in enervating the agriculture sector.[4] As a result, the productivity of labour has not risen adequately and a relatively large number of farmers continue to be required to meet the rising demand for food and raw materials for industry. The consequences of a slower decline in the proportion of the labour force on labour and land productivity have been adversely affected by two other factors: (a) the rapid disappearance of the land frontier and (b) the lack of sufficient investment in infrastructure, such as flood control, irrigation and drainage.

4. Share of primary commodities in total exports

Primary commodity exports have provided the main source of

foreign exchange for the development of the Asian and Pacific economies. In Japan, the initial impulse for industrialization was provided by primary commodity exports. As Professor Ishikawa points out: "The foreign currency required for the industrialization of Japan since the Meiji revolution was raised mainly by its export of raw silk to the United States of America and of cotton fabrics to underdeveloped countries".[5]

The proportion of primary commodity exports to total exports has, however, been rapidly declining in Asian developing countries, but still remains relatively large. By 1970, in many of the developing countries of the Asian and Pacific region the value of manufactures export had exceeded those of primary commodities (see figure II. 4). The decline has been due to four main factors. First, the increase in population has led to an increase in domestic consumption and an erosion of the export surplus in many consumable commodities. Second, the increase in domestic processing has reduced the share of primary commodity exports. Third the decline in the terms of trade of primary commdities has reduced the share of primary commodities in total trade. Lastly, the better access to developed country markets through the GSP (generalized system of preferences) and other measures has provided opportunities to Asian developing countries to shift their comparative advantage in favour of exports of labour-intensive manufactures.

The combined effect of these trends is reflected in table II.4, which shows that while the share of primary exports in world trade has declined generally during the last two decades, the Asian and

---

[2] The experience of the Republic of Korea in reducing the proportion of the labour force employed in the primary sector was even more successful between 1955 and 1965 when there was an absolute decline in the agricultural labour force, the proportion of which fell from 78.6 to 59.6 per cent. This initial phase of the development of the Republic of Korea was, significantly, associated with import substitution, rather than export-led industrialization (see box II.4).

[3] See S. Ishikawa, *Economic Development in Asian Perspective* (Tokyo, Kinokuniya Bookstore Co. Ltd., 1967) for a detailed discussion of these differences in initial conditions, especially in relation to the Japanese experience.

[4] For more detailed discussion, see section C below.

[5] Ishikawa, *op. cit.*

Pacific region has become the developing region least dependent on primary commodity exports. Its share of primary commodity

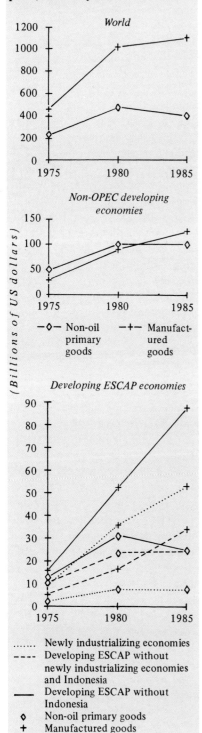

Figure II.4. Growth of primary commodity and manufactures exports, selected years

World

Non-OPEC developing economies

(*Billions of US dollars*)

—◇— Non-oil primary goods   —+— Manufactured goods

Developing ESCAP economies

...... Newly industrializing economies
- - - - Developing ESCAP without newly industrializing economies and Indonesia
——— Developing ESCAP without Indonesia
◇ Non-oil primary goods
+ Manufactured goods

exports was only marginally higher than the world average.

However, large differences exist between the countries of the region. Many countries — mainly low-income or least developed — still depend on commodity exports for well over 50 per cent of their export earnings. The region's newly industrializing economies are among the least dependent on primary commodity export and are major importers of primary commodities in the region. Owing to their large weightage and the high proportion of manufactures in their total exports, the developing ESCAP region's share of primary commodity exports is the lowest among the world's developing regions. Two of the three developed countries of the region are also among those highly dependent on primary commodity exports. In 1984, Australia's primary commodity exports share of 55.6 per cent and New Zealand's 77.7 per cent were, except for Iceland far above the corresponding share in developed countries. On the other hand, Japan is the least dependent on commodity exports. This pattern of country composition largely explains why

the region's share in world commodity exports is so low.

B. STRUCTURE OF PRIMARY COMMODITY PRODUCTION AND EXPORTS IN THE ESCAP REGION

1. General

The primary sector in the ESCAP region comprises largely agriculture, non-fuel minerals being important only in a few countries. The impact on overall development is also much greater in the case of agriculture than of non-fuel minerals. Within agriculture, short-cycle crops, especially cereals, dominate production and utilization of land and labour resources. A high proportion of these crops is domestically consumed (see table II.5). Tree crops use relatively few resources, but their production is destined largely for exports. In 1984, 63.8 per cent of primary commodity exports of the developing ESCAP region consisted of food products, 23.9 per cent of agricultural raw materials and the remaining 12.3 per cent of non-fuel minerals. The corresponding percentages in Australia were

Table II.4. Major world and ESCAP regions. Shares of primary commodities in total merchandise exports, 1970 and 1984

(Percentage)

	1970	1984
World	27.0	17.6
Developed market economies	21.8	17.0
Australia	73.5	55.6
New Zealand	88.1	77.7
Socialist Eastern Europe	21.4	9.7
Developing countries	50.3	22.1
Non-oil developing countries	69.3	35.3
Africa	58.0	23.8
Latin America	69.0	41.7
Developing ESCAP countries	45.8	19.6
Non-oil developing ESCAP countries	51.3	21.5

Source: UNCTAD primary commodity trade data on tapes, secretariat calculations.

102

Table II.5. Selected primary commodities in the developing ESCAP region. Exports as percentage of production, selected years

	Developing ESCAP region			
	1970	*1975*	*1980*	*1985*
Agricultural products				
Wheat	0.2	–	0.1	0.3
Rice	1.7	1.4	2.0	1.6
Maize	3.8	3.6	2.9	10.5
Sugar (total)	1.0	1.4	1.4	1.0
Copra	22.5	24.1	10.3	8.1
Palm oil	79.1	97.0	94.6	84.7
Bananas	4.2	8.9	8.0	7.5
Coffee green and roasted	69.3	61.1	62.9	74.6
Tea	56.1	54.0	50.4	45.5
Cotton lint	7.3	10.9	8.9	9.1
Jute and similar fibres	23.8	17.0	15.1	5.1
Tobacco unmanufactured	10.0	12.6	12.2	5.4
Natural rubber	96.3	84.0	87.7	85.7
Wool greasy	5.9	3.4	1.9	0.6
Fishery products[a]				
Fish, fresh, chilled or frozen	–	80.0[b]	101.8	43.3
Fish, dried, salted or smoked	–	1.4[b]	1.5	1.4
Crustaceans and molluscs, fresh, frozen, dried or salted	–	98.8[b]	122.2	114.3
Fish products and preparations	–	20.0[b]	27.5	33.8
Crustacean and mollusc products and preparations	–	73.7[b]	52.6	36.1
Oils and fats, crude or refined of aquatic animal origin	–	41.2[b]	121.4	35.2
Forest products				
Sawnlogs and veneer logs (non-coniferous)	47.5	36.4	31.4	21.4
Fuelwood and charcoal	0.1	0.1	0.2	0.2
Sawnwood (non-coniferous)	14.0	13.8	18.9	14.2
Wood-based panels	57.7	63.3	65.8	49.9
Paper and paperboard	2.5	3.7	4.3	3.3

Sources: FAO Trade Yearbook, various issues; *FAO Production Yearbook* various issues, and Computer Printout, 1987; *Yearbook of Forest Products,* various issues; and *Yearbook of Fishery Statistics, Fishery Commodities 1986.*

[a] The figures contain large margins of inaccuracies since production data for some of the products in some countries were lacking. Re-exports from some countries may partly account for high percentage exports in total regional production. [b] 1976.

43.0, 17.4 and 39.6, while in New Zealand they were 65.2, 27.2 and 7.3, respectively.

In individual countries, however, a few commodities form the bulk of commodity exports. Table II.6 gives an overview of country-commodity dependence on primary exports. With few exceptions (Australia, Burma, Pakistan and Thailand), cereals do not figure prominently in the ESCAP region's primary commodity export basket. Tropical beverages (tea and coffee), fibres (jute and cotton) –

exported mainly by South Asian countries – oil-seeds and fats, rubber, tropical wood – mainly exported by the South-East Asian and Pacific island countries are among the most important commodity exports of the region. The pattern of commodity export is, however, undergoing considerable change with progress in agricultural and industrial development. Many developing countries of the region which have successfully overcome their concerns about food scarcity are now poised to export cereals

and other agricultural products, including fish, fruits and vegetables for which there is a growing demand in the world market. On the other hand, many primary commodities, at present exported in unprocessed forms, are likely to be exported after processing or as manufactures.

2. Institutional structure of commodity production

Most of the agricultural production in the Asian and Pacific

(Percentage)

	>50	>25<50	>10<25
Bangladesh	Jute		Fish
Burma		Rice, tropical wood	
Fiji		Sugar	
India			Tea
Indonesia[b]		Tea, coffee, rubber, tropical wood	
Lao People's Democratic Republic	Coffee	Tropical wood	
Malaysia			Palm kernel oil, palm oil, coconut oil, copra, rubber, tropical wood
Maldives		Fish	
Nepal			Tropical wood, jute
Pakistan			Rice, cotton
Papua New Guinea		Gold, copper, coffee	Tropical wood, copra, palm oil
Philippines			Coconut oil
Samoa		Coconut oil	Tropical wood
Solomon Islands			Fish, tropical wood, copra, palm oil
Sri Lanka		Tea	Rubber
Thailand		Rice, maize	Rubber
Tonga		Coconut oil	Bananas, spices
Vanuatu		Copra	Fish
Viet Nam			Fish, copra, rubber
Australia			Wheat
New Zealand		Meat	Wool

Source: UNCTAD commodity tape.

[a] Approximate shares of indicated commodities in total merchandise exports. [b] Total merchandise exports excluding oil exports.

region is for domestic consumption and only a few crops are exported. Thus the majority of farmers in the region are not directly dependent on export of primary commodities. However, in the case of fibre and tree crops a much larger proportion of output, either in raw form or with limited processing, has traditionally been exported. The institutional arrangements governing the production, processing and marketing of these commodities vary across the countries and among different crops. The information on institutional arrangements concerning some of the region's major export commodities, e.g., jute, rice, sugar-cane, rubber, tea and palm oil presented below is intended to help in understanding the problems of efficiency as well as welfare aspects of primary commodity production.[6]

(a) Small-holders versus plantation estates

Most primary commodities in the ESCAP region are produced and partly processed by small

---

[6] The latter aspect is discussed in some detail in chapter IV.

peasant farmers, but some, such as tea, rubber and palm oil, are also grown on large plantations or estates. In recent years there has been a noticeable trend towards increasing the share of smallholders in some of these products. For example, the share of estates in the total acreage of rubber in Malaysia has decreased from 32 per cent in 1970 to 24 per cent in 1983. The proportion of smallholders in rubber plantation is even higher in Indonesia and Thailand, the two other major rubber producers in the region, accounting for 80 and 96 per cent of total acreage, respectively. In Thailand, smallholders are defined as those having a holding of less than 15 rai (1 rai = 0.16 hectare). The productivity per acre of small farmers is considerably lower than that of larger estates, being only 37 per cent in Indonesia and 70 per cent in Malaysia, compared with the productivity of larger estates.

In the production of palm oil the share of smallholders was lower, i.e. about a half in both Malaysia and Thailand in 1984, but the share in Malaysia had risen from 4 per cent a decade earlier. In Malaysia, which produces more than half of the world's and three fourths of the region's palm oil output, about 670,000 people, mainly smallholders, were dependent on palm oil output as a source of income and employment. In sugar-cane the picture is somewhat mixed. In Thailand, for example, sugar-cane growers are mainly small farmers, but in the Philippines sugar-cane is grown in estates in Negros, while in Luzon it is grown mainly by small farmers. On the whole, large-scale estate operations account for 4 per cent of the total farms and 42 per cent of the acreage, while small farmers accounting for 79 per cent of farms take up only 23 per cent of the acreage. While productivity is higher per acre in large estates, unit costs are lower for small farmers.

In the case of rice, a major export crop, in Thailand approximately 6 million farm households are estimated to be involved in rice production. Rice producers constitute 30 per cent of Thailand's labour force, about half of the total agricultural labour force. An average rice farm in Thailand is 3 hectares with 59 per cent of the farms from 1.6 to 6.4 hectares, 24 per cent being between 0 and 1.6, and 17 per cent between 6.4 and 22.4. Only 0.3 per cent of the rice farms are above

22.4 hectares. Thus, rice, like jute, in Thailand and other countries in the region, is produced by a very large number of small farmers, unlike in the land-rich North American and Australian continents.

3. Transnational corporations

The transnational corporations have in the past played a key role in both the production and trading activities relating to primary commodities. Plantations were the preferred form of transnational corporations involvement in the production of agricultural crops since they provided economies of scale, a captive supply of raw materials and a labour force which could be made dependent on plantation work. Crops for which plantation was the common mode were banana, sugar, tea, rubber, cotton and tobacco. Where peasant farming was more efficient or administratively convenient, the transnational corporations assumed the role of resident trading companies buying primary products from the peasant farmers for local processing and/or export. In some cases this was combined with selling imported manufactures to the farmers. This enabled the exercise of combined monopsony/monopoly power.[7]

The above pattern started disappearing in the ESCAP region during the post-war decolonization period as many Governments in the region took measures for land reforms and public ownership of national resources. Transnational corporations involved in production have been affected by the breaking up of large estates into smaller holdings or outright nationalization with operation by state enterprises;

---

[7] See Norman P. Girvan, "Transnational corporations and non-fuel primary commodities in developing countries", *World Development*, vol. 15, No. 5 (Oxford, Pergamon Journals Ltd., May 1987), pp. 713-740.

transnational trading companies were affected either by regulation of prices paid to farmers or by their replacement by state marking enterprises. In the mining sector there has been a gradual elimination of concessions for production based on royalties by more equitable contracts, joint ventures and state mineral enterprises.

The purpose of these measures was to ensure a fairer distribution of gains from trade in primary commodities and the appropriation of a larger share of retained earnings in commodity production by the developing producing country. This has, however, tended to reduce the incentives for transnational corporations and to increase their risks. They have responded to these measures of developing countries by diversifying into such activities as provision of management, marketing and technology transfer, of which the developing countries continue to have a growing need. There has also been an increase in the risk premium sought by the transnational corporations for their involvement in the commodity trade and production of developing countries in the form of reduced taxation and a better investment climate, as well as greater political safety. The transnational corporations have, over time, shifted away from production to trading and processing primary commodities, which offer them better opportunities for exercising their bargaining power over their suppliers and purchasers through horizontal and vertical integration of their activities, product diversification and differentiation as well as through increasing use of research-and-development-innovation in marketing. Recent years have also seen the formation of conglomerates through mergers and acquisitions which have given even greater advantage to the transnational corporations in terms of opportunities for capturing economic rents and effective use of their bargaining power.

However, in spite of the general decline in the importance of transnational corporations in primary commodities, especially in production, they continue to play a significant role in both agricultural and non-fuel mineral primary commodities. Thus they continue to have an important presence in the production of rubber, tin and palm oil in Malaysia, sugar in Fiji, hardwood in Indonesia, and copper and gold in Papua New Guinea. In recent years the role of transnational corporations in the production of primary commodities has been more indirect, mainly through marketing, transfer of technology and processing arrangements. The examples of production of cassava pellets for export from Thailand to EEC, the production of MSG (monosodium glutamate) from tapioca and the collaboration for producing radial tyres in Japan provide important evidence of the continued involvement of transnational corporations in primary commodities in the region.

The prominent role of transnational corporations in marketing and trading in primary commodities in the ESCAP developing region is evidenced by the high level of assets of transnational trading corporations in the region. For example, the assets of such corporations of the United States origin trading in Asia and the Pacific alone surpassed $1 billion in 1981. In Hong Kong, India, Singapore and Thailand each foreign investment in wholesaling and trading (mainly of primary commodities) exceeded $100 million.[8]

A major concern about the

    [8] For details, see *Transnational Corporations and Primary Commodity Exports from Selected Developing Countries,* ESCAP/UNCTC publication Series B, No. 5 (ST/ESCAP/321).

activities of the transnational corporations in primary commodities is the continuing low ratio of domestic value added in traded primary commodities. Studies on transnational corporation in primary commodity exports in the ESCAP region show that the share of the Asian and Pacific developing country producers in final users' prices is still quite low for many commodities. The combined mark-ups of exporters in the producing country and importers, wholesalers and retailers in the consuming country exceed 100 per cent for many products. This has induced many countries of the region to assume an increasing role in the marketing of primary products in order to internalize the gains from trade in primary commodities.

C. AGRICULTURAL GROWTH AND TRADE IN THE ESCAP REGION

1. The developmental role of agriculture in the ESCAP region

The role of agricultural development in the majority of the developing economies of the ESCAP region is central to their overall development. As the largest sector in terms of employment and output generation, it has a key role to perform in providing incomes and the most basic of all necessities, food, to a growing population and in earning foreign exchange through exports (generally, non-cereals) or through import substitution of food supplies. In addition, its dynamic role throughout the crucial phases of the economy's structural transformation is to generate and transfer a continuing flow of resources to other sectors of the economy for its balanced development. However, for the sector to be able to perform its dynamic role

in the economy, its own vitality and vigour needs to be continually ensured. The pivotal role of the agriculture and primary goods sector in the recent upsurge in the growth of China and Thailand are discussed in box II.3 and box II.4, respectively.

Many developing countries in the ESCAP region have learned through hindsight the harmful effects of siphoning off too prematurely or too intensively the agricultural sector's surplus. They have also learned the high cost of attending too inadequately to its needs for investment in infrastructure, human resource development and extension services which would enhance its capacity to generate larger surpluses. In the early decades of development there was a tendency to look upon the agriculture sector mainly as a source of transferring money, people, food and raw materials to the urban-industrial sector. The domestic obstacles of such transfers were not well recognized and their implicit costs were considered negligible. As a result, unanticipated problems of uneven structural change, excessive rural-urban migration, infrastructural bottlenecks, social imbalances and environmental depredation arose and frustrated the planners' dreams in most Asian and Pacific developing countries. The terms of trade in agriculture generally deteriorated and domestic demand for industrial goods did not expand sufficiently in many countries. This presented particularly difficult problems for countries which had import-substituting industrial strategies.

The population explosion and inadequate attention to agriculture in most developing countries in the ESCAP region in the early phases of their development resulted in large deficits in basic foods, mainly cereals. The region became the largest importer of cereal food in the world in the 1960s and the 1970s as a result of the need to avert serious food shortages and, in some countries, to avoid the risk of famine. This imposed severe burdens on the balance of payments in many countries. Food shortages and the high prices of wage goods, in turn, caused inflationary pressures, which frustrated industrialization efforts and created other imbalances such as increasing poverty and income inequalities. These factors eventually made it inevitable for policy makers to revert their attention to increasing domestic food production and agricultural development. However, since the development strategies continued to have a high urban-industrial bias, many of the policies pursued in the 1960s, such as low procurement prices offered to producers and subsidized supplies of food to urban consumers, continued to have overall disincentive effects on agriculture.

Agricultural productivity remained low in most countries of the region until well into the mid-1960s when the advent of the green revolution and the availability of high productivity wheat and rice strains relieved some of the imbalances mentioned above. The "green revolution" helped, to some extent, in achieving a greater balance between the harmful effects of lower prices on farmers and future food production and the beneficial effects on consumers (mainly urban-industrial workers and landless labour). The transfer

---

Box II.3. The role of agriculture in the economic transformation of China

The economy of China has undergone substantial structural transformation since 1950. From a predominantly agrarian economy, with agriculture contributing two thirds in the value of gross industrial and agricultural products and providing 80 per cent of employment, it has reached a stage of development where agriculture's share in these products was slightly more than a quarter in 1985. However, agriculture's contribution to total employment remained high, at around 60 per cent.

Despite its vast land area and plentiful natural resources, per capita availability is very low owing to heavy population pressure. Arable land per capita, for example, amounts to only about one third of the world average and the possibility of increasing cultivable land is limited. This relative scarcity of land required the application of new technological and scientific methods to bring about the necessary increases in land productivity. The Government adopted policies to encourage the use of such methods. However, pressures for rapid industrialization, and pricing, and taxation policies followed, and the introduction of the commune system during the late 1950s and the 1960s, led to relative stagnation of the agricultural sector and a rapid decline in agriculture's share in national output.

Policy reforms introduced since 1978 (dismantling the commune system, allocating land to household units for private organization of production, giving price incentives, reducing tax burdens, etc.) have stimulated agricultural growth to an average level at 3.5 times higher during 1978-1985 than the average growth rate during the 20-year period prior to 1978. The average rate of growth in gross agricultural products at 1980 constant prices reached 8.4 per cent during 1980-1985.

Acceleration of agricultural growth put the economy as a whole on a more balanced development path. Agriculture's rapid decline in economic output was halted and its share in total national income rose during the early 1980s above its level in 1978. Since then the share has been declining, but at a much slower rate than in the past.

The policy reforms aimed at bringing dynamism in agricultural production were based on the recognition that agriculture still constituted the base of China's economy, which contributed more than a third of national income, two fifths of employment and a quarter of its foreign exchange earnings. Despite recent growth in agricultural production and exports, the importance of primary commodity exports has dropped from about 60-80 per cent of the total in the 1950s, 50-60 per cent in the 1960s, and about 50 per cent in the 1970s to 25 per cent in the 1980s. This trend is largely the result of falling commodity prices. China has also suffered owing to the sharp drop in the price of oil, one of its main exports. However, it has succeeded in stepping up other primary products, especially agricultural products. For example, although once a net importer of maize and cotton it has now become a significant exporter of those products. In 1986 it was second only to the United States of America as a world-wide exporter of cotton as well as an exporter of maize to Japan. Higher production has been absorbed mostly in domestic use, for both consumption and industrial purposes. Only 4.98 per cent of agricultural output value was exported in 1985, almost the same share as in 1957 (4.31 per cent), but double the share of such exports in the 1960s and the 1970s.

Growth in agriculture has benefited the economy in many other ways. Chronic food deficits have been eliminated and even small surpluses of cereals have emerged for export. An important policy objective, namely, food self-sufficiency, has been met. The rise in agricultural income, on which more than 60 per cent of the population still depends, has created additional demand for both agricultural and industrial products in the vast rural areas of the country, and has stimulated production through its feedback effects. Rural industrialization, an essential element in the development strategy of China, has greatly benefited from agricultural growth which saw two-digit level rates of expansion in the production of crops such as oil-seeds, sugar, fruits, jute, cotton, rubber and aquatic products. Rural industries (village and township factories), which currently employ 80 million people, or 14 per cent of the total labour force, greatly benefited from these expansions in agricultural production. In 1985-1986, one fifth of the village and township factories were involved in the processing of agricultural products and foodstuffs.

Box II.4. Transition to a newly industrializing economy: experiences of the Republic of Korea and Thailand

The transition of the Republic of Korea from an agricultural economy to a newly industrializing economy within two decades has raised high expectations among many developing economies of the ESCAP region. Predictions are rife that Thailand will be among the region's next newly industrializing economies – the only unanswered question is how soon.[a]

It is, therefore, interesting to compare the performance of Thailand's economy in the 1980s with that of the Republic of Korea between 1965 and 1975 in order to have some idea of how close Thailand is to becoming a newly industrializing economy. In 1965 the two economies had roughly comparable per capita incomes. The more rapid export-led growth in the Republic of Korea, however, raised its GDP per capita 66 per cent above that of Thailand by 1975 and by 1980 the per capita GDP of the Republic of Korea was more than double that of Thailand.

The two economies, however, had rather different endowments and other characteristics before they embarked on the course of rapid economic development. The Republic of Korea was a relatively more resource-poor, labour-abundant and closed economy at the start of its development process in 1955, with about half the GDP contributed by, and 80 per cent of labour force employed in, the primary sector, and with a share of exports of only 1.6 per cent in GDP.

The Republic of Korea had two distinct phases of industrialization. The first, broadly between 1955 and 1965, consisted mainly of import substitution activities. Production was

largely for the domestic market – although the ratio of exports to GDP grew during the period from 1.6 per cent in 1955 to 8.5 per cent in 1965. However, primary exports were more than 80 per cent of total exports until 1962. Moreover, the import-substitution phase of industrialization in the Republic of Korea, unlike in many other developing countries, was highly labour-intensive. GDP grew in this phase by about 5 per cent per annum. While the primary sector output expanded by 3.5 per cent annually, growth reached 6.1 per cent in the non-primary sector, thus reducing the share of the former from 48.0 to 43.0 per cent. At the same time the labour force in the primary sector declined by 2.3 per cent per annum and that in the non-primary sector grew by 7.1 per cent per annum, resulting in a fall in the proportion of the labour force in the primary sector from 78.6 to 59.6

per cent.[b] Thus the growth of primary sector output was maintained through higher labour productivity in agricul-

[b] This was made possible by a high growth rate of population of 2.8 per cent in the Republic of Korea during 1955-1965, which implied that almost the entire increase in labour force due to population growth was absorbed in the non-primary sector. After 1965 the population growth rate fell to 1.8 per cent and some of the increase in labour force was absorbed by the primary sector, as well. See, Sung-Hwan Jo, "The impact of the raw materials sector on employment generation in the process of South Korea's industrial growth (1955-1978)", World Employment Programme Research Working Papers (Geneva, International Labour Office, August 1980), p. 9, table I-1.

Republic of Korea and Thailand. Share of primary sector in GDP, exports and labour force, 1960-1985

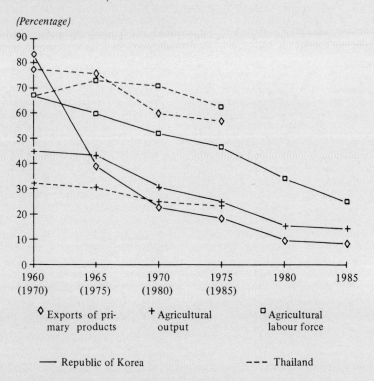

Note: The years in brackets are the bench mark period for Thailand.

[a] A recent study by the Thailand Development Research Institute found the current Thai situation to be comparable to that of the Republic of Korea around 1975. See *Prospects for Thai Economic Development* (Bangkok, Thailand Development Research Institute, Macroeconomic Policy Program and Human Resources and Social Development Program, November 1987).

ture, in spite of a significant outflow of labour into the non-primary sector.

In the export-promotion phase of the Republic of Korea, between 1965 and 1978, the economy not only grew faster — at an average rate of 10.4 per cent in real terms per annum — but also achieved a remarkable growth in exports, mainly of manufactures. Between 1965 and 1978, the share of the primary sector in total output, labour force and exports fell from 43.0, 59.6 and 38.9 per cent to 25.8, 39.2 and 11.3 per cent, respectively.

Developments in the economy of Thailand have, however, been somewhat different. While the share of agriculture declined from 40 to 17 per cent of GDP between 1960 and 1986 and is lower than that of the Republic of Korea in 1978, the share of the labour force employed in and the share of exports generated by the agricultural sector remains much higher than they were in the Republic of Korea about a decade earlier. Both these ratios have, however, declined markedly in Thailand since the 1960s — from 84 to 67 per cent in 1986 for the labour force and from over 90 to about 40 per cent in 1986 for the proportion of primary commodity exports to total exports.

The economy of Thailand, much better endowed with land and other natural resources, has not faced the same tight constraints in expanding agriculture as the Republic of Korea had encountered in its initial phase of development. However, the growth of its agricultural sector, along with the rest of the economy, slowed down to an average of 3.9 per cent, thus contributing to an overall GDP growth of 6.4 per cent during 1973-1984, compared with 5.4 and 7.2 per cent respectively, during 1958-1973. Growth decelerated considerably during the 1980s, with agriculture growing at the annual rate of 2.9 per cent and real GDP at 4.8 per cent in 1981-1986. Both external and domestic factors contributed to the slow-down.[c]

The difficulties faced by agriculture in Thailand in 1985 and 1986 were largely attributable to the sharp decline in the prices of the country's major export commodities. They also arose as the "extensive margin" for further expansion of land areas (including fishing and forestry grounds) had been almost exhausted. Agricultural productivity has been comparatively low despite substantial past investments. Further investments to boost productivity in traditonal crops appeared hardly justifiable in the face of continuing oversupply and the low world prices of the commodities on which Thailand depends.

The response of Thailand to its problems has been to diversify its economy — in both agriculture and industry — and to reduce its dependence on traditional exports. The country's performance in the last two years, 1986 and 1987, has been quite impressive, especially in the field of exports of manufactures. In current United States dollar terms, nominal manufactures exports from Thailand grew by 39.5 per cent in 1986 and are estimated to have increased by about 42.5 per cent in 1987, the highest manufactures export growth rate among all the economies of the ESCAP region.[d] Exports are expected to continue to grow by more than 20 per cent in 1988.

In both 1986 and 1987, manufactured exports have been the main source of growth in the Thai economy, the traditional agricultural sector remaining depressed owing to low commodity prices combined with a bad drought for two years in a row. In current prices, the contribution of manufacturing to GDP has overtaken that of the whole agricultural sector since 1984, their shares being 20.6 and 16.7 per cent respectively in 1986.

In agriculture, which continues to play a significant role in the economy's growth, efforts have also been made, with a considerable measure of success, to diversify the traditional crop patterns and to encourage horticultural, fisheries and livestock production. However, the infrastructure investment, technological and skill improvements needed to effectively pursue the course of industrial and agricultural diversification cannot be easily undertaken in the absence of large capital inflows such as those that were available to the Republic of Korea during its comparable period of development. An improvement in the external economic environment relating to both trade and capital inflows, which the Republic of Korea had the good fortune to benefit from, would greatly shorten the time needed for structural transformation of Thailand into a newly industrializing economy.

[c] See Ammar Siamwalla and others, "Agricultural pricing policies in Thailand" (Bangkok, Thailand Development Research Institute, 1987).

[d] In baht terms, the export growth rate was respectively 32.8 and 38.9 per cent in 1986 and 1987.

of agricultural surplus was made less painful.[9] Most food deficit countries adopted and expanded

[9] As Per Pinstrup-Andersen and Peter Hazell argue, "Since the green revolution generates an economic surplus by more efficient use of resources and reduced unit costs, consumer gains need not imply producer losses. Both may gain". See the "Impact of the green revolution and prospects for the future", *Food Review Internatonal,* vol. 1, No. 1 (1985), pp. 1-25.

as quickly as possible the cultivation of high-yielding varieties of rice and wheat. The new input requirements of water and fertilizer were made available through government efforts, often at subsidized prices. The spread of these high-yielding varieties raised the yield rates per land acre and helped boost total production throughout the region.

Thus the agriculture sector has been called upon to perform two basic developmental roles in the developing ESCAP region. First, to provide a degree of food security for its growing population which would enable it to pursue its developmental goals without the disruptive effects of inflation, frequent balance-of-payments difficulties and the social and economic tensions that food shortages bring in their wake. The second important role of agriculture has been to generate sufficient surplus resources, especially foreign exchange, to enable the economy to diversify itself. There are, of course, other roles which the agriculture sector plays in a developing economy, such as the supplier of inputs and wage goods to the industrial sector and as a market for industrial goods. The intersectoral linkages and interdependence of these are discussed in section D. The green revolution has greatly strengthened these important direct and catalytic roles of the agriculture sector in the development of the economies of the developing ESCAP region.

2. Special conditions of Asian agriculture

The progress of the green revolution in Asia was, however, a challenging task owing to a number of peculiarities of Asian agriculture. First, the Asian region is subject to the monsoon rainfall pattern that imparts a distinct seasonality to agriculture and dependence on rainfall which is heavily concentrated at high levels for four to five months per year. Second, the population density in rural Asia is three times or more that of other developing reigons. Farm land is intensively cultivated and farm size tends to be extremely small. Undeveloped land with agricultural potential is scarce in Asia and, for most countries, there is no new frontier left. Third, in some countries (such as India, Pakistan and the Philippines) the concentration of holdings and inadequate progress in land reforms, limited the spread of green revolution technology to large farmers.

In view of these structural characteristics of Asian agriculture and notwithstanding concerted efforts to reduce its dependence on adequate monsoon rainfall through irrigation and better crop varieties, until the late 1970s the food

security situation in the developing ESCAP region remained fragile and seriously vulnerable to the fluctuations in the world market. The situation was dramatically highlighted by the fourfold increases in grain prices between 1972 and 1974 as a result of crop failures in China and the Union of Soviet Socialist Republics and shortfalls associated with drought and pest attacks in South and South-East Asia.

The food situation in South-East Asia improved only marginally between 1965 and 1975; that in South Asia, including India, deteriorated sharply. Net cereal imports in South Asia rose from 2.7 million tons in 1972 to 11.5 million tons in 1975 as shortfalls worsened in Bangladesh, India, Pakistan and Sri Lanka. China's net imports of cereals more than doubled in 1973 from 1972 levels, and rose to over 6 million tons in 1974. In the Association of South-East Asian Nations (ASEAN) region, despite a small surplus in 1971 by 1973 there was a huge shortfall of 2.8 million tons which forced Indonesia to resort to large-scale importation of grain.

3. Changes in policy objectives and stances

The heightened concern about food security in the region has led to a more intensive reappraisal of policies towards agriculture and a more vigorous pursuit of consummating the green revolution in Asian agriculture. To accelerate the pace of agricultural development, increased reliance was placed on agricultural price policy. However, the pricing policies in the agricultural sector pursued by Governments have tried to strike a delicate balance among multiple objectives. This has been an exercise in political economy in most countries and has not always served the basic interest of making agricul-

ture more productive as a foundation for sound and sustained economic development. Besides low output prices, export and other taxes and exchanges rate disincentives, the fiscal and financial policies pursued by most Governments have tended to discriminate in favour of the industrial sectors. The adverse effects of these measures on agriculture have been calculated in many studies in terms of the differential rates of nominal and/or effective rates of protection to agriculture *vis-à-vis* the industrial sector. Most of these studies find that the rates of protection to agriculture were pronouncedly negative in the 1950s and 1960s and, despite recent progress in policy reforms, they continue to be negative in many cases.[10]

In many respects, policies have been reformed and liberalized in more recent years to varying degrees in different countries in the region. The recent successes in agricultural development in the region, are at least partly owing to the policy reforms that have been carried out. Real agricultural GDP has grown during 1975-1985 at compound rates exceeding 3 per cent per annum in the major agricultural countries in the region such as Bangladesh, Burma, China, India, Indonesia, Malaysia, Pakistan, the Philippines, Sri Lanka and Thailand. In some cases the growth rates have exceeded 5 per cent.

The success in agricultural production in Asia is reflected in achievement of rice self-sufficiency

---

[10] See World Bank, *World Development Report 1986* (New York, Oxford University Press, 1986); Ammar Siamwalla and others, *Agricultural Pricing Policies in Thailand* (Bangkok Thailand Development Research Institute, May 1987); Cristina C. David, "Economic policies and Philippine agriculture", working paper 83-02 (mimeographed) (Philippine Institute for Development Studies, 1983). Also see chapter V below.

in Indonesia, which was transformed from being the largest rice importer in the world in the 1970s and early 1980s to having a small surplus in the mid-1980s. India's achievement of self-sufficiency in cereals would have been thought nearly impossible only a decade ago. Given the poor external conditions and weak initial conditions for growth for Asian countries like Bangladesh, China, India, Indonesia, Pakistan and Sri Lanka, their success must be at least partially attributed to policy initiatives by Governments that helped overcome various constraints. In particular, there is strong evidence that incentives for agriculture were improved in most of these countries. This is seen in the improvement since the late 1970s in agricultural terms of trade in countries like India, Indonesia and Pakistan. At the farm level, there was improvement in paddy prices relative to fertilizer prices in many Asian countries despite the rising costs of chemical fertilizer as a result of the oil shocks.

Some recent studies point out that there is a tendency in the region for the negative protection to agriculture to be reversed and that there is even a rise in positive protection.[11] In contrast to the experience of the developing countries, where agriculture is often taxed rather than protected, the experience of developed countries shows that agriculture tends to be positively protected as the economy advances, the importance of agriculture in the economy shrinks and its continued sustenance becomes dependent on increased subsidies. However, the average levels

of nominal protection for important traded commodities (grains, livestock and sugar) between 1965-1974 and 1975-1983, have fallen more in Asian developing countries, with few exceptions, compared with the levels in some major African, Middle Eastern and Latin American countries.[12]

4. The unfinished tasks and emerging challenges in agricultural development

(a) Food security

The preceding discussion on the evolution of agricultural strategies and policies and their impact on agricultural development in Asia should not give an exaggerated view of the region's accomplishments. The green revolution has not yet run its full course in most of the region and large sections of the farming population continue to use sub-optimum levels of modern inputs owing to lack of complementary irrigation, infrastructure, marketing or credit facilities. The region is still a net importer of cereal food (table II.7). Per capita production and food availability have fluctuated considerably during the period 1975-1985 although the overall trend has been perhaps slightly upward. However, imports of cereal food still exceed exports. The rate of growth in food production still lags behind population growth rates in many countries, such as Afghanistan, Bangladesh, Nepal and other low-income economies.

The major agricultural economies of China, India, Indonesia, Pakistan and the Philippines which

have achieved a measure of success, food self-sufficiency remains quite precariously balanced from year to year. This has underscored the need for food storage capacities in these countries to be able to smooth out supplies between good and bad agricultural years — even though it is sometimes considered a costly investment.

A complicating factor has been the increase in the degree of variability in year-to-year production and prices of food grain following the green revolution.[13] The yields of crops grown with new technologies may be more sensitive to year-to-year variations in input use owing to changes in their availability or prices. The degree of price instability can be quite high in countries where only a high portion of total output is consumed on the farm and markets are relatively thin. In India, for example, where only a third of total output is marketed farm price variability for wheat and rice has more than doubled since the mid-1960s.[14] This has increased the importance of keeping considerable margins in achieving the self-sufficiency goal pursued by many countries and the necessity for large food reserves. However, there exists considerable scope for pooling food reserves at the regional and subregional levels.

The dramatic improvement in world food supplies in the 1980s from the bleak and precarious situation in the 1970s in which the

[11] See for example, Rodney Tyers and Kym Anderson, "The price, trade and welfare effects of agricultural protection" in Kym Anderson and Yujiro Hayami, eds., *The Political Economy of Agricultural Protection* (Sydney, Allen & Unwin, 1986), pp. 50-62.

[12] Don B. Gunasekera and Rodney Tyers, "Distortions in international food trade and their impact on the ESCAP region" (mimeographed) (Canberra, National Centre for Development Studies, Australian National University, September 1987), p. 47.

[13] See S. Mehra, "Instability in Indian agriculture in the context of the new technology", Research Report 25 (Washington D.C., International Food Policy Research Institute, 1981); and R. Barker, E.C. Gabler and D. Winkelman, "Long-term consequences of technological change on crop yield stability" in A. Valdés, ed., *Food Security for Developing Countries* (Boulder, Colorado, Westview Press).

[14] See Per Pinstrup-Andersen and Peter Hazell, *Food Review International*, vol. 1, No. 1 (1985).

Table II.7. Developing ESCAP region cereal supplies, 1975-1985

	Production	Export	Import	Supply[a]	Production per capita (kg)
		(Millions of tons)			
1975	509	6.7	29.8	532	240
1976	512	8.0	27.8	532	237
1977	522	8.3	29.2	543	236
1978	566	8.2	33.6	591	251
1979	569	9.9	38.3	597	248
1980	581	10.1	40.4	611	249
1981	606	10.4	41.7	637	255
1982	623	11.5	43.7	655	257
1983	695	10.5	46.1	731	282
1984	716	15.4	42.2	743	285
1985	700	17.4	34.0	717	274

Sources: FAO computer printout dated 1 June 1987, *FAO Trade Yearbook*, various issues; and ESCAP, *Handbook on Agricultural Statistics for Asia and the Pacific* (Bangkok, 1985) (ST/ESCAP/459).

[a] Supply = production − export + import.

developing countries of Asia have played an important part has to some extent taken away the attention of public policy from the still serious problems of the food availabilities and nutritional adequacy for millions of poor in Asia. Their situation, though not as grave as in famine-ravaged Africa, still does not brook complacency. In periods of recession and adjustment, the vulnerability of the poorer sections of the population increases, despite an abundance of food supplies and falling prices. As Professor A.K. Sen has aptly pointed out: "Starvation is the characteristic of some people not *having* enough food to eat. It is not the characteristic of there not *being* enough food to eat. While the latter can be the cause of the former, it is but one of the many plausible causes".[15] A brief survey of empirical evidence on the negative impact of the current reces-

sion in primary commodities on employment and incomes is presented in chapter IV.

(b) Trade possibilities

As per capita incomes rise, the demand for food consumption shifts away from cereals to animal-based diets, such as meat, poultry and milk. At present, the diets in most Asian countries are predominantly cereal-based — with over two thirds of otal calorie-intake being derived from cereals (see figure II.5). Although the region has achieved a degree of self-sufficiency in basic cereals for satisfying these inadequate calorie intake levels, the progress is still limited. The region is more than self-sufficient in rice, but imports significant proportions of wheat and coarse grains.

With rising per capita incomes, the demand for livestock and poultry products will rise. However, the demand for cereals will rise even faster, as they will be used for feeding both humans as well as animals, who are poor converters

of protein. The calorie-equivalent grain-meat conversion ratios vary from 2:1 for poultry to 7:1 for grain-fed beef. Thus both the need for higher calorie-intake and the shift in demand for animal-based diets in the developing ESCAP region is likely to increase demand for cereals at a much higher rate, even if demographic factors are kept in check.[16]

To meet these emerging challenges, the developing Asian and Pacific economies will have to continue their efforts to accelerate agricultural development. While the strategic goal of food self-sufficiency will probably continue to

---

[15] A.K. Sen, *Poverty and Famines: An Essay on Entitlement and Deprivation* (Oxford, Clarendon Press, 1981), p. 1.

[16] For detailed implications of this shift and the emerging food-feed competition in developing countries, see Rajiv Chaudry and C. Peter Tanmer, "The impact of changing affluence on diet and dietary patterns for agricultural commodities", World Bank Staff Working Paper 785; and Pan A. Yotopoulos, "Middle-income classes and food crises: the new food-feed competition, *Economic Development and Cultural Change*, vol. 33, No. 35 (April 1985), pp. 463-484.

Figure II.5. Food consumption, average per capita per day in selected developing economies of the ESCAP region, 1981-1983

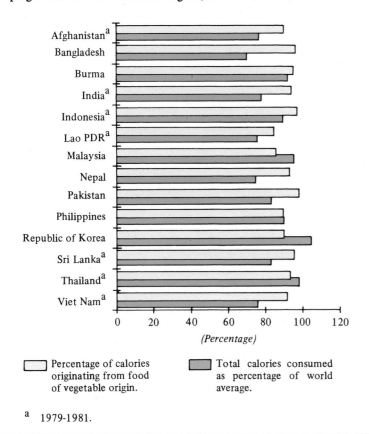

Afghanistan[a]
Bangladesh
Burma
India[a]
Indonesia[a]
Lao PDR[a]
Malaysia
Nepal
Pakistan
Philippines
Republic of Korea
Sri Lanka[a]
Thailand[a]
Viet Nam[a]

(Percentage)

☐ Percentage of calories originating from food of vegetable origin.

▨ Total calories consumed as percentage of world average.

[a] 1979-1981.

be pursued by most countries of the region, there will be increasing scope for international trade in a number of agricultural commodities both among the developing countries of the region and in the rest of the world. For this to be achieved, however, adequate investments will have to be undertaken in the agriculture sector to enable it to respond flexibly to changes in the external environment and domestic consumption patterns.

The improved performance of the agricultural sector in the ESCAP region in recent years has been reflected in a generally rising trend in exports and in import substitution of major food products except sugar. Thus the exports of coarse grains in the developing ESCAP region more than doubled during 1981-1985, while that of rice increased by 17 per cent, of beef and veal by 34 per cent, and of all other meats by 23 per cent during the period. Sugar exports fell marginally during the period, but the developing region's dependence on outside supplies increased 3.5 times. This was mainly due to the large imports by China and some shortfalls in India, Indonesia and Pakistan — which are likely to be considerably reduced. The main exporters of sugar in the region, Fiji, the Philippines and Thailand, however, face considerable competition from subsidized sugar exports from developed countries. There was a large increase in the net exports of rice from the region, largely owing to a reduction in imports by about 40 per cent by other importing countries of the region.

The attainment of self-sufficiency in basic food supplies has also enabled many countries in the region to diversify their agriculture with a view to developing new exports or substituting current food imports. This has led to considerable increases in the volume of intraregional trade in several commodities, such as that in edible oil between South-East and South Asian countries, and of sugar between China on the one hand and, the Philippines and Thailand, on the other. However, many importing countries are striving to achieve self-sufficiency in these and other products, which either reduces the possibility of mutual trade or contributes to increased supplies in the world market and further depresses commodity prices. The situation calls for greater efforts for promoting regional understanding in production and trade planning, which would give due consideration to comparative advantage before embarking on massive investments for the production and export of new commodities.

A considerable upsurge in the demand for meat, dairy products and coarse feed-grains is likely to take place in the region in the medium term, mostly in relatively high-income developing economies although a rising trends is likely in other countries also, with continued growth in per capita income levels. This will lead to large increases in imports by countries with limited land or other resource constraints. At the same time, it can provide opportunities to countries having such resources to develop exports of livestock and dairy products. This suggests a possibility of regional co-operation among countries of the region with differing resource endowments, although surpluses of the developed countries generated with heavy subsidies at low market prices are likely to be the main obstacle to such a possibility.

D. INTERDEPENDENCE BETWEEN THE PRIMARY AND OTHER SECTORS OF THE ECONOMY

1. Overall linkage effects

A salient feature of the technological changes which have been associated with the green revolution in agriculture and the growth of a domestic industrial sector is the increase in economic interdependence or linkages between the primary and the modern sector. This has considerably reduced the "enclave" nature of the primary export sector which characterized it during the colonial period.

A number of empirical studies on Asian agriculture have shown that there exist substantial indirect effects between agriculture and the rest of the economy. Thus an empirical study in India[17] found that a 1 per cent addition to the growth rate of the agricultural sector resulted in a 0.5 per cent growth rate of industrial output and a 0.7 per cent growth rate of national income, which implied an indirect effect on the economy of about 0.3 per cent increase in the overall growth rate. Studies in Malaysia[18] and the Philippines,[19] though somewhat limited in scope,

---

[17] C. Rangarajan, "Agricultural growth and industrial performance in India, Research Report 33 (Washington, D.C., International Food Policy Research Institute, 1982).

[18] Clive Bell, Peter Hazell and Roger Slade, *Project Evaluation in Regional Perspective* (Baltimore, Maryland, Johns Hopkins Press, 1982).

[19] Arthur Gibb, Jr., *Agricultural Modernization, Non-Farm Employment and Low-Level Urbanization: A case study of a Central Luzon Sub-region* (Ann Arbor, University of Michigan, 1974).

found similar indirect effects. The Malaysian study of technological change in rice showed that for each dollar of income created directly in agriculture by the project, an additional 80 cents of value added was created in the local non-farm economy, while the Philippines study, for example, found that each 1 per cent increase in agricultural income generated 1 to 2 per cent increase in employment in most sectors of the local non-farm economy.

The direction of the multiplier effects of changes in rural income transmitted to the economy depend on the nature of backward and forward linkages that characterize a given economy. In the Malaysian study, about two thirds of the 80 per cent income multiplier was due to increased rural household demand for consumer goods and services and only one third agriculture's increased demand for inputs and processing, transport and marketing services. In the past, there has been a tendency to ignore these consumption linkages; however they are becoming increasingly important as rural incomes rise significantly above the subsistence level. The existence of strong consumer expenditure linkages between households and the non-farm economy also creates additional benefits to the rural economy if there exist non-farm activities in the rural areas and rural employment if, as often is the case, the goods and services demanded are produced by small labour-intensive enterprise.

2. Processing of primary commodities

A major instrument of strengthening the linkages between the primary and industrial sectors of a developing economy is through the promotion of industries for downstream processing of primary commodities. Besides the considera-

tion of linkages, however, other arguments in favour of increased domestic processing of primary commodities also exist. Among these are the increase in value added, the reduction or cushioning of export earnings fluctuations (more valid for agricultural commodities), access to more distant export markets (through canning or packaging) and the appropriation of economic rents (mainly for natural resources such as minerals).

In general, the arguments about processing rest on an appropriate delineation of economic benefits (and costs) at each technological stage of production. This, in general, is not possible due to the inherent arbitrariness in the definition of various stages of production and determination of their benefits and costs. The profitability of processing activities can be affected by a number of factors, including availability of financial and human resources, as well as the access to export markets.

Simple processing of primary commodities has formed the basis of industrialization of most developing economies in the ESCAP region. Around half the value added in the manufacturing sector in the medium-sized primary-producing countries of the region (Indonesia, Malaysia, Pakistan and the Philippines) is contributed by the domestic processing of primary commodities. In the least developed economies, the proportion is much higher. In Bangladesh, for instance, the value added of food products, tobacco and textiles, together formed about 70 per cent of total value added in manufacturing in 1981. In the larger and more industrialized economies, such as China, India and the Republic of Korea, the proportions of primary processing industries' value added was less than a third. In the case of the Republic of Korea, however, a high proportion

114

of processed primary products were imported.

The growth of primary processing industries has often led to substantial reduction in the export supply of the commodities in their primary form (see table II.5). While having several beneficial effects, including the reduction of the glut in primary commodities and aiding the industrialization of the region, it has also given rise to some problems. First, reduction in raw material supplies has encouraged processing industries traditionally located in the developed countries to shift to substitutes competing with the natural products. This has initially led to shifts in "sourcing" to other countries, rather than outright substitution — but the long-term effects have generally been towards such technical substitution. Second, domestic processing industries have not always been able to maintain the product quality standard and specification to suit the taste of the developed country consumers who have shifted to substitutions. This points out the need for better market research in consuming countries and the possibility of establishing dowstream processing or designing facilities in consuming countries with a view to monitoring changes in tastes and adapting production. Third, escalating tariff and non-tariff barriers to trade in processed and semi-processed products (see chapter V) have further encouraged the above processes of substitution in both production and consumption in the developed countries. Finally, both final consumption and intermediate demand for these products being mainly located in the developed countries, there has been little intraregional trading in these commodities except largely as entrepot trade from Hong Kong and Singapore. Producing countries in the region have, as a result, found themselves competing against each other in developed country markets which have tended to shrink over time.

It is difficult to satisfactorily discuss in the present *Survey* the problems facing the developing countries of the region that wish to increase the total value added, as well as total foreign exchange earnings, derived from their primary commodities, through increased processing. A recent study undertaken by the United Nations Conference on Trade and Development (UNCTAD) secretariat, which included four developing countries of the region and four primary commodity processing activities: India (bauxite and phosphates), Indonesia (bauxite and tropical timber), Malaysia (palm type oils and tropical timber) and the Republic of Korea (bauxite and tropical timber), has identified a number of important barriers facing their development.[20]

Among the important domestic factors identified in the study was the importance of a continuous flow of both the basic and secondary raw materials, especially energy supplies. Some countries, such as Indonesia in the case of timber, have ensured this through a vertical integration of raw materials and processing industries. A second domestic policy element has been government support services, such as preferential export policy, development of necessary infrastructure, support for training, quality control and research and development activities. For example, the Malaysian Government has provided the palm oil processing industry research, training and marketing support without resorting to government ownership or control of marketing. A supportive policy environment is considered more essential than direct subsidies.

The transnational corporations according to the UNCTAD study, have played a somewhat ambiguous role in the development of processing activities. When a country offers an attractive local market (e.g., bauxite in India), it becomes an interesting investment proposition for the transnational corporations, but if the project would produce for export in competition with existing products of other locations, the status, size and the dynamics of the world market are more relevant considerations. Their dominance of final product markets — through superior marketing, advertising and product differentiating techniques — are often a formidable barrier to the entry of local processing firms.

The development of technology and technological research is also a major problem in processing primary commodities. Although the capacity for indigenous research is expanding, especially in larger countries such as China and India, technology research and development is expensive and most technologies continue to be bought or licensed from large firms, through ownership arrangements, tied sales and management contracts. Here negotiating expertise — both technical and legal — is an essential element for success.

E. PROBLEMS AND PROSPECTS OF MINERAL DEVELOPMENT

As pointed out in section B, the contribution of non-fuel minerals to total value added in GDP is small in most developing countries of the ESCAP region. This is partly a reflection of the relatively poor endowment of natural resources of the region, of the inadequate investment in prospecting and evaluating the potential for these resources and of the lack of even primary processing of most minerals. The recent recession in the world econo-

---

[20] "The local processing in developing countries of primary commodities" (UNCTAD/ST/CD/2) (August 1986).

my, reinforced by widespread technological changes affecting the use of metals (discussed in chapter I), have resulted in further downward pressure on mineral prices and on the incentives for exploration of new deposits and of domestic processing of minerals.

In terms of exports, although in most developing countries of the region minerals do not contribute very significantly to total exports, they do provide a substantial source of foreign exchange in many countries. The exports of some of the major minerals form a high proportion of exports in individual countries, as shown below:

Mineral	Country	Percentage of country's exports
Iron ore	India	4.0
Copper	Papua New Guinea	29.0
	Philippines	9.0
Tin	Malaysia	8.0
	Thailand	8.0

The developing ESCAP region has a significant share in world trade of a number of non-fuel minerals, such as nickel, chromite, cobalt, tin, tungsten and copper. Despite the current depressed state of commodity markets in metals and minerals, developing countries, including those of the ESCAP region, have continued to expand the production and exports of minerals in order to augment their foreign exchange reserves. For example, the production of iron ore expanded in spite of the depressed demand for iron and steel in the world in the 1980s. There was substantial growth in the iron ore production in Australia, China and India between 1981 and 1984. A recovery in world steel output and the emergence of new markets for iron ore resulted in a substantial increase in iron ore production and sales from Australia; in 1984 its exports increased to more than the levels of the mid-1970s. China

gained steadily from 107 million tons in 1982 to almost 122 million tons in 1984. Iron ore production in India fluctuated between 1981 and 1984, declining by some 9 per cent in 1983 over a total output of 38.6 million tons in the previous years, while in 1984 production rose to about 41.5 million tons. The total deposits of iron ore in India are estimated at some 13.5 billion tons.

The production of bauxite in the region continued to increase from 32.5 million tons/year in 1981 to about 42 million tons in 1984. Australia remains the world's leading producer of bauxite: its economic bauxite resources total 4.3 billion tons.[21] It accounts for 20 per cent of the world's bauxite reserves and 35 per cent of world production. Developing Asia's bauxite reserves are estimated at over 1.6 billion tons, or about 7 per cent of the world's reserves and production of 5.6 million tons or about 5.5 per cent of world total. China, India, Indonesia, Malaysia and Pakistan are among the major producers of bauxite in the region.

The principal producers of copper in the region registered gains in copper output in the 1980s, with the exception of the Philippines. The output in the Philippines, although continuing to lead the region in mine production,

---

[21] ESCAP, *The Triennial Review of Mineral Development Activities in the ESCAP Region, 1982-1984,* Mineral Resources Development Series No. 55 (United Nations publication, Sales No. E.87.II.F.5). p. 28.

declined substantially by 26 per cent to 225,216 tons in 1984 compared with 305,262 tons in 1981. Mine production of copper increased in Australia, China, India, Indonesia, Malaysia and Papua New Guinea (see box II.5).

The region's tin production declined continuously during the

Box II.5. Mineral

The 16 developing Pacific island economies in the ESCAP region occupy a land surface area of less than 0.53 million square kilometres but their exclusive economic zones extend over 22 million square kilometres of the middle Pacific Ocean. Much of the rich fishery resources, however, remain to be fully exploited by these islands because of their limited capability to invest in the infrastructure, such as fishing fleets and canning factories, needed for large-scale harvesting, processing and marketing of these resources.[a]

The few other known natural resources of great commercial potential which have been discovered and/or are under exploitation are concentrated largely in a few islands. Nauru is rich in phosphate and this resource is expected to last until the end of this century. The income from phosphate exports has made this island one of the world's richest countries in terms of per capita income, in spite of its having the highest population density within the Pacific island subregion.[b]

Phosphate exports used to account for about four fifths of the merchandise export earnings of Kiribati in the 1970s. The exhaustion and consequent cessation of mining on Banaba (also known as Ocean) Island after 1979 eliminated minerals as a

---

[a] See, *Survey,* 1985, pp. 53-54 and pp. 58-59; *Survey,* 1986, p. 60; and D.M. King, "Global tuna markets: a Pacific island perspective" in D.J. Doulman, ed., *Tuna Issues and Perspectives in the Pacific Island Region* (Honolulu, East-West Center, 1987), pp. 279-296.

[b] Nauru is not an aid recipient, but provides small amounts of assistance to others in the subregion (*Survey,* 1985, fn. 1, p. 53).

period, owing to the weakness of international demand and the consequent collapse of the International Tin Agreement in 1985. That agreement had been considered the epitome of a co-operative agreement between producers and consumers; its collapse highlighted the difficulties of the mineral producers of the region and the constant need for monitoring demand and supply changes. Demand fell largely owing to technological changes, such as galvanoplasty, can molding and processing techniques, pressing and welding techniques, as well as the emergence of cheaper alternative materials such as aluminium and TFS (tin-free steel). The level of demand in the United States, the largest consumer in the world, fell by 30 per cent between 1975 and 1985. At the same time, production of countries outside the International Tin Council (ITC) grew rapidly, while repeated im-

resources in the Pacific

major source of exchange earnings; it also caused GDP in real terms to fall by almost 40 per cent in 1980.[c] The adverse impact of such a drastic economic loss on government revenue has been cushioned by interest income from the Revenue Equalization Reserve Fund, which had been set up from the accumulated proceeds of the phosphate tax, which were then invested in bonds denominated in several major international currencies. The current value of the Fund's holdings was over $A 178 million as of September 1987, compared with the initial balance of $A 0.56 million in 1956.[d]

In absolute terms, Papua New Guinea is perhaps the most richly endowed Pacific island, in terms of both potential and current exploitation. Deposits of hydrocarbons, particularly gas, of commercial potential have been discovered. The large-scale, capital-intensive mining and export of gold and copper, in particular, have transformed the country from an agriculture-based to a minerals-based primary exporting country. The first copper/gold mine at Bougainville was commissioned at an estimated investment of $A 400 million in 1972 and reached full production capacity a year later. Exports of copper concentrates (plus the gold and silver contained therein) contributed about one half of total export receipts during 1973-1980.

The second large-scale, capital in-tensive gold/copper mine, developed at Ok Tedi at an estimated cost of over one billion United States dollars, started yielding significant gold exports in 1985; copper exports are expected to rise considerably during 1987 with the commissioning of the first stage of processing facilities in late 1986. Gold exports, which had been almost stagnant at around 19 tons annually during 1982-1984, went up by almost two thirds (to 32.1 tons) in 1985, and a further 14 per cent (to 36.5 tons) in 1986. Exports of gold and copper (plus a small amount of contained-in silver), at about 526 million kina, consequently accounted for 56 per cent of the annual domestic merchandise earnings during 1985-1986; agricultural commodities, by comparison, provided around 35 per cent of domestic export value during the same period.

The development of mineral resources has helped propel the economic growth of Papua New Guinea but has also rendered the growth process more vulnerable to exogenous economic shocks, especially changes in mineral commodity prices. However, the adverse domestic impact of such cyclical instability, particularly on the flow of public expenditure, has been offset to some extent principally through the operations of the Mineral Resources Stabilization Fund.[e] The Fund distributes annually to consoli-dated fiscal revenue a relatively stable flow of resources receivable from normal and excess profits taxation, dividend withholding taxes on non-resident shareholders, and the Government's share of dividends from its equity holdings in the relevant mining enterprises.[f] The important role of this innovative counter-cyclical institution is clearly evidenced from the uneven flow of Fund receipts which reached, for example, 109 million kina in 1980 and averaged 25 million kina in 1982-1983.

Mining for precious metals, gold and silver in particular, constitutes only a minor production and export activity in Fiji, with an estimated share of less than 1 per cent in GDP.[g] In value terms, mineral exports are dominated by gold, and to a much less extent, silver. Fiji's gold exports had been rising rapidly, from 0.95 ton in 1981 to about 2.9 tons in 1986, reflecting the exploitation of new reserves, the granting of special mining leases to a joint venture in 1983, and the influence of rising gold prices. Consequently, earnings from this commodity went up from an annual average of $F 13.7 million, or 7 per cent of domestic export value during 1981-1982, to reach $F 38.6 million, or 16 per cent, in 1986.

[c] United Nations, *Special Economic, Humanitarian and Disaster Relief Assistance — Assistance to Kiribati* (E/1985/67), pp. 10 and 12.

[d] National Planning Office, *Kiribati Sixth National Development Plan, 1987 to 1991* (Tarawa, Ministry of Finance, 8 December 1986), statistical appendix table 5.

[e] For a detailed analysis of this innovative counter-cyclical institution, see N.V. Lam, "Government responses to export instability in Papua New Guinea", *Malayan Economic Review*, vol. 26, No. 2 (October 1981), pp. 29-32; and James Guest, "Problems in managing the Mineral Resources Stabilization Fund", Bank of Papua New Guinea, *Quarterly Economic Bulletin*, vol. XV, No. 2 (June 1987), pp. 17-24.

[f] The Mineral Resources Stabilization Fund Act was also amended in November 1986 to cover designated petroleum enterprises, besides hard-rock mining companies. Fund receipts so far have come from Bougainville Copper Limited as Ok Tedi Mining Limited is not yet liable for corporate taxes: it began commercial production only in 1984 and is still in its capital recovery stage.

[g] Central Planning Office, *Fiji's Ninth Development Plan 1986-1990* (Suva, November 1985), p. 79.

position of quotas reduced the share of the ITC-controlled markets from 80 to 53 per cent in 1984.

Although the present fall in commodity prices has affected non-fuel minerals much more than other primary commodities, there seems to be much greater opportunity for developing countries, including those of the ESCAP region, to develop their mineral sector in the medium and long term. This arises from the asymmetry in the configuration of demand and supplies in global agricultural and mineral primary commodities. While in the agricultural sector, the supply pressures have arisen from both the developed and developing countries — and are likely to continue to do so — in the mineral sector there is a tendency to contract mining output in developed countries primarily because of the relatively high energy and labour costs.[22] At the same time, the demand for mineral goods has fallen in developed countries owing to structural and technological changes, while in developing countries the substitution effects are not yet widespread. Further, the dominance of multinationals in mining production has been considerably reduced and barriers to entry in the international market have been correspondingly lowered.

If and when the prices of non-fuel minerals begin to rise through a conjuncture of supply reductions in developed economies and stronger demand in the developing economies, it is likely that profitability of mineral production and investment will rise significantly. The developing economies may also be able to attract multinationals to invest in mining activities, as perceptions of profitability increase as a result of the better investment environment in such economies. In view of their need for foreign exchange resources and the likely impetus vertically-integrated mineral industries can provide to industrialization efforts, the developing countries of the the ESCAP region need to weigh the option of developing their mineral resources more seriously than the currently low prices of minerals induce them to do.

---

[22] See John Toye, "The recession, the third world and the base metal industries", *World Development,* vol. 12, No. 9 (September 1984).

III. CHANGING PATTERN OF THE ESCAP REGION'S TRADE IN PRIMARY COMMODITIES

The preceding chapter has highlighted the varied nature of dependence on commodity trade in the ESCAP region as measured by the share of primary commodities exports in total merchandise exports. Although the aggregate figure would suggest that the ESCAP region is not so heavily dependent on primary commodity trade as the other two developing regions of Africa and Latin America, it hides large differences among countries of the region, many of which depend on commodity exports for well over 50 per cent of their export earnings. In addition many countries, in particular some of the lower-income countries, are almost completely specialized in the exports of only a few, sometimes not more than 2 or 3, primary commodities. The analysis presented in this chapter focuses on the changing importance, composition, growth performance and direction of primary commodity trade in the ESCAP region. It assesses in detail the changes that have taken place in commodity trade for individual ESCAP countries over the last two decades so as to enable a better understanding of the implications of the changing nature and importance of commodity trade to the economies of the region.

A. CHANGING IMPORTANCE OF PRIMARY COMMODITIES IN WORLD AND REGIONAL TRADE

The changing importance of primary commodity exports in total world trade in aggregate and by commodity groups is a good starting point for assessing movements in their comparative importance for the ESCAP region. The changing importance is also well reflected in the relative shares for particular commodity groups of the ESCAP region in world commodity trade. Trade shares by major commodity groups are shown in table II.8 for main world regions and for the developing ESCAP region. The table also shows the share of commodity trade in total merchandise trade by regions.

An overview of the trends at the aggregate level indicates that the developing countries' share in world primary commodity trade between 1970 and 1984 declined from 34.3 to 31.8 per cent. Socialist countries of Europe, whose shares have been rather small, also experienced a decline. Thus the gain in shares accrued to developed market economies, which increased their share to 63 per cent of non-oil commodity exports in 1984. In terms of total merchandise trade, the importance of primary commodity exports fell for both developed market economies and developing countries. However, for developing countries, primary commodity exports as a percentage of total merchandise exports fell much more sharply, from 50.3 per cent in 1970 to 22.1 per cent in 1984, while the corresponding fall in developed market economies was from 21.8 to 17.0 per cent.

The decline in the importance of primary commodities in the merchandise trade of developing countries partly reflects the rapid increase in other categories of exports, particularly manufactures and petroleum exports, but partly it is also a reflection of deteriorating terms of trade for primary commodities. However, primary commodities assume much more importance in the exports of non-oil developing countries, with their share falling by just a half between 1970 and 1984, from 69.3 to 35.3 per cent. Hence, more than one third of exports from non-oil developing countries still consist of primary commodities.

Among the main groups of developing countries shown in table II.8, African countries experienced a sharp decline in their share of primary commodity trade, but Latin American countries roughly maintained their share. In contrast, ESCAP developing countries significantly increased their share in primary commodity trade from 9.6 per cent in 1970 to 11.4 per cent in 1984, in spite of the decline in the importance of primary commodities in total merchandise trade of the region.

Table II.8 also reveals some interesting changes in trade by broad categories of primary commodities (see box II.6). For developing countries as a whole, the market share of agricultural raw materials and minerals and metals fell perceptibly during 1970-1984, while the share of food products exports remained relatively stable at around 34-35 per cent. Equally interesting are the regional differences. There was a precipitous fall in Africa's share

Table II.8. Selected country groupings and ESCAP developing region. World commodity trade shares and commodity export dependence, 1970 and 1984

(Percentage)

	Total merchandise exports		All primary commodities[a]		Food products		Agricultural raw materials		Minerals and metals	
	1970	1984	1970	1984	1970	1984	1970	1984	1970	1984
World	100.0	100.0	100.0	100.0	100.0	100.0	100.0	100.0	100.0	100.0
	(100.0)	(100.0)	(27.0)	(17.6)	(14.6)	(11.0)	(5.0)	(2.8)	(7.3)	(3.9)
Developed market economies	71.6	65.3	57.8	63.0	57.9	62.8	55.2	62.6	59.3	63.5
	(100.0)	(100.0)	(21.8)	(17.0)	(11.8)	(10.6)	(3.9)	(2.7)	(6.1)	(3.8)
Australia	1.5	1.3	4.2	4.1	3.1	2.8	6.2	4.5	5.0	7.3
	(100.0)	(100.0)	(73.5)	(55.6)	(29.9)	(23.9)	(20.1)	(9.7)	(23.5)	(21.9)
New Zealand	0.4	0.3	1.3	1.3	1.6	1.3	2.3	2.2	0.0	0.4
	(100.0)	(100.0)	(88.1)	(77.7)	(57.5)	(50.6)	(29.4)	(21.2)	(0.6)	(5.7)
Socialist Eastern Europe	10.0	9.5	7.9	5.2	6.7	3.4	10.2	8.1	8.8	8.4
	(100.0)	(100.0)	(21.4)	(9.7)	(9.9)	(4.0)	(5.1)	(2.4)	(6.4)	(3.4)
Developing countries	18.4	25.2	34.3	31.8	35.4	33.8	34.6	29.3	32.0	28.1
	(100.0)	(100.0)	(50.3)	(22.1)	(28.1)	(14.7)	(9.4)	(3.2)	(12.7)	(4.3)
Non-oil developing countries	11.7	14.1	29.9	28.3	30.8	31.1	29.0	24.5	28.9	23.4
	(100.0)	(100.0)	(69.3)	(35.3)	(38.6)	(24.2)	(12.4)	(4.8)	(18.1)	(6.4)
Africa	4.2	3.5	8.9	4.7	8.2	4.3	8.7	5.0	10.4	6.1
	(100.0)	(100.0)	(58.0)	(23.8)	(29.1)	(13.2)	(10.5)	(3.7)	(18.4)	(6.8)
Latin America	5.4	5.7	13.8	13.6	16.0	15.8	6.8	5.1	14.0	13.0
	(100.0)	(100.0)	(69.0)	(41.7)	(43.5)	(30.3)	(6.3)	(2.5)	(19.1)	(8.8)
ESCAP developing countries	5.6	10.2	9.6	11.4	9.1	11.6	16.4	17.3	5.9	6.5
	(100.0)	(100.0)	(45.8)	(19.6)	(23.6)	(12.5)	(14.6)	(4.7)	(7.6)	(2.5)
ESCAP non-oil developing countries	4.5	8.3	8.5	10.1	8.4	10.8	13.6	14.2	5.2	5.3
	(100.0)	(100.0)	(51.3)	(21.5)	(27.6)	(14.4)	(15.2)	(4.8)	(8.5)	(2.5)

Source: UNCTAD primary commodity trade data on tapes, secretariat calculations.

Notes: First line: percentage of world exports. Second line (in parenthesis): percentage of total exports of each grouping or country.

[a] Note that the definition excludes cotton yarn (SITC 651.3) and jute products (SITC 654.5, 658.1 and 651.98). (See box II.6.)

of food product exports in total world commodity exports from 8.2 per cent in 1970 to 4.3 per cent in 1984. There were also perceptible declines in its share of the other two categories. The Latin American region also suffered declines in its share of all three sub-groups. However the developing ESCAP region improved its share in all major subcategories and emerged as by far the largest agricultural raw material exporter and the second largest food exporter.

Its share of exports of minerals and metals, which was the lowest among the developing region in 1970, surpassed that of Africa but remained about half that of Latin America.

As noted earlier, Australia and New Zealand have a much larger degree of dependence on primary commodities than the average developing country of the region. Both countries maintained their share in world primary commodity trade roughly constant between

1970 and 1984. In 1984, about 5.4 per cent of all primary commodity exports originated from Australia and New Zealand. With a 4.1 per cent share in world primary commodity exports in 1984, Australia was the largest commodity exporter in the world.

The developing ESCAP region has gained substantially in food products exports, in which its world market share increased from 9.1 per cent in 1970 to 11.6 per cent in 1984. This performance is particularly remarkable considering the high domestic demand growth rates owing to high population and income growth rates in the region.

This is largely the result of the rapid rise in the output of food products, in particular of food grains, in the ESCAP region between 1970 and 1984, with several countries reaching near self-sufficiency (e.g., China, India and Indonesia) or being able to produce larger exportable surpluses (such as Pakistan and Thailand for maize and rice).[1] Although declining in relative terms to 12.5 per cent in 1984 down from 23.6 per cent in 1970, food products also represent by far the largest category of primary commodity exports from the ESCAP region.

---

[1] See ch. II, this *Survey*.

The developing ESCAP region exported 17.3 per cent of world agricultural raw materials in 1984. The region increased slightly its share in the world market compared with 1970 and accounted for about two thirds of the developing countries' exports of this category in 1984. They amounted to about 5 per cent of the region's total merchandise exports.

In minerals and metals, the ESCAP region's world market share slightly increased, from 5.9 to 6.5 per cent. This is a creditable performance in view of the region's relatively poor endowment, the relatively steeper fall in the prices of minerals and the decline in the shares of the other two developing regions.

B. DIFFERING IMPORTANCE OF AND EXPOSURE TO CHANGES IN COMMODITY TRADE

1. Developing economies

The market share of developing countries of the ESCAP region, as a whole, in primary commodity trade is rather small and not much different from its share in world merchandise exports — a little over one tenth in 1984. Unlike trade in manufactures, the other most important category of total trade for the region, the exports of primary commodities are much less heavily concentrated among a few developing countries of the region. Two of the largest developing country exporters of the region, China and Malaysia, account for a little over 2 per cent each of world commodity exports or about 20 per cent each of the developing ESCAP region's commodity exports. India, Indonesia and Thailand — the next largest exporters — accounted for another 3.4 per cent of total world exports. Thus the five large primary commodity exporters account for about 70 per cent of the developing ESCAP region's primary commodity exports.[2,3] Except for the five largest primary commodity exporters, no other country had a world market share above 1 per cent.

The world market share of the developing countries of the ESCAP region in primary commodity trade rose from 9.6 per cent in 1966 to 11.4 per cent in 1984. However, only a few countries, mainly in East and South-East Asia, saw any significant increase in their world market shares. China, Indonesia, Malaysia and Thailand were among the countries which experienced such increases; their aggregate share rose from 4.9 per cent in 1966 to 6.9 per cent in 1984. The Philippines was the only South-East Asian country which suffered a significant decline in its share — from 1.2 per cent in 1966 to 0.7 per cent in 1984. Papua New Guinea and Thailand saw a doubling of their shares during the last two decades. Surprisingly, the largest percentage increase in the share of primary commodity exports took place in the Republic of Korea, which saw a 150 per cent increase in its world market share in primary commodity exports, while the proportion of such exports to total merchandise exports fell from 20.1 to 5.4 per cent between 1966 and 1984.[4] South Asian countries saw their market share eroded

by 20-25 per cent between 1966 and 1984.

While changes in the world share of exports of individual countries depend on a complex interplay of factors, both domestic and external, an increase in a country's market share can be taken as evidence of its revealed comparative advantage in primary production and indicative of its success as an efficient primary producer. Among the factors which seem to have accounted for the increase in the market shares of the countries in the region, diversification into new primary commodities appears to have been an important factor (see box II.7). Indonesia and Thailand seem to be the economies which have succeeded in broadening and shifting their commodity base over time, while countries which have failed to change the pattern of their commodity specialization have generally not done well.

Although the change in the share of primary commodities is to some extent modified by changes in share in other categories of exports, especially manufactures, for the major primary-producing countries of the region, the share of total exports in world merchandise exports has improved only in cases where the share in primary commodity exports has increased as well. This indicates to some extent the complementary, rather than competitive, character of primary commodity trade in the region. This is in contrast to the evolution of trade both in the developed market economies and developing economies, as a whole. For the developed market economies, while the total shares in exports have fallen, the shares in primary

commodity exports have risen, and vice versa for the developing economies.

Large world market shares are likely to be associated with a stronger production base, allowing price fluctuations to be compensated by volume changes, thus reducing overall export earnings instability. In addition large producers and exporters probably are not only more competitive but also have a much stronger marketing infrastructure, allowing them to keep their markets at the expense of small exporters when demand deteriorates. Small exporters might thus be marginalized, hence the larger fluctuations in their export earnings growth.

Primary commodity problems, however, are important not only to countries having a large share in the world commodity economy but also to those which have a high degree of dependence for their export earnings on a few such commodities. The pattern of this dependence was brought out in chapter II.[5] The changes in this pattern are shown in figure II.6. Many countries of the region, including most of its least developed countries, continue to depend on primary commodity exports for a very high proportion of their export earnings. Thus, while Burma and Samoa depend practically exclusively on primary commodities as exports, Papua New Guinea, Tonga and Vanuatu also depend more than 80 per cent on primary commodity exports for foreign exchange earnings. In the case of Fiji, Nepal, the Solomon Islands, Sri Lanka, Thailand and Viet Nam, dependence on commodity exports is more than 60 per cent. For other economies, such as India, the Lao People's Democratic Repub-

    [2] In contrast, the five largest exporters of manufactures in the developing ESCAP region (China, Hong Kong, India, the Republic of Korea and Taiwan (a province of the People's Republic of China)) accounted for 73.2 per cent of total manufactured exports of the region.

    [3] The country with the next highest market share, Singapore, is an entrepôt trader and most of its exports originate from Malaysia.

    [4] The dramatic increase in the Republic of Korea's share, however, is largely due to the increase in fishing, and is related to the increase in its fishing fleet.

    [5] See this *Survey*, ch. II, tables II.5 and II.6.

lic, Malaysia, Maldives, Pakistan and the Philippines, primary commodity export earnings continue to play an important role in financing development and in macro-economic management.

A developing country's dependence on primary commodity trade is also considerably exposed in the instability and growth in its export earnings. Although these issues are discussed in greater

---

Box II.7. Emerging new export commodities in the ESCAP region

While the analysis of the main primary commodity exports is useful in demonstrating the main trends in the commodity trade of the ESCAP region and its impact on overall economic growth, the aggregate figures do not provide sufficient information about the constant changes in the commodity composition of such trade and the continuing entry of "new" commodities in the primary commodity market. Indeed it is the emergence of these new export commodities which has enabled the ESCAP region to maintain its market share.

Sometimes the "new" products entering trade are "traditional" commodities whose scale of production has been boosted through public and private sector development efforts to expand their production and marketing. Sometimes commodities which have not been produced before in a country or region have been introduced to diversify and to discover new sources of exports and incomes. Among the first category of products, the exports of coffee and vanilla by Tonga, fishery products by Bangladesh and chicken, fishery products and different kinds of fruits and vegetables from Thailand and the Philippines are significant examples. Among the new export products emerging in several countries of the region are cashew nuts and coffee in Thailand and tropical flowers in Singapore.

Amongst the traditional products, poultry meat, both fresh and frozen, has been a particularly rapidly expanding export product for several countries of the region, especially Thailand. Exports of chicken by Thailand have expanded very rapidly since 1973. Exports of frozen chicken have grown particularly fast in recent years at an average annual rate of over 50 per cent during 1984-1986. They have now attained a share of 1.3 per cent in total Thai exports, comparable with those of other fast-growing and important export products of Thailand, such as canned pineapple or footwear. Japan is the

major market for Thai chicken exports, but vast market potential exists in the Middle Eastern and European countries.[a]

The vast marine resources of the region and the rapid expansion of aquaculture have enabled several countries of the region, besides such traditional exporters as Maldives and many Pacific islands, to sharply increase their exports of fishery products. During the last decade, fishery exports from Bangladesh increased at an average annual rate of more than 25 per cent, making them one of the country's major exports. Other countries which have rapid growth in fishery exports are the Philippines, the Republic of Korea, the Solomon Islands, Sri Lanka, Thailand and Viet Nam. In Thailand in particular, the raising of shrimps and other aquaculture is becoming increasingly important. Fresh shrimp exports grew, for instance, by 22.3 and 27.7 per cent respectively in 1985 and 1986.

High-quality fruits and vegetables are another category of commodities emerging as an important export for some countries of the region which have paid sufficient attention to the development of horticulture. Fresh mango exports from the Philippines reached, for instance, about $7.5 million in 1985 and are emerging as an important non-traditional agricultural export. China and Thailand are also important fast-growing exporters of fruits and vegetables. For Thailand, the category represented about $38.9 million in 1986 and has been listed by the Government under the sixth development plan (1987-1991) as an export commodity having high potential. The neighbouring economies of Hong Kong, Malaysia and Singapore are major clients but the European market is expanding rapidly, in particular in the Netherlands.[b]

In recent years, temperate climate fruits and vegetables have also been

adapted to the soil and weather conditions of Thailand and have proved a major success in the foreign market.[c]

Finally, there are lesser known commodities whose exports, though small, have expanded rapidly as, for instance, fresh and cut flowers for Singapore and Thailand, and tropical fish (aquarium fish) for Thailand and several other countries of the ESCAP region.

There is in many countries of the ESCAP region an enormous potential to develop the production of new commodities for export. Several countries, such as Thailand, have gone a long way in exploring these possibilities and in such cases ECDC-TCDC (economic and technical co-operation among developing countries) should be increased between the countries of the region. In many cases, such as the exports of fish products or fresh fruit and vegetables, the continued growth in exports will depend on the investments to be made in stabilizing supply (for instance through irrigation), ensuring the high quality of the products (through improving the strains and seeds and by keeping them free from plant disease) and in acquiring the appropriate processing technology so as to obtain products which conform to the high quality and hygiene standards set by importing countries. In some cases, costly investments will have to be made in infrastructure (such as fishing vessels, cold storage and cargo air transport) as well as research and extension services. The problems and costs encountered in the development of new export commodities are thus not negligible and need to be carefully assessed in each case.

---

[a] Bangkok Bank, *Monthly Review,* vol. 27, No. 5 (May 1986).

[b] *Made in Thailand,* vol. 2, No. 2 (November 1987).

[c] Kamolluck Tosakul, "Processed fruit and vegetables — an agro-industry producing for export" in Bangkok Bank, *Monthly Review,* vol. 27, No. 5 (May 1986).

Figure II.6. Selected developing ESCAP economies. Commodity export dependence, 1970 and 1984[a]

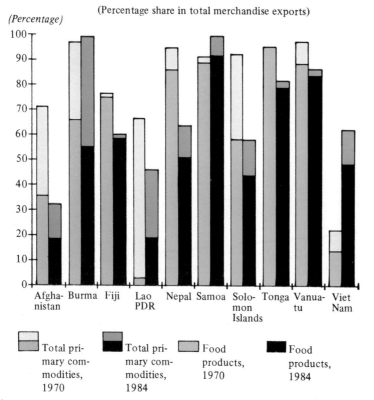

(Percentage share in total merchandise exports)

(Percentage)

Total primary commodities, 1970

Total primary commodities, 1984

Food products, 1970

Food products, 1984

[a] Data represent 1982 in the case of Afghanistan and 1983 in the case of the Lao People's Democratic Republic.

detail in the next chapter, some general trends relevant in the context are discussed below.

Several countries of the region simultaneously experienced very low commodity export growth rates (less than half the average for the region as a whole) and high instability in their growth rates. They happen to be economies with the most unfavourable commodity specialization and with a high dependence on and vulnerability to the evolution of commodity markets. This group of countries comprises Bangladesh, Bhutan, the Islamic Republic of Iran, Nepal, Tonga and Vanuatu. Four of these countries are least developed countries.

A second group of countries, with a somewhat better situation, with growth rates of about 3-4 per cent below the region's average and high instability, consists of Burma, Fiji, the Lao People's Democratic Republic, the Philippines, Samoa and Sri Lanka — three of which are least developed countries.

These two groups of countries comprise about half of the 26 developing countries of the ESCAP region included in the analysis and the majority of the least developed countries.

Thus, while on the aggregate the commodity export growth performance of the region was quite strong over the last two decades, at least half of the countries of the region, including almost all of the least developed countries, fared very poorly in terms of commodity exports. In addition, for these countries and for many others

of the region, large yearly fluctuations characterized commodity export growth, thus rendering the planning of economic development more difficult. Furthermore, the trends in the last decade show a general deterioration in both growth and stability in primary commodity earnings.

2. Developed economies

As pointed out earlier, two of the developed countries of the region, Australia and New Zealand, are major exporters of primary commodities, which in 1984 provided nearly 56 and 78 per cent respectively of their export earnings. However, unlike other countries of the region with high dependence on primary commodity exports, the importance of such exports for them has not significantly declined during the period 1970-1984.

In terms of broad commodity categories presented in table II.8, Australia and New Zealand roughly maintained their share in the world export markets of food products, and in the case of New Zealand, also of agricultural raw materials. The Australian share in this latter category has declined steadily from 6.2 per cent in 1970 to 4.5 per cent in 1984. Australia, however, significantly increased its share in the minerals and metals market from 5 per cent in 1970 to 7.3 per cent in 1984.

The importance of the minerals and metals market for Australia is obvious, with exports representing about 22 per cent of its total exports in 1984, almost equivalent to its exports of food products (23.9 per cent). For New Zealand, exports of food products represent more than half of its merchandise exports, followed by agricultural raw materials with over 20 per cent of total exports, and minerals and metals with about

6.0 per cent. The exports of minerals and metals has, however, increased rapidly compared with 1970, when they were negligible (0.6 per cent of total exports).

A detailed analysis of world market shares by main commodities shows, as might be expected, that the commodity composition of the trade of Australia and New Zealand differs substantially from that of the developing countries of the ESCAP region. In this sense the commodity trade issues faced by both countries are rather different from those of the developing part of the region, although for some categories of products strong commonality of interests exist. This is underlined by the fact that both Australia and New Zealand are among the most primary-commodity-dependent economies of the region.

Australia and New Zealand have sizeable shares in the world market for live animals and meat, dairy products, fishery products, hides and skins and wool. Australia is also an important producer of cereals, sugar and minerals, iron and nickel among other commodities. Meat exports represented more than 20 per cent of New Zealand exports in 1984 and about 5 per cent of Australian exports. Both countries had a 6-7 per cent world maket share.

The importance of dairy products has declined considerably though for New Zealand it still represents about 15 per cent of total exports. Both countries lost about half of their world market share between 1966 and 1984. Exports of fishery products expanded rapidly over the last two decades, particularly for New Zealand. Fishery product exports represented nearly 5 per cent of New Zealand exports in 1984, up from only 1.6 per cent in 1970. Cereals, mainly wheat, account for over 10 per

cent of Australian exports, which amount to nearly 6 per cent of the world market. Australia managed to increase its world market share by over 1 per cent between 1966 and 1984. Australia is also a large exporter of sugar, supplying about 6 per cent of the world market. Australia's share in the sugar market has remained rather stable over the last two decades whereas all sugar exporting developing economies of the ESCAP region, except Thailand, have experienced sharply declining world market shares.

Australia and New Zealand dominate the market for wool supplying together over 80 per cent of the world market. Their dominance in this market increased significantly between 1966 and 1984. As a proportion of their respective total exports, the importance of wool has, however, declined considerably. For Australia, wool exports represented about 7 per cent in 1984, compared with 17 per cent in 1970. For New Zealand, the share fell from 18.7 per cent in 1970 to 13.6 per cent in 1984.

Australia has emerged as a major exporter of several minerals and metals accounting for, for example, nearly one fifth of the world iron ore market, about one third of that of nickel ore and one quarter of that of tin ore in 1984. Australia also accounts for 10 per cent of the world supply of bauxite. In 1966, the share of Australia in all these markets was very small, amounting to 1-2 per cent. Altogether, about one fifth of Australian exports were minerals and metals in 1984. The Australian economy is thus particularly vulnerable to the volatile metals and minerals market. Most developing countries of the ESCAP region, in contrast, are only small exporters of minerals and metals, as discussed in the preceding chapter (see pp. 115-118).

As regards the growth performance of their commodity trade, Australian and New Zealand commodity exports grew slower than the average for all developed market economies, especially in the case of New Zealand. Food products exports of Australia grew at about the same rate as the average for the developed market economy countries, 12.2 per cent. Growth in the exports of agricultural raw materials, and of minerals and metals was, however, very low and about 2 per cent below the world averages. It was even below the average for all developing countries. For both the countries, instability in trade growth has been very high, in fact, much above the average instability levels for either developed or developing countries.

Hence, while their commodity export structure is generally very different from that of the developing countries of the ESCAP region, both Australia and New Zealand face the problems of slow export value growth, deteriorating commodity terms of trade and export instability in common with the developing ESCAP region.

C. CHANGING COMPOSITION OF PRIMARY COMMODITY TRADE

Figure II.7 indicates the commodities for which the developing ESCAP region accounted for a substantial share of world exports in 1984 – ranging from over 20 per cent for fishery products to almost 100 per cent for jute products.[6] Between 1966 and 1984 some important changes in the ESCAP region's world market

---

[6] For a few commodities such as natural rubber, vegetable oils and tin, the world trade share of the region might be somewhat overestimated because of the important entrepôt trade of Singapore.

Figure II.7. Developing ESCAP region. Exports of major primary commodities, 1966 and 1984

(Percentage of total world exports of each commodity)

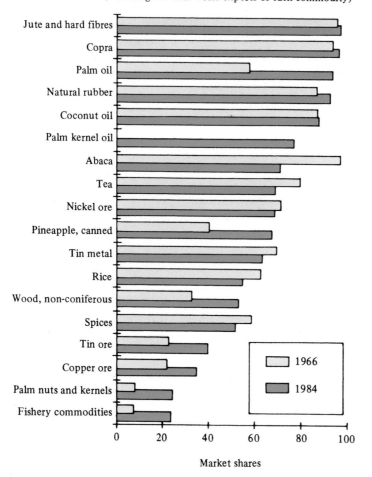

Market shares

shares for different commodities have occurred. The shares of palm oil products, canned pineapple, tin and copper ore, and fishery products increased tremendously. Significant declines occurred in abaca, tea, rice, spices and tin metal.

Amongst the commodities for which the ESCAP region's world market share was less than 20 per cent, remarkable growth was observed for poultry meat, pineapples, coffee, cocoa products, cotton and nickel intermediate products, while that for sugar fell by about 50 per cent between 1966 and 1984.

While aggregate trends in the region's market shares reflect changes in the region's competitiveness in world markets, the extent to which individual countries within the region respond to the changing situation are reflected in the changes in their market shares. In this section the performance of the region's developing economies in respect of their market shares of major commodities is discussed in some detail.

Agricultural exports accounted for about 90 per cent of total primary commodity exports in the developing ESCAP region in 1984. Of these, the predominant subcategory was that of food, which accounted for about 65 per cent of total commodity exports. Agricultural raw materials, in which the developing ESCAP region has a high world market share (17.3 per cent in 1984), accounted for about a quarter of the developing ESCAP region's primary commodity exports. Minerals and metals was a relatively less important category of primary commodity exports, both in terms of the developing ESCAP region's world market share and in terms of the share in the region's total primary commodity exports (6.5 and 12.6 per cent, respectively, in 1984).

Food exports were also the fastest growing category of primary commodity exports of the region. Their importance is bound to grow further as the developing ESCAP region increases its food supplies and as food demand moderates both with the deceleration in population growth rates and with the stronger assertion of Engel curve effects. The developing ESCAP region's world share in food exports, however, remains small and was about the same as that in total primary commodity exports in 1984. Whereas the developed market economies' world share of food exports was 62.8 per cent and Latin America's 15.8 per cent, the region's share was only 11.6 per cent in 1984.

Among the categories for which significant growth in the market shares of the region occurred during 1966-1984 are poultry, fish, pineapple, tropical beverages (except tea) and oils and oil-seeds. The commodities in which the developing ESCAP region suffered substantial losses of world share are cereals and sugar.

In the meat products category, the most remarkable change was the emergence of the region as a large exporter of poultry meat, mainly due to exports from China and Thailand, which rose from insignificant levels in 1966 to over 3 per cent of world market share.

China is also a significant exporter of live animals.

Fishery products have emerged as one of the most successful export commodities for a large number of developing countries of the ESCAP region, particularly for Bangladesh, China, the Republic of Korea and Thailand. Fishery products exports are, however, also vital for Maldives, the Solomon Islands, Vanuatu and Viet Nam.

In the cereals category, the region lost about two percentage points of its world market share of about 10 per cent between 1966 and 1984. Pakistan and Thailand each nearly doubled their market share for rice while Burma, China and Nepal lost a large part of their market. For Burma and Nepal, this is due to slow growth in production, leading to a decline in exportable surplus.

Among fruits, pineapples exports, both canned and fresh, are one of the fastest growing exports of the region. The Philippines and Thailand have been remarkably successful in carving out for themselves a large share of the world market in canned pineapples and in raising the developing ESCAP region's share of the world market from 41 per cent in 1966 to 68 per cent in 1984. For bananas, the Philippines replaced China as the region's major banana exporter and managed to take nearly 10 per cent of the world market.

In 1966, the ESCAP region supplied about one fifth of the world sugar market; by 1984, its market share had dropped by a half. This again is probably an indication of increased self-sufficiency within trade zones such as the Europeon Economic Community (EEC). Nearly all exporting countries lost sizeable market shares but the changes are particularly dramatic for Fiji which in 1984 still depended on sugar for about 40 per cent of its total exports. Nevertheless, some countries of the region, especially Malaysia, the Republic of Korea and Thailand, were able to make inroads into a falling world market.

While the ESCAP region's total share of the tropical beverages market increased marginally between 1966 and 1984 to reach about 20 per cent, its share for the main commodity exported, tea, dropped by nearly 10 per cent with the emergence of exporters outside the region, especially in Africa. However, the region still dominates the tea market, with a 70 per cent market share in 1984. The large tea exporters of the region, India and Sri Lanka, each had substantial losses in their market share, with a combined drop from 61.7 per cent in 1966 to 44.5 per cent in 1984. Bangladesh, which depends on tea for 10 per cent of its exports, lost nearly two thirds of its market share between 1966 and 1984. China nearly doubled its share in the world tea market. Indonesia was the most successful country in expanding its exports of all tropical beverages, coffee, cocoa and tea: its aggregate market share increased from 1.3 per cent in 1966 to 4.4 per cent in 1984.

Supplying about half of the world market, the ESCAP developing region experienced only a marginal drop in its market share of spices. The main supplier, India, maintained its share at about 20 per cent. Bangladesh, Bhutan, the Islamic Republic of Iran and Sri Lanka lost much of their importance in the world spices market.

The ESCAP developing region supplies about one fifth of the world oil-seeds, fats and oils market and generally increased its share between 1966 and 1984. For some products, however, such as copra, coconut oil, palm kernel oil and palm oil, the region supplies most of the market. The region's share in the case of palm kernel oil and palm oil increased spectacularly from supplying about half of the market in 1966 to becoming the predominant supplier in 1984. Malaysia, in particular, was extremely successful in increasing its world market share for both commodities, while Indonesia virtually lost all of its share in the palm oil market. In the case of coconut oil, Indonesia, Malaysia, the Philippines and Samoa gained sizeable market shares. For Samoa this is particularly significant, as coconut oil represents about 60 per cent of its exports, while Sri Lanka's share evaporated from 16.0 per cent to only 1.3 per cent. For copra, the Pacific island countries such as Papua New Guinea, the Solomon Islands and Vanuatu gained sizeable world market shares over the period reviewed; while the share of the three ASEAN producers rose in the aggregate, Malaysia was a substantial gainer and Indonesia and the Philippines heavy losers of their respective shares. Pacific island countries thus dominate the world copra market and depend very heavily on it for their livelihood, as can be seen in table II.9.

In the case of agricultural raw materials, although the developing ESCAP region has a high share in the world market and its share has slightly increased, unlike that of other developing regions whose shares have fallen, this category of primary exports grew more slowly than food and metals and minerals. Among the commodities for which the region's shares have increased are: tobacco, natural rubber, wood and cotton. Except for wood, these commodities have not had buoyant demand in world markets.

For tobacco, India, the Republic of Korea and Thailand are the main exporters and have increased markedly their world market share which remain, however, rather small at about 2-3 per cent. Indonesia and Pakistan, however lost most of their market share.

Table II.9. Selected commodities. Export dependence of developing ESCAP countries: shares in total exports, 1970 and 1984

(Percentage)

Commodities	Countries	1970	1984
Fishery commodities	Maldives	66.7	41.6
	Solomon Islands	15.0	15.3
	Vanuatu	40.2	16.6
	Viet Nam	—	17.4
Cereals	Thailand	30.9	21.6
Rice	Burma	49.5	42.2
	Pakistan	5.5[a]	16.1
	Thailand	17.0	14.8
Total sugar	Fiji	53.7	39.8
Tropical beverages	Papua New Guinea	39.6	24.1
Coffee	Lao People's Democratic Republic	2.5	48.5[a]
Cocoa and products	Samoa	28.8	8.2
Tea	Sri Lanka	55.0	42.3
Oil-seeds	Malaysia	6.8	15.8
	Papua New Guinea	22.1	21.5
	Philippines	16.9	11.9
	Samoa	38.0	69.7
	Solomon Islands	40.7	26.5
	Tonga	50.2	49.0
	Vanuatu	41.6	60.7

Commodities	Countries	1970	1984
Vegetable oils	Papua New Guinea	21.4	21.4
	Philippines	15.6	11.1
	Samoa	38.0	67.9
	Solomon Islands	40.7	26.5
	Tonga	50.3	49.0
	Vanuatu	41.6	60.7
Copra	Solomon Islands	40.7	16.8
	Vanuatu	41.6	60.6
Coconut oil	Philippines	8.5	10.9
	Samoa	—	59.9
	Tonga	—	49.0
Natural rubber	Malaysia	33.4	9.5
	Sri Lanka	21.6	8.9
	Thailand	15.1	7.4
	Viet Nam	4.7	12.3[a]
Wood, non-coniferous	Burma	22.2	33.0
	Lao People's Democratic Republic	24.5	22.6
	Malaysia	17.4	12.8
	Nepal	4.8	9.4
	Solomon Islands	31.2	14.1
Total cotton	Pakistan	19.3	12.7
Jute and products	Bangladesh	63.5	50.8
	Nepal	12.2	11.9
Copper ore	Papua New Guinea	—	29.1[a]

Source: UNCTAD primary commodity trade data on tapes, secretariat calculations.

[a] Estimate.

Over 90 per cent of the world supply of natural rubber originate in the developing ESCAP region, slightly more than in 1966. Malaysia, along with Indonesia and Thailand supply the bulk of the world market. While Indonesia expanded its market share by about 5 per cent between 1966 and 1984 to reach 26.9 per cent, Thailand nearly doubled its share, from 8.5 per cent in 1966 to 15.6 per cent in 1984. Malaysia maintained its share, while Sri Lanka's share was reduced by almost a half of its level in 1966 to 3.7 per cent in 1984. The region's developing countries supply about 50 per cent of world exports of tropical wood. Indonesia and Malaysia have emerged as major suppliers during the last two decades, increasing enormously their world market share, which together reached about 40 per cent in 1984, while the Philippines, lost a large part of its world export share.

In cotton, jute and other hard fibres, the ESCAP region's overall world market position generally improved between 1970 and 1984. In cotton, China made impressively large gains in its trade share to reach 7 per cent of the world market while the shares of other traditional exporters in the region, such as India and Pakistan, whittled down. Bangladesh increased its dominance of the world jute market, while the other major producer, India, experienced a decline of nearly 50 per cent in its world market share. China and Thailand emerged as important jute producers. More than 80 per cent of all jute exports come from the ESCAP developing region. In abaca, the Philippines remains the dominant world exporter though its share dropped by over 20 per cent between 1966 and 1984. At 71 per cent it still remained high.

Finally, while the developing ESCAP region has only a small share in the world market in min-

erals and metals a few countires are major exporters. Among the region's important exports are tin, copper and nickel. Besides Papua New Guinea, which has become a major exporter of copper, Indonesia and the Islamic Republic of Iran have also emerged as important exporters. However, the Philippines suffered a large drop in its market share, from nearly 21.8 per cent in 1966 to only 7.0 per cent in 1984. Nickel is a major metal exported by the ESCAP region. The Philippines has become a main exporter, its share in the world market increasing from 0 in 1966 to 32.6 per cent in 1984. However, Indonesia experienced a sharp drop in its world market share. Nickel intermediate products have become important exports from Indonesia. Tin has traditionally been a major export from the ESCAP developing region. Indonesia, Malaysia and Thailand are large tin metal exporters. Malaysia, however, lost a sizeable share of the world market while Indonesia increased its share very rapidly.

A general trend in primary commodity trade between 1966 and 1984, as noted in table II.10, is that the exports of developing countries grew more slowly than those of developed market economies. In addition, instability of export earnings was higher for developing countries. The primary commodity exports of the ESCAP region, however, grew even faster than those of the developed market economies, for all commodities as well as for each major commodity group except agricultural raw materials.

The high rate of growth of primary exports of the developing ESCAP region was, however, accompanied by a high degree of instability. The instability was not only higher than that in the developed market economies but also higher compared with the developing countries' total com-

modity trade and for each broad category. This is a rather significant and disturbing finding, with important adverse implications for the macro-economic management of the region's developing economies.

D. DIRECTION OF THE COMMODITY TRADE OF THE ESCAP REGION

The first part of this section examines the geographical distribution of the ESCAP region's trade in primary commodities by main SITC groups. The second part reviews the main intraregional trade flows.

1. World directions of ESCAP commodity trade

Table II.11 provides a summary of the flows of primary commodity trade from developing countries of the ESCAP region to main world regions and economic groupings of countries. The developed market economies, as a whole, provide the largest market for the primary commodity exports of the region, accounting for about 50 per cent of such exports, while about 3.3 per cent go to socialist countries of Eastern Europe and the remaining 46 per cent to developing countries. Intraregional trade represents more than a quarter of total trade. Japan, with a market share of about 20 per cent, represents the single largest market. EEC and North America follow with shares of 17.0 and 11.7 per cent respectively. Africa is a larger market than the socialist countries of Eastern Europe, while trade with Latin America is much smaller.

(a) Trade directions by main aggregate commodity categories

The developed market economies absorb the largest share of all the major categories of primary commodities from the region ex-

Table II.10. Selected country groupings and developing ESCAP region. Average annual growth rate and variability[a] of primary commodity export values, 1966-1984

(Percentage)

	Total merchandise exports	All primary commodities	Food products	Agricultural raw materials	Minerals and metals
World	13.8	10.9	11.7	9.3	9.7
	(0.5)	(0.5)	(0.4)	(0.8)	(0.9)
Developed market economies	13.3	11.7	12.2	10.4	10.3
	(0.4)	(0.5)	(0.5)	(0.8)	(1.0)
Australia	12.5	11.3	12.1	6.9	7.2
	(0.6)	(0.8)	(0.9)	(1.6)	(0.8)
New Zealand	11.4	10.6	10.4	9.4	24.9
	(0.8)	(0.8)	(0.8)	(1.3)	(3.6)
Socialist Eastern Europe	12.6	6.8	2.3	5.6	7.8
	(0.3)	(0.5)	(0.7)	(0.6)	(0.6)
Developing countries	16.1	10.0	11.1	8.3	9.2
	(1.0)	(0.6)	(0.5)	(1.0)	(1.0)
Africa	11.5	4.4	4.2	4.8	5.8
	(1.2)	(0.8)	(0.7)	(1.0)	(1.2)
Latin America	14.8	10.5	11.0	7.2	9.6
	(0.8)	(0.6)	(0.6)	(0.8)	(1.0)
Developing ESCAP region	17.0	11.8	12.9	10.2	11.6
	(0.8)	(0.7)	(0.6)	(1.2)	(1.2)

Source: UNCTAD primary commodity trade data on tapes, secretariat calculations.

Notes: First line: percentage of average annual growth rate. Second line (in parenthesis): coefficient of variation.

[a] Variability is measured by the coefficient of variation, defined as the average absolute deviation from trend value (standard error of estimate of log-linear trend regression) divided by the mean of the data series.

cept food, for which developing countries are the most important market, accounting for more than half of the region's food exports. About 70 per cent of the region's minerals and metals exports and over 50 per cent of agricultural raw materials exports are destined for the developed market economies.

Japan is the most important single-country market for the region's primary commodities, with a share of about 20 per cent of the region's primary commodity exports, about 40 per cent of its minerals and metals and over 20 per cent of its agricultural raw materials exports. EEC and North America rank as the next most important markets. For exports of food products, all the three major developed market economy regions have comparatively lower shares. Japan's market share is particularly low compared with that of the other two categories of primary commodities. This is an indication of high protection to domestic agriculture.

Africa is a relatively large importer of food products from the ESCAP region, its share reaching over 7.0 per cent, much larger than the socialist countries of Eastern Europe and, in fact, only about half of Japan's share. Socialist countries of Eastern Europe are the only significant importers of agricultural raw materials, taking up about 5 per cent of ESCAP exports.

(b) Trade directions by main SITC commodity trade divisions

Developed market economies absorb a large variety of primary exports from the region. Thus, about three quarters or more of the ESCAP region's exports of fish products (SITC 02), fruits and ve-

getables (05), and metalliferous ores (28) are exported to developed market economies. For meat (SITC 01), tropical beverages (07), hides and skins (21), rubber (23), and wood (24), the shares are over 50 per cent. More than 40 per cent of the region's sugar (SITC 06), animal feed (08) and tobacco (12) exports are absorbed by developed market economies while for dairy products (02) — a small export category for developing countries of the ESCAP region — oil-seeds, nuts and kernels (22) and oils and fats (42), the share is about 30 per cent. Cereal exports to the developed market economies are very low, representing only 7.4 per cent.

EEC is a large importer of fruit and vegetables, coffee and tea, animal feed, tobacco, hides and skins, rubber and metal ores. However, it has a relatively low share of sugar exports, fish products, oil-seeds and, mainly, cereals. Japan is a large importer of the region's meat and fish products, wood and metalliferous ores; its imports of these represent about 50 per cent of the ESCAP region's exports. It is rather surprising to find that Japan has a comparatively low export share of cereals, fruit and vegetables, sugar, tropical beverages, animal feed, tobacco, oilseeds and nuts, and vegetable oils.

Although about a half of the exports of the developing ESCAP region are imported by developing countries, the share of such countries outside the region, especially those in Africa and Latin America, is relatively small. Both high transport costs and the fact that these regions also produce similar tropical commodities account for such a small proportion. Most of the primary commodity exports from the region are intraregional exports or they are destined for Western Asia. About 30 per cent of the region's total commodity exports, 32.5 per cent of food exports, 26.6 per cent of agricultural raw materials and 23.3 per cent of mineral and metal exports are absorbed within the region. Western Asia and neighbouring developing countries absorb over 10 per cent of the region's primary exports, mainly food and agricultural raw materials. The only significant exports of primary commodities to developing countries outside the region are those to Africa, which takes about 7 per cent of the region's food exports.

2. Intraregional primary commodity trade flows

The regional trade matrix for each of the SITC categories presented in table II.11 has been computed for 1984.[7] As mentioned

[7] Excluding trade with Australia, Japan and New Zealand.

in the previous subsection, intraregional trade flows are important for several commodity categories of particular interest to the developing ESCAP region. Some salient features of the main intraregional commodity trade flows are detailed below.[8]

Intraregional trade in fishery products (SITC 03), which are important exports for the Republic of Korea and Thailand and an important emerging export for Bangladesh, is fairly small, amounting to 1.1, 9.7 and 10.5 per cent respectively of total exports of the above-named countries. The Republic of Korea exports to Hong Kong and Singapore, while Thailand exports 4.5 per cent of these products to Malaysia, followed by Hong Kong (2.8 per cent), and Singapore (2.2 per cent). Hong Kong, the Republic of Korea, Singapore and Thailand import about 2 per cent each of Bangladesh fishery exports.

The Islamic Republic of Iran provides a major market for cereals (SITC 04) exports from Pakistan and Thailand, with export shares of 25.3 and 6.8 per cent of each of the countries respective cereals exports, out of about 30 and 45 per cent, respectively, of their cereals exports received by the region as a whole. Malaysia takes 3 per cent of Pakistan's exports and 12.0 per cent of Thailand's exports, while Bangladesh, China, Hong Kong, India, Indonesia, the Philippines and Singapore are the other important markets for Thailand's cereal exports, with shares between 0.7 and 7.5 per cent. The developing ESCAP region provides a market for nearly half of Thailand's rice exports.

For fruits and vegetables (SITC 05) exports, important for Malaysia, the Philippines, Sri Lanka and Thailand, the largest market in

[8] All percentages are calculated in terms of total exports of the respective countries.

the region was Singapore followed by Hong Kong. Pakistan (6.4 per cent), India (1.9) and Maldives (1.3) provide a market for most of the 10.5 per cent of Sri Lanka's fruit and vegetable exports to the region. China, Hong Kong, the Republic of Korea and Singapore each provide a market of about 2 per cent of Thailand's exports under SITC 05.

Sugar (SITC 06) exports from the developing ESCAP region are important mainly for Fiji, the Philippines and Thailand. For Fiji, Malaysia (20.2 per cent), China (2.6 per cent), Singapore (1.3) and the Republic of Korea (1.1) were major markets in the region, which account for a total of 27 per cent of its sugar exports. For Thailand, which exports 44 per cent of its sugar products to the region, China (17.6), the Republic of Korea (14.0) and Malaysia (6.9) are the main regional export markets.

For tropical beverages (SITC 07), among the countries for which data are available in 1984, Sri Lanka's main exports to the region were destined to the Islamic Republic of Iran (5.2 per cent), Pakistan (3.1 per cent), India (1.5) and Singapore (0.6). For Indonesia, Pakistan (4.3), Singapore (4.4), the Republic of Korea (1.1) and Hong Kong (0.9), were among the largest regional markets for its exports of tropical beverages.

For tobacco (SITC 12), among the main exporters for which data are available relatively little is exported to the region — Thailand exports 18.8 per cent, Indonesia 6.8 per cent and the Republic of Korea 4.5 per cent to the region. For Thailand, China (13.0 per cent) is the largest market, while Singapore and Hong Kong are the important regional markets for such exports of Indonesia and the Republic of Korea, respectively.

Intraregional trade in oil-seeds and nuts (SITC 22) is important,

Table II.11. Developing ESCAP region. Direction of ESCAP primary commodity trade, 1984

(Percentage)

Total exports of	Developed market economies	EEC	Canada and United States	Socialist Eastern Europe	All developing countries	Africa	Latin America	Others including Western Asia	Developing ESCAP countries	Japan	Australia	New Zealand
Primary commodities[a]	50.2	17.0	11.7	3.3	46.0	4.6	0.8	10.9	29.6	19.3	1.5	0.2
Food products	44.9	16.6	11.5	2.6	52.1	7.1	0.2	12.3	32.5	14.2	1.7	0.3
Agricultural raw materials	53.2	16.2	13.2	5.2	41.1	1.8	2.2	10.4	26.6	21.6	1.4	0.2
Minerals, ores and metals[a]	68.9	21.3	8.4	1.7	29.0	0.2	0.1	5.4	23.3	38.5	0.4	0.1
SITC 01: meat and preparations	61.3	4.0	3.7	0.0	38.7	0.7	0.0	3.7	34.3	52.6	0.7	0.1
SITC 02: dairy products and eggs	29.3	0.2	2.3	0.0	70.4	0.8	0.0	15.0	54.6	26.6	0.2	0.0
SITC 03: fish and preparations	87.5	10.0	21.6	0.0	12.3	0.2	0.1	2.9	9.1	52.3	2.8	0.2
SITC 04: cereals and preparations	7.4	3.3	1.4	2.6	89.4	21.0	0.7	29.8	38.0	2.0	0.3	0.0
SITC 05: fruit and vegetables	68.8	42.3	10.7	0.8	30.2	0.5	0.1	7.6	22.0	13.2	0.9	0.3
SITC 06: sugar and preparations, honey	44.9	17.0	6.5	1.1	53.5	3.1	0.7	8.0	41.7	19.0	0.2	0.6
SITC 07: coffee, tea, cocoa, etc.	52.8	20.7	20.1	3.8	43.3	9.9	0.3	13.3	19.7	7.0	3.5	0.8
SITC 08: animal feeding stuff	45.8	31.7	2.5	0.2	54.1	0.0	0.0	6.5	47.5	5.7	5.1	0.3
SITC 12: tobacco and manufactures	41.3	24.5	11.9	0.4	58.0	2.6	0.2	8.4	46.8	2.5	0.9	0.5
SITC 21: hides, skins and furs	64.1	50.0	3.2	0.0	35.9	0.0	1.9	24.2	9.8	10.4	0.1	0.0
SITC 22: oil-seeds, nuts and kernels	25.4	9.7	0.3	0.0	74.4	1.1	0.0	11.0	62.3	11.2	0.6	0.2
SITC 23: crude rubber	54.5	18.1	22.5	9.2	35.2	1.8	4.0	4.6	24.8	11.9	0.9	0.3
SITC 24: wood, lumber and cork	61.4	13.6	1.8	0.0	38.5	1.5	0.0	15.8	21.2	42.9	2.9	0.1
SITC 26: textile fibres	27.5	11.9	1.2	3.8	68.6	3.9	0.5	13.2	51.0	13.0	0.3	0.1
SITC 28: metalliferous ores	82.2	24.8	4.6	1.4	16.4	0.1	0.1	3.4	12.8	52.0	0.5	0.0
SITC 42: vegetable oils and fats	30.9	15.8	8.9	5.7	62.4	4.2	0.0	9.1	49.0	4.4	1.4	0.1

Importing markets

Source: United Nations trade data on tape.

a Excluding SITC 522.56: aluminium hydroxide.

amounting to 62.3 per cent of the region's trade in this commodity. A substantial share of the exports of the two main producers (Malaysia and Indonesia) goes to Singapore for re-export, with 73.7 per cent of Malaysia's and 23.7 per cent of Indonesia's exports transiting through Singapore. Indonesia also exports to the Republic of Korea (8.3 per cent) and Hong Kong (2.4 per cent) while Malaysia exports 16.0 per cent of such products to Pakistan and 9.4 per cent to the Republic of Korea.

For rubber product exports (SITC 23), Malaysia, the main producer, exports 31 per cent of its total rubber exports to the region, with 13.7 per cent going to Singapore for re-export, 7.3 per cent to the Republic of Korea, 6.9 per cent to China, and 1.3 per cent to India and the Islamic Republic of Iran. Indonesia transits its regional exports through Singapore, which absorbs 23.9 per cent of Indonesia's 24 per cent export share to the region. Singapore re-exports its regional imports to China (7.1 per cent), the Islamic Republic of Iran (2.2 per cent) and the Republic of Korea (3.5 per cent). A quarter of Thailand's rubber exports go to the region, 2.6 per cent to the Republic

of Korea, 6.7 per cent to China and 12.3 per cent to Singapore.

For wood (SITC 24) exports, 21.7 per cent of Malaysian exports are absorbed in the region, 11 per cent going to the Republic of Korea, 5.1 to Singapore, 2.1 to China, 1.9 to Thailand and 1.5 per cent to Hong Kong. The Republic of Korea, Singapore, Thailand and Hong Kong are also Indonesia's main markets. The percentage of Indonesia's wood exported to the developing ESCAP region is 23.8. Thailand exports 67.3 per cent of its wood to the region, with 41.9 per cent going to Malaysia, 15.3 per cent to Singapore, 6.6 per cent to Hong Kong and 2.0 per cent to the Republic of Korea. Important bilateral trade flows for this commodity exist between Thailand and Malaysia.

For textile fibres (SITC 26), about 40 per cent of Bangladesh exports (mainly jute) are absorbed by the region, Pakistan (23.0 per cent) and India (10.4) being its major markets. Hong Kong, Bangladesh, the Republic of Korea, Indonesia, the Islamic Republic of Iran, Sri Lanka and Thailand are the largest markets in order of magnitude for the 25 per cent of Pakistan's SITC 26 (mainly cotton) ex-

ports to the region.

Finally, for fixed vegetable oils and fats (SITC 42), Indonesia and Malaysia, the largest palm oil and kernel oil exporters, export respectively 21.8 and 53.6 per cent of their exports to the region. For both countries, Singapore is a large re-export centre, absorbing all of Indonesia's exports to the region and 23.1 per cent of Malaysia's total exports. Malaysia exports 17.4 per cent of its SITC 42 exports to India, 6.6 per cent to Pakistan and about 1.4 per cent to Bangladesh and the Republic of Korea.

The above analysis makes evident that important regional trade flows exist, particularly in respect to food products, with food deficit countries of the region representing large markets for food surplus countries. Over the longer run the pursuit of active food self-sufficiency programmes by most food deficit developing countries of the ESCAP region will have no doubt far-reaching consequences for the export market of food surplus countries such as Thailand. Food products provide an important area for regional co-operation in trade, particularly between South Asian and South-East Asian countries.

IV. INSTABILITY AND DECLINING TREND IN PRIMARY COMMODITY TRADE

A. MOVEMENTS IN EXPORT PRICES AND EARNINGS

The instability of the merchandise export earnings of developing countries in the ESCAP region, which in the short term is considerably greater than that in developed countries, arises largely from dependence on primary commodities. This instability is greater in the case of the least developed countries, and the developing Pacific island countries and territories, which depend predominantly on primary commodity exports. In these economies, the short-term instability of export earnings was about twice as high as the regional average during the past two decades, which added to their already disadvantaged and fragile economic situation.[1]

For some countries, such as China and those in the Association of South-East Asian Nations (ASEAN) group, export instability is compensated for by faster growth in the medium term. In the least developed and small islands, however, the combination of high instability and low growth has a pronounced effect on export and economic performance.

The relative instability, which is calculated as the relative mag-

nitude of fluctuation around the trend of the concerned variable,[2] and the growth performance of various groups of economies are depicted in figure II.8. It appears that the greater instability of overall merchandise export earnings of country groups such as the least developed, small island, and ASEAN, directly relates to their greater dependence on primary commodities. Merchandise export earnings of the developed market economies and of the region's newly industrializing economies, which are mainly from manufactures, are much more stable.

Fluctuations in export earnings

arise from fluctuations in prices or quantities or in both. However, the magnitude of short-term instability and the secular growth of merchandise trade receipts have often been significantly modified by compensating variations in prices and quantities. In the following sections of this chapter the trends in prices, quantities and earnings relating to the region's trade in 32 non-oil primary commodities of considerable socio-economic significance are analysed for the period 1964-1985. Many of these commodities are also of great significance to the external world.

1. Short-term instability in primary commodity trade

(a) Prices

With few exceptions, both the nominal and real (or deflated)[3] unit values of primary commodity exports from the ESCAP region have shown large fluctuations during the period 1964-1985. The pattern of price instability, whether considered in real or nominal terms, varies greatly among commodity groups. For example, the prices of certain categories of food products, such as meat and fish, appear to be relatively stable, while those of cereals, mainly rice and wheat, tropical beverages, such as coffee and cocoa, vegetable oils, and most raw mate-

---

[1] For a discussion of the causes of instability and growth of all merchandise export earnings, see the *Survey*, 1985, ch. IV, pp. 161-165.

[2] All indicators of instability in this chapter are calculated in the form of instability indices. The instability index is defined as the ratio of the standard error of estimated trend values over the mean value of the relevant variable. The trend is approximated as the coefficient of variable t estimated from the log-linear regression of the form log (X) = a + bt where "X" represents the relevant variable, and "t" represents time. The index is a pure number and indicates the magnitude of fluctuations around the trend. For ease of presentation, the decimal has been moved three digits to the right.

All money values are in United States dollars, and all data are obtained from official publications of the United Nations and the Asian Development Bank, among others. The base for all serial indices extends from 1974 to 1978. This time span helps avoid biases due to the selection of a single year bench mark; it covers almost one complete economic cycle and conveniently lies between the first and second oil shocks.

[3] Adjusted by the unit value index of manufactured imports from the developed market countries.

Figure II.8. Average instability indices and growth rates of merchandise export earnings, 1964-1985 and 1973-1985

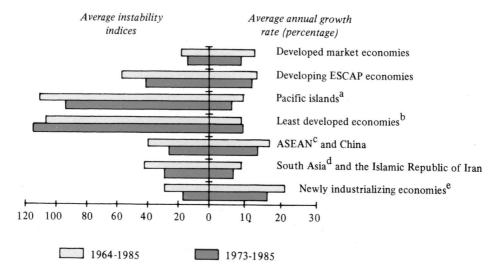

Average instability indices   Average annual growth rate (percentage)

□ 1964-1985   ■ 1973-1985

[a] Consisting of Cook Islands, Fiji, Papua New Guinea, Solomon Islands and Tonga. [b] Consisting of Afghanistan, Bangladesh (1974-1985 only), Malaysia, Nepal, Samoa and Vanuatu. [c] Excluding Singapore. [d] Consisting of Burma, India, Pakistan and Sri Lanka. [e] Consisting of Hong Kong, Republic of Korea, Singapore and Taiwan (a province of the People's Republic of China).

rials, are highly volatile (see table II.12).

The more moderate fluctuations in world prices for meat and fish products are due to more stable supplies, existence of storage facilities (mainly in Australia and New Zealand) and, unlike in agriculture, the absence of marked seasonal swings in output.

The instability index of current and deflated sugar prices over the past two and a half decades was almost twice as high as that of most other primary products, despite successive international agreements on this commodity. The volatility of sugar prices is due to several factors. Special trading agreements cover a large part of the trade, and a variety of protective and subsidy measures in the industrial market countries shift the burden of adjustment to changes in demand or supply to the small residual free market for sugar. Since only about one fifth of global annual production is traded internationally at free market prices, even a moderate

production swing can produce a pronounced market impact. The greater instability in sugar prices also stems from production conditions. First the crop yield and sugar content are sensitive to marginal changes in climatic conditions and second the long production cycle of 8 months (beet sugar) to 15 months (cane sugar) causes a considerable lag in any production response to price changes. Other rigidities include the economic viability of successive harvests from the same cane crop, and the high (fixed) costs of the processing plant and equipment.[4]

Rice and wheat, the two main staple food crops of the region, are also subject to volatile price swings. However, the major determinant of instability in their prices are conditions of global demand and supply, including changes in stocks held in

the major importing and exporting countries.[5]

Other commodities subject to relatively pronounced price instability include cocoa and coffee, coconut and palm oils, tropical wood, rubber — mainly tree crops — and wool and coal. One characteristic of most of these products is the delayed supply response through price-induced investments largely owing to a long gestation period before commercial production. Rubber, wool and coal prices also reflected the steep hikes in mineral oil prices during the mid-and-late-1970s. Oil price adjustments raised significantly the prices of synthetic or natural substitutes for these primary products. In addition, the major end uses of rubber, coal and, to a less extent, wool, are in cyclically sensitive industries.[6]

---

[4] IMF, *Primary Commodities — Market Developments and Outlook* (Washington, D.C., May 1986), pp. 21-24.

[5] See *Survey, 1985*, pp. 161-162.

[6] IMF, *Primary Commodities — Market Developments and Outlook* (Washington, D.C., May 1986), pp. 35, 50 and 53.

Aggregation over commodities, countries, as well as over time periods, however, hides considerable variations. The relative stability in volumes in contrast to the higher instability in prices, as pointed out above, is partly attributable to such aggregation. There is generally a much larger degree of instability in the volume of exports at the country level than is evident at the regional level. The commodities

Table II.12. Instability indices of export values, volumes and unit values. Various categories of non-oil primary products from selected economies of the ESCAP region, 1964-1985

	1964-1973			1973-1985			1964-1985		
	Value	Volume	Unit value	Value	Volume	Unit value	Value	Volume	Unit value
Foodstuffs									
Meat and fish products									
Beef, chilled and frozen	16	12	9	20	12	32	21	15	25
Lamb, chilled and frozen	10	4	23	16	8	24	14	8	29
Butter	14	5	32	12	14	23	15	12	28
Milk, dry	24	11	50	18	12	36	26	17	44
Crustaceans and molluscs	10	12	14	13	6	16	21	14	19
Fish products	30	27	4	15	9	17	33	34	30
Cereals and fruit									
Maize	12	10	43	23	20	27	20	17	48
Rice	15	7	40	16	8	39	20	8	55
Wheat	13	12	20	23	14	48	21	14	57
Banana	15	14	15	12	7	16	17	15	49
Pepper	9	13	27	23	7	32	22	10	34
Sugar, raw	20	4	48	25	9	62	33	8	78
Sugar, refined	46	20	79	50	24	68	61	29	99
Beverages and tobacco									
Cocoa	20	9	29	25	12	50	27	16	52
Coffee	8	24	40	32	4	52	27	16	52
Tea	5	3	6	15	4	26	17	4	28
Tobacco, unmanufactured	12	13	12	16	8	18	19	15	21
Vegetable oils and oil-seeds									
Coconut oil	15	10	30	24	15	55	26	13	53
Copra	11	10	31	31	26	65	26	22	59
Palm oil	20	7	39	18	4	38	25	9	50
Agricultural raw materials									
Cotton	18	13	19	19	24	20	18	21	25
Jute fibres	13	11	24	12	12	36	13	12	32
Logs, non-conifer	10	5	44	24	13	64	28	31	66
Sawn wood, non-conifer	22	14	40	20	18	31	25	22	43
Rubber	20	6	33	16	3	34	21	4	42
Wool greasy	19	3	40	12	8	20	17	8	38
Wool, non-greasy	21	7	36	14	8	22	21	9	39
Metals and ores									
Aluminium and alloy (unwrought)	35[a]	24[a]	22[a]	33[b]	17[b]	22[b]	58[c]	44[c]	25[c]
Coal	11[d]	7[d]	24[d]	26[b]	8[b]	64[b]	41[c]	14[c]	78[c]
Copper ores and concentrates	43	37	24	36[b]	13[b]	29[b]	82[e]	60[e]	30[e]
Iron ores	19	9	16	14[b]	5[b]	32[b]	40[e]	30[e]	40[e]
Tin	10	15	12	47[b]	24[b]	26[b]	42[e]	33[e]	28[e]

Sources: FAO Production Yearbook, various issues; UNCTAD, *Yearbook of International Commodity Statistics*, various issues; and United Nations, *Yearbook of International Trade Statistics*, various issues.

[a] 1967-1973.   [b] 1973-1984.   [c] 1966-1984.   [d] 1966-1973; Australian coal only.   [e] 1964-1984.

for which export volume fluctuations at the country level were considerably higher than those at the regional level included cotton, coffee, banana, sugar, rubber, cocoa, coconut oil, iron ore, copper, tin and bauxite. Supply factors often seemed to be more important than those affecting demand – which in many cases was internationally determined.

Aggregation over time can also give an exaggerated sense of homogeneity. However, separate calculations of price instability for 1964-1973 and 1973-1985, as in table II.12, reveal greater instability in 1973-1985, which, as is well-known, was a period of great turbulence in the international economy. Since 1980, however, the major development dominating world primary commodities has been the secular decline in their prices.

(b) Earnings

An analysis of the data on the principal primary commodities of the developing ESCAP region reveals – not surprisingly – that, in general, short-term instability in commodity prices is considerably more pronounced than that in commodity export earnings (table II.12). Export earnings, in absolute terms, are, by and large, stable. Adjustments in export quantities have evidently reacted to price variations. However, the revealed instability in commodity-specific regional earnings is a result of a complex aggregation process and considerably understates the degree of short-term fluctuations in export earnings from a given commodity or in total commodity exports experienced at the country level. The aggregation process tends to dampen the amplitude of fluctuations as differences in the timing and direction of the movements in price and quantity largely cancel out at the regional level. The

net result is that, with few exceptions, the degree of instability in export earnings from individual commodities or from all commodities at the country level tend to be considerably higher, averaging at least twice as high as those registered by commodity-specific earnings on a region-wide basis.

Region-wide earnings on cereals, sugar, coffee and cocoa, copra, non-conifer logs and coal were more unstable than those on most other primary products during 1973-1985. This is to be expected from the highly volatile prices of these commodities, as discussed in section 1 (a) above. Export earnings from most other commodities, with a few exceptions, despite compensating variations in quantities, were also more unstable during 1973-1985. The exceptions appear to be milk, crustaceans and molluscs, fish products, banana, palm oil, rubber, tropical sawn wood, wool and some metals.

During 1973-1985, in the large majority of cases, commodity prices and earnings registered lower rates of growth. Sub-section 2 below examines the secular behaviour of commodity prices and earnings and provides the necessary background for the subsequent discussion on the implications of these developments for countries in the ESCAP region.

2. Trend declines

There is much controversy on both theoretical and empirical grounds concerning the comparative behaviour over the long run of the export price trends of primary commodities and manufactures. Some of the major *a priori* arguments and empirical findings are reviewed briefly in the *Survey,* 1985. The evidence, on balance, appears to indicate that the commodity (or net barter) terms of trade tend to decline in the long run.[7] This tendency is confirmed

by the falling trend in the unit values of primary export commodities as deflated by the unit value index of exports of manufactures from the industrial market countries over the relatively shorter period, 1964-1985.

(a) Prices

Annual rates of growth of the cereals and fruit group of commodities averaged 5.3 per cent in nominal prices and, over 7 per cent in the case of beverages and tobacco, as well as of metals and ores during 1964-1985. However, the real rates of growth in the prices of most commodities, obtained by deflating nominal prices by the cost of manufactures' imports, declined at an annual rate ranging roughly between 1 and 5 per cent (table II.13). The rate of decline was much sharper in most cases during the sub-period 1973-1985.

The steepest falls for individual commodities were recorded by the cereals and fruit group – with the real prices of rice and maize declining by 5.9 and 4.3 per cent annually, and those for raw and refined sugar by 7.4 and 9.3 per cent during 1973-1985. The real price of copper fell at the annual rate of 5.3 per cent during the same period, while that of wheat, pepper, coconut and palm oils and wool fell at a more moderate rate of 2-3 per cent per year.

A variety of factors, affecting both demand and supply, were responsible for these large declines in real prices. As has been pointed

---

[7] For a comprehensive survey and analysis of issues and evidence, see J. Spraos, *Inequalizing Trade: A Study of Traditional North/South Specialization in the Context of Terms of Trade Concepts* (Oxford, Clarendon Press, 1983), pp. 21-68; and D. Evans, "The long run determinants of North-South terms of trade and some recent empirical evidence", *World Development,* vol. 15, No. 5 (Oxford, Pergamon Journals Ltd., May 1987), pp. 657-672.

out earlier, world demand for cereals became weaker as a consequence of higher levels of self-sufficiency in food-importing countries, including those in the ESCAP region, while at the same time excess supplies emerged in developed market economies as a result of increased subsidization of production of edi-

Table II.13. Average annual rates of growth. Deflated export values and unit values, and quantities of various categories of non-oil primary products from selected economies of the ESCAP region, 1964-1985

(Percentage)

	1973-1985			1964-1985		
	Deflated values	*Quantity*	*Deflated unit value*	*Deflated value*	*Quantity*	*Deflated unit value*
Foodstuffs						
Meat and fish products						
Beef, chilled and frozen	−0.1	0.4	−0.5	3.3	4.4	−1.1
Lamb, chilled and frozen	1.0	1.8	−0.8	1.5	1.6	−0.1
Butter	1.1	1.4	−0.4	−2.5	−0.6	−1.8
Milk, dry	1.8	2.1	−0.3	6.8	5.7	1.2
Crustaceans and molluscs	7.2	8.4	−1.2	12.5	12.6	−0.1
Fish products	20.5	21.6	−1.0	15.9	17.6	1.7
Cereals and fruit						
Maize	4.4	8.7	−4.3	4.3	5.7	−1.4
Rice	−2.2	3.7	−5.9	0.4	2.4	−2.0
Wheat	4.1	6.6	−2.5	3.4	3.8	−0.4
Banana	2.9	1.2	1.7	0.1	5.5	−5.4
Pepper	−2.0	0.9	−2.8	1.0	2.0	−1.0
Sugar, raw	−6.4	1.0	−7.4	1.4	2.6	−1.2
Sugar, refined	−4.0	5.2	−9.3	4.2	4.0	0.3
Beverages and tobacco						
Cocoa	12.2	13.1	−0.8	11.6	9.0	2.6
Coffee	7.9	7.5	0.4	7.9	6.3	1.6
Tea	3.9	2.3	1.6	−0.4	1.7	−2.0
Tobacco, unmanufactured	−0.4	−0.6	0.2	2.8	3.2	−0.4
Vegetable oils and oil-seeds						
Coconut oil	2.3	4.8	−2.5	4.3	5.8	−1.5
Copra	−9.7	−10.3	0.6	−8.3	−7.5	−0.7
Palm oil	8.6	10.8	−2.2	13.3	13.6	−0.3
Agricultural raw materials						
Cotton	5.1	6.5	−1.4	3.1	3.5	−0.4
Jute fibres	−6.2	−5.1	−1.1	−8.0	−4.0	−4.0
Logs, non-conifer	−2.9	−4.8	1.9	4.0	2.5	1.6
Sawn wood, non-conifer	4.3	4.2	0.1	9.0	8.1	0.9
Rubber	−0.6	0.9	−1.5	0.4	1.6	−1.2
Wool, greasy	−3.6	−0.8	−2.7	−3.3	−1.7	−1.5
Wool, non-greasy	4.4	6.5	−2.1	4.5	5.6	−1.1
Metals and ores[a]						
Aluminium and alloy (unwrought)	7.2	4.7	2.5	12.9	12.5	0.4
Coal[b]	10.1	8.2	2.0	15.0	10.6	4.4
Copper ores and concentrates	−3.6	1.7	−5.3	9.0	11.9	−3.0
Iron ores	0.4	0.1	0.3	6.2	8.6	−2.4
Tin	1.0	−2.0	3.0	3.1	1.0	2.2

Sources: FAO Production Yearbook, various issues; UNCTAD, *Yearbook of International Commodity Statistics,* various issues; and United Nations, *Yearbook of International Trade Statistics,* various issues.

[a] 1973-1984 and 1964-1984 for copper, iron and tin; and 1966-1984 for aluminium and Australian coal. [b] From Australia only.

ble food grains, especially cereals such as wheat and rice. Some food grains such as maize, which were also used as animal feed, also faced severe competition from other substitutes, including cassava, soybeans and, to a less extent, oil-seed and oil-nut cakes.

There are a few commodities — most notably banana, tea, tropical hardwood, aluminium and tin — whose prices exhibited a rising trend of between 1.5 and 2.0 per cent annually in real terms in the past decade. The movements of banana and tea prices were, by and large, in the nature of recovery from serious falls in their real prices, reaching 11 and 6 per cent per year respectively, during 1964-1973 as a result of oversupplies. Price movements of the other commodities reflected generally favourable demand factors, including the lack of competitive substitutes. In the case of tin, this was also attributable to the combined influence of buffer-stocking operations and export controls carried out under a series of international agreements. In fact, the International Tin Council had been successful in its defense of the floor prices for this commodity in the years prior to 1985.[8] Aluminium prices rose largely because of increases in the price of oil, since its production is highly energy-intensive.

(b) Earnings

The adverse impact of declines in real world commodity prices on export earnings in the ESCAP region was, in most cases, moderated by increases in the volume of exports. For most commodities in the food, beverages and tobacco group, the increase in volume averaged from 4 to 6 per cent during 1964-1985 or the sub-period 1973-1985, generally offsetting real price declines. Raw materials, in contrast, which had experienced a high rate of growth in export volumes — ranging from 5-6 per cent annually for vegetable oils, oil-seeds and other agricultural raw materials, to 18 per cent for metals and ores over 1964-1973 — suffered a sharp fall-off in the growth rate of their export quantities to below 2 per cent per year during 1973-1985.

Among the commodities whose real earnings were hardest hit by relatively unfavourable prices and/ or lower growth in export volume were copra, sugar, jute fibres, greasy wool and copper. Real earnings from copra fell between 8 and 9 per cent annually throughout the last two and a half decades, largely because of falling export quantities. This, in turn, was due to the greater degree of local-processing of copra into coconut oil to obtain higher value added for export. The volume of coconut oil exports, for example, expanded more strongly at a rate of almost 5 per cent per year during 1973-1985, more than offsetting the negative trend in real prices for over two decades.

Jute presents an exceptional case as it is one of the few primary products subject to substantial commodity substitution through technological innovation.[9] Developing countries of this region, principally Bangladesh, India and Thailand, which account for over 95 per cent of the global export value

and volume of this commodity, have suffered a substantial decline in real earnings, averaging 8 per cent annually over 1964-1985. Approximately one half of this decline was due to adverse price trends as demand shifted toward cheaper synthetic substitutes, primarily polypropylene. The other half was attributable partly to a decline in exportable surplus which arose from shifts to other crops, such as rice, and partly to increased local spinning and processing of this fibre. Annual jute production in Bangladesh, for example, was estimated to have fallen from an average of around 7 million bales during 1969/70 and 1970/71 to about 5.5 million during the decade ending in 1982/83.[10]

The region's sugar producers were most severely affected by a fall in free market prices, which in real terms, recorded the steepest rate of decline, almost 10 per cent, during 1973-1985. Real earnings on this commodity therefore decreased by about 4 per cent annually during the same period, in spite of a notable increase of over 5 per cent per year in the export volume of refined sugar. Among the major factors behind sugar price trends are excess supplies in a market subject to significant degrees of policy intervention concerning conditions of production and consumption, as noted earlier.

Palm oil and rubber producers were also confronted with adverse trends in prices which, in real terms, fell by an annual average rate of 4 and 5 per cent respectively for 1964-1973. The rate of decline moderated to 2.2 per cent for palm oil and 1.5 per cent for rubber in 1973-1985. A significant growth in export volumes, which reached

---

[8] The sixth International Tin Agreement broke down in October 1985 owing, among other causes, to substantial net forward market purchases in support of tin prices during a period of excess supplies. These forward purchases enabled control over larger quantities of the metal than the specified maximum size for the buffer stock. See C.L. Gilbert, "International commodity agreement: shadow and substance", *World Development*, vol. 15, No. 5 (Oxford, Pergamon Journals Ltd., May 1987), pp. 595 and 609-610.

[9] K. Raffer, "Unfavourable specialization and dependence: the case of peripheral raw material exporters", *World Development*, vol. 15, No. 5 (Oxford, Pergamon Journals Ltd., May 1987), p. 706.

[10] Takamasa Akiyama, "Jute supply response in Bangladesh", World Bank Staff Commodity Working Papers, No. 13 (1985), p. 16.

an annual rate of 17 and 11 per cent for palm oil during 1964-1973 and 1973-1985 respectively, more than offset the adverse impact of price on earnings. The real value of palm oil exports expanded by an average of over 13 per cent per year during the last two and a half decades. Higher export volumes also contributed to large increases in real overall earnings on cocoa, coffee and coconut oil despite unfavourable price trends in the last decade or so. In contrast, nominal earnings on rubber export barely kept up with the rising prices of imported manufactures owing to much lower growth in export volumes (table II.13).

The commodities displaying the most rapid rate of growth in export volumes from the ESCAP region, in spite of relatively unfavourable real prices, belong to the subgroup of fishery products in the food category. Induced by strong world demand and favourable prices in the 1960s,[11] the export volume of fishery products accelerated from an annual growth rate of less than 4 per cent during 1964-1973 to almost 22 per cent in the following decade. Such high growth was sustained despite the falling trend in real prices for these products of about 1 per cent per year, a rate of secular decline steeper than for most other kinds of food exports. It contributed to earnings growth, in real terms, of 20 per cent annually during 1973-1985 (table II.13).

The ESCAP region accounts generally for about one third of the global trade in crustaceans and molluscs. Although real prices of these commodities were falling by 1.2 per cent per year during 1973-1985, export quantities expanded by 8.4 per cent, thus helping to sustain an annual growth of 7.2

per cent in real earnings on crustaceans and molluscs. The growth of this particular group, however, has been limited largely by the rapid depletion of available resources: the export volume of crustaceans and molluscs used to grow by almost 16 per cent annually during 1964-1973. Given the relatively high income elasticity of demand for these products, and the health-related shift in demand toward poultry and fishery products generally, aquaculture represents a potentially attractive option for producers of this region.

B. CONSEQUENCES OF DECLINING TRENDS IN COMMODITY PRICES

1. The impact of declining terms of trade and price instability

The consequences of instability and the secular decline of primary commodity export earnings are transmitted into the overall economy through a variety of channels. There is the cumulative or multiplier effect of these export-sector constraints on the size and stability of income flow received by export producers and the government, and on the reserve base and money supply. The structure of domestic prices and costs, and the expectations of consumers and investors are also altered, sometimes perversely, giving rise to lower investment and sub-optimal allocation of resources. To some extent, these interactive effects may be offset by government counter-cyclical measures, but the operation of these measures themselves involves considerable opportunity cost in both the short and long term. Furthermore, there are problems relating to the adequacy, timeliness, and assymetrical nature of government intervention.

The most striking impact of instability and growth in export

earnings on the domestic economy relates to that on merchandise imports. Cross-sectional evidence from a sample of 26 developing economies of the ESCAP region indicates a very close interdependence in terms of both instability and growth between export earnings and import expenditure.[12] The rank correlation coefficient, significant at the 1 per cent level, between instability in export earnings and import expenditure reached 0.80 during 1973-1985, and 0.76 for export earnings growth and import expenditure growth during the same periods. These results imply a substantial and possibly increasing[13] degree of interdependence between developing and developed market economies in the global commodity and financial markets.[14]

The substantial decline in the real prices of a wide range of primary commodities produced in the ESCAP region during the last decade has been partly caused by the rising productivity, especially in agriculture, since the 1970s.[15] While the gains in agricultural productivity have largely served to achieve the goal of attaining greater food security in the region, they have also benefited external consumers of a considerable number of commodities — notably rice, pepper, sugar, rubber and palm oil —

---

[11] Prices in real terms were rising by about 2.8 per cent annually over the years 1964-1973.

[12] For a perspective on the changing nature of this interdependence, see the present *Survey*, part one, ch. I.

[13] The rank correlation coefficients for the entire period 1964-1985 were slightly lower.

[14] UNCTAD, *Compensatory Financing of Export Earnings Shortfalls* (United Nations publication, Sales No. E.85. II.D.3), p. 6; and A. Maizels, "Commodities in crisis: an overview of the main issues", *World Development*, vol. 15, No. 5 (Oxford, Pergamon Journals Ltd., May 1987), p. 539.

[15] See the present *Survey*, part two, ch. II.

through cheaper import prices. To the extent that these gains have been passed on to importers — despite the increasing importance of intraregional and South-South trade, a large share of the commodity exports of the developing ESCAP region are still destined for developed countries outside the region[16] — this implies a substantial transfer of resources outside the region.

While the benefits of increased commodity production have been partly shared by the region's trading partners, many of the resultant social costs, not reflected in commodity prices, have to be borne by the region's producers. Such costs, largely unmeasurable, arise from the external diseconomies imposed by the depletion of natural resources, such as forests, clean air and water and the negative ecological effects of increased use of fertilizers and other chemicals (see box II.8).

2. An estimate of terms-of-trade losses

As discussed above, most primary commodity producing countries in the ESCAP region have been able to more than compensate for the adverse trends in relative prices through higher export volumes, resulting in some, if inadequate, growth in their capacity to import. On the average, producers of meat and fish products, beverages and tobacco, and metals and ores recorded the highest rate of growth in their income terms of trade and hence import capability (figure II.9). Nevertheless, such capability would have been much larger had the commodity (or net barter) terms of trade been more favourable. In fact, it often fell considerably short of their import requirements. This erosion or lack of satisfactory growth in the purchasing power of primary commodities has been the prime mover for attempts at export diversification — principally of manufactures — in the developing countries of the region.

Any attempt to quantify the (potential) income losses through adverse terms of trade on the basis of ex-post commodity trade data is an extremely difficult empirical exercise. Generally, the available data and information on complex international trade flow matrices at specific country levels are either inadequate or highly aggregated.

Box II.8. Growing environmental concerns about commodity trade

The need to export larger volumes of commodities to sustain or increase export earnings in the face of declining prices and terms of trade has led to both extensive and intensive use of land and other natural resources by many developing countries of the region. The consequent rapid depletion and degradation of these resources have caused serious concern about environmental issues in the region. While, in general, the developing countries in the region have shown growing awareness of environmental deterioration, whose costs are often neglected when policy decisions are made, the compelling necessity of generating enough exports to pay for their import needs often does not leave them enough room for manoeuvre.

An important environmental concern relates to the region's forestry resources, which have contributed to its primary commodity exports. In 1980 forests accounted for 21 per cent of the region's land area, compared with a 32 per cent average for the entire world. The region originally had a sizeable coverage of closed broad-leaved, open broad-leaved, coniferous and bamboo forests. They have been depleted at the annual rate of between 0.6 and 2.0 per cent in recent years.[a]

Whether for domestic needs or for exports, commercial logging throughout the region has caused the loss of mature trees and associated damage such as loss of non-targeted trees and vegetation. Soil erosion, including that associated with the opening up of roads and tracks to forest areas, increase in water-logging and salinity and extinction of species, are some of the other consequences of the deforestation process. Among the various subregions of Asia and the Pacific, South-East Asia has the highest rate of forest degradation from logging. The high value of tropical hardwood, coupled with the richness of the dipterocarp forests, has made the subregion one of the world's major exporters of hardwood.

Deforestation in the region has also taken place owing to the extension of crop agriculture to forest lands to meet the growing demand for food as well as export needs. Crop production in recent years has been expanded through enhanced productivity owing to the use of chemical fertilizers and pesticides. Cross-country comparison in the generally land-scarce Asian countries indicates that the intensity of their use tends to rise with the overall level of development. However, the increasing use of pesticides and other chemicals increases the risks to human health and the lives of other species. Continuing long-term exposure to pesticides and chemical residues in food, water and the air is hazardous. Children are particularly vulnerable to these hazards. It is difficult to estimate the exact extent of damage. It is generally known that pesticides poison hundreds of thousands of people and kill many thousands of others each year in developing countries. The problem may be more serious in the Asian and Pacific region owing to the high population density, the non-existence of appropriate regulations or lack of strict enforcement of regulations, inadequate information and training opportunities for safe use, and high rates of soil erosion, which lead to pesticide contamination of the environment.

[a] ESCAP, *State of the Environment in Asia and the Pacific, Volume One: Summary* (ECU/OES/MCEA/PM/4), p. 11.

---

[16] *Ibid.*, ch. III.

Figure II.9. Average annual percentage change in the commodity and income terms of trade of various categories of non-oil primary products, 1964-1985 and 1973-1985

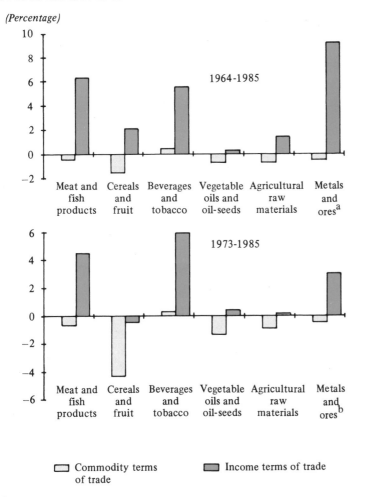

(Percentage)

are more narrowly focused and much less ambitious in scope: they relate only to the losses of potential earnings by commodity producers in the ESCAP region as a result of lower trend growth in their export prices relative to those associated with imported manufactures. The estimation approach draws upon available time series data on the quantities of commodity exports, and on nominal as well as real earnings from these commodities.

The results, like those obtained by other approaches, present only order-of-magnitude approximations and need to be used with the greatest caution and the awareness that they are based on several working assumptions — including unchanged *ex ante* demand and supply schedules, and hence prices of both the primary commodities and the manufactures traded. These assumptions are unlikely to hold if commodity prices rise so as to eliminate the disparity in the rate of growth in commodity export and manufacture import unit values. In particular, higher re-alized earnings on primary exports would induce increased supplies in the medium term, higher import demand and domestic expenditure. Higher raw material costs would affect both demand and inflation in the countries which export manufactures thus giving rise to another series of complex inter-actions in both the primary exporting and importing countries.

In spite of the many conceptual and statistical limitations noted above, the results of this approach imply an income loss of about $20 billion to the producers of the 32 significantly important non-fuel primary commodities during 1964-1985, with about four fifths of the loss concentrated in the period 1973-1985 (table II.14). These estimated losses were equivalent to 70 and 88 per cent of the increase in nominal commodity export earnings during these respec-

Furthermore, merchandise trade consists of a variety of classes and categories of goods whose different weights in exports or imports are not available in sufficient detail. In addition, the rapid changes in the composition of exports from rapidly growing economies — the newly industrializing economies and ASEAN in particular — complicate the analysis.

Apart from the difficulties of availability of data mentioned above, the estimation of terms-of-trade losses requires a satisfactory analytical framework, which takes

account of not only non-linearities in supply and demand but also their interaction in a general equilibrium model. Such an effort is clearly beyond the scope of the present study and is, in any case, not easy to achieve at a satisfactory level of aggregation.[17]

The estimates attempted below

[17] However, for a country-level exercise see B. Gibson, N. Lustig and L. Taylor, "Terms of trade and class conflict in a computable general equilibrium model for Mexico" in *Journal of Development Studies*, vol. 23, No. 1 (October 1986), pp. 40-59.

Table II.14. Estimate of cumulative losses of potential export earnings on various categories of non-oil primary products from selected economies of the ESCAP region owing to declining commodity terms of trade, 1973-1985 and 1964-1985

(Millions of US dollars)

	1973-1985			1964-1985		
	Cumulative earnings			Cumulative earnings		
	Current	Deflated	Estimated loss	Current	Deflated	Estimated loss
Foodstuffs	6 455.9	380.0	6 075.9	9 191.9	2 277.1	6 914.8
Meat and fish products	2 782.5	−23.3	2 805.8	4 607.5	1 982.9	2 624.6
Of which:						
Beef, chilled and frozen	228.3	−689.1	917.4	1 101.5	335.1	766.4
Crustaceans and molluscs	1 615.2	713.5	901.7	2 072.4	1 316.1	756.3
Cereals and fruit	3 673.4	403.3	3 270.1	11 523.4	294.2	11 229.2
Of which:						
Rice	383.2	−608.3	991.5	907.2	−350.3	1 257.5
Wheat	1 844.2	935.7	908.5	1 855.4	656.6	1 198.8
Beverages and tobacco	2 673.5	1 111.9	1 561.6	2 855.9	818.8	2 037.1
Of which:						
Tea	1 154.7	424.8	729.9	1 068.1	−108.5	1 176.6
Vegetable oils and oil-seeds	2 640.4	1 256.7	1 383.7	2 959.2	1 419.6	1 539.6
Of which:						
Palm oil	2 120.8	1 201.3	919.5	2 369.5	1 506.1	863.4
Agricultural raw materials	2 802.1	−2 576.9	5 379.0	5 687.9	−852.5	6 540.4
Of which:						
Cotton	690.4	227.3	463.1	858.5	349.5	509.0
Logs, non-conifer	32.3	−962.1	994.4	1 152.1	447.4	704.7
Rubber	902.7	−675.1	1 577.8	1 526.5	−617.1	2 143.6
Metals and ores[a]	5 285.9	2 227.8	3 058.1	7 483.0	4 905.9	2 577.1
Of which:						
Iron ores	953.5	186.9	766.6	1 632.2	1 030.0	602.2
Tin	500.5	4.2	496.3	820.6	264.7	555.9
Total	**19 857.8**	**2 399.5**	**17 458.3**	**28 177.9**	**8 568.9**	**19 609.0**

Sources: FAO Production Yearbook, various issues; UNCTAD, *Yearbook of International Commodity Statistics,* various issues; and United Nations, *Yearbook of International Trade Statistics,* various issues.

[a] 1973-1984; and 1964-1984 for iron and tin.

tive periods.[18] These estimates of the income losses suffered by the primary producing countries of the ESCAP region are comparable with the United Nations Conference on Trade and Development (UNCTAD) estimates that the loss of foreign exchange earnings by 48 developing countries owing to the fall in commodity prices over 1980-1983 was in the region of $28 billion, equivalent to about 28 per cent of their cumulative current account deficits, and to almost one half of their cumulative debt accumulation during the period.[19]

Although both the developing economies of the ESCAP region and the two primary commodity exporting developed economies, Australia and New Zealand, suffered heavily from the decline in primary commodity prices during the last decade, the loss was much greater for the developing

[18] In comparison, losses of potential income reached only one quarter of the increase in nominal export earnings during 1964-1973.

[19] UNCTAD, *Trade and Development Report, 1985* (United Nations publication, Sales No. E.85.II.D.16), p. 79. The estimated losses reached $38 billion during 1980-1984. See UNCTAD, *Trade and Development Report, 1986* (United Nations publication, Sales No. E.85.II.D.5), p. 46.

economies. While these economies suffered an estimated decline of $10.93 billion or 91 per cent of their cumulative nominal commodity export earnings during 1973-1985, the corresponding figures for Australia and New Zealand were $6.53 billion and 83 per cent. These losses more than offset the gains during the commodity boom period of 1964-1973, in which producers of beef, powdered milk and a variety of minerals (except tin) gained substantially in real terms. For Australia and New Zealand, such a gain totalling $0.5 billion, was equivalent to almost a quarter of the cumulative growth in nominal export earnings on these commodities.

The above estimates of losses in potential export income borne by commodity producers in the ESCAP region, like others made on the basis of movements in the net barter and income terms of trade, must be regarded as broad order-of-magnitude rather than as precise estimates. Nevertheless, these losses are substantial in absolute terms or in relation to other relevant financial flows. Between 1973 and 1985, for example, the non-oil merchandise trade deficit of the developing primary exporters of the ESCAP region registered a combined increase of over $11.28 billion.[20] Another telling comparison is that the combined amount of official development assistance to the developing ESCAP region (excluding the newly industrializing economies) rose by $3.73 billion in the same period,[21] or approximately one third of the estimated potential income losses.

C. WELFARE EFFECTS OF FALLING COMMODITY PRICES IN THE DEVELOPING ESCAP REGION

There is growing concern that the economic difficulties facing the developing countries since the beginning of the current dacade, and — in the context of the ESCAP region — largely related to the fall in prices of primary commodities, have a distinct welfare dimension (or "human face") which deserves greater attention.[22] Earlier attempts to treat these difficulties purely as problems of economic adjustment and efficiency not only have been inadequate, but have created additional socio-economic problems and tensions. However, owing to the continuing neglect of the welfare aspects of economic development, the statistical data for analysing them are not generally available in sufficient detail or timeliness. Nevertheless, on the basis of the data available an attempt is made below to assess the direct or specific effects — on the incomes of commodity producers, employment, poverty and real wages. Additionally, the indirect or more general economic and social effects brought about largely as a result of enforced curtailment of expenditure in pursuance of adjustment policies are examined.

1. Direct effects

The impact of low commodity prices on income and employment depends on the nature of the crop produced, as well as the institutional

structure of its production. The severity of the impact also varies according to whether it is of short- or long-term nature. For annual crops a short-term price decline is relatively easily borne by the farmer who can switch to other crops if it is technically feasible to do so. Its impact can be softened if credit is available or crop insurance schemes exist, which is generally not the case. As a result, the farmer is forced to shift to a less remunerative crop — to the extent such a shift is technically feasible. For example, with a fall in jute prices, some jute growers may shift to paddy cultivation while others may not have such an option. Since rice requires a higher input of water than jute, jute growers in flood plains and lowlands are able to shift easily to rice production but those cultivating upland and medium lands find such a shift difficult or even impossible. The adjustment to lower prices is also harder on the hired worker, who is likely to be thrown out of employment or suffer a reduction in real wages, than the peasant cultivator who may have other sources of income and ownership of assets providing him some security.

For producers of permanent crops, both short- and long-term adjustments are more difficult and costlier. Where production is organized in smallholdings, as is the case for most commodity production in the region,[23] a price fall has to be absorbed by the small-holder as a loss of income. In plantations, where wage employment is the norm, low prices are more likely to press wages rather than profits down, unless public intervention, trade union pressure or labour shortage should prevent it.

Data on change in employment, wages and income over time

---

[20] Consisting of $109 million from the developing Pacific islands, $873 million from the least developed countries, $8,054 million from ASEAN (including Brunei Darussalam but less Singapore, a newly industrializing economy), and $2,245 from South Asian countries.

[21] Consisting of $112 million to the developing Pacific islands, $894 million to the least developed countries, $854 million to ASEAN (excluding Singapore), and $1,870 to South Asian countries.

[22] See UNICEF, *Adjustment with a Human Face, Vol. 1, Protecting the Vulnerable and Promoting Growth*, G.A. Cornia, R. Jolly and F. Stewart, eds. (Oxford, Clarendon Press, 1987), p. 94.

[23] See part two, ch. II, this *Survey*.

are generally not available for the rural agricultural sector of the economies in the ESCAP region. The inadequate data available indicate a worsening of the employment and income situation of farmers and workers in the agricultural sector where a large concentration of poverty already exists.

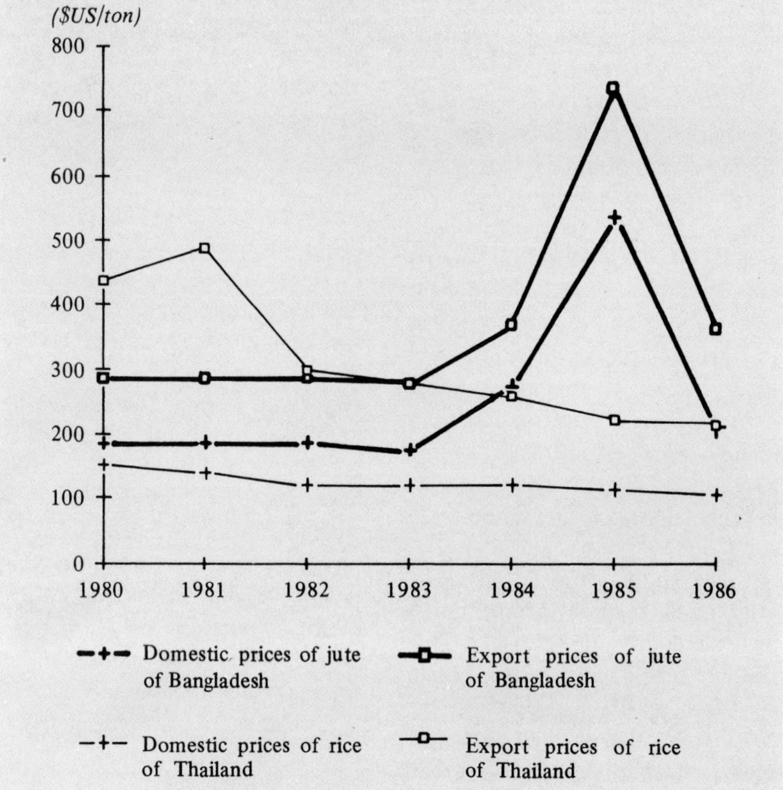

That the prices received by the producers of annual export crops move very closely with export prices – though the gap between the two has varied over time – is clearly seen in the cases of rice in Thailand and of jute in Bangladesh (see figure II.10). When the price of rice falls, not only farmers with marketable surpluses suffer a reduction in their income but a sizeable section of the farming community is also affected. The 24 per cent of rice farmers in Thailand whose holding size does not exceed 1.6 hectares and who already live below the poverty line may gain marginally to the extent that they meet their rice consumption requirements by market purchases – although this is offset by decline in wage incomes. However, the two thirds of the rice farmers in Thailand who have farm holdings of 1.6 to 6.4 hectares were badly hit when rice prices at the growers' level were pushed to $110 in 1985 and $102 in 1986, as many of such farmers were pushed below the poverty line.

Sugar is another commodity which has been hit hard by recent price declines in the international market. The Philippines and Thailand are the two countries worst affected. Whereas in Thailand a 70:30 per cent revenue-sharing arrangement between the planters and millers has largely succeeded in mitigating the unfavourable effects on the farmers, the consequences have been catastrophic for plantation workers in the Philippines, where low commodity prices were a major factor

Figure II.10. Domestic and export prices of jute and rice, 1980-1986

of economic decline during 1983-1985. The Philippines, which produced an average of 20 million tons of sugar-cane between 1979-1984 with an employment of above 300,000 workers, saw its sugar production fall to 16 million tons as a result of reduced quotas by importing countries, bringing about a corresponding fall in employment levels.

These developments have resulted in the rising indicence of poverty in rural Philippines, which is estimated at 62 per cent compared with 56 per cent in the urban areas. Relative poverty in rural areas has worsened over the years, as witnessed by a decline in the ratio of average rural family income to average urban family income from .67 in 1975 to .46 in 1985. Real wages in agriculture fell by about a quarter during 1980-1984; sugar-cane workers in Negros Islands

and Central Luzon suffered the most.

Prices of tea, which have been well below their 1980 level during the years through 1981-1987, with the exceptions of 1983 and 1984, have affected economic welfare in Sri Lanka, not only because tea workers form the largest segment of agricultural workers but also because of their impact on government revenues generated by tea estates which mostly belong to the public sector. Although real minimum wages have been maintained in the face of falling tea prices and rising consumer goods prices, many of the welfare programmes, including food subsidy schemes, had to be curtailed. Tea and other plantation workers in Sri Lanka, besides being generally low paid and economically vulnerable, are socially disadvantaged and have limited scope for mobility.

Many of the workers employed are women and youth and their hardship tends to increase in times of low prices.[24]

Rubber prices have fallen almost uninterruptedly since 1980 to about half their levels in 1985. Real wages for rubber-tappers fell by 10.5 per cent in 1984 over 1980. In 1983, a year in which rubber prices firmed up somewhat, the percentage of poor households rose to 61 per cent, compared with 41.3 per cent in 1980 (see table II.15). In Malaysia, almost all primary producing households, except oil palm smallholders, had a high proportion of poverty in 1980 at the beginning of the current commodity recession, which generally increased in 1983.

---

[24] See K. Jayawardena, *The Plantation Sector in Sri Lanka: Recent Changes in the Welfare of Children and Women,* in R. Jolly and G.A. Cornia, *The Impact of World Recession on Children* (Oxford, Pergamon Journals Ltd., 1984).

2. Indirect effects

The macro-economic and balance-of-payments impacts of the recession in primary commodities get easily translated into cut-backs in investment and government expenditures. The adjustment process, which is inevitable in any case, is further accentuated if the country is a significant borrower in the international market or applies for stand-by credits from the International Monetary Fund (IMF) or structural adjustment loans from the World Bank to help tide over the balance-of-payments disequilibrium. In the first half of the 1980s there was a sudden jump in the number of developing countries seeking such assistance as a result of the abrupt cutting off of the supply of external finance at the same time as their foreign exchange earnings were being eroded by declines in primary commodity prices. As many as 13 countries in the region had IMF-assisted adjustment.

In assisting a developing country undergoing programmes of non-transitory balance-of-payments difficulties during 1980-1985,[25] IMF and the World Bank, at the request of the Government of that country, prepare a package of domestic policies designed to correct such imbalance. Such policy packages have in recent years been subjected to considerable unfavourable comment from both the recipient countries and independent analysts. The burden of this criticism has been that they are in conflict with the pursuance of growth and pay little attention to the problems of distributive justice.[26] However, many analysts

---

[25] These were Bangladesh, Burma, China, India, Lao People's Democratic Republic, Nepal, Pakistan, Philippines, Samoa, Solomon Islands, Sri Lanka and Thailand.

[26] See, for instance, S. Dell, "Stabilization: the political economy of overall" in J. Williamson, ed., *IMF Conditionality* (Washington, D.C., Institute for International Economics, 1983).

Table II.15. Peninsular Malaysia. Number of poor households by sector, 1983[a]

	Total households (Thousands)	Total poor households (Thousands)	Incidence of poverty (Percentage)	Percentage among poor
Rural	1 489.5	619.7	41.6	86.4
Agriculture	906.6	497.6	54.9	69.4
Rubber smallholders	405.8	247.9	61.1	34.6
Oil palm smallholders	23.0	1.5	6.5	0.2
Coconut smallholders	31.0	10.1	32.7	1.4
Padi farmers	138.9	75.0	54.0	10.5
Other agriculture	161.7	87.3	54.0	12.2
Fishermen	40.5	18.1	44.7	2.5
Estate workers	105.7	57.7	54.6	8.0
Other industries	582.9	122.1	20.9	17.0
Urban	881.2	97.9	11.1	13.6
Mining	5.2	2.1	41.0	0.3
Manufacturing	222.2	28.0	12.6	3.9
Construction	38.0	5.2	13.7	0.7
Transport and utilities	92.3	14.4	15.6	2.0
Trade and services	523.5	48.2	9.2	6.7
Total	**2 370.7**	**717.6**	**30.3**	**100.0**

Source: Malaysia, *Fourth Malaysia Plan 1981-1985* (Kuala Lumpur, 1981), p. 80, table 3-2.

[a] The calculations took into consideration the effects of programmes implemented during the latter part of the 1970s and the period 1981-1983 as well as changes in other factors, such as prices and costs.

point out that at least in the 1960s and 1970s "the costs associated with the external adjustment effort appear to have been less severe than has sometimes been suggested by participants in the controversy on Fund conditionality" [27]

In the 1980s, however, the adjustment policies began to hurt more severely as the period was characterized by greater external shocks and decline in resource inflows to developing countries. Although the policy packages contain a number of specific elements and some, such as supply expansion policies and institutional policy reforms, are designed specifically to promote growth, an essential element of all adjustment policy packages is on demand restraint policies. According to an IMF study of 78 Fund-aided adjustment programmes,[28] it appears that demand restraint policies were implemented in almost all the countries analysed. For example, limits on credit expansion were applied in 99 per cent of the cases, restraint on central government expenditure in 91 per cent, reduction of the budget deficit to GDP rates in 83 per cent and wage restraint in 60 per cent. Potentially growth-stimulating supply expansion policies were adopted less frequently. Pricing policies were introduced in about 40 per cent of the cases, exchange rate policies in 54 per cent interest rate reform in 27 per cent, and restructuring of particular sectors in 65 per cent of the 78 cases. This composition of policy packages is predominantly deflationary in the short run and possibly in the medium run as well, as there are substantial time lags.

In contrast to the other developing regions, the adjustment policies pursued in the developing countries of the ESCAP region have had a less contractionary effect on growth, especially over the entire first half of the decade.[29] However, investment growth – a better indicator of medium-term growth – has declined in almost half the cases undergoing adjustment payment during 1980-1983. Current account balances also improved only in half the cases during 1980-1984. An asymmetrical characteristic of balance-of-payments changes has been that they have been made to improve in the years (e.g., 1982 and 1983) in which investment and GDP were falling. The strategy of improving balance of payments through economic contraction has been self-destructive as it has created greater foreign exchange shortfalls.

Adjustment policies generally require government expenditure to be reduced. During 1980-1984, real government expenditure per capita fell in over half the countries of the world. The necessity for adjustment and reduction of aggregate government expenditures is inescapable for a developing country trying to correct its dis-equilibrium in balance of payments and to resume its growth. However, at issue is whether such adjustment should result in across-the-board reductions or in selective increases and decreases. Generally, adjustment policies have implied selective rates of decline in different categories of expenditure. In the *Survey,* 1986 it was noted that the proportion of development expenditure had declined in a number of countries of the region.[30] In some countries, especially those in which per capita incomes have declined, per capita government expenditure has also declined and the burden of such curtailment in government expenditure has been borne largely by the education and health sectors.

In an analysis of the impact of reduction in aggregate government expenditure on different categories during 1979-1983 in Asia, it was revealed that expenditures on goods purchased by government were most vulnerable, followed by subsidies and capital expenditures. In these categories the expenditure cut was larger than aggregate reduction in government expenditure in 75 per cent, 63 per cent and 60 per cent of the sample countries.[31] The development expenditure on health and education suffered relatively more than other sectors in Asia, unlike in other developing regions. The effect of adjustment policies on human welfare is illustrated by the experience of the Philippines and Sri Lanka, two of the region's economies worst affected by the decline in primary commodity prices (see box II.9).

[27] D.J. Donovan, "Macroeconomic performance and adjustment under fund-supported programs: the experience of the seventies", *IMF Staff Papers,* vol. 29, No. 2 (June 1982), p. 197.

[28] IMF, *Fund-Supply Programs, Fiscal Policy and Income Distribution* (Washington, D.C., 1986).

[29] See G.A. Cornia, "Adjustment policies 1980-85: effects on child welfare" in UNICEF, *Adjustment with a Human Face, Vol. 1, Protecting the Vulnerable and Promoting Growth,* G.A. Cornia, R. Jolly and F. Stewart, eds. (Oxford, Clarendon Press, 1987), pp. 48-72.

[30] *Survey,* 1986, pp. 73-74.

[31] IMF, *Government Financial Statistics Yearbook,* vol. IX (Washington, D.C., 1985).

Box II.9. The human impact of recession on the Philippines and Sri Lanka[a]

Among the economies of the ESCAP region on which the impact of recession caused by declining commodity prices and deflationary demand management policies was most keenly felt were the Philippines and Sri Lanka. Their experience illustrates vividly the risks of pursuing macro-economic policies for adjustment to the external environment, without giving adequate consideration to their human welfare consequences.

The Philippine economy, which was one of the region's most dynamic economies in the 1960s, faced the first oil shock reasonably well, largely through its ability to borrow in the international market. However, like many other developing country borrowers, the facts of world economic recession, high interest rates and falling commodity prices confronted it soon after the second oil shock. Debt-servicing obligations and external and internal balances grew to unsustainable proportions. By 1982, the current account deficit was 8.1 per cent and the budget deficit 4.3 per cent of GNP, while the debt-service ratio had risen to 36.6 per cent[b] and the inflation rate was over 10 per cent. A sudden deterioration in the political situation in 1983 led to capital flight and rapid depletion of foreign reserves.

The economy was in the midst of its worst recession when deflationary measures were introduced to control inflation and to reduce the balance-of-payments deficit in 1984. The stabilization programme undertaken with the agreement of the International Monetary Fund restricted government expenditures and increased taxation. Controls on credit creation, and reforms of tariffs, public investment and energy policies were introduced. While the reforms were largely effective in achieving the desired

macro-economic objectives – principally of reducing the balance-of-payments and budget deficits to sustainable limits and of reducing inflation – the costs were heavy in terms of growth, employment, real incomes and human welfare. Employment fell in every sector but services. Declining real incomes and employment led to an increase in poverty and income inequality, already among the highest in the region.

The stabilization measures introduced by the Government in the 1980s reduced public expenditures, which fell overall by 17 per cent per capita between 1979 and 1984. Expenditure on education per capita fell by two thirds and that on health and community amenities by one third. The human impact of these developments was evidenced by rising

rates of malnutrition and a slow-down in the fall in infant mortality rates. In the worst-affected region of Negros, infant mortality rates registered a sharp rise. The worst-affected sector was education, which showed a deterioration in both access to and quality of elementary education, as well as in falling rates of participation, retention and cohort survival. Also on the increase were the more visible signs of social misery, such as street begging and scavenging for a living, along with a rise in stealing and other petty crimes.

In Sri Lanka, which has a long tradition of welfare policies, since the late 1950s slow growth, unemployment and balance-of-payments difficulties have created pressures for economic diversification. In the late 1970s, the Government adopted an

---

[a] Based largely on information contained in UNICEF, *Adjustment with a Human Face, Vol. 1, Protecting the Vulnerable and Promoting Growth*, G.A. Cornia, R. Jolly and F. Stewart, eds. (Oxford, Clarendon Press, 1987), pp. 44, 117-119 and 121-122.

[b] IMF/IBRD definition.

Per capita real government expenditures on food subsidies, calorie intake by the bottom 20 per cent of the population, and child malnutrition in Sri Lanka, 1970-1982

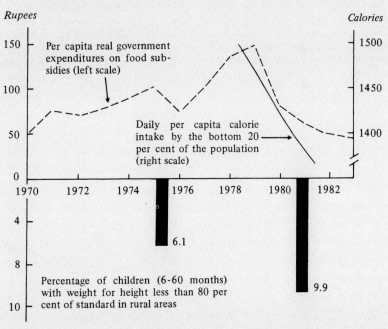

Source: Figure reproduced from UNICEF, *Adjustment with a Human Face, Vol. 1, Protecting the Vulnerable and Promoting Growth*, G.A. Cornia, R. Jolly and F. Stewart, eds. (Oxford, Clarendon Press, 1987).

(continued overleaf)

(continued from preceding page)

export-oriented strategy and decided to scale down some of the welfare measures. Policy reforms included devaluation, import liberalization, reduction in the role of public sector monopolies and improved producer prices for farmers. These reforms accelerated the average annual rate of growth of the economy from 2.9 per cent during 1970-1977 to 4.7 per cent during 1978-1984. The investment rate rose from an average of 15.7 per cent during 1971-1978 to 27.7 per cent during 1978-1984, with both private and public investment having almost an equal share in total investment. However, during 1979-1983 the share of foreign savings in total investment increased considerably, financing more than half the total investment in some years. Foreign capital inflows began to fall in 1983 and had fallen to 3.4 per cent of GDP in 1984 from a high of 19.8 per cent in 1980.

Since 1983, the combination of the falling resource inflows, the high debt-servicing burden of past debts and the falling prices of its main commodity exports have considerably reduced public resources for expenditure, a large part of which is now devoted to maintaining law and order in the country. The increasing budget deficit has also caused inflationary pressure. Both the change in the development strategy since 1977 and the change in the external environment

since the early 1980s have had significant effects on Sri Lanka's social welfare programmes.[c] Although, unlike in the Philippines, adjustment in Sri Lanka has raised the GDP growth rate, the rise has not been strong enough to protect the standard of living of the poorer sections of the population. Expenditure on the social service sectors as a whole fell from 33 per cent of the budget in 1977 to 22 per cent in 1983, the fall being largely due to the decline in food subsidy expenditure. The health and education sectors have suffered from a shortage of finance for repairs and maintenance and for supplies.

---

[c] The debate on the effects of changes in development strategy on social welfare is, however, inconclusive and is still continuing. Some recent contributions to this debate include: Paul Glewwe and Surjit Bhalla, "Growth and equity in developing countries: a reinterpretation of the Sri Lankan experience", *The World Bank Economic Review,* vol. 1, No. 1 (Washington, D.C., World Bank, September 1986), pp. 35-63 and Comments on the above by Graham Pyatt and Paul Isenmann and Response by Paul Glewwe and Surjit Bhalla in the same journal, vol. 1, No. 3 (May 1987), pp. 515-531.

The most significant effect, however, has been on the nutritional status of the Sri Lankan population, which had markedly improved during 1976-1979 as a result of the rice ration programme covering almost 50 per cent of the population. However, in 1979 the scheme was first restricted to low-income groups and later replaced by a food stamp scheme with fixed food value. As a result of the withdrawal of food subsidies in 1980 and the consequent rise in the price of food items, which more than doubled between 1979 and 1982, there was a sharp reduction in the quantity of food available under the food stamp scheme. The stagnant or declining incomes of those in the lower deciles of the population, together with the rapid erosion of the value of the food stamps, resulted in a decline in caloric intake even allowing for some substitution of cheaper rice for wheat. The daily per capita calorie consumption of those in the bottom two deciles of the population declined from 1,500 in 1978/79 to 1,405 in 1980/81 and 1,370 in 1982 (see figure). There was also a significant increase in wasting, i.e. in the proportion of children aged half-a-year to 5 years with a weight or height less than 80 per cent of the standard for the reference population. A comparison for 1975/76 and 1981/82 shows an almost 50 per cent increase in wasting for the rural areas.

V. GLOBAL MACRO-ECONOMIC TRENDS AND AGRICULTURAL PROTECTIONISM

The policies of developed market economies exercise a strong influence on the world economy with which developing economies have become increasingly integrated in recent years. Despite the fact that the primary sector is relatively unimportant in their domestic economies, the former plays a dominant role in the trade in primary commodities, especially agricultural trade. An increasingly larger part of world agricultural output is being traded in world markets and most of the increased export surpluses are originating from developed market economies. Thus during 1960-1980, while world agricultural output grew by 2.5 per cent per annum, trade in agricultural commodities grew by 4.3 per cent per annum. At the same time the share of developed market economies in world exports of major agricultural commodities rose from 54.3 per cent in 1967 to 65.0 per cent in 1980.[1]

Much of the increase in production and export surpluses of developed market economies has come from growing subsidization measures of domestic agriculture. According to Alberto Valdés, "In no other major sector is such a high proportion of production sold on world markets at less than domestic prices. This is, to a great extent, a direct effect of domestic farm policies of developed countries."[2] As a consequence, growing sur-

pluses enter world markets and depress prices of several agricultural commodities that are of interest to developing countries to levels which are too low to reflect either marginal costs to efficient producers or real scarcities.

The growing interdependence of the world economy is, perhaps, nowhere more evident than in the context of agriculture. The economies of both the developed market countries and, more so, the developing countries grew much faster during 1970-1980 than during 1980-1986. This slow-down resulted in a decline in the annual growth rate of the agricultural exports of developing countries to developed market economies from 13.2 per cent during 1970-1980 to 2.0 per cent during the 1980s. However, the growth of exports of the agricultural products of developed market economies to developing countries dropped dramatically from an average annual increase of 22 per cent in the 1970s to a decline of 4 per cent per annum in the 1980s. This reflected partly the conversion of the United States of America from a net exporter of agricultural products to a net importer with the developing countries largely as a result of the increasing balance-of-payments constraints faced by many developing country importers.

The recognition of this growing interdependence, the need for agricultural reform in the Organisation for Economic Co-operation and Development (OECD) countries and the need to ensure a better environment for developing countries is reflected in the OECD Ministerial Press Communique of 13 May 1987; which stated, *inter alia:*

"Commodity-dependent developing countries face difficult problem in view of the outlook for many commodities. An acceleration in world growth would improve the prospects for these countries. New efforts should be made to diversify their economies and to address the structural and development dimensions of commodity dependence. Action to remove measures distorting trade in commodities will make an important contribution to export prospects for commodity-dependent developing countries....

"Agricultural reform is not solely in the interests of (OECD) Member countries. Developing countries which are agricultural exporters will benefit from a recovery on world markets. Developing countries which are importers of agricultural produce will be encouraged to base their economic development on more solid ground, by strengthening their own farm sector....

"Economic cooperation with developing countries must

---

[1] See OECD, *Agricultural Trade with Developing Countries* (Paris, 1984).

[2] Alberto Valdés, "Agriculture in the Uruguay Round: interests of developing countries", *The World Bank Economic Review*, vol. I, No. 4 (Washington, D.C., World Bank, September 1987), p. 573.

respond to varying capacities and needs in the critical areas of development, trade, debt and finance. Developed countries must strive to ensure a better environment for developing countries' growth and exports in the interest of these countries as well as of the international economy more generally."

In this chapter, the various aspects of policies adopted by developed market economies which affect commodity trade are discussed. Section A summarizes some of the effects emanating from the macro-economic policy changes introduced in major developed market economies since the early 1980s. Section B concentrates on commodity sector-related policies and their effects on developed market economies. Section C is devoted to surveying attempts to assess the impact of these policies and the likely effect of liberalization in them on the export earnings of developing countries in general and of the ESCAP region in particular.

A. MACRO-ECONOMIC POLICY ENVIRONMENT

Since 1980 there have been significant changes in the macro-economic policy environment in developed market economies affecting trade in primary commodities. Their main impact has been through the slowing down of economic activity in these countries. However, there have been significant effects resulting from exchange rate realignments and interest rate changes which have also contributed to the decline in demand and prices of primary commodities in the 1980s. To some extent, the macro-economic policies have also strengthened the trend towards protectionism in agriculture which has a much longer history in the developed market economies and which has remained relatively untouched, unlike trade in manufactures which has been considerably liberalized over the years.

After growing at the remarkable rates of 25 per cent per annum during the first half and 20 per cent during the second half of the 1970s, the international market for non-oil primary commodities collapsed dramatically in the early 1980s and has not yet recovered. This was almost directly attributable to the severe recession, which initially hit the developed market economies but was quickly transmitted to the rest of the world. In 1980-1981 world economic growth decelerated to 1.8 per cent from an average of 4 per cent during 1975-1980. World trade also declined by the same percentage, reversing for the first time the trend of rapid growth in the 1970s. In 1981-1982, while global economic activity stagnated, world trade declined by nearly 6 per cent.

However, the deceleration in economic growth and in import demand in developed market economies was more marked than in the developing or in the centrally planned economies. While imports for all three major categories of non-oil primary commodities declined sharply in the developed market economies (see table II.16), imports in the developing countries and the centrally planned economies were still mostly rising. In 1982 and 1983, the pattern of decline seems to have spread around the world and brought about the sharpest decline in world demand for and trade in primary commodities. The recovery in 1984, derived largely from an expansion in the United States economy, was less than full and short-lived. Demand and prices plunged again in 1985 and 1986 as part of a continuing downward trend in demand for and prices of primary commodities.

Among the non-oil primary commodities, import demand for agricultural raw materials and metals and minerals fell much more than for food and beverages. Exports of agricultural raw materials are more sensitive to business cycle fluctuations than food products, because raw materials are inputs into manufacturing and construction which are more sensitive to recession than other sectors of the economy.

The greater severity of the impact of recession on demand for metals and minerals than on agricultural commodities (see figure II.11), partly reflects the greater incidence of the recession on the output of durable goods industries which are major users of metals and minerals and partly the trend decline in demand for metals and minerals. The emergence of synthetic substitutes and improvements in the efficiency of the use of metals and minerals has resulted in the fall in long-run demand for these inputs. The ratio of aggregate minerals and metals consumption to industrial production in the developed market economy countries declined by 9 per cent between 1979 and 1984, or by an average of 1.8 per cent per annum, compared with an annual average decline of 0.9 per cent during the 1970s; in 1981-1984, the ratio fell to 15 per cent below the level of 1971-1974.[3]

A disturbing aspect of the relationship between the level of economic activity and demand for primary commodities is that the economic recovery since 1982 has, by and large, bypassed the commodity economy almost entirely. In earlier business cycles an upsurge in the developed market economy countries led to an increased volume of international trade in primary commodities and an increase in their prices. The recent recovery, although hesitant, does not

---

[3] UNCTAD, *Trade and Development Report 1986* (United Nations publication, Sales No. E.86.II.D.5), p. 43.

seem to be any weaker than the recovery phases of earlier cycles. Yet, after brief signs of rather weak recovery in 1983-1984, commodity prices relapsed again and remained very depressed in 1985-1986. This has led some analysts to speculate that the world commodity economy has become "delinked" with the industrial economy.[4] An alternative explanation is in terms of long cycles in the prices of primary commodities (see box II.10).

However, part of the reason for the difference between the present and the earlier patterns may lie in the geographical pattern of economic recovery. Although the overall pace of economic recovery

was broadly the same in 1983-1984 as during 1976-1977,[5] the 1983-1984 recovery reflected mainly a

---

[4] See part two, ch. I, fn. 19 of the present *Survey*.

[5] As measured by changes in the year-end index numbers. Year-over-year average growth was much lower in 1983 (3 per cent) than in 1976-1977 (6 per cent). See IMF, *World Economic Outlook,* Occasional Paper No. 27 (Washington, D.C., April 1984), p. 139.

Table II.16. Annual average growth rates of GDP and of imports. World and by country groups, 1970-1984

(Percentage)

Variables/country groups	1970–1975	1975–1980	1980–1984	1980–1981	1981–1982	1982–1983	1983–1984
A. GDP (1980 prices) growth							
World	3.5	4.0	2.3	1.8	0.3	2.4	4.5
Developed market	2.9	3.5	2.4	1.5	−0.2	3.0	5.1
Developing market	6.4	5.5	1.9	2.7	1.8	0.2	2.8
Centrally planned	5.6	——5.6——		3.7	5.4	6.9	8.9
B. Growth in imports							
Total imports							
World	35.9	45.7	−1.2	−1.8	−5.8	−2.3	5.3
Developed market	32.1	26.9	−1.6	−5.9	−6.6	−0.7	7.5
Developing market	49.9	26.3	−1.5	9.6	−6.1	−7.9	−0.7
Centrally planed	53.0	8.3	1.7	−0.5	−0.4	3.5	4.0
Manufactures							
World	32.6	24.7	1.3	−0.2	−3.6	−0.7	10.2
Developed market	28.0	26.1	2.2	−4.3	−2.5	4.2	11.9
Developing market	46.0	25.3	−1.1	11.2	−6.9	−8.2	0.8
Centrally planned	36.5	14.9	0.6	−5.2	−2.4	−10.8	23.7
Non-oil primary commodities							
World	25.1	19.8	−2.9	−5.4	−7.8	−4.0	5.3
Developed market	20.0	19.6	−3.4	−10.5	−7.8	−1.7	6.6
Developing market	53.8	22.4	−1.5	4.5	−10.4	−6.2	7.1
Centrally planned	33.7	16.3	−2.4	5.4	−2.2	−10.4	−2.4
Food and beverages							
World	30.4	18.5	−1.5	−0.1	−6.3	−3.6	4.2
Developed market	25.7	16.1	−1.7	−5.3	−3.6	−1.8	4.0
Developing market	68.0	23.0	−0.4	7.7	−11.5	−2.7	6.3
Centrally planned	35.9	22.7	−1.9	13.6	−6.4	−12.6	−0.6
Agricultural raw materials							
World	17.3	24.4	−3.1	−7.4	−10.4	0.6	4.9
Developed market	16.0	23.1	−3.6	−12.2	−11.3	1.5	8.3
Developing market	24.7	30.1	0.4	−2.5	−11.3	5.2	11.7
Centrally planned	17.1	24.8	−5.7	12.8	−5.7	−7.9	−21.2
Metals and minerals							
World	22.7	19.8	−4.8	−11.5	−8.9	−6.8	7.3
Developed market	15.6	23.1	−5.3	−15.8	−11.7	−3.2	9.7
Developing market	51.0	19.1	−17.8	1.9	−8.1	−16.8	6.4
Centrally planned	39.6	7.9	−1.6	−9.8	7.6	−8.2	5.0

Sources: UNCTAD, *Handbook of International Trade and Development Statistics, 1984, 1985* and *1986;* and IMF, *International Financial Statistics Yearbook, 1986.*

substantial rebound of economic activity in the United States. In the European countries and Japan, on the other hand, the rise in industrial output was much more subdued and significantly less than in 1976-1977. As these countries are much more dependent on imported primary commodities than the United States, this divergence of growth rates could explain the more moderate rise in commodity prices during the recovery phase of the current price cycle than during the earlier one (see figure II.12).

Part of the explanation for the weak association between growth in industrial production and commodity prices in the 1980s may lie in the structural changes that are taking the economies of the industrial countries away from basic and heavy industries towards lighter manufacturing (particularly in electronics) and service industries.[6] While such changes were already under way in the 1970s, they were given additional impetus by the sharp rise in energy prices during 1979-1980.

Restrictive monetary policies initiated in the early 1980s and the resulting high interest rates were helpful in fighting the high rates of inflation in most OECD countries in 1979-1980. The expectation that interest rates would decline substantially once inflation was under control, however, was not realized in the face of high current and prospective government deficits in the United States.[7]

Thus, in the early 1980s, nominal and real interest rates in the OECD countries reached historically high levels. Although nominal interest rates in the United States have been declining and in 1985 reached only 50 per cent of the

<hr>

[6] See part two, ch. I, this *Survey*.

[7] Robert E. Baldwin, "U.S. trade policy and Asian development", *Asian Development Review,* vol. 2, No. 2 (1984), pp. 43-68.

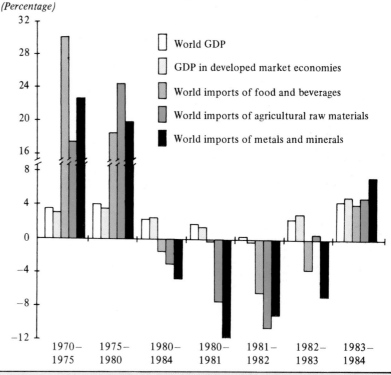

Figure II.11. Annual average growth rates of GDP and imports of primary commodities. World and the developed market economies, 1970-1984

(Percentage)

□ World GDP

□ GDP in developed market economies

World imports of food and beverages

World imports of agricultural raw materials

■ World imports of metals and minerals

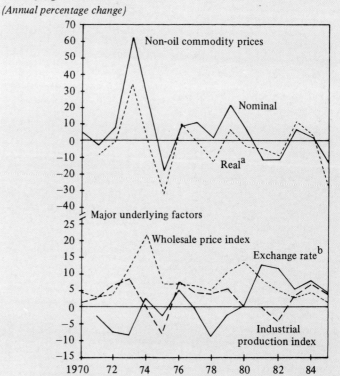

Figure II.12. Movement in index of non-oil commodity prices and major underlying factors, 1970-1985

(Annual percentage change)

Non-oil commodity prices

Nominal

Real[a]

Major underlying factors

Wholesale price index

Exchange rate[b]

Industrial production index

[a] Deflated by the export unit value index of manufactured goods. [b] Effective exchange rates: IMF – Multilateral Exchange Rate Model (MERM) of the United States dollar against other industrial country currencies.

1981 levels, real interest rates continued to stay at levels higher than 4 per cent per year.

The main direct effect of interest rate rises on commodity prices has been through stock holding and inventory-management policies. High interest rates raise the cost of holding stocks, particularly at the last stages of the distribution chain in consuming countries. This has discouraged the accumulation of stocks, thereby cutting demand, and has provided an incentive to unload existing stocks, thus adding to supply. In particular, in the metal sector, the limitation of stocks held by end-using companies has been made possible by the adoption of the new "just-in-time" inventory management system responding to the need for these companies to cut down costs in a recession-ridden market. Just-in-time methods are now becoming established and it is possible they may not be reversed in all cases by decline in interest rates. On the direct effect of interest rates on commodity prices, the results from one econometric study indicate that a 1 percentage point rise in the real three-month Eurodollar rate was associated with a more than 0.8 per cent decline in commodity prices.[8] The results of another study were less conclusive, but showed an inverse relationship between interest rates lagged by one quarter and prices for agricultural raw materials and metals.[9]

However, the indirect effects of interest rate rises on primary commodity prices are both less ambiguous and more important. First, high interest rates have been the main factor in slowing down the growth rates in developed market economies which, in turn, has had a depressing effect on the demand for primary commodities. Second, by increasing the debt-servicing

---

Box II.10.   Prospects for world economic recovery: is there a long wave?

The average rate of economic growth in the developed market economies slowed to 3.2 per cent during 1970-1980 compared with an average of 5.6 per cent during the period 1948-1971 (a 24-year period). The rapid rate of post-war economic expansion, which achieved the highest acceleration during the 1960s, thus appeared to have come to a definite end in 1971. Growth since 1980 further decelerated to an average of less than 2 per cent during 1980-1986, confirming the general down trend since 1971. Long waves or cycles are believed to exist in economic activities in market economies, characterized by long periods of expansion followed by equally long periods of slow-down. A Russian economist, Nicholai Kondratief, is credited with the discovery of cycles governing economic activities in the developed market economies, lasting roughly for a period of 50 years – 25 years of boom followed by 25 years of slump.

Kondratief came to his conclusion on the basis of observations on wages and commodity prices in the United Kingdom of Great Britain and Northern Ireland, France and the United States in the nineteenth and early twentieth centuries, ending with 1920. He concluded that after the industrial revolution had begun towards the end of the eighteenth century, western economies expanded and contracted in a roughly 50-year-long wave, with approximately 25 years of expansion and 25 years of contraction in each cycle.

Kondratief did not offer a hypothesis to account for these long cycles. But others have tried to provide the theoretical underpinning. Rostow,[a] for example, offered the explanation in terms of the oscillation in the relative prices of raw materials, which in turn reflect perpetual over- and under-shooting of supply and demand in markets for manufactures, food, and raw materials. According to Rostow, boom years are associated with declining relative prices for raw materials since they lower industrial costs, while rising relative raw material prices affect industrial output adversely, thereby generating slumps.

Empirical support for Rostow's explanation can be claimed from the post-war economic boom coinciding with a period of declining relative commodity prices and the post-1970 slump coinciding with rising relative commodity prices, although Rostow did not suggest a regular cycle but only a process of oscillatory adjustments to perpetual shocks.

Others have also tried to explain the economic slow-down in the 1970s in terms of high commodity prices, including the price of oil.[b] As stated in the text, this association between commodity prices and the boom cycle in economic activities seemed to have been lacking in the 1980s when lower commodity prices failed to revive sufficient economic expansion.

Critics have expressed scepticism over the adequacy of the statistical time series for empirically verifying the existence of the Kondratief long-wave cycle. Others question the existence of autonomous long waves and predetermined booms and recessions in the economic process. However, the recent stock market upheaval, and the continuing predictions of low economic growth and falling or depressed commodity prices right into the 1990s, strengthen the belief that the world economy is in the downward phase of a Kondratief cycle.

---

[a]   W.W. Rostow, *The World Economy*, 1978; *Getting from Here to There*, 1979; and *Why the Poor Get Richer and the Rich Slow Down* (London, Macmillan, 1980).

[b]   Michael Beenstock, *The World Economy in Transition* (London, George Allen & Unwin, 1983), ch. 7.

---

[8]   See UNCTAD, *Revitalizing Development, Growth and International Trade: Assessment and Policy Options* (United Nations publication, Sales No. E.87.II.D.7), p. 107.

[9]   Ke-Young Chu and Thomas K. Morrison, "The 1981-82 recession and non-oil primary commodity prices", *International Monetary Fund Staff Papers*, vol. 31, No. 1 (March 1984), pp. 93-140.

burden, high interest rates have forced the developing countries to increase their volume of exports by competitive devaluations and worsening terms of trade.

Another major factor influencing the international economy over the past decade has been the swings in the value of the United States dollar. The dollar fell to a historically low level in the late 1970s, but rose sharply over the period 1981-1984 partly as a consequence of the restrictive monetary policies followed in the United States. By the beginning of 1985, the dollar was generally considered to be overvalued by between 20 to 40 per cent. During 1985, the dollar depreciated by about 20 per cent and has been falling further in 1986-1987. These wide fluctuations in the value of the dollar have had implications for all major traded goods, especially primary commodities.

Floating exchange rates have constituted a source of instability in markets for primary commodities. Although increased exchange rate volatility is not the sole factor responsible for greater instability of commodity prices, empirical evidence suggests a strong relationship between the two. Since the introduction of floating exchange rates, commodity price instability has significantly increased in all currencies, including the special drawing right, but this increase has been most pronounced for prices expressed in the United States dollar.[10] This factor was important, especially in the 1972-1974 period and during 1981-1984 when the sharp appreciation of the United States currency served to further depress commodity prices in dollars.[11] Asymmetrically, however, the depreciation of the dollar since late 1985 has resulted in a much

more limited rise in commodity prices (see box II.2, p. 91).

The control of inflation since the beginning of the 1980s is considered a major achievement of the fiscal and monetary policies followed by developed market economies. In the seven largest OECD countries, the rate of increase in consumer prices was brought down from an average of over 12 per cent in 1980 to about 3.5 per cent in 1985, the lowest for more than two decades.

Although the control of inflation in the OECD countries was achieved through a variety of fiscal, monetary and structural measures, it was in no small measure contributed by the decline in commodity prices, which were depressed to historically low levels largely as a result of the slow-down in the growth of developed market economies. The linkage between changes in commodity prices and world economic growth is an aspect of the new interdependence in the world economy, the neglect of which is an important factor in the continuing global imbalances in international balance of payments.[12]

B. RISING TRENDS IN AGRICULTURAL PROTECTIONISM

Protectionism in agriculture is generally a more complex and less transparent phenomenon than in manufactures. While in manufactures trans-border measures, such as tariffs, quantitative import restrictions and export subsidies are the main instruments used, in agriculture non-tariff barriers, domestic subsidies, taxes as well as other non-border trade influences, including macro-economic policies,

are additionally significant. There has been an upsurge in the proportion of agricultural trade subject to non-tariff barriers such as quantitative restrictions, health and sanitary restrictions, packaging and labelling regulations and, more recently, voluntary export restraints.

In addition, a wide range of support and intervention measures in favour of agriculture are practised in various developed market economies. The stated objectives of these policies have included food self-sufficiency and security, and the maintenance of per capita farm incomes at close parity with levels in other sectors of the economy, as well as such policy concerns as regional development and the protection of the environment. However, as revealed by a number of studies, the extent of support provided has far exceeded such concerns and has distorted the structure of agricultural trade and production.[13] The successful conclusion of the Uruguay Round of trade negotiations launched in 1986 with

[10] See UNCTAD, *Commodity Survey 1980-1985* (TD/B/C.1/274); and Chu and Morrison, *loc. cit.*

[11] IMF, *World Economic Outlook,* Occasional Paper No. 27 (Washington, D.C., April 1984), p. 140.

[12] See part one, ch. I, this *Survey.*

[13] The following is a selected list of references. World Bank, *World Development Report 1986* (New York, Oxford University Press, 1986); OECD, *Problems of Agricultural Trade* (Paris, 1982), *Agricultural Trade with Developing Countries* (Paris, 1984), *National Policies and Agricultural Trade* (Paris, 1987); Alberto Valdés and Joachim Zietz, *Agricultural Protection in OECD Countries: Its Costs to Less-Developed Countries,* Research Report No. 21 (Washington, D.C., International Food Policy Research Institute, December 1980); *The Costs of Protectionism to Developing Countries: An Analysis for Selected Agricultural Products,* World Bank Staff Working Papers No. 769 (Washington, D.C., 1986); Timolty Josling, *Developed-Country Agricultural Policies and Developing Country Supplies: The Case of Wheat,* Research Report No. 14 (Washington, D.C., International Food Policy Research Institute, 1980); S.J. Anjaria, Naheed Kirmani and Arne B. Petersen, *Trade Policy Issues and Developments,* Occasional Paper No. 38 (Washington, D.C., International Monetary Fund, 1985).

agricultural trade on the agenda is expected to remove many of these measures (see box II.11).

1. Tariff barriers

Under the General Agreement on Tariffs and Trade (GATT) system, tariffs, as opposed to quantitative or other restrictions, constitute the principal form of permissible trade protection. Tariffs, however, have been recognized to constitute serious obstacles to trade, and tariff reduction has been the focus of efforts to liberalize trade through negotiations under successive GATT rounds. They have achieved remarkable success in reducing industrial tariffs, which, with the full implementation of the Tokyo Round agreement to be completed by January 1988, may come down to an average of 3 to 4 per cent in the developed market countries compared with their average of more than 40 per cent in the 1940s.

Despite the success in the reduction of most-favoured-nation tariffs, the institution of GSP (generalized system of preferences) schemes by most of the developed countries offering preferential tariff margins to developing country exports, and the fact that most raw material exports from the developing countries enter duty free in developed country markets, tariff barriers remain an important, though

---

Box II.11. Negotiating proposals before the GATT Committee on Agriculture

Within a year of the agreed Punta del Este Declaration, formal proposals were submitted to the GATT Committee on Trade in Agriculture in which the negotiations on agriculture were to take place in the New Round. The United States of America, the 14-member Cairns Group of countries, the European Economic Community, and Canada, submitted their proposals, which specified the issues to be negotiated, the method of conducting the negotiations and the method of implementation of rules and disciplines governing agricultural trade which might be agreed upon. Japan had not yet submitted its formal proposals to the Committee but had made statements on principles which, in its view, should govern trade in agriculture. The developing countries agreed to participate effectively in the process of negotiation.

The various proposals submitted before the committee were in agreement on the broad objectives of (1) liberalization of agricultural trade by improving market access through, *inter alia,* the reduction in or elimination of import barriers, (2) a phasing out of agricultural support and subsidies which directly or indirectly affect trade and (3) harmonization of health and sanitary regulations on internationally agreed standards so as to avoid disguised barriers to trade.

The proposals differed mainly on the emphasis in two major areas. The first related to the extent of support measures to be included in negotiations for their possible concerted reduction or elimination. The second concerned the speed with which support to agriculture should be reduced or eliminated. Most of the proposals favoured a comprehensive commodity coverage and inclusion of the overall levels of support – in particular those which distort production, consumption and trade. The producer subsidy equivalent, with suitable modification for use as a negotiating instrument, found favour as the basis of the measurement of support levels, although there were some reservations about its accuracy and suitability as a comparator.

Regarding the speed with which support, including subsidies and import access barriers, should be removed, some proposals favoured a complete phase-out of all support measures over a period of 10 years after the negotiations were ended. In other proposals no definite time limit for complete elimination of support measures was set. Most of the proposals, however, required negotiations and support reductions to be carried out in stages. The stages included very short-term or emergency measures such as a freeze on subsidies, a halt on the introduction of new access barriers, including sanitary or phytosanitary regulations, and an orderly release of stocks so as to avoid short-term market disruptions. In the interim, commitment would be undertaken by countries to reduce or eliminate trade distortion policies in the form of a schedule of reductions in individual countries. In the longer-run framework, GATT rules and disciplines should be agreed to remove all restrictions to the free flow of trade in agricultural commodities and to prohibit the use of all subsidies and other government support measures having an effect on agricultural trade. Any exceptions should be set within strictly defined limits and trade in agricultural products should be fully integrated into the generally applicable provisions and mechanisms for consultation, surveillance and dispute settlement within the GATT system.

Some of the proposals explicitly recognized the need for differential and more favourable treatment for the developing countries.

There appeared to be consensus that the long-term objective of agricultural policies affecting international trade should be to allow market forces to function more effectively. However, some countries felt that consideration should be given to social and other concerns such as food security, environmental protection and overall employment, which are not purely economic concerns.

The speed with which major agricultural trading countries had submitted their formal negotiating proposals was itself a sign of progress and an indication of the earnestness with which the negotiations had been viewed by major trading nations. The GATT secretariat expressed its satisfaction with the progress as of the end of 1987. More significant progress could be expected in 1988 since all parties have committed themselves to doing more. The final conclusion could be expected to reflect the true needs of world agricultural trade.

by no means the only impediment to the developing countries' commodity trade. Most of the tropical products exported from the ESCAP region still face high duties and their rates rise with increases in the stages of processing.

Since 1980, the GATT and the United Nations Conference on Trade and Development (UNCTAD) secretariats have prepared extensive documentation on the commercial policy situation and trade flows with respect to tropical products covering coffee, cocoa, tea, banana, spices, oils and oilseeds, rubber, jute and jute products, plant and vegetable materials, tropical wood, tropical roots, tobacco, and tropical fruits and nuts and their products. Their results show that the levels of tariffs on these products in many industrialized countries remain considerably high despite the implementation of the Tokyo Round agreements on most-favoured-nation tariffs, and of the preferential treatments under GSP schemes. Moreover, in some cases such tariffs are also openly discriminatory against developing country exports. Import tariffs on plywood exports and boneless chicken meat from some South-East Asian countries in some developed country markets provide examples of such discrimination.

A more disturbing problem facing developing countries is that of tariff escalation. While most of the natural-resource-based and tropical agricultural raw materials face zero or low duty rates in the developed countries, the same products in processed forms are subject to higher tariff rates, which results in an amplified rate of effective protection to value added by domestic industries in the importing countries. Table II.17 illustrates the degree of such escalation of tariffs by degree of processing in the case of several categories of products which are of interest to the developing countries in the ESCAP region.

The data in table II.17 show clear evidence of escalation, as in all cases the nominal tariff for the final stage exceeds that for the primary goods, while the escalator indicators also show some increase as a result of Tokyo Round tariff changes, which have brought about a greater percentage reduction in tariffs on the primary product than on its processed form. Subsequent analysis in terms of the 1983 applied rates of tariffs in 11 industrial countries also confirmed the tendency of tariffs to escalate over given processing chains.[14] With these escalations, the apparently low nominal tariffs constitute very high rates of effective protection when they are applied to processed products which have relatively low value-added contents. Moreover, since the demand for processed products is generally more elastic than the raw materials, even equal nominal rates of tariffs on both will have a more demand-restraining effect for the processed product than for the raw material. With the rates escalating on the processed products, the demand-restraining effects become magnified. Together with non-tariff measures in the structure of which escalation is also present, they constitute an important restraint on the efforts of the developing countries to process their primary commodities and to export value-added products (see chapter II).

A number of commodities, especially tropical beverages, are subjected to internal taxes in the developed countries. They are an important source of government revenue. To the extent that these taxes raise internal prices significantly, they tend to decrease consumption and imports. They thus act as a barrier to trade expansion in the products concerned. More-

over, to the extent that the product may compete, as in the case of tropical fruits like banana, with domestically produced alternatives, the internal tax is in effect no different from any other tariff or non-tariff trade protection.

2. Non-tariff barriers

Non-tariff barriers are a more important hurdle to trade in primary commodities. They have greatly proliferated in recent years and take a variety of forms. Hence their impact is harder to analyse. Two indicators have been widely used to measure the extent of this proliferation. The first is the frequency ratio, calculated in terms of percentage of the 4-digit Customs Co-operation Council Nomenclature product groups affected by the given non-tariff barrier to the total number of 4 digit product groups in a given category (e.g., product section). The second is the import coverage ratio calculated as the percentage of the value of imports covered by the given non-tariff barrier.

Volume-restraining measures, including quotas, licensing, import permits and authorizations, and voluntary export restraints, are the non-tariff barriers that affect trade most and form the hard-core of non-tariff barriers. In the case of several groups of products, such as animals and animal products, and textiles, tariff quotas are a major impediment. In the case of animals and animal products, vegetable products, fats and oils, prepared food, tobacco, and sugar, the system of variable levies constitutes a high barrier to trade, next to volume-restraining measures in their importance.[15]

---

14 UNCTAD, "Protectionism and structural adjustment" (TD/B/1126, part I, January 1987), p. 21.

15 UNCTAD, "Protectionism and structural adjustment" (TD/B/940, February 1983), tables 1 and 2. Also see Sam Laird and Michael Finger, "Protectionism in developed and developing countries" (Bangkok, Thailand Development Research Institute, 1986).

Table II.17. Pre- and post-Tokyo Round tariff escalation on products imported from developing countries into 10 industrial markets[a]

Stage of processing	Product description	Customs Co-operation Council Nomenclature	Average tariff rate[b] (Percentage)		Percentage reduction in pre-Tokyo tariff	Stages compared	Direction of change in escalation indicator[c]	
			Pre-Tokyo	Post-Tokyo			Absolute difference	Percentage difference
1	Fish, crustaceans and molluscs	0301-3	4.3	3.5	18.6			
2	Fish, crustaceans and molluscs, prepared	1604-5	6.1	5.5	9.8	2 with 1	increased	increased
1	Vegetables, fresh or dried	0701, 0704-6	13.3	8.9	33.1			
2	Vegetables, prepared	2001-2	18.8	12.4	34.0	2 with 1	reduced	no change
1	Fruit, fresh, dried	0801-9, 0812	6.0	4.8	20.0			
2	Fruit, provisionally preserved	0801-11, 0813	14.5	12.2	15.9	2 with 1	reduced	increased
3	Fruit, prepared	2001, 2003-7	19.5	16.6	14.9	3 with 1	reduced	increased
1	Coffee	0901	10.0	6.8	32.0			
2	Processed coffee	2102 ex	13.3	9.4	29.3	2 with 1	reduced	increased
1	Cocoa beans	1801	4.2	2.6	38.1			
2	Processed cocoa	1803-5	6.7	4.3	35.8	2 with 1	reduced	no change
3	Chocolate products	1806	15.0	11.8	21.3	3 with 2	reduced	increased
1	Oil-seeds and flour	1201-2	2.7	2.7	–			
2	Fixed vegetable oils	1507	8.5	8.1	4.7	2 with 1	reduced	reduced
1	Unmanufactured tobacco	2401	56.1	55.8	0.5			
2	Manufactured tobacco	2402	82.2	81.8	0.5	2 with 1	no change	no change
1	Natural rubber	4001	2.8	2.3	17.9			
2	Semi-manufactured rubber (unvulcanized)	4005-6	4.6	2.9	37.0	2 with 1	reduced	reduced
3	Rubber articles	4011-14, 4016	7.9	6.7	15.2	3 with 2	reduced	increased
1	Raw hides and skins	4101	1.4	–	100.0			
2	Semi-manufactured leather	4102-8, 4110, 4302	4.2	4.2		2 with 1	increased	increased

Table II.17 *(continued)*

Stage of processing	Product description	Customs Co-operation Council Nomenclature	Average tariff rate[b] (Percentage)		Percentage reduction in pre-Tokyo tariff	Stages compared	Direction of change in escalation indicator[c]	
			Pre-Tokyo	Post-Tokyo			Absolute difference	Percentage difference
3	Travel goods, handbags, etc.	4202	8.5	8.5	—	3 with 2	no change	no change
4	Manufactured articles of leather	4203-5	9.3	8.2	11.8	4 with 2	reduced	reduced
5	Footwear	6401-5	11.6	10.9	6.0	5 with 2	reduced	reduced
1	Vegetable textiles yarns (excl. hemp)	5706-7	4.0	2.9	27.5			
2	Twine, rope, and articles; sacks and bags	5904-6, 6203	5.6	4.7	16.1	2 with 1	increased	increased
3	Jute fabrics	5710	9.1	8.3	8.8	3 with 1	increased	increased
1	Silk yarn, not for retail sale	5004-6	2.6	2.6	—			
2	Silk fabric	5009	5.6	5.3	5.4	2 with 1	reduced	reduced
1	Semi-manufactured wood	4405-14, 16, 17, 19	2.6	1.8	30.8			
2	Wood panels	4415	10.8	9.2	14.8	2 with 1	reduced	increased
3	Wood articles	4420-28	6.9	4.1	40.6	3 with 1	reduced	reduced
4	Furniture	9401, 9403	8.1	6.6	18.5	4 with 1	reduced	increased

Source: UNCTAD, "Protectionism and structural adjustment in the world economy" (TD/B/981), February 1984, table 18.

[a] Australia, Austria, Canada, EEC, Finland, Japan, New Zealand, Norway and Sweden. [b] Unweighted average of tariffs actually applied to the products in question, whether most-favoured-nation or preferential. [c] Two indicators have been used as rough measures of the extent of change in tariff escalation: the absolute difference between the average tariff on two successive stages of processing and the percentage relationship between the two average tariff rates.

According to the preliminary findings of a recent analysis of non-tariff barriers applied by selected developed countries, conducted similarly in terms of trade coverage and frequency ratios, trade intervention in general increased significantly between 1981 and 1986. For primary commodities, the percentage of imports of all food items affected by non-tariff barriers went up from 40.8 per cent in 1981 to 42.5 per cent in 1986; for oil-seeds and nuts, they went up from 7.5 to 11 per cent and for animal and vegetable oils they went up from 9.1 to 12.5 per cent. For agricultural raw materials, the percentage of coverage went up from 2.8 in 1981 to 8.4 in 1986, and for ores and metals it went up from 12.7 to 24.7 per cent.[16] The increased incidence of intervention most certainly has affected the exporters of the products concerned in the ESCAP region.

The other major concern of the primary commodity exporting countries in the ESCAP region relates to export subsidies given to developed country exporters, which act as a barrier to import not so much into the countries giving subsidies but to third country markets. The structural surpluses of several commodities, which have resulted from policies of high internal support prices in the developed countries, have been released at subsidized prices in the international market. They have had the effect of lowering the prices of the commodities concerned and tend to deprive the

developing countries of their market share for commodities, including grains, sugar, oil-seeds and cotton. The recent efforts by the United States to regain its lost market share in commodity exports, which it perceived was lost to subsidized exports from other countries, resulted in a heightening of this concern in the region. This is because the United States action directly affected a number of commodity exports from the region which bear hardly any subsidies, and has threatened to escalate further the competitive subsidization of exports by others. The lowering of the market prices of grains, sugar and cotton in 1985-1986 was to a large extent the consequence of the measures introduced through the United States Food Security Act of 1985.

There are other examples of specific trade actions in recent years affecting specific export products from countries in the region. These include safeguard actions to protect seafood processors in some developed countries, which affect canned tuna exports from the region; health and other product standards affecting fruits and seafood exports; frequent changes in import regulations in response to the domestic growing season and size of harvests, affecting exports of banana for example, from the Philippines; imposition of additional levies on canned pineapples from the Philippines and Thailand in certain markets because of the sugar contents of these fruit products; the recent reduction of United States sugar quotas affecting the Philippines and Thailand; and the restraint on Thai tapioca exports to the European Economic Community (EEC) market under a voluntary restraint agreement.[17]

3. Total costs of protection

In order to capture the effects of overall, economy-wide costs of

protection in OECD countries a number of measures have been used. The three measures most often used, in increasing degrees of comprehensiveness and sophistication, are discussed below:

(a) Budgetary costs

The budgetary costs of support, although they do not fully reflect total cost, are themselves very large and have escalated in several cases in recent years. OECD estimates these costs in the United States at $57.0 billion in current dollars, or 4.1 per cent of total Federal Government disbursement in 1985 compared with $25.9 billion or 2.9 per cent of the total in 1980. Other estimates suggest an expenditure of $30 billion in 1986 compared with $3.5 billion in the early 1980s. In the EEC after rapid escalation throughout the 1970s, the budgetary costs of the Common Agricultural Policy seem to have stabilized recently in the face of growing budget constraints. EEC price supports under the Policy cost $23.5 billion in 1984 compared with $5.6 billion in 1974. In 1986 direct subsidy costs of the Policy amounted to $23 billion. An additional $2-3 billion was spent on surplus disposal. More than two thirds (72.8 per cent in 1985) of the EEC budget have been spent on the Policy in recent years.

Japan subsidized its farmers at the rate of $10.5 billion in 1985, although the level of budgetary support has been stabilized or reduced over the past several years. Agricultural spending amounted to 3.1 per cent of government spending in 1985 com-

[16] Percentages indicate share of the value of imports covered by selected non-tariff barriers which exclude health and technical regulations as well as excise taxes. Data covered 8 developed countries plus EEC(10). Ratios were computed by using 1981 import trade weights. Computations were made at tariff line levels and the results were aggregated to relevant product group levels. See UNCTAD, "Protectionism and structural adjustment" (TD/B/1126/Add.1), p. 3, table 1.1.

[17] See, for example, Surakiart Sathirathai and Ammar Siamwalla, "GATT law, agricultural trade, and developing countries: lessons from two case studies", The World Bank Economic Review, vol. 1, No. 4 (Washington, D.C., World Bank, September 1987), pp. 595-618.

pared with 4.9 per cent in 1980. Public spending related to the implementation of agricultural policy has tended to remain stable in proportionate terms in other OECD countries such as Australia, Austria, Canada and the Federal Republic of Germany, although their absolute levels have increased. In France, New Zealand and the United Kingdom the proportion of expenditure on this account has tended to decline at least in constant price terms.[18] However, in these calculations national government expenditures do not include EEC expenditures, and the EEC expenditures exclude the expenditures of EEC member countries.

(b) Nominal costs of protection

Domestic prices are often kept well above border prices through import restraints, domestic support measures and other institutional means. For example, in Japan consumers are estimated to pay around 60 per cent higher prices for food than would be the case if the fall in world prices and the yen appreciation since 1985 had been reflected in internal agricultural prices.[19] Some reports suggest that domestic prices of rice in Japan are maintained at levels 6-10 times higher than the international price.

The nominal costs of protection provide a way of measuring the influence of tariff and non-tariff barriers on domestic prices. The nominal protection coefficients measure the protective effect of measures which raise domestic prices relative to border prices. The nominal protection coefficient measures, however, fail to take account of product quality differences, the impact of domestic protective and support measures on world prices, and the protective effects of domestic input subsidies, deficiency payments and acreage controls. Despite such weaknesses the nominal protection coefficient estimates indicate the degree of variation in the level of protection over countries and commodities.

The estimated nominal protection coefficients expressing producers' prices as indices of border prices for several products in the developed countries are given in figure II.13. The weighted average price of wheat, coarse grains, rice, beef and lamb, pork and poultry, dairy products and sugar was found to be 40 per cent above the world price level in the concerned countries in 1980-1982. Variations across countries and commodities were substantial.

The measure of *ad valorem* tariff equivalence of various protective measures in selected countries for wheat, maize and rice, based on the differences between domestic producer and consumer prices and the world market price, also indicated very high levels of protection for all the three commodities in the EEC and Japan.[20]

(c) Producer subsidy equivalent

Various measures have been devised in recent years, the producer subsidy equivalent among them, to provide relative indices of the extent of intervention across countries and commodities on a common basis. These measures indicate the domestic price effects and producer gains resulting from policy interventions. The measures of producer and consumer subsidy equivalents establish an equivalence of the estimated amount of revenue that would be required to compensate producers (consumers) if existing government programmes were eliminated. They are thus measures of producer (consumer) gains resulting from interventionist government policies, all of which are not reflected in direct budgetary costs to Governments. These measures, although they lack precision in many ways, are more satisfactory than the size of budgetary outlays, which is often cited as an indicator of the level and extent of government support. The producer and consumer subsidy equivalents[21] take account of the usual budget outlays that finance intervention; they also include policies such as tariffs, import quotas, permits and variable levies that do not result in specific budget outlays. The results constitute an index of government intervention and provide a common basis for cross-country and cross-commodity comparisons.

The Food and Agriculture Organization (FAO), the United States Department of Agriculture (USDA) and OECD have estimated the producer subsidy

---

[18] The various figures quoted here are from the following sources: *National Policies and Agricultural Trade*, p. 37, table 4; see also World Bank, *World Development Report 1986* (New York, Oxford University Press, 1986), p. 121; "GATT negotiators under fire", *The Economist*, vol. 304, No. 1507 (18-24 July 1987); G. Miller, *The Political Economy of International Agricultural Policy Reform* (Canberra, Department of Primary Industry, 1986), pp. 1-2; and United States Department of Agriculture, "Government intervention in agriculture: measurement, evaluation and implications for trade negotiations", FAER-229 (mimeographed) (April 1987), p. 13.

[19] Miller, *op. cit.*, p. 2.

[20] OECD, *Agricultural Trade with Developing Countries* (Paris, 1984).

[21] Measures of consumer subsidy equivalents are developed in studies by USDA and the OECD. These measures generally estimate the effects on consumers of policies that separate domestic and external prices. These are not discussed in detail in the present *Survey*. It should be noted, however, that where policy instruments are functionally linked, such that they jointly affect producers and consumers, the producer subsidy equivalents measure the net effect of the package of policies. See United States Department of Agriculture, "Government intervention in agriculture . . .", p. 21.

Figure II.13. Nominal protection coefficients for producer prices of selected commodities in industrial countries, 1980-1982

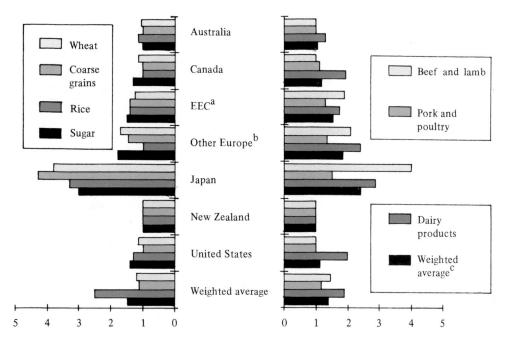

^a Excluding Greece, Portugal and Spain.   ^b Austria, Finland, Norway, Sweden and Switzerland.   ^c Averages are weighted by the values of production at border prices.

equivalents of all transfers to farmers effected through domestic support programmes and trade measures. FAO estimated them for five commodities, namely wheat, rice, maize, milk and sugar. The transfers, measured as proportions of receipts from sales of the respective commodity, indicated high levels of subsidies, especially for sugar and also for wheat and rice in some markets.[22]

The USDA and the OECD secretariat also measured producer subsidy equivalents which expressed policy transfers as a ratio or percentage of gross domestic value of production including direct net payments, such as deficiency payments less producer levies. The number of commodities included

in both the USDA and the OECD studies were 11, although the groupings of the commodities in the two studies are somewhat different. In the USDA study, producer subsidy equivalents are calculated for grains (wheat, rice, maize, sorghum and barley), oil-seeds (soybeans and other oil-seeds), cotton, sugar, livestock and dairy products for 17 developed and developing countries.

The results of the USDA study show that sugar in th United States, dairy in Canada, beef in the EEC, and beef, pork, soybeans, sugar, barley, milk, rice and wheat in Japan, are the commodities most protected. In the United States and EEC support levels for most commodities fall in the middle range of 25 to 50 per cent. In countries such as Australia, Canada and New Zealand support levels are at a low or moderate level ranging from 0 to 25 per cent. In some developing

countries such as India, the levels of support for commodities such as cotton, wheat, rice, sugar and oil-seeds are negative or very small.

The percentages of producer subsidy equivalents attributed to policies linked with border measures in the developed countries have been separately calculated. The USDA study shows that the highest percentage (75-100) of subsidies to dairy and sugar in the United States, rice and sugar in Australia, barley, beef, wheat, corn, milk, poultry meat, rice and sugar in the EEC and beef, milk, pork, rice and sugar in Japan, are accounted for by border measures or policies linked with border measures, which are more directly trade-restrictive. In Canada, New Zealand and the United States such measures account for the lowest percentage of total support.

The OECD study included the following 11 commodities for cal-

[22] FAO, "International agricultural adjustment, fifth progress report" (C. 85/21) (Rome, August 1985), p. 11, table 1.7.

culation of producer subsidy equivalents: dairy, wheat, coarse grains, beef and veal, pig meat, poultry meat, sugar, rice, sheep meat, wool and soybeans. It calculated the producer subsidy equivalents for the period 1979-1981 in individual and groups of OECD countries and found high average levels of support for the commodities concerned in Japan, the Nordic countries and the EEC .

Although the producer subsidy equivalent is the most comprehensive indicator of total support to commodity producers in different countries so far devised, it falls short of a fully comprehensive measure of effective rate of assistance for a number of reasons.[23] First, there are limitations of data for a fully satisfactory coverage of all protectionist measures. The producer subsidy equivalents fail to take account of the price effects, for example, of intermediate inputs owing to assistance provided to the industries producing these inputs. Second, the external reference prices used in the calculations, which are derived from observed market prices, already include effects of government policy actions in agricultural and financial markets. Third, external reference prices vary as a result of exchange rate changes that may be entirely unrelated to behaviour in agricultural markets. Finally, the producer subsidy equivalent does not capture the large country effect on the world reference price.

Despite its limitations, the producer subsidy equivalent is the most comprehensive measure devised so far and is useful for a quantitative comparison of levels of support and protection among countries for different commodities. The estimates so far made demonstrate that in general the support levels are higher in the importing than in the exporting countries, and higher in the developed than in the developing countries which, in many cases, provide negative protection to agriculture. The levels of support and protection are quite high in developed market economies on commodities such as rice, corn, sugar and cotton, in which developing countries of the ESCAP region compete for export markets.

The policy measures undertaken by the OECD countries and evaluated above have had several adverse consequences for world agricultural production, supply, demand, trade and prices. First, artificially high domestic prices have encouraged production and discouraged consumption in the developed countries and contributed to the supply-demand imbalance that has developed. Second, surplus production has led to rapid commodity stock buil-up, especially of cereals in the developed countries. Thus, the world stock of cereals rose from 247.6 million tons in 1981 to 395.7 million tons in 1986 and was forecast to rise to 448 million tons in 1987.[24] Stocks in the developed countries rose much faster from 145.4 million tons in 1981 to 269.0 million tons in 1986 and were forecast to rise to 324 million tons in 1987. The most noticeable rise in stocks took place in the United States (table II.18). Third, disposal of surplus production and stocks, often at subsidized prices on the world market, has served to depress and destabilize world market prices. Fourth, an escalation of competitive subsidization of exports by major developed country exporters, in which the United States moves since 1985 have been rather precipitous, has driven developing country producers to the verge of bankruptcy. Fifth, by altering trade flows in favour of OECD countries *vis-à-vis* developing countries which do not promote their exports in a comparable way, world trade in agriculture has become more distorted.

C. LIKELY IMPACT ON THE ESCAP REGION OF AGRICULTURAL TRADE LIBERALIZATION BY OECD COUNTRIES

It is obvious that any trade liberalization measure by developed market economies will generally have a large effect on the prices of agricultural commodities and hence their foreign exchange earnings. To investigate the impact of such hypothetical trade liberalization measures, a number of studies based on simulation models have attempted to explore their implications.

One of the first such attempts was made in 1980 by the International Food Policy Research Institute (IFPRI). That study indicated a $3 billion gain in export earnings of developing countries, out of a $8.5 billion per year increase in world trade in constant 1977 values resulting from a 50 per cent reduction across the board in tariffs and non-tariff barriers for 99 commodities in 17 developed OECD countries.

An updated version of the IFPRI model in 1986 found that developing countries would have increased their export revenue by an additional $6 billion in 1985 prices, which represented an 11 per cent increase for developing countries as a whole. The figures were calculated taking 1977-1979 levels of protection and trade flows. It was noted, however, that trade flows and OECD protection had

---

[23] "Price adjustment GAP and world agricultural policy reform", *Quarterly Review of the Rural Economy,* vol. 9, No. 2 (Canberra, Bureau of Agricultural Economics, June 1987).

[24] The forecasts for 1987 were being revised later in the year in the face of poor crop prospects due to weather effects and some effects of acreage control measures in developed countries.

Table II.18. World stocks.[a] Estimated total carryover of cereals, 1981-1987

	\multicolumn{7}{c}{Crop year ending in:}						
	1981	1982	1983	1984	1985	1986 Preliminary	1987 Forecast
				(Millions of tons)			
Total cereals	247.6	295.7	335.7	274.7	321.5	395.7	448
held by:							
Main exporters[b]	119.4	166.7	210.5	135.4	167.2	242.4	293
Others	128.2	129.0	125.2	139.3	154.3	153.3	155
By grains							
Wheat	98.2	106.9	119.8	129.8	144.6	148.1	156
held by:							
Main exporters	47.2	55.2	65.9	64.0	73.3	82.4	89
Others	51.0	51.6	53.9	65.8	71.4	65.7	67
Coarse grains	105.6	143.5	172.9	97.5	123.7	194.8	243
held by:							
Main exporters	51.3	88.6	119.0	45.6	63.7	134.4	182
Others	54.3	54.9	53.9	51.9	60.0	60.4	61
Rice (milled basis)	43.8	45.2	43.0	47.4	53.1	52.8	49
held by:							
Main exporters	20.9	22.8	25.6	25.8	30.2	25.6	23
Others	22.9	22.4	17.4	21.6	22.9	27.2	26
By regions							
Developed countries	145.4	187.7	229.9	152.6	189.8	269.0	324
of which:							
North America	83.9	125.6	169.4	92.7	111.0	195.8	251
Canada	14.0	16.2	18.5	13.3	12.2	14.7	24
United States	69.9	109.4	150.9	79.4	98.8	181.1	227
Others	61.6	62.1	60.4	59.8	78.8	73.2	73
Australia	2.7	5.2	2.5	8.2	8.9	6.1	6
EEC[c]	21.3	18.8	23.1	15.4	30.7	31.0	27
Japan	8.8	7.1	5.2	4.5	4.8	5.7	6
USSR[d]	14.0	14.0	14.0	19.0	20.0	19.0	22
Developing countries	102.1	107.9	105.9	122.2	131.7	126.7	124
of which:							
Asia	84.5	87.3	88.7	108.3	117.2	105.6	102
Africa	5.8	7.5	6.3	4.9	4.5	8.9	11
Central America	4.7	4.5	2.9	3.0	4.2	4.7	4
South America	7.2	8.6	8.0	5.9	5.7	7.5	7
World stocks							
As percentage of consumption	17	19	22	17	20	24	26

Sources: OECD, *Outlook for Agricultural Policies and Markets: Commodity Notes* (Paris, 1987), p. 11, table 3. Based on FAO data.

[a] Stock data are based on an aggregate of national carryover levels at the end of national crop years and should not be construed as representing world stock levels at a fixed point in time. [b] Major exporters of wheat and coarse grains are: Australia Argentina, Canada, EEC and the United States. For rice, the countries include: Burma, China, Pakistan, Thailand and the United States. [c] Twelve member countries. [d] FAO estimates.

increased since 1977-1979, so that the benefits of liberalization would be substantially greater in 1985. While for most commodities the price increase ranged between 2 and 10 per cent, for commodities that faced little or no protection in the OECD markets, the world price change was nil. The latter category of commodities included cotton lint, jute, natural rubber, sisal and hemp tow. Sugar and sugar derivative and meat were identified as the most promising of commodities, capturing approximately 47 per cent of the potential increase in export revenues in the developing countries.

The results of the 1980 IFPRI study indicated that for a number of countries in the ESCAP region a 50 per cent reduction in overall trade barriers would result in both increased exports and import expenditures on account of commodities. With a few exceptions, the countries could achieve net gains in foreign exchange earnings from their overall commodity trade (table II.19). Importers of cereals, such as Bangladesh, however, were likely to incur net losses owing to the probable increase in the price of cereals. In fact, the increased expenditures on imports indicated in most cases are largely due to cereal imports. With the attainment of greater self-sufficiency in cereals, these losses were likely to be smaller in more recent years. However, for the poorer countries the trade

effect on imports tended to outweigh that on exports because these countries either exported few agricultural products and/or exported commodities facing low rates of protection, and imported foods bearing high rates of protection (subsidies) in the OECD countries. Trade liberalization, however, may stimulate more production in food deficit countries, as most studies point out, owing to higher prices resulting from liberalization of policies.

An OECD study[25] simulated the impact of an average 10 per cent reduction in assistance in the OECD countries on world prices of the 11 commodities studied and found that world prices of livestock products, dairy products, wool and sugar would increase, while those of wheat, coarse grains, soybeans, and livestock feeds would

fall when assistance in OECD countries was reduced.

The price effects of the reduction in the OECD assistance level were of rather small magnitudes, the highest rise of about 5 per cent was indicated for dairy products expressed in terms of milk equivalents, and the highest fall of just above 1 per cent was indicated for soybeans. The OECD data, however, related to the years 1979-1981 when commodity prices were generally much higher than have prevailed since then and the level of assistance also was much lower than in more recent years.

A study commissioned by the ESCAP secretariat for the purpose of the present *Survey*, simulated with the help of a seven-commodity[26] thirty-country econometric model the effects of liberalizing food markets in industrial coun-

---

[25] See OECD, *National Policies and Agricultural Trade* (Paris, May 1987), ch. III, p. 31, table 2; and the explanatory text, p. 26.

[26] The commodities are: wheat, coarse grain, rice, ruminant meat, non-ruminant meat, dairy products and sugar.

Table II.19. **Potential trade effects on selected developing economies of the ESCAP region from reducing trade barriers[a]**

	Change in export revenues	Change in agricultural import expenditures	Increase in agricultural export revenues	Most affected export commodity in absolute terms
	(------Thousands of US dollars------)		(Percentage)	
Asia				
Bangladesh	2 017	−5 511	5.3	Beverages/tobacco
Burma	6 344	−466	3.0	Rice
Hong Kong	723	−16 168	16.2	Fats
India	254 872	−181 576	18.4	Sugar
Indonesia	42 461	−29 256	6.1	Vegetable oils
Malaysia	49 314	3 626	6.4	Vegetable oils
Nepal	1 034	−605	2.3	Rice
Pakistan	14 850	−52 631	4.5	Beverages/tobacco
Philippines	154 356	−12 480	10.7	Sugar
Republic of Korea	34 986	1 739	22.9	Sugar
Sri Lanka	14 841	3 823	4.1	Beverages/tobacco
Thailand	105 518	−106	6.6	Sugar

Source: Alberto Valdés and Joachim Zietz, *Agricultural Protection in OECD Countries: Its Cost to Less-Developed Countries,* Research Report No. 21 (Washington, D.C., International Food Policy Research Institute, December 1980), ch. 4, p. 33, table 4.

[a] Calculations use the base period 1975-1977 for the 99 selected agricultural commodities only.

tries on food self-sufficiency levels in selected countries in the ESCAP region in 1995, as shown in figure II.14. The study also quantified the trade effects of policy liberalization in the industrial countries on the ESCAP region which, *inter alia,* shows that imports of the products concerned in the traditionally importing countries will decrease and exports from the traditionally exporting countries will increase, and for some products exports will take place from some newly exporting countries, most importantly dairy products from China and India. On the basis of assumed/predicted levels of protection in industrial countries, simulations predict prices and production to be much higher in 1995 than in 1980-1982. Producers in the ESCAP region, except in Japan, would experience welfare gains whereas consumers would sustain losses, except in Japan where consumers will gain substantially. Net economic welfare losses (balancing losses and gains to producers and consumers) are indicated for most developing countries in the region, whereas gains accrue to the three developed countries, substantially so to Japan. Net welfare losses for the developing countries may however be less significant economically because the gains to producers may stimulate production which will of greater and longer-term benefits to the countries concerned.

It appears that the gains from liberalization of trade, though substantial, would not be uniform among country groups and countries within a group. It has been pointed out, however, that a feature of the structure of assistance in the OECD countries is the existence of policies which in many cases have evolved to counteract the effects of other policies. There is therefore an urgent need for policies to be rationalized with the multiple objectives of reducing

Figure II.14. Effects of liberalizing food markets in all industrial market economies on food self-sufficiency in major countries of the ESCAP region, 1980-1982 and 1995

(Ratio of domestic production to consumption of selected products)

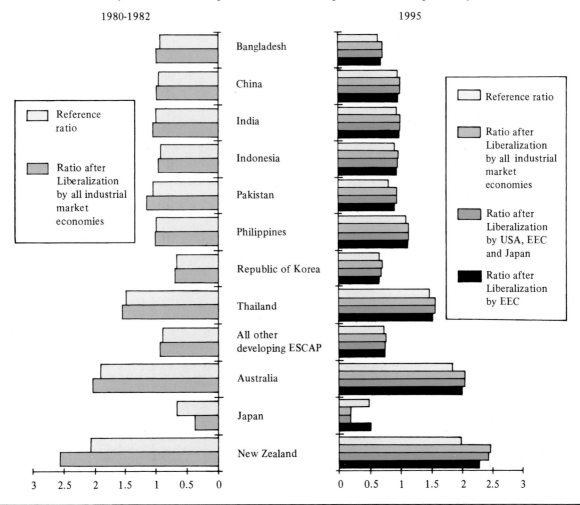

market distortions arising from assistance programmes, making the sector more flexible and more responsive to world market signals; reducing the cost to the economy of agricultural assistance and the disparity of benefits among producers; and of improving international relations in agriculture. If progress is to be made in resolving the serious problems confronting all OECD member countries, a multilateral, multi-commodity approach to the analysis and the resolution of these problems should be urgently pursued.[27]

While any liberalization of trade by OECD countries in temperate zone products is likely to confer benefits to developing countries, including those in the ESCAP region, it is evident that developing countries stand to gain more from liberalization of trade in tropical products. A wide range of tropical products therefore needs to be included in liberalization efforts which aim to eliminate tariff and non-tariff barriers which greatly hamper trade, especially in the processed products.

---

[27] OECD, *National Policies and Agricultural Trade* (Paris, May 1987), pp. 34 and 36.

VI. POLICY ISSUES AND OPTIONS IN PRIMARY COMMODITY TRADE

A. INTRODUCTION

The preceding chapters have analysed the various issues relating to trade in non-fuel primary commodities confronting the ESCAP region in the context of its changing role in the process of development. While the importance of such trade in overall commodity trade for the world, as well as for the developing countries of the region, has declined considerably in recent years, its strategic role in world trade and as a vital source of foreign exchange earnings for many developing countries makes it an important item on any current agenda of international trade issues. For developing countries its importance stems not merely from its role as a net foreign exchange earner but also as an important source of employment and income to a majority of their population and a source of funds for their overall development. For developed countries, except such countries as Australia and New Zealand, trade in primary commodities has been a small proportion of total merchandise trade but their world share of this trade is more than a half and has risen in recent years. However, the population that is dependent on primary production, especially agriculture, as a full-time occupation in developed countries is small and is now less than the proportion of unemployed in those economies.

A major source of concern for developing countries is their declining share in world exports of primary commodities. The loss in world market share of developing countries has been the result of both developed and developing country policies. The former have pursued policies of protecting their agricultural sectors and subsidizing export surpluses, thereby restricting and depressing commodity markets in which developing and developed markets compete with similar products, for example, temperate zone agriculture and tropical substitutes such as oil-seeds which compete with butter and oils. This has been by far the most important structural factor in depressing commodity prices in the 1980s. The supply increases have been largely generated in the developed market economies.

Most developing countries, on the other hand, have been handicapped by an inherited pattern of specialization in products such as tropical beverages, cotton, jute and hard fibres for which demand grows more slowly and inroads from synthetics continue to pose a serious threat. However, some individual countries or country groups have been able to increase their market shares, often at the expense of some other countries, by following more liberal policies towards their agriculture, especially exports.

In general, the developing countries, unlike developed countries, have taxed rather than subsidized their agriculture and to that extent their share of world agricultural output and trade is much lower than it would be in the absence of these distortions. Although the developing ESCAP region has been able to maintain its share, it could have achieved much more in the absence of the export subsidization by developed countries.

The second major problem that has continued to confront the developing countries, including those of the ESCAP region, is the short-term fluctuation in the primary commodity export earnings. This problem is of much greater significance to smaller economies which are heavily dependent on a few commodities and where possibilities of diversification remain low. Fluctuations in commodity prices in such countries have large domestic macro-economic impact and bring economic misery to vulnerable social groups.

Finally, there is concern about the impact of the changing interdependence between developed and developing countries. The growth in primary commodity trade in the past was largely linked to growth in the industrial countries. In recent years, there have been some signs of a weakening in that link, especially in the use of raw materials. However, growth in the developed market economies still exercises a positive influence on the demand for primary commodities. Moreover, although the nature of interdependence between developed and developing countries has been changing, the latter do not have the passive role that they had earlier. They provide a substantial market for the exports of the developed market economies which serve to stimulate growth in developed countries.

Therefore, in spite of the changing nature of complementarity (or interdependence) between the industrialized market countries and the primary exporting economies, there are many mutually-reinforcing benefits to be derived by both consumers and producers of primary commodities in their joint efforts to stabilize and maintain reasonably remunerative prices for primary commodities.

In the longer run, however, growing world trade relationships would necessitate accommodating "structural adjustment" in the economies of both trading partners for a more harmonious interdependence. It is apparent that changes in both the commodity composition and geographical flows of trade are inevitable at the national level. This is necessary in order to take full advantage of the domestic resources endowment in relation to the dynamic movements in international comparative advantage as well as for deriving greater benefits from regional co-operation in trade and production planning among developing countries of the ESCAP region.

These major problems relating to primary commodity trade require – and have evoked – policy responses at the international, regional and national levels. A comprehensive evaluation of these policy responses is neither possible nor necessary in this *Survey*. A brief account of the current international policy initiatives is given in section B, while regional co-operation efforts are discussed in section C. In section D, some of the major policy options emerging from the findings discussed in the previous chapters of this study are spelled out in greater detail. Section E puts forward some tentative suggestions for increased regional co-operation among the member countries of ESCAP.

B. INTERNATIONAL POLICY INITIATIVES

Instability in the prices of primary commodities has been a major public concern in both developed and developing countries for over half a century. Schemes for securing "remunerative and stable prices" for the main agricultural crops have been in existence since 1930, patterned after the agricultural price support programme of the Roosevelt Administration. Many developing countries have experimented with marketing boards and similar stabilization schemes. Keynes, who is recognized as one of the intellectual architects of the current international system of multilateral economic co-operation, had proposed the establishment of an international agency for stabilizing commodity prices – more ambitious in scope than the Common Fund under the Integrated Programme for Commodities (IPC) proposed by the United Nations Conference on Trade and Development (UNCTAD).[1] The main aim of Keynes' proposal was to ensure a stable supply of commodities to industrial countries without causing inflationary pressures and to ensure investment in new capacity in primary products at an adequate scale.

However, despite the agreement reached in 1980 on the establishment of the Common Fund, a major component of the IPC, it has remained non-operational. The required number of ratifications were reached in 1986 but the capital subscribed fell somewhat short of the required two thirds. The decision to ratify in 1987 by two more countries, the Union of Soviet Socialist Republics and Côte d'Ivoire has improved the prospects of entry into force of the Agreement to establish the Common Fund for Commodities in the near future.[2] The general weakness in commodity markets since 1980 has cast a shadow on the prospects of the emergence of new international commodity agreements or the effective continuance of the old ones. The international commodity agreements which the Fund was designed to support have, in the meanwhile, been dealt a considerable blow by the collapse in 1985 of one of the most important and well-functioning agreements, the International Tin Agreement. There are only five currently or recently active international commodity agreements — on sugar, coffee, cocoa, rubber and tin — with price support and, to a less extent, enhancement, as major objectives. For a variety of reasons, the success of these agreements has been limited.[3]

Another international initiative to support primary commodity trade, the Compensatory Financing Facility, administered by the International Monetary Fund (IMF)

[1] For details, see Nicholas Kaldor, "The role of commodity prices in recovery", *World Development,* vol. 15, No. 5 (Oxford, Pergamon Journals Ltd., May 1987), pp. 551-558.

[2] UNCTAD, *Final Act of UNCTAD VII* (TD/350), para. 76, p. 25.

[3] The agreements on sugar and tin, with pricing provisions, have become inoperative in this respect, while the performance of the agreements on cocoa and natural rubber is, at least, mixed. However, the agreement on coffee appears to have been more successful as an international price enhancement measure. See C.L. Gilbert, "International commodity agreements: design and performance", *World Development,* vol. 15, No. 5 (Oxford, Pergamon Journals Ltd., May 1987), pp. 600-614.

since 1963, is designed to help alleviate the domestic impact of export earnings shortfalls through short-term balance-of-payments assistance. The Facility was extended to cover earnings on services (namely, workers remittances and tourism) in 1976 and instability in cereals imports in 1981. However, several recent modifications of the scheme have resulted in the loss of a semi-automatic compensation element through the application of stricter test of co-operation with IMF introduced in 1983. The access limits of the CFF were also lowered from 100 per cent to 83 per cent of a country's quota.

Global drawings under this facility totalled special drawing rights 16.1 billion of which special drawing rights 15.4 billion or almost 96 per cent were made by the developing countries as of September 1987. The developing economies of the ESCAP region accounted only special drawing rights 4.4 billion or 27 per cent of the global drawings. There is a growing need for an alternative or supplementary scheme for export earnings stabilization. However, the several proposals for supplementary multilateral action and funding, in particular the UNCTAD proposal for a complementary compensatory financing facility,[4] have so far failed to evoke a response from the developed countries commensurate to the urgency and seriousness

of the commodity problem being faced by developing countries.

The STABEX scheme sponsored by the European Economic Community (EEC) has the same objective as the IMF Facility. It is a regional and commodity-specific scheme, with a high grant element and generous repayment conditions. However its financial impact is much more limited in absolute terms as well as in comparison to the financial resources disbursed under the Facility. Funding for the scheme amounted to about $400 million for 1975-1979 and $500 million during 1980-1984. In particular, the peak year for claims under STABEX was 1981 when a total of $327 million was finally approved. The announcement by the EEC in October 1985 that STABEX would be extended to cover the least developed countries (including six in the ESCAP region) outside the present African, Caribbean and Pacific States is, however, an encouraging development.[5]

The new round of multilateral trade negotiations under the auspices of GATT (the Uruguay Round) has raised much expectation because trade in agricultural commodities, whether in processed or semi-processed form, is now on the agenda for the first time in four decades (see box II.11). In addition, there appears to be a broad measure of agreement, backed by a certain level of political will expressed at various forums

— the OECD Ministerial Council meeting in May and the Venice Summit in June of 1987, and the Cairns Group (of 14 developed and developing primary exporters) in particular — concerning the urgent need for more liberalized agricultural trade and production conditions. It is, however, difficult to predict the likely outcome of the Uruguay Round of multilateral trade negotiations whose benefits would in any event take many years to become apparent. Nevertheless, it is undeniable that the commodity a problem has global dimensions which require a co-ordinated international approach by both the producing and consuming countries for its relief and resolution.

C. REGIONAL CO-OPERATION EFFORTS

Regional co-operation for strengthening the economic position of primary producers in the ESCAP region has existed for over two decades but, unfortunately, has not acquired the momentum that present challenges call for. Regional co-operative arrangements exist for a number of primary commodities, including coconut, pepper, rubber, tin, tropical timber, silk and jute, although the scope and intensity of their activities vary greatly. Two of these arrangements, for pepper and tin, have non-regional members, although the majority belong to the ESCAP region. Many of these regional initiatives have been undertaken under the auspices or with the help of ESCAP.

Among the earliest regional commodity arrangements to be established in the region is the Asian and Pacific Coconut Community, established in 1969. The Federated States of Micronesia, India, Indonesia, Malaysia, Papua New Guinea, the Philippines, the Republic of Palau, Samoa, the

---

[4] The proposed scheme is designed to reduce supply instability in specific primary commodity sectors consonant with national and international policies and arrangements. The facility would operate basically on self-financing and commercial principles, with voluntary contributions from donor countries used to cover any elements of concessionality for primary-producing, low-income and least developed countries (UNCTAD, *Compensatory Financing of Export Earnings Shortfalls* (United Nations publication, Sales No.E.85.II.D.3), p. 24).

[5] The allocated STABEX budget of 925 million European currency units for 1985-1990, however, was earmarked for African, Caribbean and Pacific (ACP) countries only. No claim was submitted by the non-ACP least developed countries up to 1986. For further details, see A.P. Hewitt, "Stabex and commodity export compensation schemes: prospects for globalization", *World Development,* vol. 15, No. 5 (Oxford, Pergamon Journals Ltd., May 1987), pp. 617-631.

Solomon Islands, Sri Lanka, Thailand and Vanuatu, are members of APCC. The Association of Natural Rubber Producing Countries, at present comprising India, Indonesia, Malaysia, Papua New Guinea, Singapore, Sri Lanka and Thailand, was established in 1970. The International Pepper Community, in which the participating countries are Brazil, India, Indonesia and Malaysia, was created in 1972.

The activities of the three regional commodity organizations involve all aspects of the respective industry, including production, processing, marketing, transport and shipping, research and development and training. Among the major activities of these organizatins are: (a) the collection and publication of statistics and other information on the performance of the commodity in each of the producing countries as well as in the international market place (information which is vital for policy-making); (b) the study of the cost structure of production and the adequacy of returns to farmers (information which is needed for both shaping domestic policies and negotiations at international levels on prices); (c) the study of shipping and transport problems; and (d) the study of medium-term and long-term demand prospects.

The intergovernmental co-operative/counsultative forums are relatively new arrangements in the region. The Government Consultation Among Jute Producing Countries comprising Bangladesh, Burma, China, India, Nepal and Thailand was formed in 1979, which helped to bring about agreement among the producing countries on the establishment of the International Jute Organization (IJO), a body consisting of representatives of both producing and consuming countries and aimed at the general improvement of the world jute economy.

The Intergovernmental Consultative Forum of Developing Tropical Timber Producing/Exporting Countries came into existence in 1981 with a view to adopting a co-ordinated policy approach by Governments of concerned countries in areas of common interest. Indonesia, Malaysia, Papua New Guinea, the Philippines and Thailand are members of the Forum, which meets periodically at the governmental level to devise ways and means to co-ordinate efforts towards the improvement of the timber industry.

The Regional Consultative Group on Silk was established in 1982, with China, India, Indonesia, Malaysia, the Philippines and Thailand as members. Among its objectives are identification and implementation of co-operative activities in the production, processing and marketing of silk. Besides periodic consultation on and monitoring of the implementation of various co-operative activities, including comparative studies of techniques of production and processing which have evolved in response to local conditions, efforts have been made to promote the sale of regional silk products by organizing Asian Silk Fairs in 1984 and 1986.

For tin, the Association of Tin Producing Countries (ATPC), with Malaysia, Indonesia and Thailand as leading Asian members, has drawn in other tin-producing countries such as Australia, Bolivia, China, Nigeria and Zaire to collaborate in research and development efforts in the face of the serious long-term threat to tin from substitutes. Recently these countries have also attempted to co-ordinate their production and marketing activities through the auspices of the Association with a view to minimizing the damage to their economies owing to the collapse of the international tin market.

Two recent regional initiatives at the subregional level also deserve mention, although their immediate purpose is somewhat different from the other regional efforts discussed earlier. These are the proposals for the building up of an emergency reserve of 200,000 tons of food grains by members of the Association of South-East Asian Nations and more recently the decision of the South Asian Association of Regional Co-operation countries to build up a similar reserve for the South Asian countries. It is not unlikely that these could lead to greater co-operation in food security matters among the member countries of the two subregions.

D. EMERGING POLICY ISSUES AND OPTIONS

The underlying concern of developing countries of the ESCAP region about the prospects of growth in export earnings from primary commodity trade is the uncertainty that surrounds them. This uncertainty stems from a variety of sources, including the external economic environment, policies of developed market economies and competing developing countries *vis-à-vis* particular primary products, technological changes and, last but not least, changes in weather. Perceptions about the importance of primary commodity trade undergo periodic change based on the interaction of these factors.

The present decade has been characterized by great pessimism about the future growth of primary export earnings in developing countries. Most forecasters believe that the weakness in commodity prices is likely to continue well into the next decade. In 1987, an upturn in some commodity prices, especially in minerals and metals, which had been depressed for a long time, has raised some optimism. Prices of food grains, especially rice, also began to rise strongly as a result of drought-induced crop failures and increased demand in some countries. As a result, large countries such as China and India, which were hoping to become major exporters of food grains, faced the prospects of running large import bills to ensure food security for their populations. These uncertainties considerably limit the scope for policy options and constrain planned development in primary-producing developing countries. The basic concern for food security and avoiding large balance-of-payments deficits greatly limit the policy options available to developing countries of the ESCAP region heavily involved in the production and trade of primary commodities.

Nevertheless, over the past two decades, many economies in the region which have specialized in primary production and trade, have now become leading exporters of manufactures. Others have reinforced their comparative advantage as primary producers and exporters by introducing new commodities and establishing downstream industries for processing. Many of these policy options are subsumed under the broad rubric of diversification. Diversification adds to the resilience of an economy and to its capacity to withstand external shocks in an increasingly uncertain world.

However, the policy of diversification is not without problems. First, it raises the possibility of a "fallacy of composition" or "crowding out" effect if the same trade diversification options are chosen by a number of countries simultaneously in the context of a shrinking or slowly expanding market demand. It then becomes a zero or negative sum game, in which the benefits to any one

developing country may be positive but take place at the expense of other developing country producers and reduce the competitors' market shares. There are many examples of such diversification efforts. Foreign exchange earnings from tea exports in South Asia were reduced as a result of the expansion, partly financed by World Bank loans, of smallholder tea production in East Africa. The success of Malaysia in commercial agriculture diversification has had adverse effects on earnings from traditional palm oil and cocoa exports by African producers.[6] Trade diversification may thus result in a "beggar-thy-neighbour" approach to development from the standpoint of the developing countries of the region as a whole. The policy could, however, succeed in an expanding market situation or in a situation where high-cost producers are willing and able to shift to production of other commodities.

Second, the world market for non-traditional exports, including manufactures, may not expand at a sufficient rate to absorb the higher flow of the exports of developing countries. However, the available evidence points to comparatively brighter prospects concerning effective demand for such products in industrial countries.[7]

---

6 A. Maizels, "Commodities in crisis: an overview of the main issues", *World Development,* vol. 15, No. 5 (Oxford, Pergamon Journals Ltd., May 1987), p. 545.

7 For example, manufactures from the developing ESCAP region constitute less than 12 per cent of the aggregate value of manufactures imports ($629 billion in 1981) into North America, the European Economic Community and Japan. Besides, a modest income growth of 2 per cent would enlarge apparent consumption in these regions by $76 billion, of which well over one billion could be met by ESCAP region exporters under the existing patterns of trade. See *Survey,* 1985, p. 222.

The emerging factor relates to the entrenchment of a variety of tariff and non-tariff measures in the industrial countries, despite the substantial resource costs involved. The viability of diversification into non-traditional exports would certainly be much less promising if such a policy option evokes a stronger protectionist response in the major importing countries.[8]

Third, diversification is not a costless option and resource limitations often limit the scope and extent of such measures. For example, production of new crops may require extension to and/or improvement in upland areas in countries where they exist, once the possibilities in the wet flat plains have been exhausted. This would require new investments, including those in human resources, for upland farming such as cattle-raising or tree-cropping, which are generally quite capital-intensive. Any large-scale effort to diversify would require a substantial increase in infarastructure investments.

Fourth, marketing difficulties and market aecessibility may limit the prospects of a viable export sector based on such diversification efforts. Investment needs in marketing infrastructure may be quite large in many countries. Requirements for processing, packaging and quality standards for foreign markets may be difficult to meet. Already many of these products face severe barriers in their access to markets on account of these very factors.

Finally, commodity diversification through downstream processing poses similar problems. In ad-

---

8 Conversely, a reduction in the existing barriers to trade would substantially widen the available access for developing country exports of manufactures and commodities. See chapter V, this *Survey.*

dition to new capital investment needs, there remains the problem of product quality improvement, cost competitiveness and intra-industry product diversification to successfully withstand the competitive challenges from substitutes. The escalating barriers to market access for processed products also stand in the way of such efforts.

The objective of diversification, nevertheless, needs to be pursued by all economies even in the face of the above-mentioned difficulties. However, the choice of directions in which to diversify is likely to be dictated by each country's resource endowment and stage of development. The larger agricultural economies of Asia, such as China, India and Pakistan, are likely to pursue a diversification strategy which would maximize their gains from trade subject to guaranteeing minimum food security. The Pakistan Agricultural Commission, for example, has recommended a compromise between an export-oriented option and minimum food self-sufficiency goals in food grains, sugar, edible oils and other essential food commodities. Besides cotton and rice, the traditional exports, the Commission has recommended accelerated growth in high-value agricultural exports, such as fruits and vegetables, meat, milk, fish and forestry products.[9]

A problem with large economies, such as those of China and India, is the increasing pressure on exportables owing to domestic absorption, especially of primary products, as population and incomes increase. Often the increase in domestic absorption is greater than in domestic production and "in so far as such a domestic demand pull improves the relative profitability of sales in the home market *vis-à-vis* exports, it has a further adverse effect on export performance"[10] Policies to insulate the domestic market from the export market may, therefore, be necessary to generate larger export surpluses.

For the South-East Asian countries, the opportunities for diversification are generally much greater in both agriculture and industry, and they have steadily taken advantage of those opportunities to reduce their dependence on commodity exports. Nevertheless, the traditional primary commodities remain an important part of their economy and continue to affect their economic performance. Their best option seems to be to reduce the number of people dependent on primary commodities through labour-intensive industrialization based on the processing of their primary commodities. Many countries in South-East Asia are moving towards the export of more finished products, especially of wood and forestry products. Several countries have imposed a ban on exports of log and rattan and encouraged exports of sawn timber, plywood and rattan furniture. Processing of food, fruits and vegetable products also has been expanded in many countries, for both local consumption and export. Expansion of these activities has been sought as a source of value added in production and exports, employment generation, and as a means to strengthen the linkages between primary production and industrialization.

The problems of small and medium-sized economies among the least developed and Pacific island countries of the region, whose dependence on primary commodity exports is heavy, are more serious. However, they have the advantage of having rather small individual shares in primary commodities, which makes the impact of their extra export effort on the overall volume of international trade rather small for any of the commodities concerned. They may therefore be able to introduce certain extra exports without a threat to the level of prices and the terms of trade or of a protectionist reaction from the developed countries.

Towards this end, institutional and policy-oriented measures are needed to promote new primary products and exports. These would include improvements in product quality and marketing through even rudimentary processing, quality control, refrigeration, canning and packaging. However, these would require considerable investments in such service sectors as transport, marketing and other infrastructure. For this to be possible, the level of international support currently being made available to the least developed and Pacific island countries of the region would need to be raised substantially.

E. INCREASING SCOPE FOR CO-OPERATIVE EFFORTS IN PRIMARY COMMODITIES

In the previous sections, some of the policy issues in primary commodity trade have been identified and their national, regional and international dimensions highlighted. National efforts are obviously the core of any policy initiative for solving a country's problems. However, in today's interdependent world there are serious limits on the efficacy of national efforts, limits which regional and international co-operation can help remove. Some of the initiatives already undertaken or under way

---

[9] Government of Pakistan, "Report of the National Commission on Agriculture" (Islamabad, 1987) (mimeographed).

[10] Deepak Nayyar, "India's export performance, 1970-85, underlying factors and constraints", *Economic and Political Weekly*, vol. XXII, No. 19, 20 and 21 (May 1987).

at the regional level were discussed in section C. Additional efforts which may be undertaken at the regional level are discussed below.

1. Intraregional trade

Despite the general presumption of the existence of lack of complementarity between the developing countries of the region, there exist considerable opportunities for intraregional trade in primary commodities. Both exports and imports of raw and semi-processed materials in the region have been traditionally concentrated in developed country markets. However, in recent years, markets for several products, including jute and jute products, rubber and rubber products, edible oil-seeds and cotton, have already been diversified to a certain extent to other developing countries both within and outside the region. The expansion of trade among the developing countries of the ESCAP region has increased the share of such trade to over a quarter of total primary exports, largely in food products and agricultural raw materials. The observed trend towards expansion can be further aided by co-operative endeavours among the developing countries of the region.

At present intraregional trade is hampered by various tariff and non-tariff barriers and their reduction or removal can benefit non-traditional commodity trade. The trading arrangements set up under the Bangkok Agreement and subregional arrangements such as the ASEAN Preferential Trading Arrangement provide mechanisms for multilateral negotiations. Improved bilateral contacts, understanding and co-operation can also be useful for exchange of mutually beneficial trade. Counter-trade mechanisms need to be more fully explored. A number of countries in the region have tried to solve their balance-of-payments problems through such trade involving primary commodities and manufactures and even services (such as construction).

The developed countries of the region can also play a major role in this respect. Japan is a major importer of most categories of primary exports from the region. Japan can assist the developing countries in the region by giving better access to its markets for their primary products and by providing greater technical and financial assistance to imrprove production, processing, marketing and distribution of their primary products. Such financial assistance, along with contributions from other developed countries, could conceivably be channelled through a regional commodity development fund especially to benefit more vulnerable countries. Australia and New Zealand, themselves being major commodity exporters, import very little at present from the rest of the region, and can presumably increase their imports of some categories of products from the developing countries in exchange for their increasing exports of meat and dairy products to the region.

There also exist considerable possibilities for collaboration among both developing and developed countries of the region in intensifying the development of minerals and metals exports, which have so far played a rather minor role in the developing ESCAP region's primary exports. The resurgence of interest in these commodities is reflected in the recent rise in their prices, which owes largely to the dissipation of the excess supplies and stocks, which were generated in the past. A careful planning and weighing of alternative possibilities of mineral exploration and development may serve to increase the region's potential for generating minerals and metals exports and in increasing the region's share in world exports of primary commodities.

2. Institutional arrangements

First, there seems to be a need for systematic collection and assembly of data on regional and possibly global production (including technological developments affecting production), consumption, stocks, trade and prices of individual primary commodities, especially the newly-emerging commodities, of interest to the region. This could assist in the development of an early warning and alert system on future trends in demand and supply of, and technological changes affecting, particular commodities. Existing regional commodity arrangements could be strengthened or the establishment of new organizations considered for the purpose among other things of collection and exchange of data and information. Among the commodities for which new arrangements could be considered are oil-seeds, cotton, fisheries, poultry and horticultural products. These arrangements could effectively supplement, at the regional level, the work of the global organizations such as the Food and Agriculture Organization of the United Nations, the World Bank and the International Monetary Fund.

Second, countries could come together to develop common production, trade and marketing strategies for the primary sector. Periodic meetings of national economic planners at the regional, or subregional level with interchanges between subregions, may be a useful device to harmonize development strategies and planning activities in the field of primary commodities and thereby avoid duplication and promote complementarity while undertaking programmes of agricultural and industrial diversification and restructuring.

Third, the countries could pool their resources for a joint marketing strategy with a view to effecting economy and efficiency. Establishing joint marketing institutions for the purpose may appear too ambitious initially, but may be feasible in cases where interests converge on the basis of both commodity identity and geographical proximity, that is, subregionally.

Fourth, the possibility of pooling and sharing of research results with regard to production planning and marketing may be considered.

Fifth, the possibility to share existing transport, marketing and banking facilities for intraregional and international trade in the region's primary commodities may also be considered.

Finally, the possibility of evolving common production and marketing strategies aimed at strengthening the bargaining and negotiating positions of the commodity-producing countries of the region may be considered with a view to co-ordinating the production and marketing activities in the absence of wider international agreements which have been slow in emerging.